A Concise History of China

Also by J. A. G. Roberts

China through Western Eyes: The Nineteenth Century

China through Western Eyes: The Twentieth Century

A History of China: Prehistory to c.1800

Modern China: An Illustrated History

A Concise History of China

J. A. G. Roberts

Harvard University Press
Cambridge, Massachusetts
1999

Printed in Hong Kong

First United Kingdom publication 1999 by Macmillan Press Ltd
as *A History of China.*

ISBN 0–674–00074–9 hardcover
ISBN 0–674–00075–7 paperback

Library of Congress Catalog Card Number 99–71606

This book is printed on paper suitable for recycling and
made from fully managed and sustained forest sources.

Contents

List of Maps

Preface

In 1991 Jung Chang published *Wild Swans*, a personal history of China as seen through the eyes of her grandmother, her mother and herself. The book was immensely popular and it introduced many of its readers to a subject entirely new to them: the making of modern China.

This one-volume account of the entire span of Chinese history also attempts to reach a new audience. It assumes no prior knowledge of China's past and is intended for a wider readership, one which is aware of the current interest in China's history and which recognizes the importance of the role that China will play in world affairs in the twenty-first century.

Chinese personal and geographical names have been transliterated into pinyin, the official system of romanization, rather than the traditional Wade–Giles system. Pinyin is now used in newspapers and is being adopted generally in scholarly works, although Wade–Giles is still used in the ongoing 15-volume *Cambridge History of China*. All Chinese personal and place names have been transliterated into pinyin. Thus Mao Tse-tung is rendered as Mao Zedong, and rather less familiarly Chiang Kai-shek is referred to as Jiang Jieshi. Likewise, Peking is transliterated as Beijing, Canton as Guangzhou and Hong Kong as Xianggang. Direct quotations which contain spellings in the Wade–Giles system have been amended to pinyin. When familiar names first appear in unfamiliar forms, the familiar form is also quoted and this practice is also followed in the index.

For the most part, pinyin spelling approximates to the phonetic values of English, with the following notable exceptions:

c	is pronounced 'ts' as in Tsar
i	is pronounced 'ee', except when it follows c, ch, r, s, sh, z and zh, in which case it is pronounced approximately 'er'
ian	is pronounced 'ien'
q	is pronounced 'ch' as in cheap

r   is similar to the English 'r' but is pronounced with
         the tongue behind the front teeth
x   is pronounced 'sh' as in sham
z   is pronounced 'ds' as in hands
zh   is pronounced 'j' as in jasmine

When citing Chinese names, the family name is given first, followed by the given name. However, in the notes, to maintain consistency with the citation of other names, the Western practice of putting the surname last is observed.

Following the usual practice, Chinese emperors are designated by their reign titles, not by their personal names. Non-Chinese names, for example Mongol or Manchu names, are cited in the form in which they are best known in the West.

Acknowledgements

This book is a direct descendant of Juan Gonzalez de Mendoza's *History of the Great and Mighty Kingdom of China*, which was published in Rome in 1585 and which was both the first, and the first one-volume, history of China. Like all writers who have followed in Mendoza's footsteps, I owe a tremendous debt to my predecessors, to the many scholars who have written about China. What I have written is a synthesis of the labours of others, particularly those whose efforts in recent years have deepened our understanding of Chinese society and transformed our concept of Chinese history.

I must thank my colleagues and students, past and present, at the University of Huddersfield, who have given me their time and ideas. I owe a debt of gratitude to the staff of the University of Huddersfield Library Services and to Mr Steve Pratt, the University's cartographer. My most substantial debt is to my wife Jan, who has endured my prolonged commitment to the task which has now been completed.

Introduction

The People's Republic of China, excluding Taiwan, has a surface area of 9,560,900 sq. kms, slightly larger than that of the United States. Only the Russian Federation and Canada are larger than China. Its population, which now exceeds 1.2 billion,* is greater than that of any other country in the world. Modern China is divided into 22 provinces, three municipalities (Beijing, Shanghai and Tianjin) and five autonomous regions. In terms of both area and population the single province of Sichuan is much larger than Germany.

These statistics illustrate one of the problems of writing a history of China. Modern China is a continental country, which contains within its borders a very wide range of ethnic, linguistic and regional variations. As it is not possible to encompass all aspects of this complex society in a one-volume history, the approach adopted has been to concentrate on the national picture and to make only sporadic reference to developments at regional or provincial levels. In the past this decision might have been excused on the grounds that there were few good regional studies, but this is no longer true. For example, John W. Dardess has used the exceptionally rich sources of Ming date for Taihe county, Jiangxi province, to explore the relationship between the county and 'the national matrix in which it was so firmly and inextricably embedded'.[1]

An important feature of this book is the emphasis which is placed on historical interpretation rather than on historical narrative. On a number of topics the variety of views which have been expressed is summarized briefly. However, Chinese history has also provoked wider debates which have had profound effect on historical interpretation. The influence of some of these debates may be discerned in the presentation of events, but they are not referred to explicitly. It is convenient to identify and discuss four of them briefly at this point.

---

* 1 billion = 1 thousand million.

THE 'DIFFERENTNESS' OF CHINA

In the eighteenth century some French *philosophes* regarded China as a model for Europe and suggested that features of Chinese society should be adopted in Western states. By the nineteenth century this admiration had been replaced with condescension. Western travellers delighted in identifying Chinese 'contrarieties', pointing out the ways in which Chinese custom was the direct opposite of Western practice.

The idea that Chinese society was in some fundamental way different from the societies of the West was given fresh impetus by Karl Marx. He posited that all human societies would pass through four stages: communal, slave, feudal and bourgeois society, before advancing to communism. However, he had also referred to an 'Asiatic mode of production', characterized by isolated village communities, large-scale public works projects, particularly for education and defence, the absence of private ownership of land and the absence of a meaningful class struggle. By identifying an 'Asiatic mode' he implied that Asian societies had not evolved on the lines followed by those of Europe, an apparent contradiction of his general thesis. A variation on this theme was developed by Karl Wittfogel in *Oriental Despotism* (1957). Wittfogel argued that in a 'hydraulic society' such as China, where the farm economy depended on the control of water resources, the government had to be able to mobilize vast numbers of peasants for irrigation and flood control works. This situation ensured that government remained autocratic, and that commercial and industrial development was inhibited. References to an Asiatic mode of production continue to appear in Marxist studies of Chinese history. For example, in a recent book Li Jun has argued that the Asiatic mode of production remains a valid concept, but it was the dominant mode of production only in the Western Zhou period (?1122–771 BC).[2]

References to an 'Asiatic mode of production', even in its attenuated form, distance China's historical experience from that of other societies. Of course Chinese society, like any other society, is *sui generis*, that is to say it has its own unique characteristics. The richness of Chinese culture, the complexity of China's political experience, the drama of China's recent past, might seem to justify treating China as a special case. Nevertheless in these pages the history of China is presented as being in no fundamental way different from the history of any other nation or society.

THE PERIODIZATION OF CHINESE HISTORY

Traditional Chinese historiography divided the country's history into dynastic periods and explained the divisions by reference to a dynastic cycle. According to that view, dynasties were founded by able and virtuous rulers but their successors failed to maintain the standards that their forefathers had set. If later rulers did not respond to repeated warnings, which took the form of portents, the mandate of heaven was transferred to the founder of a new dynasty. Some modern historians, while accepting that the personal qualities of its rulers had some influence on a dynasty's fortunes, have argued that the dynastic cycle was essentially the product of economic and administrative factors. When a new dynasty was founded the ruler eliminated his rivals, established an effective government, levied moderate taxes and secured the frontiers. Under later rulers the costs of government rose, powerful families began to evade taxation, and the frontiers became over-extended. In time, officials became corrupt, public works were neglected and the burden of tax borne by the peasants increased. Finally the peasants rose in rebellion and overthrew the dynasty.

Even if the concept of the dynastic cycle has some validity, a repetitive cycle is not a consistent feature in imperial history. For prolonged periods, for example between 220 and 589, no one dynasty ruled over the whole of China. At other times the dynasty changed but there was no evidence of a cyclical pattern – the continuity between the Sui and the Tang, for example, was very marked. Some of the most important historical turning points in China's history have come in the middle of a dynastic period. Although the rebellion of An Lushan had a devastating effect on the Tang dynasty, the Tang emperors remained on the throne for another 150 years. On the other hand, the change from one dynasty to another might coincide with a major social transition. The Japanese historian Naito Torajiro put forward what has become known as the 'Naito hypothesis'. He argued that modern

Chinese history began not with the arrival of Westerners in China, but at the end of the Tang and the beginning of the Song periods. That point, he claimed, marked the end of aristocratic government and the beginning of the period of autocratic rule. From the above, it will be apparent that the division of Chinese history into dynastic periods is often questioned. Nevertheless, periodization by dynasties remains the most commonly used chronological framework. As it is the organizational principle which is most accessible to the reader, it has been used in a modified form in this book.

HAN NATIONALISM

The Chinese call themselves Han Chinese, a reference to the Han dynasty (206 BC–AD 220), when Chinese culture first spread across the territory which is now called China. Inevitably a history of China is a history of the Han Chinese. It will make only passing reference to China's minority nationalities, who comprise 8 per cent of China's population, and it will adopt a Chinese perspective on the long periods in Chinese history when part or all of China was ruled by non-Chinese peoples.

In 1967 Ho Ping-ti, then President of the Association for Asian Studies, gave an address entitled 'The significance of the Qing period in Chinese history'. He began by asserting that the Manchus, the founders of the Qing dynasty, had established the most successful dynasty of conquest in Chinese history. He then argued that the key to the Qing success was the adoption by the early Manchu rulers of a policy of systematic sinicization. Thirty years later Evelyn S. Rawski, also giving the Presidential address, responded to his predecessor. He began by drawing attention to the wealth of Manchu-language materials which until recently Western and Chinese scholars had spurned as being mainly translations of Chinese documents. He suggested that the picture which was now emerging from close study of these materials contradicted Ho's assertion that Manchu success was based on sinicization.

The new scholarship suggests just the opposite: the key to Qing success, at least in terms of empire-building, lay in its ability to use its cultural links with the non-Han peoples of Inner Asia and to differentiate the administration of the non-Han regions from the administration of the former Ming provinces.

Such a view acts as a corrective to the imbalance created by unreflective Han nationalism, which has denigrated the periods in Chinese history, for example the Yuan or Mongol dynasty, when China was under foreign rule.

CHINA'S RESPONSE TO THE WEST

Much of China's modern history, particularly since the Opium wars, has been presented in Western historical literature as a 'response to the West'. The most important dynamic in China's modern development is assumed to be the reaction to the West's 'challenge' and the question is then posed: why did China not respond more rapidly and more effectively to that challenge? Such an approach defines the dynamic in nineteenth-century history as Sino-Western contact – which means a concentration of interest on the treaty ports, Western economic imperialism, etc., while ignoring the broader context of cultural and social changes already taking place in Chinese society.[3] The 'response to the West' approach also assumes that the Western impact on China, whether beneficial or oppressive, was the catalyst which enabled China to escape from the confines of 'traditional' society. This view has been challenged in a number of recent works which take as their starting point the perception that Chinese society was not unchanging, nor were Chinese intellectuals unthinking. In these books there has been a conscious effort to present a more 'China-centred' history of China. It is hoped that something of the same emphasis is to be found in this volume.

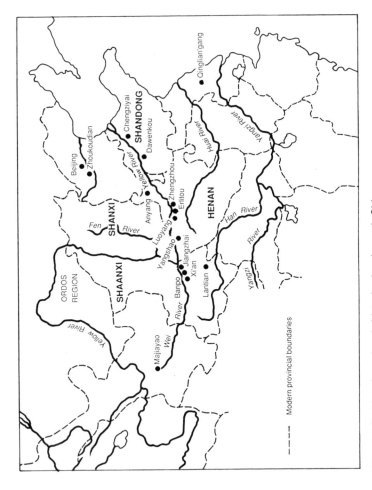

Map 1 Prehistoric and early historic sites in north China

xvi

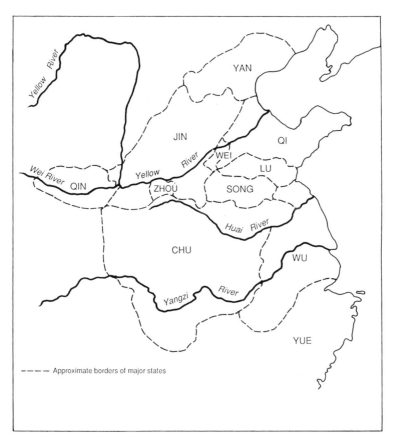

Map 2   China at the time of Confucius, *c*.551–479 BC

Map 3 China Proper on the eve of the rebellion of An Lushan

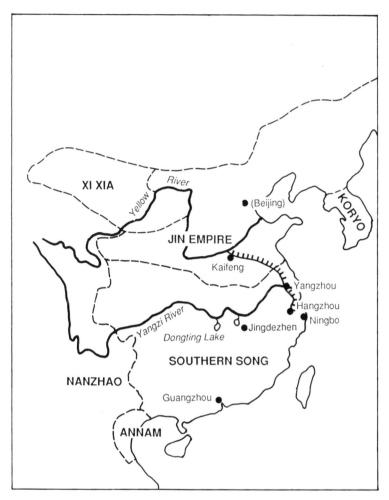

Map 4 China under the Southern Song and the Jin, *c.*1140

Map 5 China in the seventeenth century: the Manchu invasion and the Revolt of the Three Feudatories

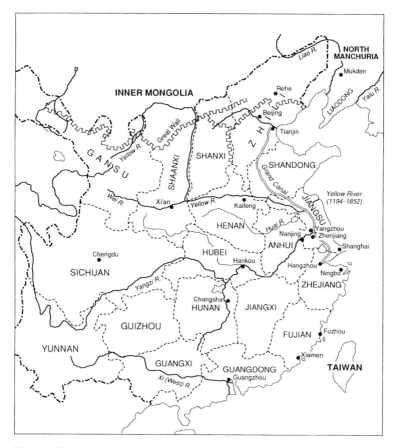

Map 6 China Proper *c*.1800

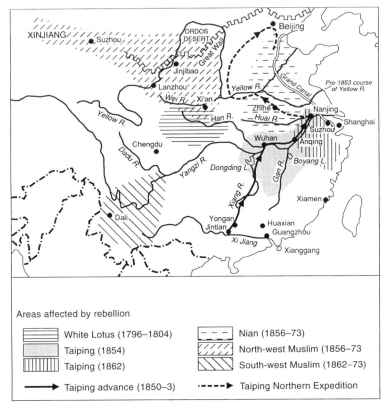

Areas affected by rebellion

White Lotus (1796–1804)		Nian (1856–73)
Taiping (1854)		North-west Muslim (1856–73)
Taiping (1862)		South-west Muslim (1862–73)
Taiping advance (1850–3)		Taiping Northern Expedition

Map 7   The rise of rebellion, 1796–1873

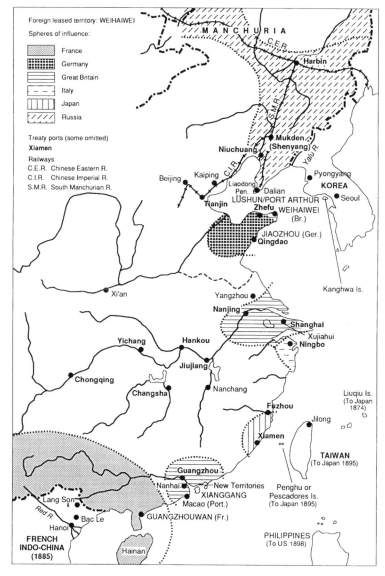

Map 8 Foreign encroachment on China, c.1900

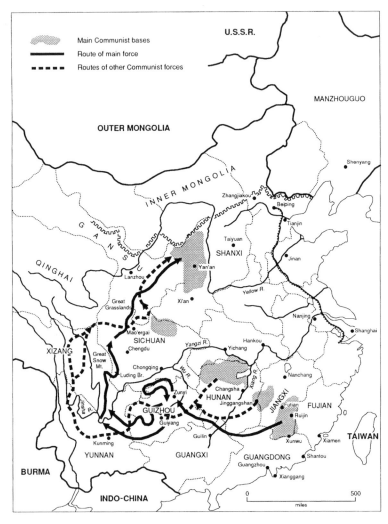

Map 9 The Long March, 1934–5

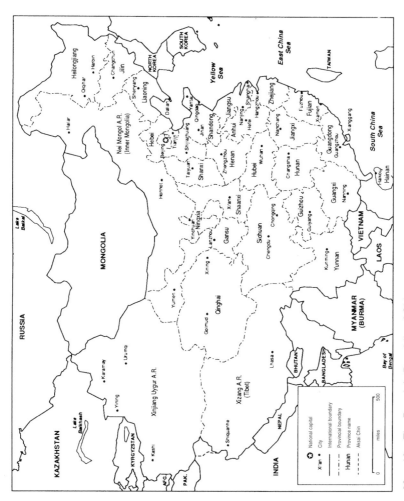

Map 10 The People's Republic of China

I

The Prehistory and Early History of China

PREHISTORIC AND PROTOHISTORIC CHINA

The physical origin of the Chinese people is a subject not yet fully understood. In 1927 remains of early man were found at Zhoukoudian, 30 miles south-west of Beijing. Beijing man, who had hominid features, was a hunter-gatherer who used stone tools and made fire. Further remains of *homo erectus*, a predecessor of *homo sapiens*, who lived between 400,000 and 200,000 BC have since been found at a number of other sites in China. Early homo sapiens inhabited sites in China between 200,000 and 50,000 BC. The best-documented find of early human remains was made at the Middle Cave at Zhoukoudian. This find, which included three restorable skulls, has yielded an unconfirmed radiocarbon date of 16,922 BC. The physical characteristics which these remains exhibit are regarded as more typical of North American Indians than of Mongoloid peoples. It is therefore questionable whether this group was ancestral to the modern Chinese.

In the Neolithic period, which in China dates approximately from 12,000 to 2000 BC, extensive settlement took place by people who were indubitably Mongoloid. At one time it was supposed that Chinese neolithic culture had originated in one area of the North China Plain, but recent archaeological discoveries have revealed a more complex picture, and two or three cultures are now considered to have achieved the transition from food-gathering to food-production. The two confirmed examples are

the Qinglian'gang culture of the lower Yangzi region and the
Yangshao culture of the middle Yellow river, and to these may be
added the Dapenkeng culture on Taiwan. The Qinglian'gang culture, which emerged in the fifth millennium BC, was characterized by the cultivation of rice and the use of painted pottery. The
better-known Yangshao culture was named after a village in
northern Henan, where in 1921 the Swedish archaeologist J.
Gunnar Andersson had found a fragment of painted pottery. Its
most famous site is at Banpo, near Xi'an, which was occupied
from about 4500 BC. Banpo was a village of some 45 houses. Its
inhabitants cultivated millet and kept pigs and dogs. They produced pottery which was not only decorated but also bore
incised markings. As similar markings have been found on pottery excavated at other sites within the region, it has been suggested that these are not simple potters' marks but an early stage
in the development of Chinese characters.

   In 1928, at Chengziyai in north-west Shandong, specimens of
a different type of pottery were found, which became known as
Longshan ware. Whereas Yangshao pottery was red and was
sometimes painted with stylized renditions of birds and flowers,
Longshan ware was unpainted, more finely made and usually
elevated on a circular foot or on tripod legs. Because the first
examples of Longshan ware had been found in Shandong, it was
assumed to be the culture of eastern China, whereas Yangshao
was regarded as the culture of the Central Plain. When the site at
Miaodigou in Henan was excavated, Yangshao ware was found
below Longshan finds, and this gave rise to a second theory, that
Longshan culture was later than, and derived from Yangshao culture. However, the evidence to support a developmental theory
has not been forthcoming; it now seems probable that the two
cultures developed separately and that Longshan culture, which
was widely distributed in eastern China, gradually spread to the
Central Plain, where the painted pottery tradition was already
dying out.

THE XIA DYNASTY

According to Chinese legend, human beings had their origin in
the parasites on the body of the creator, Pangu. After his death a

succession of sage rulers introduced the key inventions and institutions of human society. The first sage ruler was Fuxi, who domesticated animals and instituted marriage. He was followed by Shennong who introduced agriculture, medicine and trade. Then came Huangdi, the Yellow Emperor, to whom was credited the invention of writing, ceramics and the calendar. Some centuries later came the Emperor Yao, who ruled wisely and introduced flood controls, but whose particular claim to fame was that he decided his son was unworthy to be his successor and chose instead a humble sage named Shun. The reigns of Yao and Shun were later regarded as a golden age in Chinese history. Shun in turn awarded the succession to his faithful minister Yu. It is at this point that China's prehistory begins to merge with history. Yu, whose reign according to tradition began in 2205 BC, allegedly founded the Xia dynasty, the first of the three dynasties of ancient China. The Xia dynasty may have existed between approximately 2200 and 1750 BC along the Yellow river near Luoyang and to the north of that area, in the Fen river valley. The pottery finds suggest that Xia culture derived from Longshan. The most important site identified with the Xia is Erlitou in Henan, where palace-like buildings and tombs have been excavated and the earliest known bronze vessels have been found.

THE SHANG DYNASTY

The second of the ancient dynasties was the Shang, the traditional dates of which are 1766–1122 BC. It was once supposed that the three ancient dynasties were successive, but it is now understood that Shang was already a powerful entity before it overthrew the Xia, and that the three dynasties overlapped both in time and in territory. The Shang state had a series of capitals, the most important of which were Zhengzhou, the capital in the earlier or middle period of the dynasty, and Anyang, which was occupied c. 1300–1050 BC.

At Zhengzhou a city wall some four miles long enclosed a large settlement. The wall and the buildings within were constructed using the 'stamped earth' technique. The houses and workshops which have been found there indicate that Shang society was highly organized and socially stratified. This evidence confirms the impression of Shang society which was obtained from the finds made at the late Shang capital at Anyang, first excavated in the 1930s. Outside Anyang, at Xiaotun, the remains have been uncovered of what perhaps was the ceremonial and administrative centre of the late Shang state. At Xibeigang, two miles north of Xiaotun, 11 very large cruciform graves have been found, which may belong to the 11 Shang monarchs who were recorded as having reigned at Anyang.

Much has been written about the Shang, but here the discussion will be limited to three themes: the character of the Shang state, the significance of the oracle bones, and the implications of the Shang bronzes. The Shang rulers performed an important ritual role, but they were also involved in the administration of the state and were served by officials who had specialized functions. They were supported by aristocratic clans with whom they had either kinship or marriage connections. Aristocratic society practised military skills and fought using horse chariots. The relationship between the Shang kings and the clan leaders was a personal one, but it was formalized through ceremonies of investiture which gave the king the right to demand services from the clans, which included labour services and military duties. The Shang kings, or their aristocratic supporters, waged aggressive campaigns against their neighbours, thereby obtaining prisoners and loot. The extension of Shang authority was also achieved by commissioning the establishment of new towns and the opening of new land for farming. Through these means the late Shang state extended from its core along the Yellow river to the Wei valley and to the north of present-day Shanxi. The Shang also established relations with a state named Shu, which may refer to the culture that had developed independently in Sichuan. The discovery at Sanxingdui, a settlement just north of Chengdu, of two underground caches of bronzes which are quite different in character from those of the Shang, was one of the most remarkable archaeological finds of the 1980s.

The economic basis of the Shang state was agriculture, the most important cultivated crop being millet. The climate of the North China Plain was warmer and moister than it is at present, and the area was well-forested, thus requiring considerable amounts of labour to clear for planting. It has often been asserted, particularly by Marxist historians such as Guo Moruo, that the labour to perform this and many other tasks was slave labour, and that Shang society should be defined as the slave-society stage in China's social evolution. This view has been supported by the evidence of the human sacrifices which accompanied royal burials and by references in oracle inscriptions. Recently Jun Li has suggested that the bulk of the population were not slaves, in that they were not bought or sold, nor were they deprived of their personal freedom. Nevertheless they were subject to coercive work, building city-walls and performing agricultural tasks, and they were conscripted for military duties.

Much of the information available on Shang society comes from inscriptions made on the shoulder-blades of oxen (scapulimancy), or less commonly on the shells of turtles (plastromancy). At one time such items were described as 'dragon bones' and ground up for medicine. In the late nineteenth century the bones and their inscriptions were recognized for what they were. Over 150,000 fragments of Shang oracle bones have now been identified and these provide a major source of evidence about the Shang state. Many of the inscriptions refer to future events and they have been translated as questions addressed to an oracle. Recently it has been argued that the inscriptions are not questions but statements or predictions and that the divination process formed part of a sacrificial rite. Once the bones had been inscribed, a heated bronze tool was applied to them and the cracks which appeared were interpreted as a response to the question or prediction. Some of the inscriptions relate to the actions of the king and his allies and from these information may be gleaned about the organization of the Shang state. Others refer to the weather, to the planting and harvesting of crops and to the siting of buildings. The inscriptions use a vocabulary of more than 3000 different graphs and they include a dating system based on a 10-day week and a 60-day cycle.

The most prized archaeological finds from the Shang period are the bronze vessels and implements, many of which were made for ceremonial purposes. Because the vessels are very sophisticated, and because evidence had not been found of an earlier and more primitive stage in bronze work, it was long assumed that the technology for their production had been imported into China. However, the evidence accumulated in recent years supports the hypothesis of the independent discovery of metallurgy in China and the rapid transfer of skills from pottery to the manufacture of bronzes. The production and use of bronze was controlled by the king, and the quantity of bronze objects found indicates that the extraction of metal ore and the manufacture of bronze objects was a major industry, employing large numbers of skilled craftsmen. Early bronze technology in the West used the lost-wax technique, but early Shang vessels were cast in several moulds and the parts assembled later. The lost-wax technique was used later, in the Zhou period, and may have been introduced from the West. The earliest bronze vessels have been found at Erlitou and important finds of bronze vessels were made at Zhengzhou and Anyang, the two Shang capitals. These vessels had a ritual function. An early bronze vessel found at Zhengzhou, which has a lobed body and a tripod of legs, a shape derived from a Longshan pottery prototype, was used for the preparation of sacrificial meats. Other ritual vessels were intended for the heating of wine. Many of these vessels are decorated with stylized surface decorations, the most famous motif being the *taotie*, a monster mask intended to avert evil. Jade was also used for ritual purposes, as it had been in the Longshan culture. Two jade forms were common: a pierced disc known as a *bi* and a tube of square cross section known as a *cong*.

The Shang kings were buried in vast pits, which would have required the labour of many hundreds of men to excavate. Their corpses were placed in wooden coffins and these were surrounded by grave goods. On the ramps leading to the bottom of the pit lay human bodies and those of horses. The human victims, who may have been prisoners of war, had sometimes been beheaded. The main royal tombs at Anyang were robbed a very long time ago but the tomb of Fu Hao, the consort of a Shang king who died *c.* 1250 BC, was discovered intact in 1976. It contained about two hundred bronze vessels, some in the shape of animals. The bronzes in Fu Hao's tomb are much larger than those found in some other aristocratic graves, and this has been taken as a sign of social stratification.

From the evidence of the oracle bones and bronze vessels, and from the burial practices followed, some understanding may be obtained of Shang religion. The Shang people worshipped many deities, most of whom were royal ancestors, some were nature spirits, and others perhaps derived from popular myths or local cults. This veneration of ancestors was practised by much of the population, and it has remained an essential part of Chinese religious practice until modern times. It has long been assumed that Shang religion also had a single supreme deity, referred to as Di, who was part ancestral figure, part natural force, who presided at the apex of a complex Shang pantheon. A recent study has rejected the idea of Di as a high god, and has claimed that in Shang religion *di* was the term used to refer collectively to 'the gods', and that it was only under the Zhou that the idea of a supreme god emerged. From the evidence of the tombs it is clear that the Shang believed in an afterlife, and divination may have been addressed to departed ancestors. The Shang court may have been attended by shamans, and the king himself was perhaps a shaman. If these suggestions are correct, then the character of Shang religion was very different from the rational approach of the philosophical schools which were to gain influence during the Zhou period.

THE WESTERN ZHOU PERIOD

The Zhou dynasty is traditionally dated from 1122 to 256 BC, and this immensely long period is divided into the Western Zhou, from 1122 to 771 BC, and the Eastern Zhou, the latter age being further subdivided into the Spring and Autumn period, from 771 to 481 BC, and the Warring States period, from 403 to 221 BC.

Long before the fall of the Shang, the Zhou had emerged as a powerful state somewhat to the west of the main centre of Shang activities. The origin of the Zhou people is not clear. According to Mencius, a disciple of Confucius, 'King Wen was a Western barbarian',[1] and some support in the past has been given to the theory that the Zhou were of Turkish origin. However, there is no linguistic evidence to indicate that they came from far afield. A more plausible theory suggests that they originated in the Fen valley in Shanxi, and later migrated to the Wei valley in Shaanxi, to the west of Xi'an. There, in proximity to the Shang state, the Zhou people came to adopt many aspects of Shang culture, a process which enabled them to acquire administrative techniques and which facilitated their seizure of power.

The establishment of the Zhou dynasty provides the first example of the right of a dynasty to rule being based on an ethical justification. According to the *Shujing*, the *Book of Documents*, one of the earliest surviving Chinese historical sources, the fall of the Shang came about because of the shortcomings of the last Shang ruler. As a result the protection or mandate of heaven was taken from him and awarded to the rulers of Zhou. Of these, King Wen was a paragon of virtue, and his son King Wu, who overthrew the Shang after a great battle at a place called Muye, an outstanding warrior. It was recorded that the Zhou headed a coalition of eight nations which included Shu, and that the Zhou and their allies gained the victory because the Shang troops were driven to mutiny by the cruelty of their ruler. These events probably took place *c.* 1045 BC, that is nearly eighty years later than the traditional date for the overthrow of the Shang.

Shortly after the conquest, perhaps in 1043 BC, King Wu died and was succeeded by his son. This arrangement was a break with the past, for under the Shang the succession had passed to surviving brothers. It established the important principle observed by later Chinese dynasties that the heir should come from the succeeding generation. However, the new King Zheng was a minor, and for the first part of his reign authority was wielded by the Duke of Zhou, one of the most famous figures in early Chinese history. The duke consolidated Zhou control over Shang territory and defeated a rebellion in the east led by survivors of the Shang royal family. However, even after the rebellion had been defeated, the Zhou continued to appoint members of the deposed Shang lineage to be in charge of territories in the east. The Duke of Zhou also waged campaigns against the Huai Yi, a people who lived in the Huai valley, who remained undefeated throughout the Western Zhou period. Expansion also took place by peaceful means, through the transfer of groups of people to newly-opened territory, where they intermarried with non-Zhou people, thus extending the influence of what may now be called Chinese culture.

Western Zhou society has been described as feudal. The use of the term was first proposed by the Marxist historian Guo Moruo in the 1930s, and its application to China is based on two assumptions. The first is that feudalism is a form of social organization which arises under certain conditions, namely the decline of a powerful centralized state and its replacement by a congeries of small states owing only nominal loyalty to a central ruler. This situation may have prevailed in China after the fall of the Shang (which Guo Moruo regarded as a slave society) and the occupation of the Shang territories by the Zhou. The transition also came about, it is claimed, because of technological improvement – the introduction of iron – and the general economic advance which that implied.

The second ground for describing the Western Zhou as feudal concerns the essential element of the feudal relationship, the granting of fiefs to vassals, who in return promise to provide their feudal lord with military support. Under the Zhou, according to the famous early Zhou text the *Shijing* or *Book of Songs*

> Everywhere under vast Heaven
> There is no land that is not the king's.
> To the borders of those lands
> There are none who are not the king's servants.[2]

Under the Western Zhou, grants of territory were certainly made and confirmed and they were formalized at ceremonies at which the king gave presents that had a symbolic meaning, and which as time went on became increasingly lavish. The ceremonies and the gifts which had been presented were commemorated in inscriptions on bronze vessels. The wide distribution of these vessels, many of which date from early in the dynasty, and in particular from the years following the Duke of Zhou's suppression of rebellion, indicate that this form of appointment played an important part in the establishment of the Western Zhou political structure over its newly-acquired eastern territories. Appointees were given graded titles of rank which have sometimes been equated with the aristocratic titles used in the West. Some of the bronzes recorded military activities, which confirm that the relationship involved military assistance, although they give the lie to the idealized picture of the Western Zhou period as a golden age of peace, a time when Chinese did not fight Chinese, although they might fight against the surrounding 'barbarians'.

Notwithstanding this evidence, the appropriateness of the term 'feudal' to describe the Western Zhou has been queried. The argument that the China of three thousand years ago was a very different society from mediaeval Europe needs no elaboration, and any close comparison between the two societies is difficult to sustain. Whereas in Europe the feudal relationship was typically impersonal and prescribed in detail, under the Zhou the dominant relationship was one of kinship and the contractual element in the relationship was not specified. In Europe feudal lordships were hereditary and enfeoffments, providing that the vassal remained loyal, were irrevocable. However, under the Western Zhou appointments required reconfirmation and could be revoked. Appointments, which might be defined in terms of particular duties, have been described as 'protobureaucratic', the implication being that whereas in Europe bureaucracies emerged as a counter to feudal society, in China the beginnings of a bureaucracy existed alongside the supposed feudal order. In Europe the term feudalism has been used to describe a particular mode of economic organization, namely the binding of the peasant to the land and the compulsory provision of labour for the feudal lord, but such a system did not exist under the Western Zhou. In short, if the term feudalism implies merely a 'system of government in which a ruler personally delegates limited sovereignty over portions of his territory to vassals',[3] it may fit the Western Zhou, but the contemporary evidence does not justify the use of the term with its more precise definition.

THE SPRING AND AUTUMN PERIOD

The Western Zhou period was characterized by rapid but unstable expansion, which saw Zhou influence extend over much of north China and as far south as the Huai valley. At first the appointment of members of the ruling dynasty and its allies to semi-independent fiefs created a viable political structure, and the power of the Western Zhou kings over them was considerable. King Yi, who reigned c. 897–873 BC, wielded sufficient authority to have Duke Ai boiled to death for supposedly criticizing him. But by the end of the ninth century BC the kings' authority had declined, their appointees and their successors had become increasingly integrated into their local society, and the fiefs were assuming the character of independent states. The early Zhou rulers had mounted expeditions to the north-west and west of their main centre in Shaanxi, but they now came under pressure from the Rong and the Di, non-Chinese peoples who inhabited the steppe regions and who may have used horses in warfare. In 771 BC a Rong invasion forced the Zhou to move their capital eastwards to Luoyang, hence the use of the term Eastern Zhou to refer to the subsequent period. The years 771–481 BC are known as the Spring and Autumn period after the annals which describe the events of those years in the small state of Lu. The key political development of the time was the rise of states which professed only symbolic allegiance to the Zhou kings, who in the end only ruled a small area around Luoyang. Up to 170 states are recorded as having existed in those years, of which about 15 were of significant size and importance. By the end of this period warfare and succession disputes had reduced the number of important states to seven, of which four deserve particular mention. One was Qi, which occupied the area of modern Shandong. In the early seventh century BC, Guan Zhong, the chief minister of the state, introduced a reform which transformed military service from the prerogative of the nobility to an obligation on the common people. The state of Jin, which was located in present-day Shanxi, also introduced reforms after a military disaster. Jin fought campaigns against the Di people, and finding that the mountainous terrain was unsuitable for chariots, developed infantry armies. Its leaders also intermarried with the Di people. To the south lay the expanding state of Chu, which occupied the middle Yangzi region, and which was regarded by the other states as semi-barbarous. Finally to the west lay the state of Qin, which had emerged at the time of the fall of the Western Zhou, and which was considered by the other major states to be non-Chinese. These states acted as sovereign bodies and have been described as 'seven different cultural spheres'.[4]

The Spring and Autumn period saw frequent wars between states and with the surrounding peoples. One calculation suggests that throughout the entire period only 38 years were peaceful. In 651 BC, in an attempt to achieve stability and to counter a threat from the north, Duke Huan of Qi invited representatives of the central states to a conference and obtained their agreement to a set of principles concerning good government. He was chosen as hegemon of the 'five leaders of the feudal lords'. But this system did not last and conflicts continued through the period. These wars reflected the rapid political, social and economic changes which were occurring at the time. At the beginning of the Spring and Autumn period, the political elite was composed of the king, the feudal lords and their hereditary ministers, each of whom had a defined status, a prescribed role in ritual performances, and an obligation to fight to defend the honour of the lineage. Under the impact of constant war, this elite began to fragment. State governments became more centralized, administrative units were established and junior members of the aristocracy were appointed to supervise them. A class of men known as *shi*, or gentlemen, began to emerge in the seventh century BC and by the fifth century *shi* had eclipsed the former elite in government.

At the same time major technological and economic changes were taking place. The use of bronze became much more widespread, and recent discoveries have shown that by this time bronze agricultural tools were in common use in the lower Yangzi valley. By the middle and late Spring and Autumn period cast iron and steel were being produced. However iron was not generally adopted for making weapons, implements and vessels until the Warring States period, considerably later than the same development in the West.

Up to this time Chinese agriculturalists had probably practised a form of communal agriculture, which was later to be described in idealistic terms as the 'well-field' system. Under this arrangement plots of land were divided into nine holdings, eight of which were farmed by individual families, with the ninth farmed communally and the produce delivered to the lord. Communal agriculture began to decline during the Spring and Autumn period, perhaps because of the spread of the iron plough, which increased productivity. In 594 the state of Lu instituted a system of land taxation which required peasants to pay taxes rather than to provide labour service. Some evidence suggests that individual ownership and a free market in land began to appear at this time. Accompanying this change was a growth in commerce and the appearance of coinage. In the Shang period, cowrie shells had been used in transactions and cloth was also used as a medium of exchange. By the late Spring and Autumn period metallic currencies had been introduced, early coins being in the form of spades or knives.

THE WARRING STATES PERIOD

The transition from the Spring and Autumn to the Warring States period was once represented as a change from an age of relative peace to one in which war was the dominant theme. It has been demonstrated, however, that wars were equally frequent in both periods; though the character of war did change, ceasing to be an aristocratic monopoly and becoming an activity which involved authoritarian leadership, standing armies, and peasants performing military service. In this period military specialists appeared – the most famous being Sunzi, supposed author of the *Art of War*, which dates back to the fifth century BC. In it he advised a commander to block up the eyes and ears of his men to deprive them of knowledge and consciousness, and so ensure that they would act solely according to his will. New weapons were adopted, notably the crossbow and the improved iron sword, and armour was developed. From the middle of the sixth century, armies composed solely of infantry began to appear and the number of combatants rose sharply, with armies of 600,000 men being recorded.

In the Warring States period the economic and social changes which had begun in the Spring and Autumn period accelerated. In agriculture, the availability of iron tools, the application of fertilizer and the use of irrigation all became more common. The number of walled towns increased and some of these developed commercial quarters. Occupational specialization and the development of trade was accompanied by the spread of the use of money. There is evidence for the existence of markets and of extensive inter-regional trade. The names of a few merchants have been preserved, including that of Lü Buwei, whose career in the state of Qin will be noted shortly. However, the implication of this evidence is disputed. Marxist historians have suggested that the most significant development was the disappearance of communal land-ownership and the emergence of a private landlord class. Other writers have argued that the rise of trade was indicative of a change to a more individualistic society. The evidence for either interpretation is at best fragmentary, and the most that can be said with confidence is that this was a period of rapid development, which was reflected in the intellectual activity of the period.

*　*　*

Kong Fuzi, Master Kong, known in the West as Confucius, a latinized form of his name, lived approximately 551–479 BC. He was born in the small north-eastern state of Lu. His parents probably belonged to the minor aristocracy and his search for an official position was perhaps typical of *shi* or gentlemen of his day. He became an expert on ceremony, genealogy and ancient lore and was appointed to a junior post in his own state until he was forced to go into exile. He visited a number of states and held office in Wei before returning to Lu for his last years. He acquired a number of followers, who recorded his sayings in a compilation made long after his death, known as the *Lunyu* or *Analects*.

Confucius's teachings were influenced by his perception that he lived in troubled times, and by his belief that in the early Zhou period China had experienced a golden age. He frequently cited the actions of Kings Wen and Wu, and those of the Duke of Zhou, as examples of appropriate behaviour. He believed that they had followed the *dao* or Way, which in this context meant 'the Way of running a state so that good order and harmony can prevail among men'.[5] His concern for the promotion of good government led him to seek a position as minister to a king who would heed his advice and practise ethical government. In order to achieve this the ruler should select good officials, set a moral example and treat his people with benevolence.

A number of other themes were prominent in Confucius's teaching. He made frequent reference to standards of conduct and to the ideal of the *junzi* or princely man, a term often translated as 'gentleman'. Two quotations from the *Analects* illustrate this concept. In the first, Zi Lu, one of Confucius's disciples, asked about the gentleman. Confucius replied:

'He cultivates himself and thereby achieves reverence.'
'Is that all?'
'He cultivates himself and thereby brings peace and security

to his fellow men.'
'Is that all?'
'He cultivates himself and thereby brings peace and security
to the people.'

In another passage Confucius distinguished between the gentleman, who is superior not because of breeding but because
of superior moral accomplishments, and the small man. 'The
gentleman,' he said, 'understands what is moral. The small man
understands what is profitable.'[6] Confucius constantly emphasized the importance of education and of self-cultivation, and
thus established a respect for book-learning which was to last
throughout the imperial period. Self-cultivation was not only a
matter of scholarship, it was also a commitment to learning how
to behave. The essential quality was *jen*, a term often translated
as benevolence, but which also connoted dealing with other
human beings as a man ideally should. One aspect of *jen* was
reciprocity: 'Do not impose on others what you yourself do not
desire.'

Confucius believed strongly in the importance of ritual and
ceremony and in the value of politeness and good manners. The
correct performance of ritual was an essential part of the government of a state. Within the family it was important to observe
the niceties of behaviour to others and to apply restraint with
regard to eating, drinking and dress. Confucius placed particular
stress on the importance of filial piety, which implied obedience
to one's parents during their lifetime and care for them as they
grew old. After their death it was essential to provide them with
a proper funeral and to observe mourning over a period of three
years. There was also an obligation to make the correct sacrifices
to the dead, in particular to male ancestors. Though referred to
as 'ancestor worship', these ceremonies did not imply the deifi-
cation of forebears. Confucius had little to say about religion,
but he did define wisdom as keeping one's distance from gods
and spirits while showing them reverence. In all his teaching
Confucius was not announcing a new doctrine but expounding
what he believed to be the principles which had been observed
by rulers and families in the past.

Confucius's most famous opponent was Mozi, who lived
approximately 470–391 BC. It has been suggested that Mozi's

family may have come from a class of prisoners or slaves, for there is a degree of rancour in his attack on Confucianists as aristocrats. Whereas Confucius had stressed what was described as 'graded love', implying reserving a greater concern for one's family and ancestors than for other people, Mozi urged men to practise universal love. By this he meant in particular the satisfaction of the ordinary people's material needs, and he condemned elaborate funerals and prolonged mourning as inappropriate expenses. He regarded ritual as superfluous and had no time for music, which played an important part in Confucius's concept of how harmony could be achieved in human affairs. But like Confucius he condemned war, and his passionate denunciation of its effects was characteristic of his teaching.

> Now among all the current calamities, which are the worst? I say that the attacking of small states by large states, the making of inroads on small houses by large houses, the plundering of the weak by the strong, the oppression of the few by the many, the deception of the simple by the cunning, the disdain of the noble towards the humble – these are some of the calamities in the world.[7]

Quite distinct from Confucius's and Mozi's concern with morality was the preoccupation with nature, which was the keynote of the philosophical ideas known in the West as Daoism. The *dao* in this context was a metaphysical concept, sometimes referred to as the absolute. The impossibility of defining it was asserted in the opening lines of the oldest Daoist text, the *Laozi*,

> The way that can be spoken of
> Is not the constant way;
> The name that can be named
> Is not the constant name.
> The nameless was the beginning of heaven and earth;
> The named was the mother of the myriad creatures.[8]

This text, otherwise known as the *Daodejing* or *The Way and Power Classic*, was supposedly written by Laozi, a contemporary of Confucius. It is now generally accepted that there was no such person and that the text is a compilation dating from the fourth century BC. Inevitably it reflected the troubled times in which it was composed. The ideal ruler was the sage, who had acquired enlightenment and who then applied it to the art of government. The most important principle was *wuwei*, which meant that the ruler should avoid interfering in people's lives

> Not to honour men of worth will keep the people from contention; not to value goods which are hard to come by will keep them from theft; not to display what is desirable will keep them from being unsettled of mind.
>
> Therefore in governing the people, the sage empties their minds but fills their bellies, weakens their wills but strengthens their bones. He always keeps them innocent of knowledge and free from desire, and ensures that the clever never dare to act.
>
> Do that which consists in taking no action, and order will prevail.[9]

The other main Daoist text, the *Zhuangzi*, is more reliably associated with a man of that name whose supposed dates are 369–286 BC. A constant theme in the book was how man might free himself from his earthly constraints. Its most famous anecdote told how Zhuangzi once dreamed that he was a butterfly,

> a butterfly fluttering about, enjoying itself. It did not know that it was Zhuangzi. Suddenly he awoke with a start and he was Zhuangzi again. But he did not know whether he was Zhuangzi who had dreamed that he was a butterfly, or whether he was a butterfly dreaming that he was Zhuangzi. Between Zhuangzi and the butterfly there must be some distinction. That is what is called the transformation of things.[10]

In all this philosophical activity Confucius's teaching was not forgotten and its main themes were to be re-stated by Mengzi, known in the West as Mencius, who lived between 372 and 289 BC. Mencius, like Confucius, gathered a group of disciples around him and it is their collection of his sayings which is the basis of the text known as *Mencius*. Mencius made three important additions to Confucius's thought. The first concerned human nature, on which Confucius had merely observed: 'Men are close to one another by nature. They diverge as a result of repeated practice.'[11] Mencius believed that what set man apart from animals was the heart, by which he meant the essential moral nature of man. Gao Zi, a critic of Mencius, likened human nature to whirling water, and said that if you gave it an outlet to the east it would flow east, and if you gave it an outlet to the west it would flow west. Mencius responded by asking whether water showed the same indifference to high and low? 'Human nature is good, just as water seeks low ground. There is no man who is not good; there is no water that does not flow downwards.'[12]

Like Confucius, Mencius had much to say on the subject of good government. He stressed that the economic welfare of the people was the basis of political stability, and advocated a return to the well-field system, the system of equal land-holding which he believed had existed early in the Zhou period. He added that if a ruler failed to rule benevolently then his people had the right to rebel.

Mention of Mencius's view of human nature leads to Xunzi, who lived between 298 and 238 BC. He famously argued, 'The nature of man is evil; his goodness is acquired.' Man, he insisted, is born with desires and passions, which if not curbed will lead to disorder.

Crooked wood needs to undergo steaming and bending by the carpenter's tools; then only is it straight. Blunt metal needs to undergo grinding and whetting; then only is it sharp. Now the original nature of man is evil, so he must submit himself to teachers and laws before he can be just; he must submit himself to the rules of decorum and righteousness before he can be orderly.[13]

Xunzi therefore emphasized education and the study of those books which he regarded as classics. Although it is not clear to which books he referred, it was at about this time that the canon of Confucian literature began to be defined. Five books were designated as classics: the *Yijing* or *Book of Changes*, a book of divination; the *Shujing* or *Book of Documents*, a collection of writings ascribed to the Shang and early Zhou periods; the *Shijing* or *Book of Songs*, an anthology of poetry and folksongs; the *Spring and Autumn Annals*; and the *Liji* or *Book of Rites*, a compilation of three works on aspects of ritual and conduct to which Confucius was believed to have contributed. Later, four works, to be known as the Four Books, became the basic texts for primary education. These were the *Analects* of Confucius, and the *Mencius*, which have already been mentioned, and two sections from the *Book of Rites*, the *Great Learning*, an essay on self-cultivation and the ordering of the family and society, and the *Doctrine of the Mean*, which is concerned with how man and his actions may be brought into harmony with the universe.

While these philosophical issues were being debated, theories relating to the order of nature were formulated into two concepts, *yin* and *yang* dualism and the 'five elements'. According to dualist theory all matter may be classified as either *yin*, which is the negative, female and yielding principle of the universe, or *yang*, which is the positive, male and active principle. These two principles are regarded as complementary and their relationship is necessary for cosmic harmony. The theory of the 'five elements', which are wood, fire, earth, metal and water, asserts that these are the five permanently active principles of nature. The five elements are related to the five directions, the five seasons, the five metals, the five atmospheric influences, etc. They are also incorporated into the divination techniques of the *Book of Changes*.

THE RISE OF QIN

During the Warring States period the most dynamic of the seven principal states was Qin, situated on the Wei river. The other states accused the inhabitants of Qin of having the same customs as the Rong and Di, non-Chinese groups living to the west and north of their territory. Qin expansion was at first achieved at the expense of the Rong, who were finally subdued in the fourth century BC. Meanwhile Qin had modernized its government and had adopted practices from other parts of China, notably the introduction in 408 BC of a land tax payable in kind rather than in labour. In its dealings with other warring states, Qin had often clashed with the state of Jin, its neighbour to the north-east. However, in 403 BC Jin was partitioned between its three most influential ministerial families. The successor states of Han,

Zhao and Wei, although still powerful entities, became involved in interstate rivalry, which was to be exploited by Qin. Qin was reputedly willing to employ able men from other states. The ruler of Wei had been warned about a young man from his state named Yang Gongsun '[he] has marvellous talents, – if he is not employed in an official post, it would be better to put him to death, lest another kingdom obtain his services!' For a time Yang served as a minister in Wei, but in about 361 BC he was attracted to Qin, where he was created Shang Yang, or Lord Shang, and placed in control of a reform programme. The programme, though unprecedented in its scope, was not entirely novel for it consolidated changes which were already under way in Qin and in other states.

Shang Yang was the first exponent of the ideas and practices later to be known as Legalism. Whereas the Confucianists had urged that rulers should rule through benevolence for the benefit of their people, and that ethical and moral issues should have primacy, Legalists argued that the interests of the state came first and that the state should be organized rationally to maximize its power against that of its rivals. To achieve this, Shang Yang supported the use of war and he himself led a campaign against his own state. He also implemented a wide range of reforms. One of his objectives was to abolish feudalism, implying ending the devolution of power to hereditary landowners in favour of direct state administration. It was at this time that the *xian*, or district, became the standard administrative subdivision. An agrarian reform abolished the 'well-field' system, in so far as it still existed, and replaced it with a free market in land. Farmers were honoured for increasing their productivity, whereas traders, whose activities were regarded as against the interests of the state, were liable to punishment.

Strict laws and punishments were instituted and fixed administrative procedures were introduced. The population was divided into groups of five or ten families and individuals were held responsible for the wrongdoing of any member of the group. A comprehensive law code was introduced which prescribed severe punishments for offences. A collection of bamboo slips, found in 1976 in the grave of a Qin official buried in Yunmeng *xian*, Hubei province, contains details of a legal code in existence before Qin united China, which may be the code established by

Shang Yang. For his part in promoting these reforms Shang Yang has traditionally been condemned, and more recently praised. To Confucianists he was a destroyer of tradition who coerced the people into submission. In the 1970s, at the time of the anti-Confucius campaign, he was cited as the example of how revolutionary violence might be used to suppress the aristocracy and to introduce radical reforms.

In 338 BC, after the death of his patron, Shang Yang was acused of plotting rebellion and put to death. Nevertheless, the direction that he had given to Qin policy remained influential. In 316, Qin began to dismember the state of Chu, first seizing the territory of Shu, centred on present-day Chengdu, and subsequently subjugating the neighbouring territory of Ba. There followed a series of campaigns against the other states, all marked by victories for Qin and reports of very heavy casualties. In 256 the remaining territory of the Zhou was annexed and the dynasty extinguished. Qin was successful in each of these campaigns because of its location in the west which gave it a secure base, because of its strict social discipline which enabled it to mobilize its manpower, and because of its strong economy which provided ample resources, to overwhelm its opponents. However, the argument that Qin won because it had better weapons, in particular iron swords, has not been supported by archaeological evidence.

By the middle of the third century BC, Qin appeared to be on the verge of becoming the dominant state, but its triumph was to be delayed for a generation. In those years a number of individuals emerged who were to play key roles in the final victory. The first was Han Fei, who had been born in the state of Han in about 280 BC, and had been a student of the philosopher Xunzi, who had taught that 'the original nature of man is evil'. Although a Confucianist by training, Han Fei turned against Confucianism. The *Hanfeizi*, which contains a number of his essays, is the most coherent expression of the ideas of Legalism. Han Fei rejected Confucian idealization of the past, and accepted something of Mozi's utilitarian view of the function of the state. He also agreed with the idea of *wuwei* as expressed in the *Laozi*, arguing that if a state has effective laws, laws which reward the people for good behaviour and punish them severely for transgressions, then there is no need for the ruler to play an active role in government.

The second individual was a wealthy merchant named Lü Buwei, who when trading in the state of Zhao had befriended Zichu, a son of the ruler of Qin, who had been sent there as a hostage. As a mark of his friendship he gave the prince his favourite concubine who, according to the account of Sima Qian, the Grand Historian, was already pregnant by Lü Buwei. The latter then went to Qin and persuaded the heir to the Qin throne, who was childless, to accept Zichu as his heir. In quick succession the Qin ruler and his heir died, to be succeeded by Zichu, who himself died in 247 after a reign of only three years. Zichu had appointed Lü Buwei as his chancellor and Lü continued in that post until 237, during the minority of King Zheng, who was supposedly his son. In that time Lü Buwei further strengthened Qin by encouraging the construction of canals and by sowing dissension between the other states. He was also a patron of the arts, commissioning a major literary compilation known as the *Lü shi chun jiu*, or *Spring and Autumn Annals of Mr Lü*, which summarized existing knowledge on a wide variety of matters. Illadvisedly he continued his liaison with the concubine who was allegedly the king's mother. The scandal which this caused led to him being forced to commit suicide in 235.

By now a third important character had appeared on the scene. This was Li Si, who had studied under Xunzi and alongside Han Fei. Whereas Han Fei was a theoretician, Li Si was a practical politician, who had come to Qin because he considered that the career prospects in his native state of Chu were poor. He attached himself to Lü Buwei, and would probably have fallen with him, had he not presented to King Zheng a document entitled *Memorial on Annexation of Feudal States*, in which he argued the value to Qin of employing advisers from other states. He did not extend this tolerance to others, for he is reported to have engineered the death of Han Fei after the latter had been sent as envoy to Qin by the state of Han.

THE QIN DYNASTY, 221–206 BC

In 230 Qin started the series of campaigns which led to the unification of China. The other states tried to form alliances to oppose the advance of Qin and in 227 Yan sent an assassin to murder King Zheng. But this attempt failed, as did all other efforts at resistance, and in quick succession the surviving states were defeated. In 221 the king of Qin assumed the title of Qin Shi Huangdi, the First Emperor of Qin. It was suggested to him that the newly-acquired territories should be distributed to a feudal nobility, but in an outspoken memorial Li Si opposed the idea. Instead, the empire was divided into 36 commanderies and prefectures under officials appointed by central government. The emperor's and Li Si's distrust of those who served them was apparent in the arrangement in which military and civil authority was separated and a third supervisory official was appointed to each commandery, thus initiating a pattern of control through division of authority which was to survive through the imperial period. Many aristocratic families were required to move to the capital at Xianyang, near present-day Xi'an. Vast quantities of weapons belonging to these families were confiscated and melted down to make statues, and city fortifications were destroyed.

After the conquest Li Si embarked on a series of measures which applied Legalist principles to the new state. A major effort was made to standardize measurements, and examples have survived of inscribed weights and vessels. Other reforms provided for a network of roads radiating from the capital and fixed the axle-width of carts using them. Standard gold and copper coins were circulated, and the form of the latter – a round coin pierced by a square hole – established the shape of future coinage. These measures served to encourage commerce, although the emperor shared the prejudice of Legalists in favour of agriculture and against merchants, who on occasions were rounded up and settled in distant regions.

The *Shiji* or *Historical Records*, compiled by Sima Qian a century later, state that Li Si carried out a reform of the written language, that he 'equalized the written characters, and made these universal throughout the empire'. The probability is that a group of scholars under Li Si's direction developed a standard script known as the Small Seal, which was used in official communications. It was also used on seven stone stelae erected in various parts of the empire to commemorate the inauguration of a new age and to record the journeys made by the emperor. The emperor's relationship with scholars was a difficult one. In 213 a scholar cited the historical record to criticize the emperor for having accepted Li Si's recommendation with regard to feudal fiefs. In response Li Si presented a memorial to the emperor suggesting that scholars, other than those attached to the court, should surrender all historical records other than those of Qin and that these should be burned. Copies of works such as the *Book of Songs* and the *Book of Documents* were collected and destroyed, but the destruction was by no means complete and many books, in particular treatises on technical and literary subjects, survived the holocaust. If that incident was not enough to earn Qin Shi Huangdi the enduring disapproval of Confucian scholars, the action he allegedly took in the following year certainly was. Having heard that certain scholars were criticizing him, he ordered that more than 460 of them should be buried alive. Descriptions of both these events are given in the account written by Sima Qian a century later. The truth of the allegations is uncertain and the latter incident may never have happened.

After the unification Qin Shi Huangdi continued the drive for territorial expansion. Expeditions were sent south to modern Guangdong and Guangxi and Chinese were sent or deported to colonize those regions. To support the military expeditions a canal, known as the 'magic transport canal', was dug to link the Yangzi and Xi (West) rivers. Meng Tian, the most famous general of the day, led a large force against the Rong and Di and forced them to retreat beyond the Ordos region, to which Chinese settlers were also sent. Meng Tian was said to have used a vast army of convicts to construct a 'great wall' extending for more than ten thousand *li* (a *li* is approximately $1/3$ of a mile: the phrase 'ten thousand *li*' means 'extremely long'). This reference has long been taken to refer to the building of *the* Great Wall. However, the Great Wall of today dates mainly from the Ming period, and Meng Tian's wall was a more modest construction, joining together earth walls which had been built in the Warring States period. Meng Tian also built the Straight Road, which ran northwards for some 500 miles from Xianyang to the Ordos desert, and which was intended to facilitate the supply of troops operating on the frontier.

During his reign Qin Shi Huangdi had become increasingly preoccupied with the theory of the five elements and the secret of immortality. As the Zhou dynasty had been associated with the element of fire, the Qin dynasty was identified with the element which fire does not overcome, namely water, and also with the colour black and the number six. In all garments black became the dominant colour and in measurements six was taken as the basis of calculation. On his tours the emperor dispatched people to collect herbs believed to grant immortality and he sent an expedition to the island of Penglai, where immortals were believed to reside. In 210 BC he travelled to the coast of modern Shandong, where in response to a dream he hunted and shot a large fish. Shortly afterwards he fell ill and died. In an attempt to manipulate the succession, Li Si and Zhao Gao, the eunuch chief minister of Qin, concealed the emperor's death by keeping his body in the sleeping-carriage and disguising the smell by surrounding it with carts loaded with salted fish. By this means they procured the succession of a younger son, who became the Second Emperor.

Even before he became emperor, Qin Shi Huangdi had started to plan his tomb. Construction began in 212 BC or earlier at a site thirty miles east of Xianyang. The position of the tomb has long been known, but it was not excavated, as records showed that it had been rifled twice. However, in 1974 a chance discovery led to the uncovering of three vast pits to the east of the burial mound. In these pits were over 7000 life-size terracotta figures of soldiers. The mausoleum itself has yet to be excavated. According to the description left by Sima Qian, it contained a model of the empire which had rivers of quicksilver and a mechanism for operating the tides. The model was lit by candles made of whale fat. The tomb incorporated boobytraps which would shoot any intruders. To guard its secrets the workers who had constructed it were also entombed, one of the last examples in Chinese history of mass human sacrifice.

The Second Emperor set out to rule as his father had done. In a famous memorial Li Si advised him about 'supervising and holding responsible', a method of control advocated by the Legalists. But very quickly things began to go wrong. Discontent had arisen over the heavy taxes levied to complete the Epang palace, which had been started by Qin Shi Huangdi. Before the new emperor had been on the throne a year a rebellion headed by Chen Sheng and Wu Guang, two poor farmers, had broken out in the former state of Chu. Less than a year later other uprisings had occurred and Chen Sheng's forces were within 30 miles of the capital. At court Zhao Gao intrigued against Li Si, who was executed by being cut in two at the market-place at Xianyang. Zhao Gao's political ascendancy increased to such an extent that in 207 BC he was able to force the Second Emperor to go into retirement and then to commit suicide. Two months later the new emperor had Zhao Gao killed, but by then the empire was lost and he was forced to submit to Liu Bang, one of the rebel leaders, who became the first emperor of the Former Han dynasty.

Early in the following century a poet and statesman named Jia Yi wrote an essay entitled 'The Faults of Qin', an analysis of the reasons for the precipitous fall of the Qin dynasty. Jia Yi criticized Qin Shi Huangdi for his overweening ambition, his disregard for the ways of former kings, and in particular for his burning of the books. Having pacified and fortified the empire he had supposed that it would last ten thousand generations. But the Qin empire had a fatal flaw: it was not ruled with humanity and righteousness and it was this which enabled Chen Sheng and others to overthrow it. Marxist historians have emphasized the role of poor peasants in the fall of the dynasty, describing their rebellion as the first great popular revolt in Chinese history. Western historians have suggested that the dynasty fell because of a combination of factors, including the moral shortcomings of its rulers, the discontent brought about by their policies, and the magnitude of the task they attempted.

THE FORMER OR WESTERN HAN DYNASTY, 206 BC–AD 9

The first of the rebellions against the Qin, that headed by Chen Sheng and Wu Guang in the north, collapsed in the face of Qin resistance and internal disputes, and both leaders were killed. In the meantime a second rebellion had broken out headed by Xiang Yu, whose family had previously been generals in the state of Chu. Xiang Yu resented the Qin centralization of power and after gaining an important victory at Julu, he put himself forward as the supreme general of the feudal states. Among his supporters was Liu Bang, a peasant from the district of Pei in modern Jiangsu, of which he had proclaimed himself the feudal lord. In 206 BC Liu Bang captured the Wu Pass, which left the Qin capital at Xianyang at his mercy, and he then negotiated the surrender of the third and last emperor of the Qin. He was said to have spared the inhabitants of the capital, to have prevented looting, and even to have rescinded the most severe of the Qin laws. However, when Xiang Yu arrived the city was looted and the last emperor was put to death. Xiang Yu then revived the feudal states, appointing 19 rulers with himself as hegemon. At this point he and Liu Bang fell out and over the next four years they fought a series of campaigns, in which Liu Bang was often defeated, but nevertheless his reputation for moderation earned him the support of a number of the feudal lords. In 202 BC, after Liu Bang had gained a decisive victory at Gaixia in modern Anhui, Xiang Yu was captured and killed.

Liu Bang, who had adopted the title of King of Han, now assumed the style of *huangdi* or sovereign emperor, and used the name of his state as the title of the new dynasty. From now on he will be known as the Emperor Gaozu. During his reign, which lasted until 195 BC, and the reigns of his two sons and his grandson, that is until 141 BC, a remarkable consolidation of political power took place and many of the features of the imperial system, which was to last initially for two centuries and subsequently for two millennia, took shape. Gaozu himself represented for all time the possibility that a man of peasant origins but of outstanding virtue might rise to become emperor. His supporters, three of whom became known as the Three Heroes of the Han dynasty, were all said to have known poverty and to have performed acts of charity on behalf of the poor and dispossessed.

Gaozu began his reign by announcing an amnesty and measures to restore the country to peace. Being aware of the limitations of his authority, he moved cautiously to assert central control. In the west of the country, and in the area around the new capital, which was established at Chang'an, he continued Qin practice and applied direct rule in the form of commanderies. But in the east and the south he accepted the existence of ten kingdoms, whose rulers professed allegiance to him. Later, in a piecemeal fashion, he replaced the rulers of these kingdoms with members of his own family. In the commanderies he rewarded senior officials, military leaders and leaders of non-Chinese groups who had submitted to the Han, by conferring on them the rank of *hou*, or marquis. These titles gave them the right to raise taxes, part of which they remitted to the state and part of which they were allowed to retain. Gaozu introduced two other important measures to ensure the stability of the dynasty. The first was to formalize the system of bureaucratic government which had been introduced under the Qin. The emperor was assisted by three senior officials, known as the Three Excellencies, and they in turn were supported by nine ministers, each of whom had a defined area of responsibility. To restrict the power of the senior officials, the terms of their appointment made them mutually dependent. Likewise ministers and military officials were often appointed in pairs with overlapping responsibilities. The other measure was less specific, but nevertheless of great significance. Gaozu was notorious for his contempt for scholars, declaring that he had won the empire on horseback and had no time for the Confucian classics. However, a Confucian scholar named Lu Jia, who had been an early supporter of the emperor, compiled for him the *New Analects*, a collection of essays which identified the shortcomings of the Qin dynasty and recommended that the new emperor's government should observe ethical standards. This may have marked the beginning of the adoption of Confucian values as the basis of imperial government, a process which was advanced further in 196 BC when an edict was issued regulating the recruitment of able persons, that is men of merit, to the administration.

During Gaozu's reign steps were taken to stabilize the frontiers of the empire. To the north the main threat came from the people known as the Xiongnu, who were once identified with the Huns, but are now described as a confederacy of steppe people originating in Mongolia. This confederacy had been established in 209 BC by a charismatic leader named Maodun. He defeated the main rivals of the Xiongnu on the steppe and established his capital at Longcheng in Outer Mongolia. He then began to expand southwards, into the Ordos region, where the Qin general Meng Tian had campaigned. Gaozu could not tolerate this challenge and in 200 BC he led a large army against the Xiongnu, but was defeated at Pingcheng in modern Shanxi and he himself narrowly escaped capture. He then switched to diplomacy, initiating a policy known as 'harmonious kinship', which involved the marriage of a Chinese princess to the Xiongnu leader, the exchange of gifts, and the recognition of a frontier separating Xiongnu and Chinese territory.

When Gaozu died in 195 BC the throne passed to his son, then a minor, and subsequently to two other descendants, both minors. During those years real power lay in the hands of Gaozu's widow, the Empress Lü. The empress herself, and the Lü family which came from the province of Shandong, later came to epitomize the danger to the imperial succession of usurpation by the empress dowager's family. While Gaozu was still alive he was supposed to have required her to swear an oath not to elevate members of the Lü clan to the rank of king. But she manipulated the succession, and killed off rivals, and from 188 BC until her death eight years later she ruled as regent. She had hoped to assure the position of her family after her death, but after the succession of another of Gaozu's sons, who became the Emperor Wendi, the Lü family was eliminated.

Under Wendi and his son, who reigned as Jingdi, that is between 180 and 141 BC, the Chinese Empire achieved new levels of stability and prosperity. It was during this period that the agricultural economy of China Proper first exhibited its characteristic features: intensive cultivation involving sophisticated techniques of irrigation and seed selection; an economic interdependence in which a free peasantry produced a marketable surplus of primary goods, and supplemented its income through domestic handicrafts; and an economic vulnerability to natural disasters and the encroachment of landlordism and state exactions. It was this last feature which encouraged migration, and in particular the drift of population to the southern provinces.

This period also saw a refinement of religious beliefs and practices concerning the dead. A vivid illustration of this was provided by the tomb of the Countess of Dai, which was discovered in 1972 at Mawangdui in Hunan. The tomb, which dates from about 168 BC, contained the mummified body of the princess and various talismans which would enable her to make the journey to paradise. These included a painting on silk which depicted the route her soul would take, first to the magical island of Penglai and then to the gates of paradise. An indication of the increased complexity of the belief in an afterlife can be found in the appearance, in tombs dating from the first century, of bronze TLV mirrors. These mirrors, which have markings like the letters T, L and V, may have been used for divination. They are ornamented with a design incorporating the twelve symbols which represent the divisions of time, and the five elements. These mirrors served to reassure the bearer, whether alive or dead, that he or she stood in the correct relationship with the cosmos. The most glorious period of the Former Han dynasty was the reign of the Emperor Wudi between 141 and 87 BC. During those years the frontiers of the empire were extended, important political reforms were instituted, and major achievements were recorded in the fields of thought and culture. However, before the end of his exceptionally long reign a variety of financial problems had arisen and tensions at court had appeared, which proved to be a forewarning of the crisis that was to overwhelm the dynasty.

When Wudi came to the throne the gravest threat was posed by the Xiongnu, who, despite the agreement made with Gaozu, had continued to raid Chinese territory and in 166 BC had penetrated to within 100 miles of the capital at Chang'an. Under Wudi the policy of appeasement on the frontier was replaced by one of divide and rule. The first step was for the Han to seek allies among the opponents of the Xiongnu. In 138 BC Wudi sent Zhang Qian to contact the Yuezhi, known enemies of the Xiongnu. Zhang Qian failed to obtain their assistance, but his epic journey extended Chinese influence for the first time into the Western Regions, that is modern Xinjiang. From 129 BC Wudi launched a series of attacks against the Xiongnu. Although the Han forces won a number of victories, they were unable to campaign on the steppe for more than 100 days at a time, and so could not subjugate the Xiongnu.

Meanwhile expansion had taken place in other directions. In 128 BC an expedition was sent to Korea and 20 years later a longer campaign led to the establishment of four commanderies in the north of the peninsula. Nor was the south neglected, for in 111 BC an expedition reached Guangzhou and subsequently commanderies were established to administer the territory of the modern provinces of Guangdong and Guangxi as well as the northern part of Vietnam.

Wudi had received a good education from Confucian teachers, and during his reign he appeared to observe the teachings of the famous Confucian scholar Dong Zhongshu (c. 179–104 BC), who had defined the 'threefold obligations of the ruler'. These were to serve the basis of Heaven by making the appropriate sacrifices and setting the correct moral example; to serve the basis of earth by performing symbolic acts such as ploughing a furrow and feeding silkworms; and to serve the basis of man by establishing schools and enlightening the people by education. The most significant of the reforms which fulfilled those obligations was to start recruiting men of talent who had been educated through the medium of the Confucian texts, to the bureaucracy. In 141 BC, and in subsequent years, senior officials were called upon to nominate candidates for the civil service who exhibited the right qualities for appointment. Five years later official posts were established for academics who intended to specialize in the interpretation of the Confucian texts. This arrangement was formalized in 124 BC with the establishment of an imperial academy where a quota of 50 students studied the classics in preparation for an examination. If they passed they became eligible for an official appointment. This reform did not immediately replace the qualification for office through birth. The kingdoms which had been established at the start of the dynasty still remained in existence, as did the marquisates, held by the second rank of nobility, which were likewise hereditary positions. In the early years of his reign Wudi had conferred a large number of new marquisates on meritorious officials, military leaders and tribal leaders. However, by 112 BC the civil service had become such an effective arm of imperial government that dependence on marquisates was no longer necessary and the great majority of them were extinguished. In Wudi's reign the most celebrated example in Chinese history of social mobility occurred. This was the case of the Confucian scholar Gongsun Hong who rose from the condition of swineherd to become chancellor in 124 BC.

In Wudi's empire scholarly activity thrived. The ruler of Huainan, a kingdom in modern Anhui, commissioned a compilation known as the *Huainanzi*, which brought together a variety of explanations of the working of the universe as understood by Daoist scholars. This project indicated the popularity of Daoist thought at the time, and illustrated the tendency to adopt an eclectic approach which was to recur in future. The Confucian scholar Dong Zhongshu, author of the treatise on the obligations of the ruler which has already been mentioned, also wrote an influential work on portents, which he claimed were 'Heaven's threats', a warning to the emperor of Heaven's displeasure. This doctrine was to provide officials with a pretext for making indirect criticisms of the throne. Dong Zhongshu also synthesized the concepts of the five elements, the *yin* and *yang* forces, and the principle of the *dao*, to form one cosmic system. At the same time Sima Qian, the Grand Historian, was working on the *Shiji*, the *Historical Records*, a comprehensive survey of the history of China, which had been begun by his father.

From what has been said it might be supposed that by Wudi's reign Confucian ideas dominated the practice of government. In fact the situation was less simple, for a complex struggle was taking place between two attitudes, which Michael Loewe has termed 'modernist' and 'reformist'. The modernist attitude looked back to the achievements of the Qin dynasty and the principles of Legalism for its inspiration. It conceived the task of the state to be the enrichment and strengthening of China, which implied intervention in the economy and the expansion of frontiers. The reformist attitude looked to the teachings of Confucius for guidance, and like him harked back to the traditional values of the kings of Zhou as the epitome of ethical rule. It emphasized the interests of the people, which it believed were best served by allowing individual freedom and only intervening in the running of the economy to protect the poorest in society. It therefore advocated frugal government and a cautious foreign policy. According to Loewe, modernist policies dominated in the first century of the Former Han, whereas reformist policies gained the ascendancy in the latter half of the dynasty's span, the point of change occurring during the reign of Wudi.

The event which provides the best evidence of this conflict of attitudes is the conference which was held shortly after Wudi's death to discuss the cause of the hardship suffered by the people. The record of the conference is known as the *Discourses on Salt and Iron*, a reference to the government monopolies which were at the heart of the debate. The modernist viewpoint was represented by government spokesmen who argued that a state-planned economy was of benefit to the population as a whole. Their critics, the reformists, responded by saying that government should be based on principles rather than on material considerations. The debate ranged widely and included criticism of the over-ambitious foreign policy which had prompted the government to try to tap new sources of revenue. It is generally agreed that the reformists had the better of the argument and that thereafter Confucian principles played a larger role in determining government policy.

After Wudi's death the dynasty experienced a series of damaging succession disputes. Wudi's successor was a minor and power was held by a triumvirate headed by Huo Guang, the most famous kingmaker in Chinese history, who retained power throughout that reign and then played a key role in the selection of a grandson of Wudi to become the Emperor Xuandi in 74 BC. The occurrence of a minority did not necessarily weaken the dynasty, for emperors rarely played an active part in the administration of the state. However, the excessive influence of a great family was undoubtedly a threat. Huo Guang was praised for his support of the interests of the common people, but his wife was reviled for having murdered the empress and then having her daughter nominated empress in her place. After Huo Guang's death in 68 BC, the emperor ordered the elimination of the leading members of the Huo family.

During Xuandi's long reign, from 74 to 49 BC, the dynasty recovered a measure of stability. The danger on the frontiers had declined, for in 60 BC rivalry between the Xiongnu leaders fragmented their power and ended their threat. In the meantime trade had developed along the Silk Road, which passed through the Western Regions.

However, after Xuandi's death the characteristic features of dynastic decline multiplied. His successors either suffered from ill health or came to the throne as minors. The court was criticized for its extravagance and for the excessive influence of the eunuchs. Economic problems emerged which were traced to government expenditure and some dramatic, if short-term, reforms were initiated, including the temporary abolition of the government monopolies. Ineffectual measures were taken to try to reverse the growing problem of the concentration of land-holding and the evasion of taxation by landlords. River defences were neglected and in 30–29 BC the Yellow river burst its banks.

THE USURPATION OF WANG MANG, AD 9–23

It was in this atmosphere of dynastic decline that the famous usurpation of Wang Mang occurred. Few characters in Chinese history have been the subject of such contrasting assessments. He was at pains to present himself as a devout Confucian and friend of the people, and he fabricated evidence of portents to enable him to claim to have heaven's mandate. Nevertheless, Confucianists denounced him as a tyrant and a hypocrite. He was a reformer and in 1928 the famous scholar Hu Shi described him as a pioneer of state socialism. More recently he has been described as one who tried to reconcile the conflicting attitudes of the modernists and reformists.

Wang Mang was born in 45 BC. He was the nephew of the Empress Wang who was the consort of Yuandi and the mother of Chengdi, the emperor who reigned from 33 to 7 BC. The Wang family, and Wang Mang in particular, had at various times held positions of authority, including that of regent. Under Aidi, who was on the throne from 7 to 1 BC, the Wang family lost influence, but under his successor, another minor, Wang again became regent. In AD 9 he usurped the throne and declared himself emperor of the Xin, that is the New dynasty.

After seizing power Wang Mang carried through a series of reforms, which he presented as an attempt to end abuses. He first attacked the increasing concentration of land-holding. In an edict dated AD 9 Wang Mang 'nationalized' the land, that is to say he abolished private land-ownership and prohibited the sale of land and slaves. In its place he called for a return to the 'well-field' system of equal land-holding. The second reform reintroduced the monopolies in salt and iron which since Wudi's reign had fallen into disuse, and applied controls to the market in grain, cloth and silk. Through other measures the coinage was devalued, the nobility was required to surrender its holdings of gold in exchange for coin, and new taxes were imposed on merchants and craftsmen. During his reign Wang Mang also suppressed a rebellion in the south-west province of Guizhou and negotiated a successful agreement with the Xiongnu. He was a patron of the Old Text school of Confucian scholarship. He also encouraged scientific research and conducted an experiment to test the claims of a man who asserted that when coated in feathers he could fly thousands of *li* and spy out the movements of the Xiongnu.

Notwithstanding these achievements, in AD 23 Wang Mang was driven from the throne and then killed by rebels. Why did the Xin dynasty last for so short a time? According to Ban Gu, the compiler of the history of the Former Han, the reason was obvious. Wang Mang was an usurper whose radical and ill-judged reforms brought disaster upon the people. This negative view has been echoed by modern writers, for example Nishijima Sadao has decried his anti-mercantile policies as both ineffective and a cause of his downfall. Hans Bielenstein, however, has argued that Wang Mang was no innovator, but a pragmatist who governed much as his Former Han predecessors had done. The true cause of his downfall was a series of disasters which began in AD 11 with the shifting of the Yellow river to its southern course. This natural disaster, which had been preceded by prolonged neglect of the river defences, brought about a tremendous loss of life and precipitated a long-term migration from the north to the south.

In the short-term it also gave rise to a massive peasant rebellion in Shandong province. The rebels, who became known as the Red Eyebrows because they painted their foreheads red, professed no political objective other than a vague demand for a restoration of the Former Han. However, their activities created such disorder that gentry families became apprehensive. One of the migrant routes passed through Nanyang in southern Henan, which was the home of the Liu, a clan which claimed imperial descent. The Liu raised a rebellion against Wang Mang, and after three years of confused fighting, in which the imperial troops were defeated and the Red Eyebrows driven back, a member of the clan, Liu Xiu, proclaimed himself emperor of a restored Han dynasty. He is better known by his posthumous name Guang Wudi.

THE LATER OR EASTERN HAN DYNASTY, AD 25–220

The restoration of the Han dynasty may be explained in the first instance by referring to the military skill and political sagacity of Guang Wudi. Despite his claim to the title of emperor, it took him ten years to defeat all opposition. His most dangerous opponent, Gongsun Shu, who had likewise declared himself emperor, came from a prominent Sichuan family. However, although the territory over which Gongsun Shu claimed to reign was very extensive, it was sparsely populated. Guang Wudi had greater resources at his disposal and this enabled him to invade Sichuan and in AD 36 to capture Gongsun Shu's capital at Chengdu.

Marxist historians have defined the fall of the Xin dynasty and Guang Wudi's victory in class terms. Wudi has been described as a representative of the landlord class which had seized the fruits of the struggles of the peasant Red Eyebrows. Such a view has been firmly rejected by Hans Bielenstein, who has argued that the struggle between the Nanyang gentry and the Red Eyebrows was not a class struggle, for both sides accepted the existing social and political order. It was essentially a regional struggle, which was eventually won by the Nanyang faction supported by some other factions. Bielenstein has argued that an important social change did occur at this time. Under the Former Han, great clans had dominated the high offices of state. At first these clans had been the followers of Gaozu, the first Former Han emperor. Later other great families had risen to national prominence, the last example being the rise of the Wang clan which was followed by the usurpation of Wang Mang. However, most of Guang Wudi's 35 chief supporters were not from the great clans but from the lesser gentry. The regional factionalism, which was apparent in the early years of Guang Wudi's reign, reflected the basis of his support and was to prove an underlying weakness of the dynasty.

The Later Han dynasty fixed its capital at Luoyang, 200 miles east of the Former Han capital at Chang'an, hence the dynasty's alternate title of the Eastern Han. Within the city walls were situated the royal palaces, government offices and the residences of nobles and officials. Outside were extensive suburbs which housed half a million people, making it the most populous city in the world at that time. Luoyang was an important centre of commerce, which the evidence suggests was as flourishing as under the Former Han. Money was widely used and part of the labour-service obligation was commuted into a monetary tax. Another sign of commercial activity was the construction of roads and bridges. This was a period of important agricultural improvements, with the widespread adoption of iron ploughshares, a greater use of draught animals and the extension of irrigation. It was also a bad time for poorer peasants who may have been unable to afford these technological improvements.

During the reigns of Guang Wudi and his successors Mingdi (r. 57–75) and Zhangdi (r. 75–88), many of the administrative practices of the Former Han were continued. At central government level the most senior official was the grand tutor, whose task was to give moral advice to the emperor. Three officials, known as the Three Excellencies, were placed in charge of finance, the military, and public works. Nine ministers supervised other aspects of the administration. Of growing importance was the secretariat, which was responsible for the receipt and drafting of documents. A more sinister development, which can be traced back to the reign of Mingdi, was the increasing influence of the eunuchs, castrated males who had been placed in charge of the imperial harem and who also maintained the imperial palace. The country as a whole was divided into about 100 commanderies and kingdoms and these in turn were divided into counties. In AD 2 there had been 1577 counties, but by AD 140 this number had fallen to 1179, an indication of the extent to which the north had become depopulated. Each commandery and each county had appointed officials, while the kingdoms were headed by the sons of emperors.

All three emperors attempted to assert Chinese influence on the periphery of the empire. The outcome was short-term success and longer-term problems. One of Guang Wudi's principal allies, Ma Yuan, led an expedition to Vietnam, where he suppressed a rising led by two sisters. To the north and west the main threat continued to come from the Xiongnu who had taken advantage of the change of dynasty to regain control of the Western Regions. However, the Xiongnu now suffered an internal split. Subsequently the southern Xiongnu entered into an expensive tributary relationship with China and were allowed to settle in the Ordos region. The northern Xiongnu remained hostile, but after a series of defeats their influence dwindled. This allowed the dispatch of the famous general Ban Chao to the Western Regions and led to contact with states as distant as Sogdiana. To the north-east, relations had been established with the Wuhuan and Xianbei. The former had been allies of the Xiongnu, but now

accepted a tributary relationship with China and were encouraged to settle beyond the Great Wall. The Xianbei had been used
by the Chinese as allies against the Xiongnu, but after the
decline of the Xiongnu, they in turn became the main threat on
China's north-eastern frontier.

The middle period of the Later Han dynasty, that is to say
from AD 88 to 168, was marked by increased factionalism at
court and the alienation of scholars. A succession of minors
occupied the throne, and power often fell into the hands of the
family of the empress. A notorious example of this was the case
of Liang Ji, brother of the Shundi emperor's consort. Between
141 and 159 he held a series of important positions and gained
an unenviable reputation for rapacity. The court eunuchs continued to grow in numbers and in influence. In 135 they gained the
right to hand down noble titles to their adopted heirs. The
eunuchs entered into the struggles at court, for example a group
of eunuchs procured the murder of Liang Ji. While these
intrigues dominated palace affairs the literati class felt excluded
from influence and some of them became concerned about the
changes which they believed were taking place in society.
Foremost among the critics was the scholar Wang Fu who raised
the alarm about the growing unevenness of the distribution of
wealth. He deplored the excessive luxury of the upper classes
and the poverty of the peasants, the producers of the essentials.

From AD 168 the Later Han dynasty suffered a series of disasters from which it was never to recover fully. The crisis began
with a succession dispute, which was eventually resolved by a
coup which placed a eunuch faction in control of the court. The
new emperor, Lingdi, could not stem the rapid deterioration in
the authority of the dynasty. The selection of officials on the cri-
terion of merit was replaced by the widespread sale of office. On
the north-east frontier the Xianbei, under Tanshihuai, formed a
great steppe confederation which inflicted a series of defeats on
Chinese forces until Tanshihuai's death in AD 180. In AD 184 the
Yellow Turban and Five Pecks of Grain rebellions broke out.
These movements were the work of impoverished peasants
inspired by the prophecies of Daoist priests who predicted the
coming of the Great Peace. The Yellow Turban movement was
centred on the lower Yangzi, that of the Five Pecks began in
Sichuan. Both rebellions spread extremely rapidly and the rebels

attacked officials whom they blamed for their misery. Both rebellions were repressed with a tremendous loss of life, but other popular movements arose in their place.

After the Emperor Lingdi died in AD 189 the dynasty subsided quickly. His death led to another succession crisis, this one notable for a massacre of the eunuchs. Thereafter, although Han emperors remained on the throne, the empire was divided between three contestants, all generals of the Later Han. The most famous of these was Cao Cao, later immortalized as the hero of the *Romance of the Three Kingdoms*. Until AD 220 the fiction of the survival of the dynasty was preserved, but after Cao Cao's death, which was followed shortly by the abdication of the emperor, it was clear that the dynasty had come to its end.

The record of the Han dynasty has sometimes been compared with that of the Roman Empire. Both empires extended to the limits of the known world, both recorded remarkable technological achievements, both developed sophisticated administrative and legal systems, and both enjoyed a similar span of power until their collapse. Similarities have also been found in the explanations for their fall: the rise of privileged families owning vast estates; the degeneracy of the imperial line and factionalism at court; and an ideological failure, precipitated in the Roman case by the rise of Christianity, in China by the attraction of popular Daoism. Both empires were threatened by 'barbarian' tribes on their frontiers and both made the fatal error of allowing these 'barbarians' to settle within their boundaries. Yet the collapse of the two civilizations led to very different outcomes, for the Chinese Empire rose again but the Roman Empire was never to be reconstituted. This has prompted a further reflection on why the Chinese Empire had the resilience to survive. Maybe it was because it was a land empire, whereas the Roman Empire was both united and divided by the Mediterranean. Maybe it was the cultural homogeneity derived from a common Chinese written language and the persistent strength of Confucianism. Maybe it was the durability of the notion of ethical rule through the imperial institution. And maybe it was the strength of its institutions, which, according to Hans Bielenstein, 'formed the most impressive system of government in the world at the time, and for centuries to come'.[14]

2

From the Period of Division to the Tang Dynasty

Between 220 and 589, apart from a brief interlude between 280 and 316, no one dynasty ruled the whole of China. Between 220 and 280 the empire was divided into three kingdoms. The Western Jin then briefly and ineffectually reunited the country, but from 316 there was a prolonged division between the north and the south. In the south, six dynasties established their capital at Jiankang, that is modern Nanjing. In the north, until 384 there was a period of extreme fragmentation known as the time of the Sixteen Kingdoms. Then the Toba, a branch of the Xianbei, established the Northern Wei dynasty with its capital at Luoyang. In 534 the dynasty split and a further period of political fragmentation ensued until Yang Jian not only conquered the north but also subdued the south and in 589, having established the Sui dynasty, reunified China. In 618 this dynasty was replaced by the Tang, and one of the most glorious periods in Chinese history commenced.

THE PERIOD OF DIVISION, 220–589

Between 220 and 280 north China was divided into three states. In the north, with its capital at Luoyang, was the kingdom of Wei, ruled by Cao Pei, the son of Cao Cao, the famous poet and general of the closing years of the Later Han. To the south-west, in the region of present-day Sichuan, was the kingdom of Shu

Han, ruled by a descendant of the Han royal family. Finally in the south was the extensive, and only partly sinicized, kingdom of Wu. In 263 Wei absorbed Shu Han and then, following an usurpation by a general named Sima Yan, subdued Wu. Sima Yan established the Western Jin dynasty and briefly ruled over a unified China. However, after his death in 290 the country lapsed into civil war and in 311 the Xiongnu sacked the capital Luoyang.

The adventures of Cao Cao and others are entertainingly described in *The Romance of the Three Kingdoms.* However, a detailed account of political developments of the time would make dull reading. Of greater interest is an important social change which had begun under the Later Han and which was to continue through to the Tang. This was the re-emergence of an aristocratic society. After the collapse of the social and political structure of the Later Han, families which in the past had achieved national importance by obtaining office at court began to concentrate on perpetuating that influence in their locality. In 220 the Wei dynasty introduced the 'nine-rank system', in which a local arbiter, a member of the local upper class, classified all candidates for office into nine ranks, according to character and ability. The higher the rank a man received, the higher the level at which he could enter the bureaucracy. As a result of this reform, and as a consequence of the changing political situation, within three generations '[b]irth, status, and office-holding became inseparably bound'.[1]

Early in the fourth century, the danger of allowing the Xiongnu to settle within China's boundaries was made manifest. Liu Yuan, a sinicized Xiongnu king, captured Luoyang and declared the restoration of the Han dynasty, thereby founding the first alien dynasty in Chinese history. Although his dynasty did not last long, it set a precedent for the political division which was to persist for several centuries, with the north of China being ruled by non-Chinese dynasties and the south remaining under Chinese control.

The first of the southern dynasties, the Eastern Jin, which had its capital at Jiankang on the Yangzi, was founded by a survivor of the Western Jin. Other great families moved south to the Yangzi valley, and were joined by large numbers of refugees, many of whom became servants of the great families, which caused tension between the old and new settlers and the rise of popular movements. The political situation was very unstable and in 420 one of the dynasty's generals usurped the throne and established the Liu-Song dynasty, which survived until 479. This dynasty, and the dynasties which followed it, made sporadic attempts to limit the power of the aristocracy. However, a more effective counter to that power came through the rapid increase in commercial traffic on the Yangzi and the growth of a merchant class, a development which was particularly apparent in the reign of Emperor Wu of the Liang dynasty (r. 502–49).

In the meantime the north had been subject to a series of invasions by non-Chinese peoples. The first incursion was by the Xiongnu who, as noted above, seized Luoyang in 311. They established the short-lived Earlier Zhao dynasty (304–20), which was to founder on the issue which was to perplex all non-Chinese invaders: should they adopt Chinese culture at the expense of preserving their own identity? The second major incursion came from the Di and Qiang, proto-Tibetan tribes from the west. In 351 the Di established the Earlier Qin dynasty centred on Chang'an. Fu Jian, their most famous leader, conquered much of north China and in 382 invaded the south, but his army, which was unused to campaigning in the damp conditions of the Yangzi valley, was defeated by the Western Jin at the battle of Feishui.

The third, and most enduring incursion was that of the Toba, a tribe of which the leadership group may have been Turkish in origin, but which came to incorporate many Xianbei who had been allowed to settle in northern Shanxi. In 386 the Toba established the Northern Wei dynasty, based at Pingcheng (near modern Datong), which they laid out according to the Chinese conventions for a capital city. This was the first example of adoption of Chinese practices, which in time led the Toba to employ Chinese as officials and to abandon the tribal system in favour of a bureaucratic state. Before this transformation could be completed the Toba had to assert themselves as the paramount power in north China. Taking advantage of the effects of the campaigns fought by the Earlier Qin, they overcame the neighbouring kingdoms, drove back the Ruanruan, a new confederation of Mongol tribes, and extended their influence into Central Asia. They achieved these victories because they were able to put massive cavalry forces into the field. By 440 the Toba had created the most powerful state in East Asia.

The sinicization of the Toba empire proceeded apace under the Xiaowen emperor, who reigned 471–99. He issued a series of decrees which amounted to 'a conscious and deliberate attempt to bring the country closer to the . . . ideal of a Han-Chinese, Confucianized bureaucratic monarchy ruling an ordered, aristocratic state'.[2] These reforms included the adoption of Chinese surnames, the encouragement of intermarriage with Chinese, and the use of the Chinese language at court and for official business. At the same time restrictions were placed on Toba religious and social customs. In 477 an important but imperfectly-understood land reform was introduced. It decreed that all land belonged to the state and that every free man and woman would receive a share which they could enjoy in their lifetime, but which would be redistributed after their death. The reform echoed Wang Mang's attempt at land equalization, but was more successful, as it remained in force until about 750. The intention of this reform may have been to check the increasing impoverishment of the Toba, who after having settled in China could no longer plunder or graze their horses, and whose increasing poverty contrasted with the growing prosperity of Chinese gentry settled in the region. An alternative explanation of the reform is that it was intended to increase grain production and curb the influence of Chinese landowners.

In the 490s the Toba court abandoned Pingcheng and established a new capital at Luoyang, 500 miles further south, a place redolent with historic associations and at the heart of the most populous and prosperous region of north China. Luoyang quickly acquired a population of half a million people and became one of the great cities of the world. The city was set out on a grid system and graced with many elegant buildings, including some 500 Buddhist monasteries and nunneries. It was an important commercial centre and it housed a large community of foreign traders.

These developments alienated the more conservative aristocratic elements in Toba society. The sinicization policy marginalized them politically. A change in frontier policy, away from aggressive intervention and towards static defence, deprived them of their military role. Tension within Toba ranks grew acute after the move to Luoyang, and when in 524 the Ruanruan crossed the frontier in force, the Toba border garrisons mutinied. This 'revolt of the six garrisons' was followed by ten years of conflict, which culminated in the abandonment and sack of Luoyang. The Northern Wei empire split into the sinicized Western Wei state with its capital at Chang'an and the more traditional Eastern Wei in the north-east.

INTELLECTUAL AND RELIGIOUS DEVELOPMENTS DURING THE PERIOD OF DIVISION

In the centuries which followed the collapse of the Han empire, important new intellectual and religious movements gained a following. These included the transformation of Daoism and the introduction and rise of Buddhism.

Even before the end of the Han period it seemed that Confucianism neither served the state well, because it endorsed filial piety which underwrote the excessive influence of the great families, nor helped the individual, who could find little comfort in its moral exhortations. This apparent failure provided the opportunity for the emergence of what has been called neo-Daoism or philosophical Daoism. A precocious exponent of these ideas was Wang Bi, who, having written commentaries on the *Laozi* and the *Daodejing*, died of the plague in 249 when only 23 years old. Wang Bi, like many other neo-Daoists, remained an admirer of Confucius and did not argue that Daoism and Confucianism were incompatible.

Other writers and philosophers were more hedonistic and anarchic in their views and behaviour. A group which called itself the Seven Immortals of the Bamboo Grove met near Luoyang and engaged in *qingtan* or 'pure conversation', which took the form of metaphysical discussions and recitals of poetry. The term *qingtan* also implied 'criticism by the pure', a theme followed up by Bao Jingyan who has been described as China's first political anarchist. Other Daoists investigated medicine, alchemy and personal hygiene. It was at this time that an important connection was established between the Daoists' predilection for communing with nature, and landscape painting, a theme explored in *Introduction to Landscape Painting* by Zong Bing

(375–443). Meanwhile Daoism had developed as an organized church with priests and places of worship. By this time Buddhism had gained its first foothold in China. Buddhism had its origins in India and it was through commercial contacts along the Silk Road that the first intimations of Buddhism reached China. The Emperor Mingdi, who reigned between AD 57 and 75, is said to have dreamt of a golden deity who was later identified as Buddha, and this prompted him to send to India for copies of the Buddhist scriptures. Evidence that Buddhism may have reached China during his reign has been found in an edict dated 65 which used the Sanskrit term for a Buddhist monk. By the end of the second century AD Buddhist communities had formed at Luoyang and in several other places, notably Pengcheng in the Huai river valley. Buddhist temples had been constructed and a start had been made to the translation of Buddhist scriptures.

It is usually suggested that the spread of Buddhism in China was slow and that this was because a variety of obstacles stood in the way of its acceptance. These included the resistance of the Chinese educated classes to a religion which elsewhere had appealed to an illiterate community; the incompatibility of the Buddhist emphasis on the renunciation of worldly concerns with the Confucian emphasis on the importance of the family; and the difficulty of translating Buddhist religious concepts into Chinese, partly because of Chinese ignorance of Sanskrit, and partly because the translators subsumed Buddhist ideas into the vocabulary used for Daoist concepts.

In time, Buddhism made inroads in both south and north China. In the south it gained its first adherents among those educated Chinese who had been attracted to neo-Daoism and who now found Buddhism intellectually attractive. An example of such a person was Zhi Dun (314–66), who engaged in 'pure conversation', using Buddhism to illuminate Daoism and vice versa. Huiyuan (c. 334–417), a Confucian scholar who became a student of the Daoist texts, converted to Buddhism and later established a religious community at Lushan in northern Jiangxi. His followers sought salvation through the worship of Amida, the infinite Buddha. Huiyuan successfully asserted the principle that on grounds of conscience Buddhist monks should not be required to pay homage to the ruler. In 399 a monk named Faxian travelled from Chang'an to India to collect Buddhist scriptures, which he brought to Jiankang, and translated them there. He also wrote an account of his travels, the *Record of the Buddhist Countries*. The most famous Buddhist convert in south China was Emperor Wu of the Liang dynasty. In 504 he ordered his family to change their adherence from Daoism to Buddhism and he then called for the destruction of Daoist temples.

Because the northern dynasties did not have the same reservations against foreign religions as did the Chinese, Buddhism made more rapid progress in the north. A monk from Central Asia named Fotudeng reached Luoyang in 310, soon after the city had been sacked. A legend relates that he conjured a display of blue lotus flowers in a bowl of water and this enabled him to obtain the patronage of the Later Zhao dynasty. Buddhism was welcomed not only for its magical powers, but also because it provided a counterbalance to the Confucian influence of Chinese officials retained by non-Chinese dynasties. The first Northern Wei ruler, conscious of the growing influence of Buddhism, appointed a monk named Faguo to administer the Buddhist communities. This appointment made him a government official and liable to pay homage to the ruler, a relationship which Huiyuan had previously declared unacceptable. Faguo's ingenious response was to declare that the ruler's virtue made him the embodiment of the Buddha and that he therefore had no scruples about subjecting himself. Nevertheless the foreign origin of Buddhism made it an object of suspicion and the Emperor Wu of the Northern Wei, who reigned 424–51, was persuaded by his Confucian advisers to carry out a pogrom against Buddhist monks. The persecution did not last long, for in 460 work began on the Buddhist cave temples at Yungang, ten miles west of the capital at Pingcheng. In the 490s, after the Northern Wei had transferred their capital to Luoyang, another complex of cave temples was commenced at Longmen. In these temples the representation of the Buddha shows a transition from Indian to Chinese artistic conventions. The inscriptions in the caves, which refer to the cult of ancestors, also demonstrate how Buddhism was becoming sinicized.

THE UNIFICATION OF CHINA UNDER THE SUI DYNASTY, 589–618

In the middle of the sixth century China was composed of four main political units. After the collapse of the Northern Wei, the north was divided between the Northern Zhou, to the north-west, and the more sinicized Northern Qi, to the north-east. On the middle Yangzi was the small state of Liang. South of the Yangzi valley the Chen empire, ruled by the last of the Six Dynasties, spread extensively although its control was ineffectual.

The Northern Zhou and Northern Qi competed for control of north China, but their actions were limited by the threat from a new steppe confederation headed by the Tujue, a Turkish people whose influence had spread from Manchuria across Central Asia to the borders of Persia. Nevertheless in 577 the Northern Zhou, with the assistance of the state of Chen, attacked and defeated the Northern Qi. Events then came to their aid, for in 582 the Turkish Empire split into an eastern and a western part and the threat from the north was reduced. This gave the Northern Zhou the opportunity to go on the offensive. In 587 they overran Liang and two years later overwhelmed Chen.

Northern Zhou society was dominated by a small group of non-Chinese aristocratic families. One such family, the Yuwen, occupied the throne. Yang Jian, the prime mover behind the events which were to follow, came from another of these aristocratic families, one which was probably of Xianbei extraction. He had been born and brought up in a Buddhist temple. His wife, who was also a Buddhist, came from a prominent Xiongnu clan and his daughter was married to the heir apparent. Yang Jian rose to prominence as a military commander during the invasion of Northern Qi. In the following year the Northern Zhou emperor died and Yang Jian's son-in-law succeeded to the throne. Within a year Yang Jian deposed him and then attempted to wipe out the Yuwen family. This provoked a civil war, which Yang Jian might well have lost if he had not received support from Gao Jiong, a wily military leader who later became his long-serving minister. In 581 he defeated his opponents and established a new dynasty to be known as the Sui. Thereafter Yang Jian is better known by his posthumous title, Wendi.

It soon became apparent that Wendi's ambitions extended

beyond achieving a military coup. He claimed to be the legitimate heir to the Han dynasty and went through the appropriate rituals to confirm this. This claim provided him with a moral justification for the conquest of the south, which he achieved with great efficiency in 589. The city of Jiankang was sacked, but the Chen aristocracy and its officials were treated leniently to win their allegiance. Wendi's determination to broaden the basis of his support was also apparent in the manner in which he placated the Confucianists by endorsing the virtue of filial piety, while at the same time ending the persecution of Buddhism which had been practised under the Northern Zhou.

During his reign, which lasted until 604, Wendi introduced many other measures to ensure the stability of the dynasty which he had founded. He commenced construction of a great new capital at Chang'an. Aware that the aristocratic and non-Chinese tradition of Northern Zhou government was unsuited to ruling a newly-unified China, he set out to reconstitute a central government which echoed the practices of the Han dynasty, but which also served the autocratic tendencies of the emperor. More Chinese were now employed in the service of the state, but the most important offices were monopolized by close relatives of Wendi and those who had previously held office in the Northern Zhou. Wendi himself served as his own chancellor. Provincial and local government was rationalized and all appointments were made by the Board of Civil Office. After appointment, officials were subject to regular supervision, and censors were sent on tour to report on their conduct. The emperor himself when travelling investigated the work of his officials. It was at this time that two enduring techniques of control were adopted, the 'law of avoidance', whereby an official was not permitted to serve in his own district of origin, and that of rotation, which limited the length of time an official could hold a post.

Although Wendi himself had scant regard for scholars, it was during his reign that the essential characteristics of the examination system took shape. Examinations were conducted by the Board of Civil Office, they were held triennially and degrees were awarded at three levels. To obtain a lower degree a candidate had to demonstrate literary ability and knowledge of a classical work. The most prestigious degree, the *xiucai*, or 'cultivated talent', assessed the candidate's broader learning. Successful candidates were appointed to official positions, although the proportion of Wendi's officials holding degrees is unknown. Wendi also initiated important reforms relating to law and taxation. He promulgated the Kaihuang Code, which synthesized northern and southern legal traditions and abolished some cruel punishments. It defined crimes and their punishments in plain terms and allowed guilty officials to commute their punishment by payment of a fine or by accepting demotion. The Kaihuang Code was to provide a model for all future imperial legal codes.

Wendi also overhauled the land and taxation systems, reviving the 'equal field' arrangement and the periodic distribution of land to the common people, and revising the tax registers. The common people were required to pay three taxes: a land tax payable in grain, a textile tax payable in silk or linen, and a labour tax requiring 20 days' labour per year from adult males.

As might be expected, Wendi also reviewed the military situation and reorganized the armed forces under central control. In 590, having completed the conquest of the south, he took the bold step of demilitarizing the population of the North China Plain, and later he ordered the confiscation of all weapons. This did not imply that Wendi had abandoned all military activity. He sent an expedition south to recover control of Champa, known in modern times as Annam. In the north he contained the Turks by establishing military colonies and by building walls.

In many of his actions Wendi received the advice and encouragement of his consort, the Wenxian empress. That a woman should play such a role was accepted in northern aristocratic families, but such a relationship was unique in China's dynastic annals.

It was on the empress's advice that the emperor's second son was nominated heir. The Yangdi emperor, as he was later known, succeeded his father in 604. His name was to be execrated by Chinese historians, for he was suspected of parricide. Because of this crime, and as a consequence of his megalomania, extravagance and licentiousness, he was said to have forfeited the mandate of heaven and thereby to have brought to a premature end the short-lived Sui dynasty. Arthur Wright however has noted that in many respects Yangdi continued the policies inaugurated by his father, and has added that he was also a faithful husband, a devout Buddhist and a connoisseur of the arts.

Two aspects of Yangdi's reign are always held up for criticism: his programme of canal-building and his fixation with the conquest of Korea. The purpose of the canal-building programme was to enable the resources of the productive land in the south to be brought to the north, by connecting the drainage of the Yellow, Huai and Yangzi rivers. The programme had been started by Wendi and in places it merely consisted of restoring or improving existing waterways. Yangdi carried the programme much further, creating a network of canals extending for about 1200 miles, which has been described as 'probably an engineering feat without parallel in the world of its time'.[3] This national system of communications was to provide the basis for the prosperity of the Tang period. However, it was achieved by large-scale state intervention in the economy and by drafting many thousands of men and women labourers, features which earned it the condemnation of Confucian historians.

Yangdi's foreign policy was shaped by his awareness of the threat still posed by the eastern Turks in what is now Mongolia. His response was to continue his father's strategies of building walls, using marriage diplomacy, and seeking alliances with the eastern Turks' potential enemies. To achieve the last objective he sent his frontier expert Pei Ju on a fact-finding tour to the western Turks and in 607 the emperor himself travelled to Yulin, where he was infuriated to hear that an embassy from Koguryo, the state occupying eastern Manchuria and the northern part of the Korean peninsula, was present. It was the threat of an alliance between the Turks and the Koreans which prompted Yangdi's disastrous expeditions against Korea. The first attack was launched in 612, but poor planning and Koguryo resistance forced the Chinese to withdraw. Further campaigns were launched in 613 and 614, with similar results, but in the meantime widespread rebellion had broken out in China. The emperor was not informed of the true extent of the disaffection until it was too late for him to take effective action. After many of his former supporters had abandoned him, in 618 he was murdered by a descendant of the Yuwen family, whom his father had deprived of the throne.

The collapse of the Sui dynasty has often been attributed to Yangdi's personal failings and his overweening ambition. Sometimes it is conceded that fortune turned against him, in that the disastrous flooding in the Yellow river valley in 611 was the prelude to the rise of rebellion. However, Yangdi is held responsible for the rebellions, which are ascribed to the harsh conscription of peasants for canal-building and to the military disasters in Koguryo. On the other hand the collapse of the dynasty may be explained by reference to the continued rivalries within the northern aristocratic clans, to the survival of separatist sentiment in the territory of the former Northern Qi, and to the willingness of Li Yuan, who was to seize the throne and found the Tang dynasty, to reach a demeaning accommodation with the Turks.

THE ESTABLISHMENT OF THE TANG DYNASTY

Li Yuan, the founder of the Tang dynasty, was a member of a northern aristocratic family which later claimed descent from the Han nobility, but which more probably derived from a Hebei family who had intermarried with the Xianbei tribal aristocracy. Under the Northern Zhou his grandfather had been created Duke of Tang. Li Yuan, like his forefathers, pursued a military career and under the Sui his success in suppressing rebellion led to his promotion to command the important garrison at Taiyuan.

It was from there that in 617 Li Yuan decided to raise a rebellion. His motives for so doing have been the subject of debate. As the situation of the Sui dynasty had deteriorated, Yangdi had grown apprehensive of the danger of an attempt on the throne, and hearing of a prophecy that the next ruler would have the surname Li, he had ordered the execution of prominent holders of that name. Fear for his own safety may therefore have prompted Li Yuan to action. According to traditional historiography, however, the real reason for his decision was the ambition of his son Li Shimin, who tricked his father into an act of disloyalty and then laid plans for a successful rebellion by negotiating secretly with the eastern Turks. This explanation, which minimizes the role played by Li Yuan, has been found to be largely the concoction of Li Shimin himself, the man who later became the famous second emperor of the Tang dynasty. According to the evidence of a contemporary account, Li Yuan had nourished plans to rebel before his appointment to Taiyuan. He had taken part in planning the revolt, and in the negotiations with the Turks in which they were promised all the booty seized by the rebels and were encouraged to believe that Li Yuan was willing to become their vassal.

Within a year of the outbreak of the rebellion Li Yuan had captured Chang'an and had declared the establishment of the Tang dynasty. He was later given the posthumous title of Gaozu, by which he will now be known. It took Gaozu another six years to complete the conquest of the country. One reason for the slowness of the conquest was the multiplicity of rebellions and claims to the throne, which required extensive military campaigns to extinguish. Another reason was the restraint exercised by Gaozu, who preferred whenever possible to win over rebel leaders and to confirm Sui officials in their posts.

The transfer of power from Sui to Tang did not imply any major shift in the locus of power. Gaozu's background, and the support he mustered, came from the same northern aristocratic clans as did that of the Sui. At first he largely continued Sui practices in central and local government and maintained their legal and taxation systems. However, it would be unfair to Gaozu to imply that he did nothing new. During his reign mints were established and a new currency was issued. A revised code of law was produced which went further than that of the Sui in incorporating features of southern practice. He revived the examination system, although he continued to appoint aristocrats to senior posts. He reduced the throne's reliance on Buddhism as a unifying force. Early in his reign he appointed Fu Yi, a Daoist priest known as a fierce critic of Buddhism, as his chief astrologer. Gaozu made his own preferences clear in an edict in which he declared that Daoism and Confucianism were key pillars of the state, whereas Buddhism was a foreign religion, whose monks' involvement in worldly affairs sharply contradicted the tenets of their faith. Gaozu's manner of dealing with the eastern Turks showed that his position remained fragile, for he was forced to retain their goodwill through bribery. However, he did manage to gain a breathing space which allowed him to consolidate his position in China.

Gaozu's reign came to a sudden end. Li Shimin, to whom had been credited his father's rise to power, was a bitter rival of his elder brother, the heir to the throne. Li Shimin had played a major part in the campaigns to consolidate Tang control in the east, and this had enabled him to build up a strong personal following. The heir apparent's strength lay at court and in the capital, Chang'an. In an atmosphere of intrigue and plots Li Shimin chose to break the deadlock by carrying out a coup. The event, known as the Xuanwu Gate incident, resulted in the death of the heir apparent, the abdication of Gaozu and the succession of Li Shimin, henceforth to be known as Taizong.

THE REIGN OF TAIZONG, 626–49

Taizong's reign, which lasted until 649, has long been regarded as a golden age in Chinese imperial history. Taizong himself, though he had obtained the throne through the murder of his brother and the enforced abdication of his father, has been regarded by Confucianists as a model ruler, a view echoed in the West where he has been described as 'probably the greatest monarch in China's history'.[4]

In the first part of his reign, that is until 636, he presented himself as a humble student of the art of civil government. He employed a succession of capable ministers who came to epitomize the ideal relationship between an emperor and his advisers. Among them was Wei Zheng, an 'unbending moralist and fearless remonstrator', who was even prepared to criticize Taizong himself. He preserved many features of the government of his father's reign, which were later to be regarded as ideal institutions. The central government comprised the secretariat which drafted edicts, the chancellery, which reviewed them, and the department of state affairs, which put them into effect. It also included the censorate, the body which investigated abuses, and the supreme court, which reviewed sentences for crimes. The country at large was divided into prefectures and districts, the former administered by prefects and the latter by district magistrates. Hitherto, service in the provincial bureaucracy had been disparaged. Now Taizong took a personal interest in the careers of those appointed to provincial posts and dispatched commissioners to check on the quality of their work. Further revisions were made to the law codes and the severity of punishments was reduced. His father had adopted the 'equal field' land system of the Sui, which included provisions for the registration of households and the periodic redistribution of land. Taizong continued to support the system, although it was already apparent that it was far too rigid and idealistic to suit the changing economic situation in many parts of China.

Taizong was a member of a northern elite which had sprung from intermarriage with non-Chinese peoples. Their enjoyments were outdoors – one of his brothers once remarked that he would rather forgo three days' eating than one day's hunting. Although Taizong never lost these preferences, it was during his reign that the distance between the emperor and his social equals and between the emperor and the common man began to increase. An example of this tendency was Taizong's concern to establish the superiority of the imperial line above that of the 'four categories of clans', the leading Chinese families of the north-east. In 638 a revised national genealogy was published, which showed the Li clan in a pre-eminent position. His actions relating to education and scholarship suggest a similar motive. A system of state schools and colleges was instituted, one of which was reserved for children of the imperial family and those of the highest officials. Many students came to Chang'an to study and a variety of scholarly projects were sponsored, notably the writing of the dynastic histories which served to legitimize the succession of the Tang. The examinations were held regularly. The great majority of officials continued to come from the great clans, but the highest positions now tended to go to those who had passed one of the literary examinations.

Whereas the Sui had used Buddhism as an integrating force, Gaozu had relegated it to an inferior position. Taizong, having gained the throne by a coup, was at first careful to avoid alienating the Buddhist community. In 629 he ordered the building of seven monasteries where prayers would be offered for the souls of those who had died in the battles which had led to the victory of the Tang. Later in his reign he adopted a harsher line, passing measures to control corruption in the Buddhist church. In 637 he promulgated an edict criticizing the prominent position which Buddhism had come to occupy in China, and decreed that Daoist clergy would take precedence over Buddhist monks and nuns. In the same year he issued a legal code which contained a section regulating the Buddhist clergy, and restricting their participation in secular life.

Although Taizong remained critical of Buddhism, in the year before he died he gave audiences to the famous Buddhist pilgrim Xuan Zang. In 629 Xuan Zang had left China secretly and had travelled overland to India to collect Buddhist texts. This journey provided the inspiration for the sixteenth-century novel by Wu Cheng'en, *Record of a Journey to the West*, which is better known in the West as *Monkey*. When Xuan Zang returned to Chang'an in 645 he was received by Taizong. Perhaps the emperor hoped to gain new insights into Buddhism, but more probably his curiosity had been aroused by Xuan Zang's knowledge of foreign countries. The most Taizong ever offered Buddhism was a 'measured patronage'.[5]

In 637 Taizong's mentor Wei Zheng had the temerity to memorialize that he had observed that whereas in the early years of his reign the emperor had always made righteousness and virtue his central concern, now, thinking that the empire was without troubles, he had become increasingly arrogant, wasteful and self-satisfied. This change in the behaviour of the emperor followed the death of his father the retired emperor in 635, and that of the empress, who had been his close confidante, in the following year. Thereafter Taizong engaged in extravagant building projects and, more significantly, pursued an expansive foreign policy.

Soon after Taizong had seized the throne the eastern Turks under their khaghan Xieli had invaded China and had come within 75 miles of Chang'an. Taizong was forced to bribe them to withdraw. However, in 628 the eastern Turks were split by an internal feud. Taizong gained the support of Xieli's enemies and two years later a large Chinese force inflicted an overwhelming defeat on Xieli's men. Xieli himself was taken prisoner and the eastern Turks were forcibly resettled on Chinese territory. Such was Taizong's domination of the situation that he himself became the 'heavenly khaghan'. Thus began a remarkable expansion of Chinese power in Central Asia. With the eastern Turks now his allies, Taizong was able to split the western Turks and to recover the influence which the Han had once exerted in the Western Regions. In 657 Su Dingfang fought a memorable engagement near Issyk Kul which reduced the western Turks to vassals of China and advanced the Chinese Empire to the borders of Persia. In the meantime China had been sending punitive expeditions against the Tuyuhun, a Xianbei people who lived around Lake Kokonor, not realizing that the reason why the Tuyuhun were raiding Chinese territory was that they were coming under increasing pressure from a newly-unified Tibet. Taizong's final campaign was directed against Koguryo, which also had once been part of the Han empire, but which more recently had been the graveyard of Yangdi's ambitions. Gaozu had pursued a more cautious policy and Koguryo had resumed tributary relations, but in the 640s the Koguryo throne was usurped and the new ruler began to menace the south Korean state of Silla, China's faithful tributary. The threat of a unified Korea was sufficient to prompt Taizong to act, and in 645 he led an invasion of Koguryo. The expedition made slow progress and had to be withdrawn before the onset of the Korean winter. A similar fate frustrated an attack in the following year. Plans were made for an even larger campaign in 649, but Taizong died before it could be launched.

Taizong's foreign wars had been conducted against a background of difficulties at court. Early in his reign he had named Li Chengqian, his eldest son, as his heir apparent. However, complaints were made that Li Chengqian was homosexual and that he behaved eccentrically, and a faction formed to support the claim of Li Tai, a younger son. Both sons attempted plots against each other and against the emperor, and in 643 Taizong settled the succession on Li Zhi, his ninth son, who was to reign as the Gaozong emperor.

GAOZONG AND THE EMPRESS WU

Gaozong, who was only 20 years old when he came to the throne, reigned until 683. He suffered from ill health and from 660 his consort, the Empress Wu, was the effective ruler. Gaozong was succeeded by two of his sons, but the empress continued to control affairs, and in 690 she herself usurped the throne and established the Zhou dynasty, thus becoming the one example in Chinese history of a female monarch.

Gaozong began his reign cautiously. He relied on advice from his father's ministers, notably his uncle Zhangsun Wuji, a notable historian. The machinery of government operated smoothly and reforms continued to be introduced, for instance a commentary on the penal code was promulgated, which was to remain authoritative for centuries.

However, Gaozong's court was riven by a continuance of the factional fighting which had emerged late in his father's reign. Although modern historians have attempted to link these factions to regional bases and policy issues, it seems more likely that their source was vendettas which had their origin in the succession dispute. After Gaozong came to the throne, Zhangsun Wuji continued to pursue those who had supported Li Tai, and this situation was exploited by Wu Zhao, who later became the Empress Wu.

Wu Zhao was born in 627 into a 'merchant' family, and her supposed background has been used to identify her as a member of a newly-emerging mercantile class. It has been suggested that the preference she showed when in power for officials who had succeeded in the examination system confirmed her support for social mobility. She came from the north-east, and this fact has been interpreted as proof of the ascendancy of the leading families of that region over the north-western aristocracy, which had played a major role in the rise of the Sui and Tang. Her decision to transfer the capital from Chang'an to Luoyang may support this view. However, there is little evidence to show that either class or regional affiliation played a significant role in her rise or in the policies that she pursued as a ruler, which largely continued those of her predecessors on the throne.

Wu Zhao had been a concubine in Taizong's harem. In defiance of convention Gaozong started an affair with her and in 652 she bore him a son. She then began to intrigue against Gaozong's consort, the Empress Wang, and incriminated the empress in the death of her new-born daughter. In 655, having secured her position by having her son declared heir apparent, she disposed of her enemies, first the former empress and then Zhangsun Wuji, who had resolutely opposed her rise. In 660, when Gaozong suffered a stroke, the empress made herself *de facto* ruler.

The Empress Wu proved to be a shrewd ruler and over the next twenty years she continued many of the policies and practices of her predecessors. Some of her actions, however, have been taken as examples of her selfish and irrational behaviour. The first con-

cerned her decision, taken in 657, to designate Luoyang as a second capital, and then to transfer the court periodically between
the two capitals, at great disruption and heavy expense, until
finally relocating it at Luoyang in 683. Her motive has been
identified as political, favouring her power base in the north-
east, but there was also a sound economic reason for the transfer.
The area around Chang'an could not produce the amount of
grain required to feed the court and garrison, and the transportation of grain up the Yellow river, traversing the Sanmen rapids,
was extremely expensive. Luoyang, however, was favourably situated at the terminus of the water route from the south. Another
claimed example of her irrationality occurred in 666, when the
empress decided to hold, and then in defiance of precedent to
participate in, the *feng* and *shan* sacrifices on Taishan, the holy
mountain in Shandong province. These costly ceremonies, which
announced to heaven the glory of the dynasty, had not been performed since the Han period. Her selfishness has been detected
in her patronage of Buddhism and in particular her commissioning of work on the cave temples at Longmen. On her orders a
large number of statues were carved, including one of the
Vairocana Buddha, the features of which were said to be those of
the empress herself.

Under Gaozong and the Empress Wu attempts to extend and
consolidate the empire continued. Koguryo was defeated and a
short-lived Chinese protectorate was established at Pyongyang.
However by 676 a resistance movement, which had started in the
southern state of Silla, forced China to withdraw. Although Silla
went on to unify the Korean peninsula, Chinese influence in the
area remained strong and Silla became China's most dependable
tributary state.

The more pressing threat to China's interests at this time was
the rise of Tibet. At the beginning of the seventh century Tibet had
emerged as a unified state. Buddhism had been introduced and, in
the form of Lamaism, had made rapid progress. Under Song-tsen
Gampo, who ruled from 620 to 649, Tibet started to send tribute
to China. At the same time the Tibetan state began to expand,
pressing on the territory of the Tuyuhun pastoralists, and moving
into parts of Sichuan and the Tarim basin. Chinese influence in
the Tarim basin was later restored, but the expansion of Tibetan
power into modern Qinghai and Sichuan proved irresistible.

THE REIGN OF EMPRESS WU, 690–705

Gaozong died in 683 and was succeeded by his third son Zhongzong. Within months the Empress Wu, now the empress dowager, compelled his abdication in favour of his brother, who remained on the throne for six years. During that period the empress dowager began to reveal 'a heart like a serpent and a nature like that of a wolf'. In 684 Li Jingye headed a revolt of those families which had been disgraced and exiled to the Yangzi valley. He was quickly defeated, but the empress dowager used the revolt as a pretext to purge her opponents at court. She formed a secret police and conducted a reign of terror, for which hostile critics have condemned her as a mass murderer, whereas her apologists have argued that the powerful prejudice against a woman's open exercise of power forced her to use terror to safeguard her position.

In 690 she usurped the throne and established a new dynasty, the Zhou. She may have taken this unprecedented step because of the threat of rebellion, but as that had been averted it was more probably a calculated move justified by the urgings of her supporters. Much was made of the discovery of a white stone bearing an inscription prophesying her elevation. She was encouraged to act by Buddhist clergy, whom she had patronized and who now hailed her as the incarnation of the Maitreya Buddha. She was presented with three petitions, one said to have contained 60,000 names and each urging her to ascend the throne, which have been taken as evidence that she had some popular support.

Two views have been expressed on the character of the Zhou dynasty. The traditional one has subsumed it within the Tang tradition and has perceived little difference between the policies that the empress pursued and those that had been followed by the preceding Tang emperors. The other is that her usurpation marked a significant social revolution, the rise of a new class, which the empress tried to use in her struggle against the traditionalist aristocracy. The truth perhaps lies somewhere in between these two views. Court intrigues and an attempt by the empress's family to establish its dominance were familiar elements in the political process. However, there is some evidence to show that the empress did try to free herself from the influence of her chief ministers and to favour officials who had advanced through the examination system. Unlike her predecessors she showed marked favour to the Buddhist community, and this led her to approve the construction of the Mingtang, or Hall of Light. Built at great expense, it was used for wild religious rites supervised by the abbot, the empress's lover Xue Huaiyi. When he fell out of favour he took his revenge by burning the building down. Thereafter the empress began to show more concern for Confucianism.

The most serious crisis of the reign arose on the north-eastern frontier, where a new tribal confederation was taking shape. It was headed by the Qidan, from whose name the word Cathay was to be derived. The Qidan, who spoke a language ancestral to Mongolian, were pastoral nomads who lived in Manchuria, in the marginal zone between the open steppe and settled areas. It has often been noted that it was from this zone that most of the dynasties of conquest were to originate. In 605 the Qidan had been severely chastised after a raid into Chinese territory and they had subsequently become vassals of China. In 695 they rebelled against Chinese maladministration and gained a dramatic victory over Chinese forces near the site of modern Beijing. This encouraged trouble at other points along the frontier, with the Turks invading Gansu and the Tibetans threatening the Chinese hold on Central Asia. The empress responded with a mixture of diplomacy and force, concluding a marriage alliance with the Turks and defeating the Qidan in battle.

The closing years of the empress's reign saw a decline in her influence. Her extravagant building programme and expensive frontier campaigns had emptied the treasury and attempts to raise new taxes exposed the seriousness of the fiscal problem facing the dynasty. The empress's behaviour continued to cause scandal. From 697 she became enamoured of the brothers Zhang, who paraded around in fancy costume and overrode the authority of senior ministers. When the Turks again invaded China in 698, she found it so difficult to raise support that she was obliged to decide an issue that she had always sidestepped, that of the succession. She agreed that in due course the throne would revert to her son Zhongzong, whom she had set aside in 684. It was not until 705 however, that a plot hatched by her senior officials accomplished the death of the Zhang brothers and forced the empress to abdicate. She died later that year. Her usurpation, her extravagance, her scandalous behaviour, the very fact that she was a women, ensured her unanimous condemnation by Confucianist historians. More recently her record of achievement in all but the closing years of her reign has been rehabilitated. She has been credited with providing strong leadership and having presided over an age of relative peace and prosperity, for which she earned the gratitude of the people.

THE REIGN OF XUANZONG, 712–56

The Tang restoration of 705 was followed by another period of court intrigues and weak leadership. However, in 712 the succession fell to a talented man of 27, who was to be known as Xuanzong emperor and whose reign was to be remembered as one of the high points in China's history. During the early years of his reign the fortunes of the dynasty were revived and high achievements were recorded in literature and the visual arts.

Xuanzong's reign has traditionally been divided into three parts, an initial period of consolidation and reform, a central period during which constructive policies were still being applied but serious problems had begun to emerge, and a final period during which the emperor withdrew from direct involvement in government and the crisis developed which led to the rebellion of An Lushan.

During the first period, which lasted until 720, Xuanzong was assisted by several outstanding ministers, notably Yao Chong, who had risen through the examination system and who had been chief minister under the Empress Wu. Yao Chong had proposed a ten-point programme to address problems of administration and several of his suggestions were now implemented. The number of chief ministers was reduced and their authority was strengthened. Those who had passed the examinations were promoted and an attempt was made to compel able officials to serve in neglected locations in the provinces. The administrative and penal codes were revised to ensure uniformity of treatment throughout the empire. Measures relating to supply and taxation were introduced. These included some improvement to the supply of grain to Chang'an and an extension of the system of 'price-regulating granaries' whereby grain was stock-piled for sale when prices were high. However, the most serious problem of the time, how to revise the tax registers so that they recorded all households, including migrant households, remained unsolved.

The most significant reforms concerned the military. Early in the dynasty troops had been recruited through the *fubing* militia system, under which men of good families served on the frontier and at the capital. This system had proved inadequate to deal with the more formidable threats of the eastern Turks, the Qidan and the Tibetans, and by Xuanzong's reign it demanded change. The frontier of the empire was now divided into nine sectors, each headed by a military governor. He commanded a large force of professional soldiers, a force capable of responding rapidly to incursions, an arrangement which allowed him considerable freedom of action. The professional forces were supported by military colonies, which supplied them with food and military reserves.

In the middle period of the reign many of these policies were continued under new ministers, but at the same time a change of emphasis occurred. Whereas under the Empress Wu, and in the early part of Xuanzong's reign, many of the chief ministers had passed an examination and might be termed literati, from 721 men of aristocratic background, whose principal qualification was hereditary privilege, increasingly obtained appointments. The political history of the period to 736 has been interpreted as a struggle between these two groupings. The first member of the aristocratic group to achieve prominence was Yuwen Rong who in 721 had proposed a solution to the problem of unregistered households. His suggestion was that 'runaway households', that is the numerous households which had migrated to escape taxation, should be offered an amnesty from arrears of tax. This measure proved remarkably successful and Yuwen Rong was promoted to a number of key positions. Pei Yaoqing, also an aristocrat, although he had passed the *mingqing* examination, tackled another chronic problem, the supply of grain to Chang'an. By reducing the distance that grain had to be carried overland, he cut the costs of transportation and greatly increased the quantity of grain available. This enabled Xuanzong to fix his capital permanently at Chang'an, rather than making periodic, expensive and disruptive moves to Luoyang.

In 736 another aristocrat, Li Linfu, rose to power and until his death in 752 was virtually a dictator. Because he was regarded as the enemy of the literati and as the author of the misfortunes which accumulated in the closing years of the reign, his name has been execrated. His elevation came after a prolonged struggle with Zhang Jiuling, who had become chief minister in 734. Zhang, who came from the south, was the epitome of the austere scholar-official. Li Linfu, who came from the north-west, had risen through intrigue, although the allegations of his lack of scholarship were probably exaggerated. Li Linfu's triumph has been seen as the victory of guile over honesty, but alternatively it has been interpreted as being a result of Xuanzong's desire to establish a strong, centralized and financially sound government, and his conclusion that he would achieve this better through the ruthlessness of Li Linfu than through the moral injunctions of Zhang Jiuling.

When in sole power Li Linfu acted to improve the efficiency of the administration. Legal reforms were instituted, changes were made to the deployment of the military forces, and currency reforms were introduced. But from the 740s the emperor, who was sixty in 745, ceased to play an active role in government, and became increasingly infatuated with Yang Guifei, the most famous beauty in Chinese history. At court the relations between aristocratic factions became embittered. These circumstances provided the context for the rebellion of An Lushan which broke out in 755.

LITERATURE AND THE VISUAL ARTS UNDER XUANZONG

The Tang period is often referred to as a golden age in Chinese culture, and the reign of Xuanzong is accounted its high point. The poetry written during that reign was later regarded as a model which all Chinese poets might try to emulate, but could never hope to surpass. An eighteenth-century anthology, the *Three Hundred Tang Poems*, has become a treasury of poems familiar to all educated Chinese.

The composition of poetry goes back a long way in China's literary history. Mention has already been made of the *Book of*

Songs, the collection of poems dating back to the Zhou period which became a classic text. Cao Cao, the military leader at the fall of the Later Han, had been a renowned poet. The most famous poet of the period of division was Tao Qian (376–427), whose poems celebrated the pleasures of a simple life in the country. In the early Tang period many poets were closely associated with the court and their poems were written to commemorate events there. However, during Xuanzong's reign a new generation of writers wrote to express their feelings, which had often been aroused by absence or exile. Wang Wei (699–759), who was also a famous painter, was master of a form of brief verse which left it to the reader to complete the sentiment implied. The following poem alludes to the custom of giving a departing traveller a piece of willow

Willow Waves

The two rows of perfect trees
Fall reflected in the clear ripples
And do not copy those by the palace moat
Where the spring wind sharpens the good-bye.[6]

Li Bo (701–62), sometimes described as China's best-loved poet, was a close contemporary of Wang Wei. He cultivated a reputation for eccentricity and in his poems made use of Daoist metaphysics. In 'My trip in a dream to the Lady of Heaven mountain' he conjured up vivid images of height and depth, of light and darkness

A thousand cliffs, ten thousand turns, a road I cannot define;
Dazzled by flowers, I rest on a stone and darkness suddenly falls.[7]

Many of his poems refer to the moon and to his love of wine, preoccupations which have been associated with some Turkish influence, perhaps from his father. The legend of his death, that when trying to embrace the reflection of the moon in water, he fell from a boat and was drowned, neatly and tragically brought those two preoccupations to a conclusion.

Whereas Li Bo's commitment was to Daoism, Du Fu (712–70), the poet with whom Li Bo's name is forever linked, was a Confucian. Du Fu's failure in the examinations had left him with a lasting disappointment and with a hard struggle for subsistence. The An Lushan rebellion separated him from his wife and children for over a year. In a poem he recalled the moment that they were reunited, by which time his hair had gone white

And then my son, pride of all my days,
With his face, too, whiter than the snows,

Sees his father, turns his back to weep –
His sooty feet without socks or shoes;
Next by my couch two small daughters stand
In patched dresses scarcely to their knees.[8]

Xuanzong's reign also saw important advances in the visual arts. Wu Daozi (c. 700–60), who has been described as the Michelangelo of China, painted Buddhist subjects and transformed 'the essentially sculptured ideals of India into the linear, painterly terms of the Chinese tradition'. Though none of his work survives, the style which he established can be traced in the frescoes at Dunhuang, the Buddhist centre on the Silk Road.[9] Another important advance was in the field of landscape painting. According to the Ming art critic Dong Qichang (1555–1636), it was at this time that the division of landscape painting into 'southern' and 'northern' schools occurred. Artists of the southern school were amateurs and scholars, the best-known early exponent being the poet Wang Wei, who was known for his evocative monochrome paintings of winter scenes. Those of the northern school were professionals and court painters, the most famous of whom were Li Sixun and his son Li Zhaodao (died c. 735). A painting entitled *Minghuang's Journey to Shu*, said to depict the flight of the emperor from An Lushan's rebels, preserves the characteristics of their style, which was marked by dramatic mountain peaks and blue-green colouring. From Xuanzong's reign dates perhaps the most famous of all Chinese paintings, *Shining White of the Night*, a depiction of the emperor's favourite horse by Han Gan (c. 715–81).

THE TANG WORLD AT THE TIME OF XUANZONG

During the Tang period China's relations with the outside world were transformed. At the beginning of the period only one neighbouring state, Koguryo, could claim to be a stable political unit. By the reign of Xuanzong, China was surrounded by states which, having borrowed culture and institutions from China, now aspired to a separate political identity.

During the Sui dynasty China had recovered control of Annam and in the early Tang period, despite a number of rebellions, Chinese dominance of the region remained secure. North of Annam was the state of Nanzhao, centred on present-day Yunnan, which was ruled by people of Tai origin who had adopted the Chinese language and features of Chinese government. In the eighth century China encouraged the emergence of a unified Nanzhao state, with its capital at Dali, to act as a buffer against the rising power of Tibet.

Tibet itself had become a centralized monarchy and had adopted Buddhism. Song-tsen Gampo (r. 620–49) had initiated a period of rapid sinicization. Thereafter the country began a phase of rapid expansion, challenging China's influence in Central Asia and advancing into modern Qinghai. In 696, during the Empress Wu's reign, a Tibetan army had defeated a large Chinese force less than 200 miles from Chang'an. During Xuanzong's reign Tibetan raiding began again, but on this occasion it was China which emerged victorious and in the ensuing peace treaty, Tibet acknowledged Chinese suzerainty and the border between the two countries was defined.

On China's northern borders, political entities were less clearly established. At the beginning of the eighth century the eastern Turks were China's most threatening neighbours. They dominated the whole of the steppe region from Manchuria to Ferghana, and their raiding had forced the Chinese to maintain an expensive defence system along the Yellow river. However, the death of the eastern Turk leader in 716, and a subsequent succession dispute, provided the opportunity for the rise of the Uighur empire in Mongolia. The Uighur, who are an important minority in modern China, speak a Turkic-related language. They had formerly been vassals of the eastern Turks, and they now became clients of the Chinese. Up to this time they had been nomadic tribesmen, but with Chinese encouragement they established a capital at Karabalghasun. For the next hundred years, until 840, the Uighur provided China with a reliable ally on the steppe, receiving in exchange enormous benefits in terms of trade and subsidies.

To the north-east, Koguryo had been absorbed by Silla, and in 676 Korea for the first time became a unified state. Over the next century Silla borrowed heavily from Chinese culture, encouraging Confucian scholarship and introducing competitive examinations. When Koguryo was defeated, refugees had fled to near Jilin in northern Manchuria. In 713 they founded a state known to the Chinese as Pohai, which like Silla was organized on the Chinese model. By this time Japan too had emerged as a unified state. After the reunification of China under the Sui, Japan had begun to adopt many aspects of Chinese culture. In 604 the regent, Prince Shotoku, promulgated the Seventeen-Article Constitution, which set out the principles of government based on Confucian doctrines. The Taiho Code of 702 was based on Chinese legal and administrative practices.

With the emergence of these states on China's periphery, states which had borrowed heavily from Chinese institutions and practices, the 'Chinese dominated east Asian cultural sphere' had taken shape.[10] States which had adopted Chinese culture, and which accepted the superiority of China even though they were independent countries, were treated by China as tributaries. At fixed intervals these states sent tributary missions to China bearing gifts and in return they were rewarded with trading privileges. However, the essential significance of these missions was not economic, but political, as the ceremonial to be performed on these occasions was an acknowledgement of Chinese superiority.

The relationship which developed with the nomadic peoples of the steppe was different in character. The economies of the nomadic and settled populations were in some respect complementary. The relationship evolved over a period of time and varied according to the relative strength of the steppe peoples and of the Chinese state. It took a variety of forms: marriage arrangements, usually with a Chinese princess becoming the bride of a steppe leader, trade agreements, and the payment of subsidies to tribal leaders. If these arrangements broke down the nomadic peoples might employ what has been described as the 'outer frontier strategy', in which they raided Chinese territory to seize or extort what they required.[11]

While China's frontiers were becoming more clearly defined, the process of Han Chinese expansion within Chinese territory continued apace and the sinicization of the non-Chinese population made stealthy progress. The main movement of Chinese settlers was to the south. The area known as Nan Yue, or southern Yue, that is present-day Guangdong and Guangxi, had been conquered during the Han dynasty, but thereafter the Yue people had recovered their independence. The region was now placed firmly under Chinese control as Lingnan province. To administer the indigenous population the *tusi* system, a form of indirect rule through the appointment of tribal chiefs as officials, was adopted. At the same time the establishment of military colonies in the south encouraged Chinese migration. The region was also used by the Empress Wu as a place of exile for her opponents. As the Chinese community grew, a few southern Chinese achieved distinction in the Tang administration, the most notable example being Zhang Jiuling, Xuanzong's austere first minister.

A similar advance was occurring in what is now Fujian province. Chinese migration to this area dates back to the Han period, but the settlement of the marshy coastal region was impeded by the prevalence of malaria and schistosomiasis. By the eighth century the draining of the marshes and acquired immunity against infection had allowed Chinese settlers to start cultivating wet rice on the coastal plains and to open up the excellent harbour of Quanzhou bay, which by the ninth century had become the main centre of trade with the South Seas.

The Tang empire of the eighth century was the most advanced civilization of its time and its capital Chang'an was probably the world's greatest city. The city had a population of about one million living within its walls and another million living in the suburbs. Chang'an was the hub of the empire, served by a network of roads and canals which linked it to the Silk Road to the west and the expanding population of the Yangzi valley to the south. To Chang'an's markets came traders bearing exotic goods from Central Asia. Its cosmopolitan population included adherents of Christianity, Zoroastrianism and Manichaeism. The country's greatest port was Guangzhou, and here too a cosmopolitan mercantile community had assembled, which included traders from India and Persia.

THE REBELLION OF AN LUSHAN, 755–63

Between 755 and 763 the Tang empire was shaken to its foundations by the rebellion of An Lushan. Although the rebellion was eventually defeated and the dynasty survived for another century and a half it never recovered its former authority or glory. So sweeping were the changes which followed the rebellion, that it has been identified as a major turning point in Chinese history.

The immediate causes of the rebellion related to the situation at court and the military arrangements on the frontier. As noted earlier, from the 740s Xuanzong had increasingly left the conduct of government to Li Linfu, while he first immersed himself in a search for personal enlightenment and then became infatuated with Yang Guifei. Although she had some powerful personal connections, she came from a family of modest standing, her father having been a local official in Sichuan. After gaining the emperor's favour, Yang Guifei obtained various court posts for her relatives, including her second cousin Yang Guozhong who became a law officer working for Li Linfu. In 746 Li Linfu began a series of bloody purges directed against his critics, and Yang Guozhong used the opportunity to advance the interests of the Yang family. From 749 Yang Guozhong began to intrigue against Li Linfu himself. When the latter died in 752 Yang Guozhong took his place as the most powerful figure at court.

The military situation derived from the division of the frontier into nine sectors each headed by a military governor. Initially this system worked well as many of the military governors came from aristocratic backgrounds and were closely connected with the bureaucracy. Some governors made their reputation by waging successful frontier campaigns, which enhanced their reputation and that of the dynasty, albeit at a heavy financial cost. However, in the 740s Li Linfu began to appoint non-Chinese governors, on the grounds that they were better soldiers and had no political ambitions. This gave An Lushan, a professional soldier who was half-Sogdian and half-Turkish, the opportunity to rise to prominence. In 742 he was given the key military governorship of Pinglu in the extreme north-east, an area where the leading families nurtured some antipathy towards the aristocracy of the region around Chang'an. His military success in this post ingratiated him with the emperor, and despite his being grossly fat he also became the favourite, and, scandal said, the lover, of Yang Guifei, who adopted him as her son. After Li Linfu's death, rivalry developed between An Lushan and Yang Guozhong. The latter held the military governorship of Sichuan, but otherwise his power base was at the court, and it was there that he tried to drive a wedge between the emperor and An Lushan.

Realizing that he was in danger, in late 755 An Lushan marched south, seized Luoyang and declared the establishment of a new dynasty. For the next eight years the country was plunged into a civil war. After Yang Guozhong had made an ill-judged attempt to recapture Luoyang, the emperor was forced to abandon Chang'an and flee north. During his flight one of the most poignant scenes in Chinese history took place, one commemorated in the famous poem by Bo Juyi (772–846), the *Song of Unending Sorrow*. The commander of the emperor's escort held Yang Guozhong responsible for the disaster and had him killed. He then demanded the death of Yang Guifei and with immense sadness the emperor ordered her execution. The emperor fled to Chengdu in the south-west and later that year abdicated in favour of his son who had gone to the north-west to rally support. An Lushan was assassinated in 757, but it was only after Xuanzong's grandson, the Emperor Daizong, succeeded to the throne in 762 that the remaining rebels were defeated with Uighur assistance.

The rebellion had a number of immediate and longer-term consequences. Some parts of the country became depopulated, others suffered severe economic and social dislocation and the state's financial machinery collapsed. The north-east of the empire became virtually independent and elsewhere provinces fell under the control of military governors. The fall of the capital deeply shocked the Tang aristocracy, some of whom moved to the south. The violence of the rebellion had a lasting impact on the minds of some writers, who thereafter concentrated their intellectual enquiries on the lessons of history. The involvement of the frontier armies in a civil war encouraged the Tibetans to advance and in 763 they briefly captured Chang'an. Although they withdrew quickly, their attacks continued, a sign that the Tang empire was no longer an expanding power, but one which had difficulty defending its frontiers.

The rebellion has been seen as a turning point in Chinese history, although according to Edwin G. Pulleyblank it acted more as a catalyst than as a cause of the most profound transformation. In his study of the background of the uprising he referred to the economic revolution which had taken place in the early Tang period, noting in particular the great agricultural expansion in the south and the movement of population to the Yangzi valley. These changes had undermined the fiscal position of the government and had weakened the authority of the north-western aris-tocracy. The importance of these changes was revealed by the dynasty's rapid collapse in the face of rebellion. Their longer-term significance was made manifest by the inability of the later Tang rulers to emulate the achievements of their predecessors.

THE POST-REBELLION RESTORATION

From the above it might be supposed that the post-rebellion period was characterized by unremitting dynastic decline. Undoubtedly the central government lost power to provincial regimes, to the extent that the 'Tang regime survived only at the cost of becoming highly decentralized'. However, after the rebellion many of the processes of government continued to operate, significant reforms to the taxation and administrative systems were introduced and a new frontier policy was applied. Only in the ninth century did unequivocal evidence of decline appear.

Some of the most important innovations concerned fiscal reform. During the Emperor Daizong's reign (762–79), an official named Liu Yan tackled the twin problems of supplying Chang'an with grain and improving the dynasty's finances. His solution was to use the profits of the salt monopoly to pay for the maintenance of the canal and the barge fleets. As the centre for salt production was the Yangzi delta and the hub of the transport system was at Yangzhou where the canal joined the Yangzi, this was a neat and practical solution. Some of Liu Yan's reforms were undone by his great rival and successor Yang Yan, who was chief minister under the reforming Emperor Dezong, who reigned 779–805. However, it was Yang Yan who put into general application the most significant tax reform of the age, the 'two-tax system'. This tax consolidated various taxes into one single tax, which was to be paid, in two instalments a year, not only by the peasantry but by all the productive classes. A second purpose of this reform was to restore imperial control over taxation, which had fallen into the hands of the financial specialists of the salt administration and the eunuchs who controlled the treasuries. This system of taxation was to remain in force for the next seven centuries.

As an example of an administrative reform, one might refer to the so-called restoration under the Xianzong emperor (r. 805–20). Xianzong aspired to regain control of those provinces which had in effect become autonomous, and he was prepared to use force to achieve this. In 806 he sent a punitive expedition to Sichuan which defeated the general who had usurped the command there and replaced him with a governor willing to accept central government direction. He followed this with other military interventions, which secured control of the central provinces but were less successful in the north-east. At the same time he instituted reforms to reduce provincial autonomy in the matter of taxation and to increase the contribution which the wealthy Yangzi provinces made to the exchequer.

The rebellion had completely undermined the Tang frontier strategy. The system of military colonies had been abandoned. China had lost to Tibet the pasture lands from where it had obtained its supply of war horses, and these now had to be purchased at vast expense from the Uighur. They demanded a large annual subsidy for refraining from attacking China. Between 780 and 787 the Emperor Dezong attempted to negotiate a settlement with Tibet, which involved signing away large tracts of territory and agreeing a frontier between the two countries, but the Tibetans would not abandon their long-term ambitions. This situation led Dezong to conclude a formal alliance with the Uighur, which involved the marriage of Dezong's daughter to the Uighur leader and a costly commitment to an annual exchange of Uighur horses for Chinese silk. In return he obtained Uighur support against Tibet. This alliance was to be the cornerstone of China's frontier policy until the Uighur empire disintegrated in 840.

THE RISE AND SUPPRESSION OF BUDDHISM

Wendi, the first emperor of the Sui dynasty, had used Buddhism to legitimize his right to rule and to provide a common faith for all people of all classes, thus providing a unifying force after a long period of disunion. The early Tang rulers had given their preference to Daoism, but at the same time they had recognized the strength of the Buddhist church, which by now had achieved very wide acceptance and had become a powerful presence within Chinese society.

> By the eighth century, Buddhism was fully and triumphantly established throughout China. Its canons were revered, its spiritual truth unquestioned. It marked and influenced the lives of the humble and the great and affected every community, large and small, in the empire of Tang.[12]

In achieving this level of acceptance, Buddhist doctrine had become sinicized and Chinese Buddhist sects had emerged. The four most influential Buddhist schools in China are the Tientai and Huayan schools, which are best known for their doctrine, and the Meditation and Pure Land schools, which are more significant for their practice. The Tientai school is entirely Chinese, being based on the teaching of Zhiyi, who established a school at Tientai, the sacred mountain in Zhejiang, late in the sixth century. His teaching centred on a minute examination of the *Lotus Sutra*, and his school offered a doctrine of universal salvation through intellectual enquiry and meditative practice. The Huayan or Flower Garden school had in effect been founded by Fazang, a man of Sogdian descent born in Chang'an in 643. This school categorized the various Buddhist sects into vehicles and claimed that Huayan doctrine combined all that was valuable in each of these vehicles, a syncretic approach typical of Chinese thought.

The Meditation school, known in China as Chan and more familiar to the West as Zen, the Japanese pronunciation of its name, traces its origin to the Indian master Bodhidharma who arrived at the court of the Northern Wei in about 520. He emphasized the importance of contemplation and his teaching later subsumed elements of Daoism. In the eighth century Chan Buddhism split into a northern and a southern school, the former

believing in gradual enlightenment, the latter in sudden enlightenment. The latter school, which stressed intuition rather than
intellect, has remained popular to this day. Bodhidharma's influence was also apparent in another field, for when he was abbot
of the Shaolin monastery, some 20 miles south-east of Luoyang,
he was so perturbed by the poor physical condition of the monks
that he introduced the Shaolin style of boxing. Another very
popular school was the Jingtu or Pure Land School, which
claimed that salvation came through faith rather than through
good works. It took its name from the Pure Land, or Western
Paradise, presided over by the Amita Buddha, and claimed that
the believer could reach that land by the frequent repetition of
Buddha's name. It popularized the cult of the boddhisattva ('one
who is to become enlightened') Avolokitesvara who became
Guanyin, the Chinese goddess of mercy.

Most descriptions of Chinese Buddhism, while readily admitting that the religion has become sinicized, nevertheless convey
the impression that it has 'a clear-cut independent tradition different from that of other types of religion'. Erik Zürcher has
challenged this and has produced evidence to show that this was
the view of Buddhism promoted by its intellectual leaders. In
fact the vast majority of Buddhist monks were barely literate,
and at the popular level Buddhism fused with Chinese indigenous religion, readily accepting beliefs and practices such as
spirit possession and spirit writing.[13]

Whereas the Sui emperors had found an ally in Buddhism, the
early Tang rulers, with the exception of the Empress Wu, held it
at a distance, although they found it expedient to conciliate the
Buddhist community from time to time. Xuanzong took a harder
line, failing to grant any of the typical signs of imperial favour,
for example the building of monasteries, the mass ordination of
monks, or the imperial participation in Buddhist rites. However,
he did attempt to strengthen the link between Buddhist monasteries and the imperial institution by requiring them to commemorate the emperor's birthday and to instal images of the Buddha
in the likeness of the emperor.

The An Lushan rebellion had a disastrous impact on the
Buddhist church. Forced to raise revenue quickly, the government permitted unrestricted ordination for all willing to pay
the official fee. As monks were exempt from taxation, this lost

the state future revenue, but for the church the more important consequence was the debasement of the quality of the clergy. The rebellion itself brought about the destruction of many monasteries and the loss of many important collections of manuscripts, which caused particular damage in the philosophical schools. On the other hand, Pure Land Buddhism gained in popularity and for the first time achieved recognition at court.

After the rebellion Buddhism at first received increased imperial patronage. Daizong became convinced that the dynasty owed its survival to Buddhism and he supported the construction of many monasteries and authorized the ordination of thousands of monks. He demonstrated his personal piety by venerating Buddhist relics and by sponsoring vegetarian banquets for the clergy. His successor Dezong was more cautious in his support, looking with favour on schemes which would reduce the economic burden the Buddhist church imposed on the state. However, he too became a great patron of monastic building and of Buddhist scholarship.

The growth of the Buddhist church had long been the subject of criticism by its opponents. In 621 the Daoist priest Fu Yi had argued that monastic communities were a burden on the state. He urged the emperor to disband the Buddhist clergy and put the monasteries to a better use. Under Dezong a Confucian official in the Bureau of Records, named Peng Yan, told the emperor that he should eliminate the abuses within the Buddhist church, citing the ignorance of the clergy, and the loss of tax revenue. He estimated that the annual cost of supplying a monk with food and clothing equalled the taxes paid by five adult males.

When in 819 the Emperor Xianzong had the supposed finger-bone of Buddha brought to Chang'an so that he could worship it, the most celebrated protest of all was heard. It came from Han Yu, a famous Confucian scholar, who presented a memorial in which he stated that he was surprised that the emperor should see fit to encourage Buddhism by greeting the relic, which he described as 'this loathsome thing'. He declared,

Now Buddha was a man of the barbarians who did not speak the language of China and wore clothes of a different fashion.

His sayings did not concern the ways of our ancient kings, nor did his manner of dress conform to their laws. He understood neither the duties that bind sovereign and subject, nor the affections of father and son.[14]

The emperor's reply was first to threaten Han Yu with death, and later to order that he go into exile in the far south.

Although these criticisms had been voiced, it was not until the reign of Wuzong (840–6) that decisive action was taken against Buddhism. Wuzong was strongly committed to Daoism and was said to hate the sight of Buddhist monks. However, there is no evidence to support the view that a Daoist pressure group was responsible for his decision. Buddhist historians have often blamed Li Deyu, the authoritarian chief minister, for the suppression. Li Deyu was a committed Confucianist, who shared the scholars' disdain for the excesses of popular Buddhism, although he did not express the outrage voiced by Han Yu. If he was involved in the decision it may have been for political reasons, to curb the power of the eunuch Qiu Shiliang, who was responsible for Buddhist affairs. However, the most compelling reason for the emperor's action, and Li Deyu's support for it, was financial. Since An Lushan's rebellion there had been a severe shortage of copper for the minting of coins. Part of this shortage was attributed to the use of copper in the casting of images and bells and chimes for Buddhist temples. More generally the Buddhist church was regarded as too wealthy and because of its tax exemption it was considered to be too great an economic burden for the state to support.

The great suppression began with the seizure of the private property of Buddhist monks and restrictions on pilgrimages. It reached its climax in 845 when Wuzong ordered all monasteries to surrender their land and wealth and all monks and nuns under the age of forty to be laicized. As a result of these measures some 4600 monasteries and a further 40,000 temples and shrines were destroyed, a quarter of a million monks and nuns were laicized, several million acres of land were confiscated and sufficient copper was recovered to allow the temporary resumption of the payment of salaries in cash.

THE FALL OF THE TANG DYNASTY

Signs of dynastic decline appeared after 820, when a series of young emperors proved unable to assert their authority over courts which were riven by factional in-fighting. This often involved the eunuchs, who controlled the imperial palace and were in a position to manipulate the emperor and determine the succession. Their influence even extended to the military, as the emperor relied on eunuch army supervisors to spy on his generals and keep them in line. Through the efforts of Li Deyu, who became Wuzong's chief minister in 840, the fortunes of the dynasty temporarily revived. His decisive action against Buddhism has already been noted. He also took steps to control the eunuchs and to restore the bureaucracy. However, he was dismissed by the Emperor Xuanzong,[15] who came to the throne in 846. The new emperor, or his ministers, did attempt a reform of the grain transport system and the salt monopoly, but the more serious problems went unaddressed. The most important of these were the growth of large landed estates, chronic fiscal problems which the government had attempted to resolve by loading the tax burden on the lower Yangzi provinces, and a deteriorating situation on the frontiers.

The fall of the dynasty came about because of a rising tide of disorder. The first wave of mutinies and rebellions had occurred in the lower Yangzi area during Xuanzong's reign, but these were suppressed. In the 860s the state of Nanzhao attacked Annam and only retreated after a campaign which exhausted the Chinese treasury and prompted another wave of mutinies. One mutinous band was headed by Pang Xun, who led his soldiers back to their homes in the lower Yangzi region, pillaging as they went.

In 874 a disastrous rebellion broke out in the area between the Yellow and Huai rivers, an area which had been overtaxed and which had suffered from a succession of floods and droughts. Its two leaders, Wang Xianzhi and Huang Chao, were heads of bandit gangs. They have been represented by Marxist historians as fighting for the interests of the peasantry, but this claim is rejected in Western accounts, which argue that they were motivated by self-interest and only became rebels when government forces attempted to suppress them. Wang Xianzhi was killed in 878. Huang Chao then made a dramatic sweep south, during which he captured and sacked Guangzhou. He returned to the lower Yangzi, where he should have been cornered and defeated, but he was allowed to escape and in 880 he captured Chang'an, forcing the emperor to flee to Chengdu. Huang Chao founded a new dynasty, but failed to establish an effective government. The imperial forces rallied, and with the help of the Shatuo, a Turkish tribe, they defeated the rebels and Huang Chao was killed in 884.

Although the emperor returned to Chang'an, the dynasty had collapsed. The imperial writ only ran in the area around Chang'an and even the traditional Tang support in that region had crumbled. To the north, large parts of the country were occupied by non-Chinese forces; in the east, military governors had seized power; much of central and south China had seceded and formed independent states. The final demise of the dynasty occurred in 907 when Zhu Wen, a former lieutenant of Huang Chao and now a military governor, who had already extended his control over a large part of north China, established the Liang dynasty.

3

. . . .

The Song and Yuan Dynasties

After the fall of the Tang in 907, China experienced another period of disunity. However, whereas after the Han it had taken over three centuries to reconstitute a centralized empire, on this occasion the period of division lasted only half a century. This has been taken as proof of the strength of the political institutions created by the Tang. Despite the frequent changes of regime the ruling elite remained the same and the personnel of the civil service which maintained the functions of government continued in office. Since that time the expectation that China should be a unitary state has been accepted as the norm and periods of disunity have been viewed as aberrations from that standard.

From 907 to the establishment of the Song in 960, the extreme north-east of China was ruled by the Qidan Liao dynasty. The rest of the country was divided into two, the northern section being ruled by a succession of five dynasties, and the southern section being fragmented into ten kingdoms. In 960 Zhao Kuangyin, a general from the last of the five dynasties, usurped the throne and established the Song dynasty (also known as the Northern Song). At its height, in the middle of the eleventh century, the Song dynasty ruled over much of China Proper. Part of north-eastern China and Manchuria was the territory of the Qidan Liao dynasty, and from about 1038 the north-west, the area of modern Gansu, was controlled by the Tangut Xi Xia kingdom. Early in the twelfth century the Qidan Liao dynasty became involved in a disastrous war with the Jurchen from eastern Manchuria. In 1125 its last ruler was captured by the Jurchen, who had established the Jin dynasty. Qidan survivors fled west and established the Western Liao kingdom in Central Asia, which lasted from 1131 to 1213. In the meantime the Jin dynasty had continued to expand into northern China and by 1127 had confined the Song to the southern half of the country. Now known as the Southern Song, they remained in power there until 1279.

THE FIVE DYNASTIES AND THE TEN KINGDOMS

This complex period in Chinese history was marked by three main developments. The first was the emergence of a new structure of power based on military strength. This development had begun in the late Tang, with the appearance of military governors of provinces, and it was to be carried further after the collapse of the dynasty. As an example of the process one could refer to the career of Zhu Wen, who had first come to prominence as a supporter of the rebel Huang Chao. After capturing Chang'an, Huang Chao appointed Zhu Wen to control a key prefecture to the east of the capital. When the rebellion faltered Zhu Wen defected to the Tang side and was made military governor of Xuanwu, in the area of modern Henan. During the closing years of the dynasty he concentrated on building up his power base, mainly by creating a professional army which was personally loyal to him. It comprised both infantry and an elite cavalry force, the latter provided by the wealthy families who supported him. By 903 Zhu Wen was in a position to dominate the court and in 907 he deposed the last Tang emperor and founded the Liang dynasty, the first of the five northern dynasties.

The second important development of the period concerned the situation along China's northern borders. It will be recalled that from the 720s the Tang had relied on the Uighur to stabilize the frontier region. However, the Uighur empire collapsed in 840, and this proved the beginning of a general disintegration of political authority throughout northern Asia. It was this situation which allowed the rise of the Shatuo Turks. They had formerly been subject to the Uighur, but early in the ninth century some Shatuo tribes switched their allegiance to China and were permitted to settle in Shanxi. Shatuo forces, commanded by Li Keyong, assisted the Tang in the recovery of Chang'an from Huang Chao's rebels. In the closing years of the Tang dynasty the Shatuo made an alliance with the Qidan of Manchuria. Their influence in north China increased and in 923 they defeated the Liang dynasty and established their own dynastic state, to be known as the Later Tang. Although this state only lasted until 937, it expanded to cover a large part of north China, anticipating the future reunification of China. The Later Tang state also set a precedent for the rule by non-Chinese people of Chinese territory inhabited by a majority population of Han Chinese.

The third significant development was occurring in the south. There the fragmentation of political authority was extreme, the region becoming divided into some ten independent states, the Ten Kingdoms. Political weakness may have encouraged development as regional economies grew rapidly and interstate trade flourished. Because of the persistent shortage of copper, the southern states permitted the use of lead, iron and even pottery for coinage. These have been described as forerunners of a paper currency, and it was at this time that promissory notes, the immediate ancestors of paper money, began to be used. The kingdoms of the Southern Han and Min (modern Guangdong and Fujian) both expanded their overseas trade. The state of Wu on the lower Yangzi was not only prosperous, but also encouraged a lively literary culture – some of the earliest printed books were produced in this region. The Later Shu state in the area of modern Sichuan became a refuge for former Tang officials, artists and poets, and consciously attempted to preserve the best features of the Tang empire. In these ways the Ten Kingdoms may be said to have contributed to the future success of the Song dynasty.

THE QIDAN LIAO DYNASTY

The ethnic identity of the Qidan is uncertain, as little is known of their language. The most that can be said is that they probably shared a common ancestry with the peoples called the Xianbei. In the seventh century they had invaded Hebei but had been defeated heavily and forced to submit to Chinese authority. As

Tang authority declined, the tributary relationship, which the Qidan had accepted, was replaced by the more aggressive stance of the military governors of the frontier provinces, and this may have been the catalyst for the unification of the Qidan tribes. An ambitious leader named Abaoji emerged who encouraged changes in the Qidan nomadic lifestyle. Chinese captives and refugees were placed in urban centres where trade and manufacturing developed. The Qidan began to farm and to produce cloth, iron and salt.

Abaoji was also a formidable warrior and under his leadership the Qidan made raids deep into Chinese territory. In 905 he reached an agreement with Li Keyong, the Shatuo leader, offering him his support against Zhu Wen, and over the next few years the Qidan became embroiled in the struggle between the successor states to the Tang dynasty in north-east China. During this time Abaoji also forced the Qidan to accept him not simply as a tribal leader, but as an emperor in the Chinese style. In 907, according to subsequent chronology, he founded the dynasty to be known as the Liao. In 916, having adopted a Chinese reign title, he laid out a capital on the Chinese pattern in the north-west of present-day Liaoning. At the same time he built up his personal power base by recruiting a bodyguard composed of warriors from different tribes.

The Qidan now began to expand their territory. In 924 a major expedition was launched to the west and obtained the subjection of the Uighur. Two years later a campaign to the east overthrew the sinicized kingdom of Pohai. Before his death in 926 Abaoji had made it clear that his next objective was north China. In 937, the Qidan intervened in a succession dispute in the Shatuo Later Tang kingdom. The price for intervention was the cession to the Qidan of the strip of Chinese territory known as the Sixteen Prefectures and the recognition by the Later Tang (now known as the Jin) of the suzerainty of the Qidan. In 947 the Qidan invaded Jin territory, and for a few months attempted to rule a vast tract of China, but realizing their mistake they withdrew to the north.

The Qidan Liao dynasty ruled part of north China and the territories beyond until 1125. The Qidan method of ruling, which owed something to the precedent set by the Toba in the Northern Wei dynasty, has been described as 'dualism'. In the northern territories they preserved many features of traditional Qidan society, and Qidan filled the important military and civil posts. The southern region, which had its capital in the Sixteen Prefectures on the site of modern Beijing, was modelled on the governmental institutions of the Tang. Many of the middle-ranking officials were Chinese who had qualified for office through success in the examinations. Whereas in the north, Qidan customary law applied, the Chinese population of the south was subject to Tang codified law. This dualistic arrangement inevitably caused tension between the two halves of the state, which hinged on the extent to which sinicization should be allowed to threaten the separate identity of the Qidan. The Qidan rulers' skill in relieving this tension provided a model for the later empires of the Jurchen Jin and the Manchu Qing dynasties.

THE ESTABLISHMENT OF THE SONG DYNASTY

The Song dynasty was founded by Zhao Kuangyin, later to be known as the Emperor Taizu. He had been a military leader under the Later Zhou, which in its brief existence from 951 to 960 had already made considerable progress towards reunifying north China. Having usurped the throne, he then used a combination of guile and persuasion to obtain the submission of the provincial commanders. Instead of attempting to defeat them on the battlefield he won them over by offering them honours and pensions. At the same time he created a professional army loyal to the dynasty. Once he had achieved the unification of the north he proceeded with similar caution to win over the states south of the Yangzi. When he died in 976 all of China Proper, apart from two independent kingdoms in Zhejiang and Shanxi and those parts of China ruled by Nanzhao and the Qidan, had come under Song control.

This process was continued by his brother, the Emperor Taizong (r. 976–97). He obtained the submission of the Zhejiang and Shanxi kingdoms. He also received tribute from the Xi Xia state, which had been founded by the Tangut in the Ordos region and present-day Gansu. Only in its contacts with the Qidan was the Song dynasty forced to compromise. In 979 Taizong invaded the Sixteen Prefectures, but was defeated near Beijing. After two further unsuccessful campaigns an uneasy truce was agreed. In 1004, after another series of campaigns had led to yet another stalemate, an agreement known as the Treaty of Shanyuan was reached. It confirmed the Qidan claim to the Sixteen Prefectures and carefully regulated the protocol for relations between the two states. The Song agreed to pay not tribute, but an annual 'contribution to military expenses' amounting to 200,000 lengths of silk and 100,000 ounces of silver. This payment has been represented as a heavy burden on the Song state, but it has been argued that the Song more than recouped the cost through increased trade. The subsidy also stabilized the Qidan economy. In short it was 'a good bargain for both parties'.[1] It has been pointed out that the Song relations with the Qidan Liao 'were the nearest thing to equality in Chinese history until modern times'.[2]

In the meantime the first Song emperors had been laying the foundations of one of the most famous dynasties in Chinese history. Its capital was situated at Kaifeng on the Grand Canal, a city more readily supplied from the south than Chang'an or Luoyang. Many features of Tang administration were revived in a modified form. Central government comprised a secretariat and a chancellery, which respectively formulated and reviewed policies before presenting them to the emperor for approval. If accepted the policies were passed to the department of state affairs, which was composed of six boards of government, for implementation. The officials at the head of the chancellery and secretariat were recognized as the chief ministers. Military affairs were kept separate from civil affairs and the military affairs bureau reported directly to the emperor. The same was true of the censorate, which oversaw the bureaucracy on behalf of the emperor and which had the power to impeach officials.

The same continuity was evident in Song provincial government. The basic administrative unit was the prefecture, formerly known as the commandery, of which there were about 300. Prefectures were responsible for many of the functions of central government, for example each prefecture had a revenue quota defining the amount of revenue it had to remit to the treasury. However, whereas in Tang times the prefecture had enjoyed a high degree of autonomy, under the Song this was reduced. Military matters became the prerogative of the state and the powers of the prefecture to make appointments or to deal with capital offences were circumscribed. A new level of administration, the circuit, was introduced to oversee the operation of groups of prefectures, an arrangement which anticipated the provincial administration of the late imperial period. This complex and sophisticated governmental structure was manned by a civil service. A bureaucracy had been in existence since Han times, and in the early Tang period its operations had been rationalized, its chain of command clarified and its importance vis-à-vis the aristocracy and local interests confirmed. It was then that the examination system began to assume the importance it was to bear in the later imperial period. However, in the late Tang and Five Dynasties period the collapse of central authority had allowed wide variations in bureaucratic practice to develop, and the authority of civil officials had become overshadowed by that of military commanders.

Under the Song, recruiting the right type of personnel to the bureaucracy was regarded as an important issue, and three responses to it may be noted. The first was the improvement and expansion of the examination system. Under Taizu, the Tang system of annual examinations, which led to the award of a variety of degrees to a small number of successful candidates, was continued. Under Taizong the number of candidates awarded the *jinshi*, the highest degree, rose from 10 a year to over 140. In response the number of candidates rose sharply. In 1002, 14,500 men who had been selected as candidates by their prefectures converged on the capital Kaifeng for the *jinshi* examinations. To deal with this rapid growth in numbers several reforms were instituted, which included the incorporation of prefectural examinations into the examination system, the definition of quotas determining how many candidates should pass at the prefectural level, and provisions for impartiality including the anonymity of the candidates. A second response was to improve educational facilities. Officially-sponsored schools had existed under the Tang, both in the capital and in the prefectures, but the provision was very limited. Under the Song, local officials began to establish new schools and to provide them with a set of the Confucian classics, which were now available in print. At Kaifeng the Imperial University, which had originally been reserved for children of officials, was opened to prefectural candidates.

The most striking response to the need to find suitable candidates for public service appeared to run counter to the principle of competitive examinations. This was the use of the *yin* privilege, a system of sponsorship which allowed certain senior officials to nominate members of their family for official appointments. This method of recruitment was justified by a saying of Confucius, 'raise to office those of virtue and talent whom you know'. Whereas the examination system might produce clever candidates, the sponsorship system emphasized character, and the candidate's suitability had to be guaranteed by the official making the nomination.

In the early Song period the bureaucracy was quite small, numbering less than 10,000 officials. By the end of the twelfth century that figure had quadrupled. Nevertheless the examinations and the sponsorship system still produced far more qualified men than there were offices. To deal with this situation there was often a protracted delay between qualification and appointment, and officials might take lengthy career breaks. Two other conventions, which had already been applied in the Tang period, affected appointments: a 'law of avoidance' debarred an official from serving in his own province, and a system of tenure regulated the length of time an official might occupy a particular post.

Did the bureaucracy of the Song period offer a 'career open to talent'? According to E. A. Kracke an analysis of the examination lists for 1148 and 1256 shows that nearly 60 per cent of the successful *jinshi* candidates came from families with no history of civil service appointment in the previous three generations. Nevertheless a candidate needed a wealthy or literate family background to be successful. Certain groups, possibly including merchants and artisans, were excluded from the examinations.[3] According to John W. Chaffee the early Song emperors, remembering how the Tang rulers had been challenged by the great families, aimed to create a meritocratic state in which the emperor rewarded achievement with office. However, the meritocratic principle was subverted by the spread of learning, which increased the competition and encouraged the imperial clan and bureaucratic families to find ways of bypassing the examination system and so maintain their privileged position.[4] Winston W. Lo has argued that the system of recruitment strengthened the dynasty by creating a body of graduates who came from both the north and the conquered south and who were ideologically committed to the service of the emperor.[5]

One might suppose that a bureaucratic state would be committed to the preservation of the status quo. However, the administration of early Song China was more concerned to rectify what were considered to be the deficiencies of the state, particularly if its record was compared with that of the Tang. The Song empire was much smaller, for it did not control large parts of Inner Asia and even within the Great Wall the territory known as the Sixteen Prefectures was ruled by a Qidan dynasty which the Song had been forced to recognize as its equal. The urge to recover these territories caused the Song to break with the practice of the early Tang period, of basing military strength on the recruitment of militia. Instead the dynasty depended on a professional army of over a million men. It has been estimated that military expenditure consumed 70 per cent of government revenue. This level of expenditure would undoubtedly have caused an early financial crisis but for the efficient revenue-collecting systems in operation and the fact that the emperor also had access to substantial private funds.

The raising of so much revenue was only possible because the economy was expanding. Between the eighth and twelfth centuries China experienced what has been described as a 'medieval economic revolution'. Mark Elvin has identified five aspects of the economy which were transformed. The first was agriculture, which supplied the driving force for the other changes. During this period migration south, and in particular to the Yangzi valley, and improvements to the techniques of wet-rice cultivation led to a large increase in food output and allowed a doubling of the population. The second important development was a revolution in water transport, with the completion of an integrated system of internal waterways. At the same time the introduction of technical improvements to ships, including watertight bulkheads and the magnetic compass, facilitated coastal and oceanic voyages. Important changes occurred in the use of money and the availability of credit. Whereas under the Tang a shortage of copper had limited monetary transactions, under the Song, copper became readily available and the annual output of copper cash rose by twenty times. At the same time the use of credit instruments and promissory notes increased. The fourth change was a vast increase in commerce, a result of the linking of the rural economy to the market mechanism. Trade was now carried out not only in luxuries, but also in necessities, and a national market developed for some commodities. One consequence of this was an urban revolution, with at least 10 per cent of the population now living in market towns and cities. Kaifeng, the capital, carried out a trade which was valued at nearly 50 per cent more than that of London in the year 1711. Finally the period saw systematic experimentation, rapid technological advances and the appearance of large-scale industry, for example for the production of iron.[6] These developments led Charles O. Hucker to observe,

> In most respects, eleventh-century China was at a level of economic development not achieved by any European state until the eighteenth century at the earliest.[7]

These developments have been interpreted as the beginnings of capitalism, and such an interpretation immediately poses the question of why this process did not continue and lead to an industrial revolution. Responses to this question often conclude that development was inhibited by particular obstacles. Etienne Balazs pointed out that the key economic and social changes had occurred in the Tang–Song period, when national sovereignty was divided and the power of the state and the scholar-official class was weak. Once the Song had become established, limitations on individual freedom, the lack of laws protecting property, above all the overwhelming prestige of the state bureaucracy, prevented the emergence of a capitalist bourgeoisie.[8] Charles O. Hucker suggested that the complexity of the economy outgrew China's managerial competence. Other writers referred to a shortage of capital, an over-abundance of cheap labour, a failure to develop a scientific outlook, and the effects of the Mongol invasions.

Albert Feuerwerker has observed that the question which should be addressed is not why China failed to proceed to an industrial revolution at this stage but why Europe achieved this later. He pointed out that despite the economic achievements of the Song period, the Chinese economy remained at the 'premodern economic growth stage'. The economy was highly productive and the state had developed sophisticated social, political and economic institutions. Europe was to face a different situation. The rise of population which began in the sixteenth century threatened a decline in living standards and this forced an early technological and organizational response. In China the potential of the technology which had been developed by the Song period was not exhausted until modern times, and a response was consequently delayed.[9]

THE REFORMS OF WANG ANSHI

From early in the Song period scholars and officials proposed schemes of reform to deal with the perceived problems of the day. During the reign of the Renzong emperor (1023–63), Fan Zhongyan advanced a ten-point programme of reform, which included measures to improve the efficiency of the bureaucracy, to raise the standard of the examinations, to increase agricultural production, and to reduce the demands on the people for labour service. Of these proposals only some educational reforms were implemented. Fan Zhongyan is also credited with pioneering the creation of a national school system and introducing anonymity for examination candidates. Another proponent of reform was the famous writer Ouyang Xiu (1007–72), who urged a renovation of Chinese society to bring it closer to the ideal Confucian society of the past. He called on able men to form a 'party' committed to reform. He was, of course, aware that the organization of an opposition was unacceptable in Chinese politics, but he justified his proposal on the grounds that his supporters would be men of principle, whereas their opponents would be men motivated solely by profit.

It was against this backdrop that Wang Anshi (1021–86), China's most famous reformer, took the stage. Wang Anshi, a protégé of Fan Zhongyan, had held a number of official positions in the provinces, and in 1058 had presented to the Emperor Renzong a document known as the *Ten Thousand Word Memorial*. In it he expressed anxiety about the current state of the empire and advocated a series of conventional Confucian measures to remedy the situation, in particular by increasing the number of capable officials available for the service of the state. However, he also made two novel suggestions: that men should be placed in positions for which they had special qualifications, an idea which ran counter to the Confucian ideal that an official should be a man of wide general learning, and that the emperor himself should do more than merely oversee the government, and should actually sponsor a programme of reform. The Emperor Renzong ignored these suggestions, but when the Shenzong emperor (r. 1068–85) came to the throne he appointed Wang Anshi his chief minister, a post he occupied until 1076 and re-occupied from 1078 to 1085.

During his first period in office Wang Anshi embarked on a reform programme to be known as the New Laws. These reforms affected the economy and taxation, security and military affairs, and the administration. He had identified a shortage of revenue as one of the main weaknesses of the state. He therefore proposed a number of novel ways in which revenue might be increased, including the purchase of surplus products in one area and selling them in another, thereby stabilizing prices and realizing a profit for the state. Another project concerned Sichuan, which up to this date was only loosely incorporated into the empire and only lightly taxed. In 1074 Wang Anshi created the Tea and Horse agency, which established a monopoly over the Sichuan tea industry, and used the tea to purchase war horses from Tibet. The agency was to operate successfully until 1126, when the north of China was lost to the Jin and the supply of horses ceased. Thereafter the monopoly ruined the Sichuan tea industry.

Other measures took account of the interests of the common people. Farmers were offered low-interest loans to enable them to escape from the clutches of money-lenders. As the money-lenders were usually landlords, the intention behind the measure was to reduce the concentration of land-holding and the evasion of taxation which accompanied it. Wang Anshi inveighed against the extravagance of the rich and threatened to take measures to restrict the manufacture and sale of luxury articles. The military reforms aimed to reduce the crippling cost of the army. To achieve this he revived the *baojia* system, the age-old system of collective security. Groups of ten households (the *bao*) were to take responsibility for local security and were also to supply men to be trained as a militia. With reference to the administration, his main reform was intended to encourage the promotion of candidates of good character. The exposition of the Confucian classics, rather than the exercise of literary skills, was now the main emphasis of the examinations. To encourage this Wang Anshi himself composed commentaries on the classics.

Although much of this reform programme fell within the Song tradition of pragmatic reform, Wang Anshi was immediately criticized. Lü Hui, a member of the censorate, attempted to impeach him, alleging that 'Wang Anshi is overbearing in his relations with his associates, and brooks no opposition.' He claimed that he was scheming to get all military and financial authority into his own hands, and that he had commissioned members of his faction to tour the country ostensibly to devise measures of financial economy but in fact to stir up trouble. Lü Hui's criticism may have been motivated by personal feelings, but other critics challenged the practicality of Wang Anshi's reforms. Su Dongpo, an official who was also well-known as a poet and calligrapher, suggested that the offer of low-interest loans to peasants might in future be used to oppress poor households. The outstanding scholar Sima Guang resigned in protest against the reforms and later wrote that the New Laws derived from Wang Anshi's desire to satisfy his own ambitions and that their effect was to oppress the poor.

Sima Guang's attack on Wang Anshi's reputation permanently blackened the reformer's reputation among Confucian scholars. Since his day more sympathetic assessments have been offered. The famous nationalist scholar Liang Qichao noted the resemblance between the New Laws and modern ideals. Marxist historians identified a class struggle behind the political criticism, claiming that Wang Anshi was a member of the bureaucrat-landlord class, and came from the south (he was a native of Jiangxi province), whereas Sima Guang came from the big landlord class (whose strength lay in the north). His reforms were supported by the dynasty as a means of containing peasant discontent, but were opposed by the big landlords because they threatened their interests. The Japanese sinologist Miyazaki Ichisada related Wang Anshi's reform programme to the impetus to reform which had marked the early Song period, and more generally to the transition from an aristocratic to an autocratic society. Miyazaki argued that the reforms, rather than causing the downfall of the Northern Song, had prolonged the life of the dynasty. James T. C. Liu stressed not only the importance of the reforms, but also the significance of their rejection. Wang Anshi had tried to introduce state economic planning and the development of economic resources, while at the same time attempting to curb administrative and fiscal abuses. Although he was suspected of being 'a Legalist in disguise' he was in fact a Confucianist, albeit an unorthodox one. The rejection of his utilitarian policies left the field to an orthodox Confucianism which stressed the moral qualities of the bureaucracy.[10]

Wang Anshi's reforms, and the conservative reaction to them, were to divide the bureaucracy and weaken the dynasty. In 1086, after the death of the Shenzong emperor, Sima Guang became chief minister and repealed several of the New Laws. However, the Zhezong emperor, who reigned from 1086 to 1101, appointed Cai Jing, Wang Anshi's son-in-law, to office, and he revived the New Laws though perhaps without Wang Anshi's high motives. Political opponents were labelled as disloyal and hounded out of government. Cai Jing remained in power under the Huizong emperor, (r. 1101–26), who is better remembered as an artist and patron of the arts than as an effective head of state. During his reign court extravagance weakened the state's finances, the bureaucracy continued to grow, corruption increased and other signs of dynastic decline appeared. In 1120 the Fang La rebellion broke out in Fujian and Zhejiang. Fang La, the owner of a plantation of lacquer trees, was incensed by the amount of tax he was expected to pay. The rebellion had secret society links and also had a connection with Manichaeism, a religion which had been brought to China in the eighth century by Uighur merchants. This rebellion, and others which broke out at this time, were the inspiration for the famous novel *Water Margin*.

However, the most serious threat to the dynasty was the rise of the Jurchen in the north. Until the beginning of the twelfth century the Qidan Liao empire had appeared to be relatively stable. The dualistic system of government was cumbersome and poorly organized, and it had not resolved the conflict of interest between the traditionalists of the Qidan aristocracy and sinicized Qidan officials who aimed to create a centralized, pro-Chinese state.

THE SONG AND YUAN DYNASTIES

Nevertheless when Tianzuo came to the throne in 1101 the succession was uncontested and relations with China, with the Xi Xia empire to the west, and with Koryo to the east were amicable.

In 1112 Tianzuo visited the eastern part of his empire. Near Harbin he entertained the chiefs of the north-eastern tribes, including the Jurchen, a semi-nomadic Tungusic people who had been subjugated by the Qidan in the tenth century. At the feast, Aguda, the chief of the 'wild' Jurchen, that is the Jurchen who lived furthest from the Qidan empire, refused to perform the dance which signified the submission of his tribe. His refusal caused a breakdown in relations between the Qidan and the Jurchen. In 1114 Aguda proclaimed the establishment of the Jin dynasty with himself as its first emperor. Tianzuo seriously underestimated the threat that this implied. Qidan forces were defeated in the field and the Qidan Liao dynasty was shaken by an internal rebellion. Moreover, the Song court had rashly involved itself in the situation by forming an alliance with Jurchen in the hope of dismembering the Liao empire and recovering the Sixteen Prefectures. In 1122 Song troops attacked, but failed to capture, the Qidan southern capital. This gave the Jurchen the opportunity to invade and occupy the entire Qidan territory and in 1125 Tianzuo was captured and forced to relinquish the title of emperor. Qidan survivors moved west and between 1131 and 1213 they ruled the Western Liao empire in Central Asia.

In the meantime the situation of the Song dynasty had become critical. Weakened by internal rebellion it was in no condition to withstand the aggression of the Jurchen Jin empire. In 1125 Jurchen forces invaded China and besieged Kaifeng. Before retiring they forced the Song to promise them an enormous indemnity. In 1127 they returned, captured and pillaged Kaifeng, and carried the emperor off as a prisoner. Over the next few years the Jurchen tightened their grip on north China and forced the Song court to retreat south of the Yangzi. However, the Jurchen did not have the capacity to conquer the south and in 1141 a peace was agreed between the Jin and Song dynasties which left the former ruling much of north China and the latter controlling the south of the country. The Song also agreed to pay to the Jin an annual tribute of 200,000 taels of silver (a tael was about 1.3 ounces of silver) and 200,000 bolts of silk.

THE JURCHEN JIN DYNASTY, 1115–1234

The Jin empire at its height encompassed north China, Manchuria and Inner Mongolia. Its history may be divided into three stages: a period of dualism, which lasted until about 1150, a period of increasing sinicization, and from 1215 a period of decline.

Through its conquest of north China the Jin had come to rule about 40 million Chinese, a task for which it had made no preparation. Not surprisingly the dynasty chose to emulate the Qidan Liao and adopted a policy of dualism. In Jurchen territory north of the Great Wall the tribal structure was retained and a separate system of taxation was applied. In north China, until a peace was agreed with the Southern Song in 1142, a series of regimes headed by Chinese puppet rulers exercised ineffectual control. Large numbers of Jurchen 'farmer-soldiers' moved south, where they acted like an occupying power, quelling Chinese rebellions harshly and forcibly resettling many thousands of Chinese in Manchuria. Their treatment of the Qidan was even more severe.

In 1150, after a disputed succession, Hailing became emperor and pressed ahead with a policy of sinicization. He established the central capital at Yanjing, present-day Beijing. Having ruthlessly curbed the power of the Jurchen aristocracy, he used the examination system to admit Chinese and Qidan into his service. He himself studied Chinese and adopted Chinese customs such as drinking tea. Nevertheless he distanced himself from Chinese tradition by sanctioning the public flogging of senior officials at court. His successor Shizong (r. 1161–89) attempted to reverse the process of sinicization by promoting the study of the Jurchen language, which was already falling into disuse, and by prohibiting Jurchen from adopting Chinese dress. However, he too pursued centralizing policies, in particular the whole-scale adoption of a Chinese form of central government, which demanded the employment of many thousands of Chinese officials and which ran counter to the traditional tribal organization of the Jurchen people. After his death, token Jurchenization was abandoned and sinicization proceeded apace, the ban on inter-marriage between Jurchen and Chinese being abandoned in 1191. By then the Jin rulers regarded their dynasty as a legitimate Chinese dynasty which preserved the traditions of the Tang and Northern Song, and this view was shared by at least a proportion of their Chinese subjects. Within the Jin empire, Chinese intellectual activity continued, but it was a conservative intellectualism which rejected the reform ideas of Wang Anshi and his followers.

The collapse of the Jin dynasty was brought about by a combination of internal and external events. In 1194 the Yellow river shifted to its southern course, causing immense damage and seriously affecting the economy. The aftermath of this disaster may have encouraged the Southern Song minister Han Tuozhou to declare war on the Jin in 1206. The Southern Song attack was easily repelled, but it was a distraction at a time when a graver danger had appeared, the rise of Genghis Khan and the threat of a Mongol invasion from the north-east. The first wave of Mongol attacks occurred between 1211 and 1213, at a time when the Jin court had been paralysed by a coup. The Mongols also attacked the Xi Xia state to the north-west. In response to the disruption caused, the Xi Xia supported a rebellion against the Jin which lost the latter much of north-west China. In 1215 the Jin abandoned Yanjing and transferred their capital to Kaifeng.

Over the next few years the principal threat was a popular rebellion, that of the Red Coats in Shandong. Genghis Khan died in 1227 and there was a brief respite from Mongol raids. However, in 1230 the new khan Ögödei renewed the attack and in 1232 besieged Kaifeng. The siege, which lasted for over a year, was notable for the endurance of the Jurchen and Chinese defenders, and also because both sides used firearms. The last Jin emperor fled the capital and appealed to the Southern Song for assistance, warning them that if the Mongols were victorious, they would be their next victims. Instead the Southern Song allied themselves with the Mongols against their Jurchen enemies. The outcome was inevitable and in 1234 the Jin emperor committed suicide and the dynasty came to an end.

THE SOUTHERN SONG, 1127–1279

After the loss of Kaifeng and the capture of the emperor in 1127, resistance to the Jurchen was led by Gaozong, a younger son of the Huizong emperor, who reigned until 1162. He established his capital at Hangzhou, and gradually reasserted Song control over southern China. Lacking the military power to suppress the separatist movements which had sprung up, he was forced to adopt a policy described as 'summoning to pacification', whereby outlaw bands were given the choice of either surrendering and being incorporated into the imperial army, or being attacked and eliminated. Behind this policy was an acknowledgement of the deep shame felt over the loss of northern China to the Jurchen, and the potential strength of loyalist feeling.

Among those who responded to the loyalist cause was a young man named Yue Fei. He played a key role in subduing rebel bands around the Dongting lake in Hunan and then campaigned against the Jurchen, in 1140 raiding as far north as Kaifeng. But then the Southern Song, in the person of the emperor's chief minister Qin Gui, negotiated a settlement with the Jurchen, accepting terms which acknowledged the Song to be vassals of the Jin. These terms gave the Southern Song security and enabled the dynasty to free itself from an unacceptable dependence on its generals. However, many on the Song side regarded the terms as a disgrace. To protect the emperor's reputation the negotiations were conducted by Qin Gui. He was also to take the blame for the execution of Yue Fei on a trumped up charge. Yue Fei's true fault was his determination to continue the war of resistance, and for his patriotism he became one of the great heroes of Chinese history.

The desire for revenge against the Jurchen Jin remained a key issue for the Southern Song dynasty. In 1161, the last year of Gaozong's reign, Hailing the Jurchen Jin emperor made an unprovoked attack on Song territory south of the Huai river, but was halted on the Fei river, a battle which became a byword for heroic resistance. Soon after this defeat Hailing was assassinated and in 1165 his successor Shizong concluded a treaty with the Southern Song which retracted the assertion of vassal status and the use of the term 'tribute', although the Song's annual payments to the Jin continued. For the next 40 years there was an uneasy peace.

Early in the thirteenth century Han Tuozhou, the Song Emperor Ningzong's chief minister, used the issue of revenge to assert his authority. Having heard reports of the damage caused by the Yellow river floods, and believing that the Chinese living under the Jin yoke would rebel if encouraged, in 1206 he invaded Jin territory. The invasion was badly planned, the Jin's Chinese population did not rebel, and the Jurchen replied with a raid deep into Song territory. This disaster led to the dismissal and murder of Han Tuozhou. When peace was agreed in 1208 the annual payments were increased and the Jin demanded and were given Han Tuozhou's head in expiation of his crimes. By now the Mongol threat to the Jin was apparent, yet the Southern Song leaders, oblivious to the danger to their own country, continued to oppose the Jin until that dynasty was extinguished.

Northern Song dynasty emperors had presided over but had not directed the administration, for that was the task of the bureaucracy. The bureaucracy was composed of scholar-officials who in theory governed according to moral principles. The administration was divided into distinct areas, with military and financial affairs kept separate from general administration. If officials failed in their duties they were liable to be impeached by the *yanguan* or 'opinion officials'. Such a system of government was centralized, but not necessarily autocratic, but this was to change in the Southern Song period. Gaozong, the first Southern Song emperor, was diligent if not officious in the performance of his role. Early in his reign he delegated power to a team of ministers who, because of the crisis situation, exercised both civil and military authority. However, in 1139 the ministerial team was dispensed with and Qin Gui became the 'sole surrogate', a chief minister who exercised power on behalf of the emperor. The immediate reason for this shift towards absolutism was the emperor's decision to make peace with the Jin, a decision which stemmed 'not from Confucian principles, but from power calculations.'[11]

This political arrangement was to continue to the end of the dynasty. In 1162 Gaozong abdicated in favour of his son, but until his death in 1187 he remained the power behind the throne. After his death his son, the Xiaozong emperor, fell into a deep depression and eventually he too abdicated. Recurrent illness was to affect all subsequent Southern Song emperors. Throughout the long reign of the Ningzong emperor (1194–1224), two chief ministers were successively in control. Han Tuozhou, the nephew of Gaozong's empress, gained office through intrigue and in particular through cultivating close ties with the eunuchs.

He conducted a vendetta against moralistic scholar-officials of the Neo-Confucian school, who were critical of his lack of formal education. His rash decision for war in 1206 may have been prompted by the domestic political struggle in which he was engaged. His murder in 1207 – he was bludgeoned to death by palace guardsmen – was perhaps tacitly agreed by the emperor. His end was welcomed by the Neo-Confucianists, but the circumstances indicated another serious departure from the principles of Confucian government, for whereas an emperor might well dismiss a minister in whom he no longer had confidence, to procure his death by violence was a very different matter.

Ningzong's second 'sole surrogate' chief minister was Shi Miyuan, who gained office after the death of Han Tuozhou. The Shi family, a well-established provincial family from Ningbo in the south-east, produced a succession of men who gained office through the examination system. On appointment Shi Miyuan reversed Han Tuozhou's policies, making peace with the Jin and rescinding the ban on Neo-Confucian teaching, all acceptable, if authoritarian, actions. However, when Ningzong died in 1224 he interfered with the succession, setting aside the heir to the throne in favour of his own nominee. The controversy which this caused preoccupied the court at the very time that the Mongols were destroying the Jin empire. Nevertheless, Shi Miyuan remained in office until his death in 1233.[12]

The most notorious of the Southern Song long-serving chief ministers was Jia Sidao, who became chief minister in 1259 and remained in office until shortly before the dynasty collapsed. His posthumous reputation was that of a licentious dilettante who had gained high office through intrigue. In fact by the time he was appointed chief minister he had twenty years of experience in a variety of official posts. His notoriety derived from two particular incidents, the first occurring in 1259 when he was accused of treachery for his dealings with the Mongols, who in that year had crossed the Yangzi and were investing the town of Ezhou on the middle Yangzi. According to his accusers, Jia Sidao, having falsely claimed to have gained victories over the Mongol forces, agreed with the Mongols that they should withdraw in return for the Song defining the Yangzi as the frontier and agreeing to pay an annual tribute. However, it has been shown that no agreement was reached on that occasion, and the reason for the Mongol withdrawal was the succession crisis caused by the death of the Great Khan Möngke.

The second incident concerned Jia Sidao's pursuit of radical agrarian and economic policies, reminiscent of the reforms of Wang Anshi. His aim was to counter the increasing concentration of land-holding and the evasion of taxation which large landowners could procure. In 1263 he introduced laws which fixed the maximum size for a landed property and provided for the compulsory purchase of excess land-holdings. The revenue from the land acquired by the state was to be used to support the army. These measures remained in force until 1275, and some land was confiscated and some revenue was raised for defence. But the measures also alienated large landowners and others who might have been expected to support the dynasty. By now the Mongols were across the Yangzi and Jia Sidao himself took command of the Song forces. The defeat which followed ensured his fall and the immediate revocation of his laws. Nevertheless, as the Mongols approached many Song gentry decided to go over to the invaders' side, an ironic confirmation that Jia Sidao was responsible in some degree for the fall of the dynasty.

INTELLECTUAL AND CULTURAL TRENDS UNDER THE SOUTHERN SONG

Whereas the political record of the Southern Song has often been criticized, the intellectual and cultural achievements of the period have long been held in high esteem. Two particular aspects of this achievement will be considered: the emergence of Neo-Confucianism, and the development of landscape painting and ceramics.

Neo-Confucianism in its broader sense refers to the Confucian revival which had begun under the Tang through the activities of Han Yu and others. Under the Northern Song the revival was continued by intellectuals such as Ouyang Xiu, whose call for a renovation of Chinese society has already been noted. Neo-Confucianism then acquired a political connotation, for its exponents ranged themselves in opposition to Wang Anshi and the reformers, who were likened to the Legalists.

During the Northern Song period Neo-Confucianism extended

its range and borrowed ideas from Daoism and Buddhism. Zhou
Tunyi (1017–73) used the *Book of Changes*, the five agents, and
the concepts of *yin* and *yang* to identify the 'Great Ultimate', the
principle from which all being derives. Zhang Zai (1020–77)
suggested that the entire universe was composed of a single pri-
mal substance, referred to as *qi*. These ideas were developed by
Cheng Hao (1032–85) and his brother Cheng Yi (1033–1107).
The former emphasized the unity of the human mind with the
mind of the universe. His writings later engendered the Neo-
Confucian school of the Mind. The latter adopted Zhang Zai's
ideas on the *qi* but added a second concept, that of *li* or principle, the original nature of all things. His ideas led to the school
of Principle. These ideas were later synthesized by Zhu Xi
(1130–1200) into a single doctrine, and it was his ideas which
became enshrined in what according to the narrow definition is
Neo-Confucianism. To the metaphysical ideas of the Northern
Song philosophers, he added a revived emphasis on the *dao*, the
Way that all individuals should strive to follow, and this required
a greater emphasis on self-cultivation and a deeper understanding of the Confucian classics. Because of Zhu Xi's emphasis on
the Way, his teaching became known as the True Way school.
This attracted many devout followers, who adopted archaic rites,
old-fashioned styles of dress and strict deportment to emphasize
their separateness from conventional career-minded Confucian
bureaucrats.

In 1195, soon after Han Tuozhou had become chief minister,
the True Way school was condemned as false learning, and Zhu
Xi, who was briefly in office, was dismissed. However, the ban
was soon lifted and after Han Tuozhou's death the True Way
school gradually became the orthodox state doctrine. As the
Mongol threat increased, and as the Mongols themselves in
north China began to adopt features of Confucianism, the
Southern Song turned to the True Way (now known as the school
of Principle) as true Confucianism. Although Neo-Confucianism
provided a sense of identity and an integrative ideology which
enabled Chinese intellectuals to survive the Mongol occupation
its effects have been described as 'China turning inward'. As a
defence mechanism it reinforced belief in Chinese cultural superiority, as a state orthodoxy it deprived scholars of the right to
criticize the growth of autocracy, and as a personal philosophy it

elevated self-cultivation above political reform or practical improvement.

It has been said of Song painting, particularly of bird-and-flower and bamboo painting, that it reflects the profound and subtle examination of the visible world which is characteristic of Neo-Confucianism. Su Dongpo (1036–1101), already referred to as a critic of Wang Anshi, said that when a scholar paints a landscape, he seldom depicts a real place. Instead he borrows the forms of mountains and trees as a vehicle to express his feelings and his ideas. The value placed on the art of painting is indicated by the attention paid to it by Huizong, the last emperor of the Northern Song, who was both a practitioner of the bird-and-flower style and the patron of an academy of painting. Under the Southern Song the restrained style of the earlier period was replaced by the more expressive style of painters such as Xia Gui (fl. 1180–1224). Chan Buddhist painting also flourished at this time. It was characterized by a concentration on certain details of the subject, with all else left undefined. The most famous exponent of this style was Mu Qi (c. 1200–70), whose painting *Six Persimmons* is well known in the West.

The Tang period had seen important technical advances in the manufacture of ceramics, including the development of porcelain. Under the Song, technical improvement continued and it was accompanied by a very high aesthetic standard. Under the Northern Song, state kilns near Kaifeng produced a variety of high-quality wares, including Ding ware, a white porcelain which was very thin and translucent and which was often incised with delicate patterns. When Kaifeng fell to the Jin, some of the potters fled south for Ding ware was later made in Jiangxi. The best-known Southern Song porcelain is that known in the West as celadon. The very best celadon, which had a greyish-green glaze, came from Longquan in southern Zhejiang. This ware became a major export item, much of it going to Japan.

ECONOMIC AND SOCIAL CHANGES

During the Southern Song period economic growth continued apace. Agricultural output was increased by the adoption of new seeds, a notable example being the introduction of fast-ripening

Champa rice from Vietnam. Irrigation was extended and multiple cropping was used more widely, and as a result in some areas seasonal unemployment almost disappeared.

By the Song period the *juntian* or 'equal field' system had finally been abandoned and had been replaced by a free market in land. All modern writers agree that this produced a new pattern of land-holding, but the characteristics of that pattern are disputed. Mark Elvin referred to it as 'manorialism', implying that this was a period of large private estates or manors, worked by tenant-serfs who were bound to the land. Evelyn Rawski, however, claimed that agriculture was dominated by free, small-scale farmers, working under a system of private ownership. More recently, Peter Golas has calculated that at the end of the eleventh century, official and first- to third-rank households, which constituted a mere 14 per cent of the population, owned 77.5 per cent of the land under cultivation, and he concluded from this that large land-holdings made up a very important part of Song agriculture.[13]

Under the Song there was a marked trend towards urbanization. Under the Northern Song, Kaifeng had been the world's largest city. That position was now taken by Hangzhou, the 'temporary residence' of the Southern Song, the city known to Marco Polo as Quinsai. In the thirteenth century Hangzhou, which was both the residence of the court and a great commercial centre, had a population of perhaps two million. It was the hub of what had now become China's most important silk-producing region, and its lively commerce encouraged the use of increasingly sophisticated commercial methods, for example the use of paper currency. Hangzhou was also a port handling foreign trade. For the first time in China's history maritime trade became an important part of the economy and tariffs became a significant contributor to the imperial revenue.

Under the Song, and particularly under the Southern Song, a new elite emerged which entirely displaced the aristocratic clans of the Tang period. A key element in the formation of this elite was the expansion of the examination system. What is less clear is whether the examination system had created that new elite, and was constantly renewing it through the introduction of new blood, or whether the elite had a different origin and was largely self-perpetuating through various means, of which the examination system was only one. According to Richard L. Davis, who studied the Shi family of Ningbo which produced the chief minister Shi Miyuan, the rise of the Shi was the product of examination success. In that system it was difficult for any family to maintain a position of power for long, and for its extended prominence the Shi clan owed much to the longevity of its leading members. However, Robert P. Hymes, who investigated the elite of Fuzhou in Jiangxi during the same period, has argued that the formation of the elite largely occurred independently of the examination system. The elite of the Song period was heavily southern in its origins, and was far more durable than reliance on examination success would imply. This durability was based on the role that elite families had established for themselves in their locality. This finding led Hymes to suggest that during the Southern Song period there was a marked tendency for the elite to shift its attention from the pursuit of office to the consolidation of its home base, and thereby to separate itself from the state.[14]

The spread of printing, and the intellectual ferment which that inspired, has ensured that more is known about Song society, and in particular about the lives of women, than about the society of any previous period in Chinese history. It used to be supposed that under the Tang, women participated in society with considerable freedom, but that under the Song, women's situation took a turn for the worst. This deterioration was exemplified by the spread of foot-binding and the condemnation of the remarriage of widows. To explain this decline, reference is made to Neo-Confucianism, alleging that Cheng Yi and Zhu Xi promoted the idea that women must value chastity. This view has recently been challenged by Patricia Buckley Ebrey, who has pointed to the contradictory evidence that women had particularly strong property rights during the Song period. She noted the spread of foot-binding but warned that to assume that it implied the subjection of women was anachronistic, for the evidence suggests that it was adopted by women to promote their attractiveness. Southern Song culture encouraged men to bookishness, to reinforce the contrast with the martial virtues of the Jurchen and Mongols. In turn this favoured a stereotype of women as beautiful and deferential. Foot-binding was originally associated with dancers, and then more generally with courtesans and concubines. It was to allow other women to match this claim to beauty that foot-binding came into general use. As for the remarriage of widows, there was certainly a strong popular prejudice against this, although the law allowed a woman to remarry. However, Ebrey argues that this prejudice has been misunderstood in modern times. During the Song period a marriage was about how families perpetuated themselves through the incorporation of new members. A man was incorporated at birth, a woman at marriage. If a husband died and the woman remarried, she renounced her loyalty to the family into which she had been incorporated.[15]

THE MONGOL CONQUEST

The traditional view of Mongol rule over China was that it was an unmitigated disaster. Hongwu, the founder of the Ming dynasty, claimed that one of his aims was to restore the integrity of Han Chinese civilization, which had been partially despoiled during the Yuan period. Three particular charges have been levelled against the Mongols: that they discriminated against the Chinese both racially and economically; that they failed to build on the technological and economic achievements of the Song period and so contributed to the introverted and noncompetitive position adopted under the Ming; and that they instituted practices – the example given is the public flogging of ministers – which contributed to the development of despotism. However, some modern historians have suggested that whereas the Mongol invasion of China caused extensive damage, the period of Mongol rule did have some positive features. The Mongols reunified China, and their adoption of the dynastic title 'Yuan' and other practices of a Chinese dynasty entitled them to a place in the Chinese dynastic record as legitimate holders of the mandate of heaven. Chinese civilization was not fundamentally altered by the episode of Mongol rule and in several ways scholarship and the arts benefited. Moreover, in some respects Mongol rule was more humane and less ideologically restrictive than that of the Song. The *pax mongolica*, the 'Mongol peace', which spread across Asia, exposed China to a wide variety of external influences. At a personal level the hostility of Chinese for Mongol was not so intense as to prevent many Mongols remaining in China after the flight of the Mongol court.

The Mongols were pastoral nomads who, by the late eleventh century, were living as a tribal society in present-day Mongolia. Already accomplished warriors on horseback who were in frequent conflict with the Tatars, their neighbours to the west, the Mongols now began to develop an ethnic consciousness. This political situation was exploited by Temujin, the son of a tribal leader, who was born in about 1167. According to *The Secret History of the Mongols*, his father had been poisoned by the Tatars and this grievance motivated him to claim the leadership of his tribe. He raised a disciplined army divided into groups of 1000 men and devised new military tactics. This enabled him to unite the Mongol tribes and in 1206 he was acclaimed Genghis Khan, the universal sovereign of the steppe peoples. He claimed to be heaven's chosen instrument and declared that all who stood in his way did so in defiance of heaven's will.

Genghis Khan then embarked on a remarkable sequence of conquests. In 1210 he invaded the Xi Xia kingdom and forced it to pay him tribute, thereby cutting China's trade routes to the north-west. In 1215 he captured the Jin capital at Yanjing, but instead of destroying the Jurchen dynasty he turned west and seized Bokhara and Samarkand. In the meantime he began to recruit Chinese and Qidan officials and appointed Mukhali, one of his most reliable generals, to administer the Chinese territory which he had occupied. In 1226 he turned to destroy the Xi Xia kingdom, but died during the campaign. He was succeeded as khaghan, or khan of khans, by his third son Ögödei and the Mongol Empire was divided between his sons and grandson. Ögödei continued the conquests, invading Korea and in 1234 completing the destruction of the Jin dynasty. In the west, Mongol forces overcame Russia and inflicted devastating defeats on the states of eastern Europe. Only Ögödei's death in 1241 halted this extraordinary expansion.

After the conquest of north China the Mongols looked for ways to exploit their gains. A famous anecdote tells how a Mongol nobleman suggested that the entire population should be annihilated and the region turned over to pasture. This led Yelüchucai, a sinicized Qidan in Mongol employ, to propose as a more effective means of exploitation the granting of an amnesty to those Chinese who had unwittingly broken Mongol law, the establishment of a new administrative system and the creation of bureaux to organize regular tax payments. Ögödei rejected entire reliance on sinicized officials and granted licences to Central Asian Muslims to farm taxes, thereby undermining Yelüchucai's fiscal strategy. Later in Ögödei's reign Yelüchucai's hope of restoring a form of Confucian rule to north China was further undermined when the khaghan awarded large landed estates to the Mongol princes and princesses. Ögödei drank himself to death in 1241 and his widow became regent. It was not until 1251, when Möngke became khaghan, that Mongol expansion resumed. Rather than make a direct attack on the Southern Song, Möngke decided to outflank them and in 1252 he ordered his brother Khubilai to attack and destroy the south-western kingdom of Nanzhao, which the latter had achieved by 1254. Möngke's next objective was the province of Sichuan, but he died in 1259 while pursuing that campaign. Once again a succession dispute delayed a decisive Mongol assault on China.

Möngke had entrusted the administration of north China to his younger brother Khubilai, who had shown a willingness to accept advice from Confucian advisers and to promote the prosperity of the region. In May 1260 he was elected khaghan and shortly afterwards adopted a Chinese reign title. His chief Chinese adviser, a former Buddhist monk named Liu Bingzhong, supposedly remarked that 'although the empire had been conquered on horseback, it could not be administered on horseback'. It was with his encouragement that Khubilai laid out a Chinese-style capital at Kaiping in Inner Mongolia. Later renamed Shangdu or 'upper capital', it became known in the West as Xanadu.

As emperor of China it was inevitable that Khubilai would at some point resume the assault on the Southern Song who continued to assert their claim to the whole of the country. By 1268 he was ready to attack, his first objective being the key city of Xiangyang on the Han river. For this campaign Khubilai had to obtain ships and engineers proficient in siege warfare. After a five-year siege, in which the Mongols used a large mangonel to batter down the walls, the city surrendered and the route to the Yangzi valley was clear. In 1275 Bayan, the leading Mongol general, met and defeated a large army led by Jia Sidao, the last chief councillor of the Southern Song. Jia's land policies had already alienated wealthy landowners and this defeat ensured his dismissal. Song resistance now collapsed and the Song court surrendered. However, it was only in 1279 that the last Song loyalists were defeated at sea and the last Song emperor drowned.

CHINA UNDER MONGOL RULE

Although Khubilai had triumphed in China his other military ventures were less successful. Twice, in 1274 and 1281, he attempted to conquer Japan, but on both occasions was driven back by fierce Japanese resistance and bad weather. On the second occasion a typhoon, referred to by the Japanese as *kamikaze*, a 'divine wind', caused the destruction of half the Mongol force. Campaigns in South-east Asia took the Mongols into terrain in which their military skills were of little value and they suffered disastrous reverses. These failures, ill-health and the death of his favourite wife cast a shadow over Khubilai's final years. He suffered further from difficulties over the succession, which was to prove a chronic problem for Mongol emperors. Whereas the Chinese practice was for the emperor to nominate one of his sons to succeed him, Mongol custom prescribed that the political succession should go to whichever of the khaghan's male relatives was acclaimed at a council of notables. Khubilai, as emperor of China, attempted to follow Chinese custom and nominated Zhenjin, his eldest son by his principal wife, as his successor, but Zhenjin died in 1285. When Khubilai himself died in 1294 it seemed that he had bestowed the succession on his second son Temür, but this was contested by his eldest surviving son. The rivalries engendered by this dispute were re-awakened every time a Mongol emperor died, and were a significant factor in the decline of the dynasty.

Temür, who reigned until 1307, continued many aspects of Khubilai's rule. His successor Khaishan, who came to the throne after a violent conflict, spent lavishly and acted arbitrarily. He in turn was succeeded by his brother Ayurbarwada, perhaps the most sinicized and cultured of the Mongol rulers, who ruled as the Renzong emperor from 1311 to 1320. After his death the court split into factions, divided partly by the struggle for the succession between the two lines of descent from Khubilai and partly by the stand taken towards sinicization. In 1323 Yesun Temür, a man hostile to the influence of Chinese scholar-officials, seized the throne and held it until his death five years later. After an even more savage succession dispute Tugh Temür, a man regarded as committed to China rather than to the steppe, held the throne for another five years. The last Mongol ruler, Toghon Temür, came to the throne as a minor, and survived until the Mongol court fled from China in 1368.

Khubilai established the pattern of Mongol rule over China. In 1272 he adopted *Da Yuan*, or 'Great Origin', as the title of his dynasty and established its claim to be a universal empire. He retained many superficial features of Song government, for example the secretariat and the six ministries, and the traditional division between the civil, military and censorial branches of government. He adopted Chinese court ceremonial and Confucian rites and even set up an office to collect materials for a history of the preceding dynasties. However, Khubilai declined to restore the examination system on the grounds that it might restrict his choice of officials to those who had a knowledge of the Confucian classics. Officials were selected with reference to birth and the *yin* privilege. Although Yuan government appeared to be highly centralized, even under Khubilai the authority of the central government did not run much beyond the metropolitan province and this tendency towards regionalism became even more marked under his successors.

One of the most notorious of Khubilai's actions, in Chinese eyes, was his division of the population into four groups: the Mongols at the top of the social pyramid, below them the *semu ren*, that is miscellaneous aliens, a reference to Western and Central Asians, then the *Han ren*, the inhabitants of north China, and finally the *nan ren*, the Chinese of the newly-conquered south. Although the division between these groups was not as rigid as may have been intended, it clearly discriminated against the Chinese. Despite this discrimination some Chinese scholars were prepared to accept office. Before the conquest of the south, Khubilai had employed a number of Chinese advisers, including Xu Heng, a notable Neo-Confucian scholar, who held the view that the duty of a scholar was not to shun the Mongols but to civilize them. Khubilai had been persuaded to establish a history office by the historian Wang E, on the grounds that the history of previous dynasties provided models for the present which all great emperors had found it prudent to observe. The bureaucracy was ethnically very mixed, and because no metropolitan examinations were held for 40 years, the opportunity existed for educated men to work their way up to a salaried official position. When in 1315 the Renzong emperor permitted the reintroduction of examinations, it was in a form which was heavily weighted in favour of Mongol candidates.

To counterbalance Chinese influence in government Khubilai and later Mongol emperors employed many foreigners in key positions. The largest and most influential group were the Turks, a group which included the Uighur, a significant number of whom were employed as top-ranking officials. They provided an infrastructure between the Mongols and the broad mass of their Chinese subjects. An important religious role was performed by Tibetan Buddhists. A Tibetan monk, 'Phags-pa, was placed in charge of all Buddhist clergy and advised on relations with Tibet. In return he identified Khubilai as the universal emperor of the Buddhist tradition. Throughout the Yuan period Tibetan Buddhism or Lamaism was granted a privileged status, and this became a source of complaint among Chinese, particularly in the south. In 1285 a Tibetan or Tangut lama named Yang, who had been made responsible for Buddhist teaching south of the Yangzi, caused particular offence by breaking open the tombs of the Song royal family and using the treasures obtained to restore Buddhist temples.

The early Mongol emperors employed a significant number of Muslims, many of whom came from Central Asia, in key positions in China. Islam was not new to China, for it had been introduced in the Tang period and Muslim traders had settled in Guangzhou and other southern ports. Islam had also made converts among the Chinese in Central Asia. However, the engagement of foreign Muslims rather than sinicized Turks and Tibetans was a distinct departure from dual government as practised by previous dynasties of conquest. Muslims in China were classified as *semu* and were granted special privileges. They performed a wide variety of specialized tasks, particularly in matters of finance, but also in the fields of medicine, astronomy, and architecture, although they were excluded from the higher ranks of the armed forces. Although Muslims did not play a major role in the administration of China, there was one notable exception in the case of Saiyid Ajall, a Central Asian Muslim who was appointed governor of the newly conquered territory of Yunnan.

The most notorious Muslim to play a prominent role in Khubilai's reign was Ahmad, who, from 1262 until his death in 1282, directed Khubilai's state financial administration. His principal task was to increase state revenue and he did this by increasing the number of households liable to pay tax and instituting profitable state monopolies on tea, liquor, vinegar, gold and silver. Ahmad also encouraged the overland trade between China and Central Asia. Much of this was financed by merchant associations known as *ortogh*. This trade was profitable to the government, for all merchants on reaching China were required to exchange precious metals for paper currency. The *ortogh* were also a source of loans for the Mongol nobility. In return for their services *ortogh* merchants were given a preferential position when raising capital to finance trade caravans.

Although Khubilai used Muslims in high office, he was aware of Chinese hostility towards them and he grew concerned about their increasing influence. Ahmad's Chinese critics accused him of nepotism, exploitation and profiteering. From 1279 Khubilai adopted a harsher policy towards Muslims and in 1282 he may have been implicated in the murder of Ahmad by Chinese conspirators.

The *pax mongolica* and the increase in trade along the Silk Road enabled the establishment of the first direct contacts between China and the West. For the early travellers the most common motive was trade, but some had a political objective, to seek allies at a time when Islam was seen as a threat by both Mongols and Christians, and for others proselytism was the prime purpose of their journey. The first European to place his journey to China on record was a Franciscan monk, John of Plano Carpini. He had been sent by Pope Innocent IV and the Holy Roman Emperor to seek an agreement with the Mongols and to convert them to Christianity. He failed on both counts, but he left a record of his travels which included a description of the enthronement of Güyüg Khan in 1246. Guillaume Boucher was one of several European artisans who were employed by Möngke Khan in the 1250s.

In about 1265, soon after Khubilai had become emperor of China, he received two Venetian merchants, the brothers Maffeo and Niccolo Polo. They returned to the West in 1269, having been commissioned by Khubilai to ask the Pope to send 100 Christian scholars to China. In 1271 they set out for China again, without the scholars but with Niccolo's son Marco. Marco Polo's *Travels*, written or dictated by him after his return to Europe twenty years later, contained a detailed description of Khubilai's court, of north China or Cathay as it was then known to Europeans, and of the great city of Hangzhou, which he called Quinsai. Some features of Marco Polo's book, for example his failure to refer to the Chinese mode of writing or to mention the Chinese habit of drinking tea, have aroused suspicion about the authenticity of the text and the question has been raised whether he actually reached China. The book certainly contains some false claims, for example the statement that Marco Polo advised the Mongols on the capture Xiangyang, whereas the city had fallen to the Mongols two years before he reached China. However, what is described as 'conclusive proof' of Marco Polo's presence in China during Khubilai's reign has now been identified.[16]

In 1287 Rabban Sauma, a Turk born in China, reached Naples and subsequently had audiences with Philip IV of France and Edward I of England. In 1295 another Franciscan monk, John of Montecorvino, reached Khanbalik, the Mongol capital, and was allowed to establish a Christian mission which survived for fifty years. Another Franciscan, Odoric of Pordenone, wrote a narrative of his travels which became the source of many of the Western stereotypes about life in China.

In Chinese eyes the period of Mongol rule was one of damage to the economy and a decline in Chinese living standards. A puzzling piece of evidence to support this view concerns the demographic record. According to taxation figures the combined population of Song and Jin China amounted to well over 100 million, but according to the census carried out in 1290, which excluded Yunnan and other areas and did not enumerate several categories of people, it was less than 60 million. So large a discrepancy led Frederick W. Mote to assume that 'there was a catastrophic reduction in China's population between 1200 and 1400, the most extreme in the history of China'.[17] This population decline has been attributed in the first instance to the Mongol invasion of the north, to the confiscation of land for distribution to the invaders and the application of heavy taxation to those Chinese who retained their land. This precipitated a wave of southward migration, though the depopulation of the north was not balanced by a population increase in the south. The Yuan dynasty also stands accused of sins of omission and commission in its subsequent management of the economy. The consequence of its failure to maintain river defences finally became evident with the massive flooding of the Yellow river in 1344.

Mongol extravagance had first been demonstrated by the building of the summer residence at Shangdu, which contained a magnificent marble palace. In 1266 Khubilai ordered the construction of a new capital at Dadu (otherwise Khanbalik, the city of the khan) near modern Beijing, and the cost of this project placed a heavy burden on the treasury. Financial problems were exacerbated by instances of official corruption. Paper money had been introduced under the Song and Khubilai extended its use to promote trade. At first this currency, backed by a silver reserve, proved a success but in 1276 the amount of paper notes in circulation was greatly increased to finance the conquest of the south. This was the beginning of a loss of confidence in paper currency, and by the beginning of the Ming period it had become entirely discredited.

Such a presentation of Mongol handling of economic affairs is certainly one-sided. Khubilai quickly recognized the need to restore the devastated economy of north China. Impoverished areas were granted tax concessions and villages affected by natural disasters were given assistance. In 1261 he established an 'Office for the Stimulation of Agriculture' which helped peasants to make the best use of their land. Khubilai also endorsed the existence of peasant self-help organizations which promoted irrigation and land reclamation. He encouraged internal trade and greatly improved the postal relay system. After the conquest of the south, measures were introduced to relieve areas affected by the war. Large landowners were allowed to retain their land and the land-tax burden was relatively light. The encouragement of maritime commerce was also beneficial to the region. Later in Khubilai's reign the Japanese campaigns and ambitious attempts to improve the canal network to facilitate the supply of grain to

Dadu imposed further heavy burdens on the treasury, but it was still possible to conclude that Khubilai left his successors 'a stable and generally prosperous state'.[18] Later Yuan emperors were less proactive in economic matters, and Ayurbarwada in particular has been cited as reverting to the Confucian ideal of cutting government expenditure and lightening taxation but doing little to encourage economic activity. As a consequence, and perhaps advantageously, the large landowners of the south were largely left to their own devices.

Another aspect of Mongol rule which in Chinese eyes amounted to discrimination related to legal matters. Whereas the Mongols had brought with them the *jasagh*, the collection of rules promulgated by Genghis Khan for the regulation of a nomadic society, the Chinese were accustomed to statutory law as codified under the Tang. Under the Yuan, Mongols and *semu ren* were tried according to Mongol law, while Chinese were tried according to Chinese law. Critics of this arrangement pointed to differences in punishment for the same offence, and in particular to the provision that a Chinese offender should be tattooed as well as receiving the prescribed punishment for his crime. However, tattooing (to identify a criminal) was not a Mongol innovation, for the provision already existed under Song law. Legal cases involving both Mongols and Chinese were dealt with in special courts, and in these actions Mongols did have some advantages, for example marital disputes involving a mixed marriage were normally adjudicated according to the law of the husband unless the wife was a Mongol, in which case Mongolian law applied. A further example of discrimination which has been quoted concerns the prohibition of a Chinese retaliating if assaulted by a Mongol. However, this example is misleading as the law elsewhere provided the Chinese with a legal remedy for the injury.

The Mongol emperors, beginning with Khubilai, sought to preserve their Mongol inheritance. Mongol religion, a form of shamanism, was preserved and Khubilai performed its traditional rituals, for example that of scattering mare's milk. No attempt was made to impose Mongol religious beliefs on the Chinese and the Yuan period was notable for its religious freedom. Möngke and later Khubilai encouraged open debate between Buddhists and Daoists, who were currently involved in bitter rivalry. In

1281, after a famous debate, Khubilai decided that the Buddhists had won the contest and that Daoist excesses should be curbed. The Mongol attitude towards Confucianism was more circumspect. Khubilai's ignorance of written Chinese debarred him from a proper understanding of the Confucian texts – not until Ayurbarwada came to the throne did a Mongol emperor have a working knowledge of written Chinese. Nevertheless Khubilai recognized the importance of Confucianism and he employed Confucian officials and promoted the translation of the Confucian classics into the Mongol language. Ayurbarwada went further in modifying the Mongolian character of the state, but the Confucian elements which were now incorporated remained superficial features. Early in Toghon Temür's reign effective power was held by his chancellor Bayan,[19] who, to the dismay of Confucian scholars, attempted to turn the tide of sinicization by abolishing the examinations as a route of entry into the civil service. Bayan was overthrown in 1340 and thereafter, until the fall of the Yuan, Confucianism recovered some of its ideological pre-eminence and the restoration of the examination system offered not only to Chinese, but also to Mongols and *semu*, a common objective and a commitment to a unified state.

In the Yuan period Confucian scholars were therefore placed in a dilemma. Some, such as Xu Heng, whose name has already been mentioned, reasoned that their Confucian duty required them to serve the Mongols in the hope of civilizing them. Wang Yun (1227–1304), author of a book which offered advice on the actions to be expected from a model ruler, a book which was translated into Mongolian, achieved the same effect by different means. But other scholars refused to condone the Mongol presence and would not compromise and accept office. A notable example of such a person was Liu Yin (1249–93), who in 1291 refused an invitation to become an academician at the Imperial College. His feelings were revealed in a poem, part of which read

The streams and hills now shelter thieves and bandits;
The fields are now abandoned to brambles and thorns.
Our heritage is a burden of moral obligations,
But we lack a ruler who grieves at committing murder.[20]

Liu Yin's refusal to commit himself to public service has been seen as an example of 'Confucian eremitism', a withdrawal of Confucian scholars from worldly affairs as a protest against Mongol rule.

Another form of protest has been identified in drama. Drama as a form of popular entertainment had emerged in the Tang period, and plays and sketches were commonly performed under the Song, but it was not until the Yuan period that plays as a distinct literary form appeared. These plays, known collectively as the 'Yuan northern drama', were mainly written for performance in Dadu, but the theatre also became popular in the south. Their popularity may be linked to the development of a sophisticated urban culture. It has also been suggested that their appearance was connected with the exclusion of Chinese scholars from government employment and with the consequent diversion of their energies into other fields. Some left the world of public affairs to become 'Confucian eremites', others earned a living and found a spiritual outlet in the world of popular entertainment. Allegedly the plays they wrote contained protests against the Mongol presence and the popular response to their productions contributed to the collapse of the Yuan dynasty. This interpretation has not stood up well to critical evaluation. The Yuan northern drama evolved from earlier dramatic forms to which both Chinese scholars and professional writers contributed. The popularity of the theatre in the Yuan period owed a lot to Mongol patronage. Few plays contained overt political criticism and the fact that plays were written in the vernacular, and hence comprehensible to Mongols, made the claim of a subversive intent implausible.

THE FALL OF THE YUAN DYNASTY

Traditional Chinese explanations of the fall of the Yuan have tended to emphasize the persistent Chinese hatred of the invaders and the Mongols' failure to modify their rule to meet Chinese expectations. It was therefore only a matter of time until a combination of dynastic decline and righteous rebellion would bring about the collapse of the dynasty.

In the early Ming period and in more recent years a rather different interpretation has been proposed. This suggests that under Khubilai and his immediate successors the Mongols devised an effective, and to an extent acceptable, means of ruling China, and that Mongol rule might have persisted for much longer but for a sequence of disastrous events occurring in the 1350s and 1360s which undermined the dynasty.

For two reasons the long-term survival of the Yuan dynasty was doubtful. The first concerned the military superiority of the Mongols, which at the time of the conquest of the south had been a decisive factor, but which did not last the span of the dynasty. Whereas the Chinese military tradition was one of conscripted forces, the Mongols were accustomed to military status being hereditary. Soon after the conquest of the south they divided all the military forces in China into four: the Mongol army, the Mongol and associated nomadic forces used to garrison conquered areas, the Chinese and Qidan forces from north China, and the 'Newly adhered' Chinese forces from the south. The first three categories were provided with plots of land and slaves (often war captives), were given tax concessions and were expected to be self-sustaining. Each Chinese military household was required to provide one soldier, but in the Mongol households virtually all adult males performed military service. This system soon proved to be impracticable, for many of the slaves ran away and Mongol households could not subsist on their own by farming. As early as the 1290s there were reports of impoverishment and a decline in military standards. By the 1340s many Mongol military households were no better off than poor Chinese peasants and the garrison system, created to repress internal disturbances, had almost ceased to function.

The second reason concerned the extent to which the Mongols were prepared to become sinicized. Khubilai had presented himself as a Chinese emperor and none of his successors entirely rejected that role, though some of them were more willing to accept it than others. At first the Mongols had ruled China as a subordinate part of a Mongolian empire, but from 1307 that situation was reversed and the Mongolian steppe was being incorporated into China. From 1328 there began a process of thorough Confucianization of the government and increasing patronage of Chinese culture. Nevertheless, in some respects all the Mongol emperors refused to allow themselves to be absorbed into

Chinese culture. They treated their empire as a feudal patrimony and rewarded their relatives and retainers with hereditary privileges, a form of advancement incompatible with the Chinese bureaucratic system. As a consequence by the time of Toghon Temür, the last Yuan emperor, the Yuan state was 'a state whose roots in Chinese society, though deep, were still not deep enough'.[21]

The crisis which was to overwhelm the Yuan dynasty began in the 1340s with the outbreak of local rebellions, with the rise of piracy which threatened the shipment of grain to the capital by sea, and with the flooding of the Yellow river. In 1351 the emperor called upon Toghto, a young and able man who had previously served as chancellor, to return to office and deal with the situation. Toghto took steps to increase revenue, control the floods and suppress the rebels, at first with some success. He embarked on an ambitious project to reopen the Grand Canal which had silted up, drafting in thousands of peasants as labourers, but this in turn aroused a new and greater rebellion. In 1355 Toghto's opponents persuaded the emperor to dismiss him and this act has been seen as marking the end of the Yuan government as an integrated political system. The dynasty now controlled only the capital and the surrounding regions, while other parts of the country were held by independent commanders. As the rebellion grew and acquired a moral dimension, a civil war broke out among the Yuan supporters. In 1368 the court fled to Manchuria and the Yuan dynasty came to its end.

4

The Early Modern Period: The Ming and the Early Qing

In January 1368, nine months before the departure of the Mongol court from China, Zhu Yuanzhang ascended the throne. He adopted the reign name of Hongwu and called his dynasty Ming, meaning brightness. His reign was to last until 1398, by which time he had established what was to prove the most durable dynasty in Chinese history. He was succeeded by his grandson, but in 1403 the throne was usurped by Hongwu's fourth son, who is known as the Yongle emperor. The reigns of Hongwu and Yongle provide examples of effective rule in the early stages of the dynastic cycle. After Yongle's death the dynasty began a long decline, briefly interrupted by a period of reform in the second half of the sixteenth century, which culminated with its collapse in 1644 in the face of peasant rebellion and Manchu invasion.

The Manchu invaders adopted the dynastic title of the Qing and, building on the experience of previous dynasties of conquest, created a highly successful form of Sino-Manchu rule. Under a sequence of three able emperors, Kangxi (r. 1662–1722), Yongzheng (r. 1723–35) and Qianlong (r. 1736–95) the Chinese Empire reached its greatest extent and Chinese culture achieved its greatest sophistication. In the late Ming period, and increasingly under the Qing, foreign contacts proliferated. By the end of the eighteenth century the dynasty was showing some evidence of decline. The implications of relations with the Western world, and the consequences of population growth, had raised questions about the capacity of the imperial system to meet the challenge of changing circumstances.

THE ESTABLISHMENT OF THE MING DYNASTY

In the preceding chapter only brief reference was made to the rise of the rebellion which led to the expulsion of the Mongols. More should be said on the subject, because the character of the movement, and the temperament of its leader, was to determine the style of early Ming government.

Zhu Yuanzhang was born in 1328 near Fengyang in modern Anhui, an area soon to be affected by the change of course of the Yellow river, by the silting up of the Grand Canal and by the depredations of pirates. The area was also under the influence of the Maitreya cult of the White Lotus sect, which anticipated the coming of the future Buddha and the establishment of a 'pure land'. From about 1340 White Lotus sect adherents turned to collective violence and became known as the Red Turbans. Zhu Yuanzhang was caught up in this disorder. After the death of his parents in the famine of 1344, he became destitute. For a time he took refuge in a Buddhist temple, then he became a beggar and perhaps a soldier. In 1351 Toghto, the Yuan chancellor, conscripted thousands of men to work on re-routing the Yellow river and dredging the Grand Canal. His coercive measures provoked the outbreak of the Red Turban rebellion, which within a year had swept through the Yangzi valley and had confined the government forces to Nanjing and the other major cities of the region. In 1352 Zhu Yuanzhang joined a Red Turban band led by Guo Zixing, which was active near Fengyang. Within a year he had recruited 24 men from his native area and had married Guo Zixing's adopted daughter. Over the next two years the forces commanded by Toghto suppressed much of the rebel activity, but in January 1355 he was dismissed and the rebel movements revived. Han Liner, the leader of the northern Red Turbans, who claimed descent from the Song, declared himself emperor. By the end of the decade the Yuan dynasty had entirely lost control of the Yangzi valley, which was being contested by several regional leaders.

From this struggle Zhu Yuanzhang was to emerge the victor.

His success may be explained in part by his military ability and his skill in making tactical alliances. As his influence grew he gained a reputation for willingness to take advice from Confucian scholars and for benevolence towards the common people. By 1355 he had established a base camp and had built up a personal army. In the following year he captured Nanjing, and began the transformation 'from leader of a populist sectarian revolt to leader of a political movement aspiring to traditional legitimacy'.[1] Each time that his forces captured a town he appointed a new civil administration staffed by scholar-officials, some of whom had previously served the Yuan. He engaged officials to supervise the repair of river defences and to promote the revival of agriculture. He gradually severed his links with the Red Turban ideology and with the northern Red Turban dynasty, which came to an end in 1367 when Han Liner was drowned. In these and other ways he demonstrated his eagerness to acquire the qualities associated with a Chinese emperor. In January 1368, having defeated his main rivals and feeling confident that the Mongol court could offer no significant resistance, he declared the founding of the Ming dynasty and assumed the reign title of Hongwu.

Hongwu's first task was to gain control of the rest of China. A military expedition was sent north where it forced the flight of the Mongol court and captured Dadu, which was renamed Beiping, meaning 'the north is pacified'. The most serious threat was posed by Kökö Temür, who in the 1360s had established himself as an independent military leader in the region around Taiyuan. In 1372 a large force pursued Kökö Temür into Mongolia and inflicted a heavy defeat on him, but he later recovered and only after his death in 1375 did the Mongol threat decline. In the meantime an expedition had been sent to recover Sichuan, which had been seized by the southern branch of the Red Turbans. In 1377 the Korean state of Koryo was persuaded to abandon its loyalty to the Yuan rulers and to recognize the Ming, and in 1379 Tibet, which had also failed to acknowledge the legitimacy of Ming rule, was brought into obedience by force.

Although Hongwu claimed to be restoring the practices of the Tang and Song periods, from necessity in the early years of his reign he continued nearly all the features of government employed by, and in some cases introduced by, the Mongols. He retained much of their military structure, in that the army continued to be treated as an occupational caste commanded by an hereditary officer class. The Ming armed forces derived from Hongwu's early followers and the bands which had surrendered to him in the course of his conquest. The latter had been promised that their units would be kept intact and that their leaders' commands would be made hereditary. From 1364 these forces were organized according to the *weiso* system, that is into guards, numbering 5000 men, and battalions numbering 1000 men. This force could not be demobilized without a risk of serious disorder, but it was too costly to maintain as a charge to the state, so Hongwu continued the Yuan practice of making the armies self-sufficient through the extension of the military colony system. The commanders of these forces, in particular those who were the survivors of Hongwu's original band of 24 men, or of those who had joined him early in his campaign, were rewarded with noble titles and ranked higher than military and civil officials.

The same principles were applied to the early Ming system of government. The Yuan central government had consisted of a Secretariat–Chancellery headed by two chancellors, who conducted all routine administrative business, a powerful and independent Bureau of Military Affairs, and a Censorate, which was more concerned with the surveillance of the operation of government than with receiving remonstrations from officials. At the intermediate level a variety of administrative bodies had been created, the most important being the branch secretariats, which administered areas which were the forerunners of the modern provinces of China. This structure had been adopted by Hongwu during his rise to power and it was retained, with some amendment to the titles of offices, through the first decade of his reign. The most significant, albeit symbolic, change was the reversal of the precedence the Mongols gave to the official designated as 'of the right', in favour of the Chinese custom of giving precedence to the left. These arrangements led Edward L. Dreyer to remark 'As originally conceived, the Ming empire was thus Mongol in form and structure; it was Chinese only in rhetoric and personnel.'[2]

The moderation and caution which had marked the early years

of Hongwu's reign came to an abrupt end in 1380 when Hu Weiyong, the chancellor of the left, was accused of conspiracy and executed. The charges levelled against him included having dealings with the Mongols, but his real fault was to have challenged the authority of the emperor by building up a power base in the civil bureaucracy. Hu Weiyong's death was followed by a ferocious purge which was said to have cost the lives of 30,000 of his supporters. It also led to important changes in government. The office of chancellor was abolished and the emperor demanded that it should never be restored by his successors, the Secretariat-Chancellery was dismantled and the authority of the military commission was fragmented. Hongwu in effect became his own chief minister.

During the remaining years of his reign Hongwu ruled as a conscientious autocrat. He followed a punishing schedule of audiences and concerned himself with many details of government, for example the promulgation of a Ming legal code, which was eventually completed in 1397. He took a particular interest in education and ordered the establishment of schools in every prefecture, subprefecture and district, with staff and students supported with public funds. This has been described as the beginning of an empire-wide, state-supported educational system. In 1382 Hongwu revived the examinations, which now became the main avenue for entry into the civil service. In 1397, when he discovered that not a single northerner had passed the *jinshi* examination, he amended the pass lists and so initiated a quota system which reserved a proportion of examination passes to certain groups. *Jinshi*, or 'presented scholars', so described because the successful candidates were presented to the emperor, numbered 871 for the entire Hongwu reign, still only a small proportion of the civil bureaucracy which comprised about 15,000 officials. However, many *jinshi* attained positions of influence and provided an important counterbalance to those who owed their appointment to heredity.

Throughout his reign Hongwu claimed to be concerned with the welfare of his people. He promoted resettlement schemes and gave some encouragement to textile production and trade. His most enduring legacy derived from his policies relating to taxation. As the first emperor of a dynasty, unencumbered by heavy financial commitments, he was in a strong position to reform the tax system. He took steps to equalize the land-tax burden, while maintaining a punitive level of taxation on ten prefectures south of the Yangzi where opposition to his rise had been strongest. His ambition was to apply a new level of detailed control over the entire land and tax system. In 1370 he ordered that each household in the country should be issued with a registration certificate which recorded details of the family, including its status and occupation, with the implication that these could not be changed. In 1381 these records were consolidated in the 'Yellow Books' or registers. Hongwu is also credited with having commissioned a monumental cadastral survey, the returns being edited into land registers called 'fish-scale books' because the topographical charts they contained resembled fishes' scales. In fact this project was neither new nor applied nationally. The emperor's priority in tax matters was control and this was demonstrated by two other measures. Rural communities were organized into the *lijia* system, under which groups of 110 households were grouped as *li* and made responsible for the payment of taxes and the discharging of labour services. Overlapping this arrangement was the tax-captain system, under which wealthy families were made responsible for the collection of grain taxes in their area.

Although Hongwu laboured hard to create an efficient centralized tax structure, his projects have been heavily criticized, firstly on the grounds that they were too ambitious for the technological means of the Ming state. The tax reforms were based on a serious misunderstanding: the country was not over-taxed but under-taxed and as a consequence state revenues were not sufficient to provide effective public services. Finally the tax system made little reference to progressive taxation or the encouragement of enterprise, and it had become so complex that it defied effective reform.

Hongwu died in 1398 and was buried on the slopes of Zijinshan on the outskirts of Nanjing, where his body still lies. His reputation has oscillated between praise for having expelled the Mongols and having founded the Ming dynasty, and condemnation for having been a tyrant whose policies established an enduring trend towards despotism. The Marxist historian Wu Han, who became notorious at the time of the Cultural Revolution, depicted Hongwu as a man of the people who betrayed the popular cause and sided with the landlord-gentry class to obtain power. Wu Han's critics have argued that Hongwu was motivated solely by his own ambition and was never a sincere supporter of the poor. F. W. Mote traced Hongwu's abolition of the post of chancellor to a trend towards despotism already evident under the Song, but suggested that his harshness and unreasonableness had its precedent only in the brutal world of the Yuan.[3] Other historians have described traits of Hongwu's personality, noting his ugliness, his suspicion of rivals, and his extreme sensitivity to supposed insults, which caused him to execute almost all his longest-standing supporters and thousands of others. The one redeeming feature of his personality was his attachment to the Empress Ma, who until her death in 1382 may have exercised a moderating influence on her husband.

THE REIGNS OF JIANWEN, 1399–1402, AND YONGLE, 1403–24

Hongwu was succeed briefly by his grandson, who reigned as the Jianwen emperor until he was deposed by his uncle, Hongwu's fourth son, the Prince of Yan, who was to be known as the Yongle emperor. It is difficult to form any precise idea of Jianwen's abilities as it was in the interests of his uncle's supporters to denounce him as ineffectual and depraved. He certainly was better educated than his grandfather and he accepted the advice of his Confucian tutors to rescind some of the despotic measures of Hongwu's reign. He also attempted to reduce the autonomy of the hereditary princedoms founded to accommodate Hongwu's sons. This prompted the rebellion of the Prince of Yan, the commander of the northern frontier army, which concluded with the reported death of Jianwen in a fire in the imperial palace.

Yongle was vulnerable to the charge of being an usurper, and so he moved quickly to consolidate his position by restoring features of government as practised under Hongwu. He did make some changes, the most important of which was the creation of a new grand secretariat to replace the Secretariat–Chancellery which is father had abolished in 1380. To it he appointed seven senior officials, four of whom were holders of the *jinshi* degree.

They enjoyed security of tenure throughout the reign and this allowed the creation of an efficient bureaucracy.

Yongle also took the momentous decision to transfer the capital from Nanjing to Beijing. The main reason for the move was to permit closer control over the military forces in the north. It was by no means certain that the Ming would adopt the Yuan choice of Beijing. To secure the food supply to Beijing required the restoration and extension of the Grand Canal, a major task which was completed in 1415. The construction of the new capital began in 1406 and involved the securing of very large quantities of timber and bricks and the deployment of many thousands of labourers and artisans. The walls and the major palace buildings had been completed by 1417 and thereafter Yongle was resident there unless absent on campaigns.

Yongle's reign was notable also for his pursuit of an ambitious foreign policy, which in some respects echoed the aspirations of Khubilai's reign. Before he became emperor he had commanded troops on the northern frontier and so it was not surprising that his first concern was for the security of that region. At the beginning of his reign the most significant threat came from the Mongol ruler known in the West as Tamerlane. Having conquered a vast Central Asian empire, in 1404 Tamerlane set out to invade China, but died en route in the following year. On China's north-eastern frontier the Urianghad and Jurchen tribes were disunited and Yongle persuaded them to accept Chinese overlordship. Further to the west, in what is now Mongolia, the Tatar and Oirat still presented a danger. Between 1410 and 1424 Yongle led five expeditions against them, on the last of which he died. Although these expeditions were recorded in Chinese annals as successful, they were extremely expensive and failed to eliminate the Mongol threat. These facts indicate that even during Yongle's reign 'sclerosis had begun developing in the Ming military establishment'.[4]

In the south, Yongle's forces eliminated surviving pockets of Yuan and tribal resistance and then moved against Annam, which since the Tang period had been an independent state sending tribute to China. In 1406 the Annamese throne was usurped and this provided the pretext for sending a Chinese army, which conquered the territory and organized it as a province. However, the Chinese administration was corrupt and the military forces were too small to enforce control. Within a decade a powerful patriotic resistance movement had emerged which shortly after Yongle's death forced a Chinese withdrawal.

The most spectacular aspect of Yongle's foreign ventures was the dispatch, between 1405 and 1421, of six maritime expeditions. Yongle's motive for launching these expensive voyages is unclear. One theory was that they were sent in search of the Jianwen emperor, who, according to rumour, had not died in the fire at Nanjing but had escaped overseas disguised as a monk. More probably the ships went in search of treasure and to aggrandize Yongle – who was an usurper – by adding to the number of foreign rulers who recognized him as emperor. The first expedition, commanded by the grand eunuch Zheng He and comprising 317 ships and 27,870 men, put in at several Indian ports. On subsequent voyages Zheng He reached Hormuz on the Gulf of Oman, and ships from his expeditions put in at Jidda and explored the African coast as far south as Malindi. After Yongle's death the voyages ended, perhaps because their political purpose no longer applied, perhaps because they did not turn in a profit. As a consequence China's lead in oceanographic knowledge and commercial enterprise was soon overhauled by the Portuguese.

THE MIDDLE YEARS OF THE MING DYNASTY – POLITICAL ASPECTS

The death of Yongle in 1424 brought to an end the expansionist stage of the Ming dynasty, and for much of the rest of the period Ming emperors pursued defensive policies. An explanation for this change can be found in an incident which occurred in the reign of the Zhengtong emperor, who came to the throne as a minor in 1436. In the 1440s the Oirat tribes were united by a leader named Esen, who then began to encroach on Chinese territory. In 1448 a very large Oirat tribute mission to the Chinese court was treated contemptuously by Wang Zhen, the chief eunuch. In the following year Esen responded by invading and defeating a Chinese force near Datong, to the west of Beijing. The 22-year-old emperor, with the encouragement of Wang Zhen but against the advice of his officials, decided to lead a counterattack. His forces, said to number half a million men, were ambushed at Tumu, 70 miles north-west of Beijing. The emperor was captured and Wang Zhen was killed.

The disastrous Tumu incident had a variety of consequences. Some officials, anticipating that Esen would now press home his advantage, suggested that the court should abandon the capital. This idea was opposed by Yu Qian, the vice-minister of war, whose resolution led to his being enshrined in Chinese folklore as a symbol of patriotic resistance. The hereditary military elite, which had been established by Hongwu and revived by Yongle, was blamed for the defeat and Yu Qian's rise to power represented a long-lasting victory of the civil bureaucracy over the military.

To reduce the leverage the Oirat exerted over the Chinese court by holding the emperor hostage, it was decided to enthrone his half-brother in his place, and the latter took the era-name of Jingtai. The deposed Zhengtong was referred to as the 'retired emperor' and after his release was excluded from power. Inevitably he became the focus of opposition to Jingtai and after he had been restored by a coup in 1457 the subsequent settling of scores, which included the judicial murder of Yu Qian, left a legacy of factionalism at court. Finally the Tumu incident forced the dynasty to review its strategy towards the Mongols. Recognizing that it did not have the resources to control the steppe transition zone, that is the intermediate zone between the steppe and the settled areas, where the threats to China from nomadic peoples usually originated, the dynasty now opted for a defensive strategy. The Mongol threat was most apparent in the Ordos region and it was there that in 1474 the construction of the Great Wall, as it is known today, began.

*　*　*

The political character of the Ming period is often referred to as 'Ming absolutism', a reference to the unchecked growth of imperial power from the late fourteenth century. This tendency was already apparent under the Song and it advanced further under the Mongols. Under Hongwu it assumed its highest form. His decision in 1380 to abolish the post of chancellor or chief minister had placed him in direct control of central government. The branch secretariats, which administered the proto-provinces, comprised a civil administration, a military commission and a surveillance office, three separate agencies. As each agency was under the supervision of the central government, the branch secretariat itself enjoyed no element of autonomy. China was a country which had large cities and numerous towns, but its citizens had failed to secure the privileges which had been obtained by civic communities in the West. Hongwu had overseen the production of a revised Ming legal code, but although this was enforced by a sophisticated judicial system, there was no means whereby the exercise of imperial power could be challenged in the courts.

This absolutist framework was supported by systems of surveillance and by harsh punishments. Hongwu believed that the laxity of the Yuan administration had contributed to the dynasty's fall and he consequently took a very severe line on official corruption. For example, an official found guilty of receiving a bribe of over 60 taels[5] of silver was decapitated, his head was spiked on a pole, and his corpse was skinned and stuffed with straw. Hongwu maintained an elaborate surveillance operation through the use of spies, secret agents and the Embroidered Guards, who carried out the major purges of his reign. These autocratic but effective policies were continued under Yongle, but were neglected by the later Ming emperors.

The agency which existed to control abuses of power was the censorate. The censorate as a separate branch of government, entrusted with the task of surveilling the work of officials through the empire, had emerged under the Han. In addition to censors, 'speaking officials' were appointed to perform the task of remonstrance, that is offering advice and warning to the emperor. Under the Yuan the censorial system was expanded and censors acquired the power to punish junior officials for wrongdoing, and also took over the duty of remonstrance. During the Ming period the censorate continued to play an active role in government. Overmighty officials, and the eunuch dictators of the latter part of the reign, were frequently impeached. Censorial officials submitted numerous memorials to the emperor offering advice on various matters, and on a few occasions criticized decisions taken by the emperor himself. However, the censors' role was marginal, they were neither agents of popular or bureaucratic resistance to imperial domination, nor agents of imperial oppression. Under strong emperors they were effective defenders of tradition, but under weak rulers, when corruption and inefficiency proliferated, they did not challenge absolutism though their frequent criticisms could immobilize the actions of government.

Another aspect of Ming government associated with absolutism was the assumption of a political role by court eunuchs. As no uncastrated male, apart from the emperor himself, was permitted to enter the imperial harem, eunuchs had exceptional access to the emperor and could exert considerable influence on him. The eunuchs' role was of particular importance if the emperor was enthroned when still a minor, as were eight of the eleven emperors who succeeded to the throne between 1435 and 1644. In 1384 Hongwu had ordered the erection of an iron tablet bearing the inscription 'Eunuchs are forbidden to interfere with government affairs. Those who attempt to do so will be subjected to capital punishment.' Notwithstanding this injunction, he sent eunuchs as his personal envoys to tributary states and to the provinces as tax-auditors. Yongle went further, entrusting eunuchs such as Zheng He with the command of major ventures. He also removed the eunuchs from bureaucratic control and appointed them to head the Eastern Depot, the headquarters of the secret police. The Xuande emperor (r. 1426–35) rescinded the ban on eunuchs being educated and established a palace eunuch school. Thereafter eunuchs gained a key position as the emperor's personal secretaries, controlling the flow of information and so bypassing the secretariat.

Emperors trusted eunuchs because they were entirely dependent on imperial favour, and in return eunuchs exploited their privileged position at the expense of the bureaucracy. The consequence was the emergence of eunuch dictators, the first being Wang Zhen whose role in the Tumu incident has already been mentioned. The next notorious example of eunuch misuse of power was the case of Liu Jin, the chief of imperial staff for the Zhengde emperor, who had come to the throne as a minor in 1506. Liu Jin was flagrantly corrupt and oppressive, and his excesses led to his enemies accusing him of plotting to kill the emperor, for which crime he was executed. The last and most infamous of the eunuch dictators was Wei Zhongxian, who achieved a total ascendancy over the Tianqi emperor (r. 1621–7), who showered him and his relatives with gifts and titles. All the eunuch dictators subverted the controls over the abuse of power by gaining the emperor's confidence and by using spies and secret police to instigate a reign of terror.

ECONOMIC AND SOCIAL ASPECTS OF THE EARLY MING

Hongwu's policy of requiring the compilation of the Yellow Books and the 'fish-scale' registers ensured that a large amount of data relating to population and the acreage of land under cultivation was amassed during the Ming period. However, much of this information was palpably inaccurate – for example in 1582 one county reported that it had 3700 households with residents over 100 years old. As a consequence only the roughest estimates can be made of the correct land and population figures. It is estimated that during the Ming period the population rose from about 65 million to about 150 million persons and that the acreage of land under cultivation increased from less than 400 million *mou* to approximately 500 million *mou*.[6] The increase in cultivated land was partly due to internal migration, most notably to Yunnan and Guizhou. There were no major advances in agricultural technology, but the slow diffusion of improved planting materials, including early-ripening rice introduced from Vietnam in the eleventh century and plants originating in the New World, the most important of which were maize, sweet potato and peanuts, which reached China in the late Ming period, enabled the food supply to match population growth. This growth might have been greater but for constraints. The decades of the 1430s and 1440s were marked by a devastating succession of droughts, floods, pestilences and epidemics, which caused severe loss of life. It is also apparent that female infanticide was widely practised, for example it was said that 'Jiangxi people are fond of drowning girls.'[7]

The great majority of the population lived in the countryside and depended on agriculture for a living. However, in the Ming period, particularly in the sixteenth century, cities and towns grew and some industries flourished. Jingdezhen, the porcelain centre in Jiangxi, claimed to have a population in excess of one million. The local magistrate complained that the fires of its kilns were so bright and the sound of its pestles so noisy, that he could not sleep. Hangzhou, the great centre of silk production, was a city of similar size. In Songjiang prefecture in the Yangzi delta numerous towns specialized in the production of cotton textiles. From the fifteenth century a division of labour had been established, with cotton spinning remaining a cottage industry, but weaving being transferred to the urban environment. Alvara Semedo, a Jesuit missionary, estimated that in 1621 200,000 looms were being operated in and around Shanghai. It was said that 'Songjiang cotton cloth clothes the empire.' Goods produced by these industrial centres were distributed widely. The city of Linqing on the Grand Canal was a major distribution centre for north China. At the beginning of the seventeenth century it claimed to handle more than 1.6 million shiploads of freight every year.

This growth of industry and of urbanization brought with it attendant social problems, but it did not precipitate an industrial revolution. Explanations why this did not occur recall the debate concerning economic development under the Song. In the case of the cotton industry it has been suggested that a combination of factors: a sufficient but not an abundant supply of raw cotton, gradual technological improvements, an excellent commercial network and the availability of cheap labour, prevented the development of bottle-necks which might have forced a switch to factory production.

The Ming government rarely attempted to intervene in the operation of this economy. However, its policies relating to currency and taxation are of some relevance in this context. Under the Yuan, paper currency had circulated widely and in the late Yuan period the reckless issue of paper notes had led to inflation and a silver shortage. Whereas the Mongols had understood that a paper currency should be convertible and should therefore be backed by silver reserves, Hongwu was oblivious to this need and issued large quantities of non-convertible paper currency. By 1425 paper notes were worth only one-fortieth of their face value and by the end of the fifteenth century paper currency had ceased to have any commercial value. The consequence was that the monetary system was restricted to a copper coinage and unminted silver.

The main sources of Ming government revenue were the land tax, which included labour services, and the salt monopoly. Hongwu's tax reforms, and in particular his establishment of a tax-quota system, had ensured that revenue would prove inadequate for future state needs, and from 1528 onwards the Ming government treasury was in deficit. In an attempt to increase revenue a wide variety of supplementary taxes were levied, with the result that the land taxes of the late Ming period have been called 'as complex as personal income tax in the twentieth-century United States'.[8] It was this situation which prompted the most ambitious reform attempted by any Ming government, the series of measures intended to simplify the tax system and improve its collection which was dubbed the Single-Whip reform, a pun on its correct title, the 'reformed single entry system'. Starting in 1531, on the initiative of two surveillance commissioners whose task was to rectify abuses in the tax system, measures were introduced to consolidate the land tax and labour-service requirement into a single payment, to be paid in silver, not in kind. Between 1570 and 1590 these arrangements were extended to all parts of the empire. These reforms have been cited as an important step towards the development of a monetary economy and 'the beginning of the modern land tax system'.[9] They may have been significant in shifting the incidence of taxation from the household to the land-holder, and thus have taken some cognizance of the fact that rural society had moved beyond a subsistence economy, and that the modest landlord class of the early Ming had given way to the larger estates and the commercial landlordism of the later Ming. However, the reforms were never carried through in their entirety, the payment of tax in kind continued, labour services were still required in some areas, and the land tax became more rather than less complicated.

*　　*　　*

It was during the Ming period that the status group commonly referred to as the gentry emerged fully. The term is used to translate the Chinese expression *shenshi*, which literally means 'officials and scholars'. Its use implies that entry into the group was achieved by success in the examination system or by the purchase of rank, and that the group existed to provide a reservoir of talent to support a bureaucratic system of government. However, this group owed its emergence as much to the economic and social changes of the Ming period as it did to the formal process of examination. The commercialization of the economy and the attendant rise in land prices had encouraged the formation of a stratum of wealthy upper gentry who controlled land and credit, who may be identified with the tax captains of the early Ming period. It had also brought into being a larger group of families prosperous enough to educate their sons for the examinations and to participate in the activities of gentry society. Viewed from this perspective the gentry were not an adjunct of the bureaucracy, but rural elites 'with a wide and flexible repertoire of strategies at their disposal, in which landowning, education, and degree-holding were usual but not necessarily indispensable elements'.[10]

This picture has been fleshed out in a number of recent studies. Hilary J. Beattie investigated Tongcheng county in Anhui and found that the families which produced degree-holders depended less on obtaining office – always a high-risk strategy – and more on the careful acquisition of land and the systematic use of marriage with other powerful lineages.[11] Timothy Brook has shown how gentry society maintained its position not only through economic and political means, but also through its cultural domination, expressed in literary and artistic pursuits. Recently John W. Dardess, in a study of Taihe county, Jiangxi, has suggested that although gentry society had deep local roots, even in the early Ming period the 'great talents' of the county had no intention of staying at home but were anxious to play their part on the national stage. For him gentry society would not have existed if its values had not been confirmed by the national context into which it was embedded.

These studies invite a reconsideration of the amount of social mobility which existed in China at this time. The classic study by Ho Ping-ti assumed that social mobility was obtained through the operation of the examination system, which ideally provided equal opportunity for all but the 'mean people', who included slaves, the children of prostitutes, and all boat people. He categorized the 14,562 men who had obtained the *jinshi*, the highest degree, between 1371 and 1904, according to whether their families had produced degree-holders in the three preceding genera-

tions. He found that in the early Ming period 57.6 per cent of
jinshi came from families which had not previously produced a
holder of a higher degree, that the proportion remained as high
as 49.5 per cent for the entire Ming period, but fell to 37.6 per
cent under the Qing. He concluded that this was evidence of an
unparalleled instance of upward social mobility in a major society prior to the industrial revolution.[12] Hilary Beattie's study,
however, suggested that the important lineages of Tongcheng
were well-established by the middle of the Ming period and
there was little subsequent movement up or down. John W.
Dardess showed that in the early Ming the number of elite families in Taihe county was increasing in response to the availability
of land and the high rate of bureaucratic recruitment, but by the
mid-fifteenth century the opportunity for rapid expansion had
gone. Now the excess children of elite families were 'purged',
that is they either migrated to other regions, or they lost their
elite status and became artisans, or in the case of daughters, concubines and maids.

THE LATE MING PERIOD

After the Tumu incident of 1449, for a century the Ming dynasty
pursued defensive and generally conciliatory policies towards
the steppe tribes. The Jiajing emperor (r. 1522–66) had to deal
with the rise of a new Mongol confederation under Altan Khan,
who raided Chinese territory to obtain supplies for his campaigns against the Oirat to the west. In 1550 Mongol forces
besieged Beijing and looted the outer suburbs. Despite efforts to
buy off the Mongols and to strengthen the defensive walls, these
raids continued until 1571 when Altan accepted a peace treaty.
Nevertheless, China's military weakness had been exposed and
her northern borders continued to be threatened by the Mongols
until the end of the sixteenth century, when a new threat from the
Jurchen, or Manchus, appeared.

The same defensive stance characterized Ming maritime affairs. Foreign relations were governed by the tribute system and
took the form of embassies and the exchange of gifts. Private
trade and unofficial contacts were discouraged. However, from
early in the sixteenth century this attitude came under challenge.

In 1514 the first Portuguese reached China and in 1517 Tomé Pires, who had been appointed Portuguese ambassador, arrived at Guangzhou and was eventually permitted to travel to Beijing, although he was not received in audience. In the 1550s the Portuguese were allowed to establish a trading station at Aomen (Macao), but were ordered to remain apart from the Chinese population. In the meantime Japanese traders and pirates had appeared in numbers along the south-east coast of China and had breached the restrictions on foreign trade. Large-scale attacks by *wokou*, or Japanese pirates, exposed the inadequacy of the coastal defences. In the 1550s raiding parties established bases on the coast of Zhejiang, threatening the whole region. In 1554 Songjiang, the centre of the cotton industry, was attacked and its magistrate put to death. Official measures and regular forces having proved ineffective, Qi Jiguang, an unconventional Chinese commander, drilled a volunteer force, used firearms as well as traditional weapons and denied the raiders any respite. It was only when the ban on Chinese participation in foreign trade was rescinded in 1567 that peace was restored. Ten years later Alessandro Valignano arrived in Macao and obtained permission for the Jesuits to establish a mission on Chinese soil. In 1598 his successor, Matteo Ricci, reached Beijing.

This failure to sustain frontier policies was an indication of the weakness of the Ming dynasty, rather than the cause of its fall. That has been explained in a variety of ways, beginning with the process of the dynastic cycle, with its emphasis on the inadequacy of emperors and the machinations of ministers and eunuchs. The Jiajing emperor (r. 1522–66) withdrew from the active supervision of the government for long periods of time. He became obsessed with Daoism and the search for the elixirs of immortality, and this eventually led to his death by poisoning. From 1549 to 1562 the most powerful official was Yan Song, whose long survival was based on obsequiousness towards the emperor and avoidance of the pressing issues of the day. The Wanli emperor's reign (1573–1620) began more promisingly, for he had the support of Zhang Juzheng, a man committed, albeit vainly and controversially, to raising government efficiency and improving the financial administration, but after his death in 1582 government fell into the hands of the eunuchs. The reign of the incompetent Tianqi emperor (1621–7) saw the rise of the eunuch dictator Wei Zhongxian, and that of Chongzhen emperor (r. 1628–45), who was active and well-intentioned, was marred by the service of untrustworthy officials.

Modern historians have looked beyond and below court politics to explain the Ming decline. One line of investigation concerns the response of the elite to the social and economic changes of the late Ming period. Timothy Brook described how Hongwu's ideal, of a society in which owner-cultivators worked within a subsistence economy, was subverted by the growth of a wealthy land-based gentry in the early sixteenth century. The gentry in turn found that the competition for examination success had increased and the risks associated with a bureaucratic career had multiplied. This brought about a change in their orientation, away from a 'state-centered vision of gentry life', with its emphasis on engagement with worldly affairs, in favour of embracing Buddhism, which implied withdrawal from public life. Buddhism provided the gentry with an alternative set of beliefs and a field of action not defined by the state, exemplified by their patronage of Buddhist monasteries.[13]

The relationship between the state and the gentry was also damaged by a Confucian revival which later engendered violent factional disputes at court. In the late sixteenth century a number of private academies were established, where scholars and ex-officials bemoaned the decline of Confucian standards and the political immorality of the court. In 1577 Zhang Juzheng, Wanli's grand secretary, was criticized by the Confucianists for failing to observe the period of mourning after his father's death. In the same year he ordered a personnel evaluation which resulted in the discharge of a number of officials, an exercise which was to be repeated by his successors. Discharged officials joined academies, the most notable example being the Donglin academy, founded in 1604, which was based near Wuxi in the Yangzi delta. Its location offers some support to the suggestions that the Donglin movement had a regional basis, or that it represented the interests of a land-owning class resentful of Ming absolutism. Donglin sympathizers were kept out of government until Wanli's death in 1620. In the early years of Tianqi's reign officials known to have Donglin connections briefly dominated the court, but they were forced to retire when the eunuch dictator Wei Zhongxian gained power. Until the dynasty fell, factionalism deriving from the Donglin movement weakened the government. Officials and scholars were alienated and thus susceptible to changing their allegiance when the dynasty collapsed.

The decline and fall of the Ming dynasty has been linked to climatic change and to the effects of the worldwide depression which began in the 1620s. In the late Ming period, and in particular between 1626 and 1640, China experienced unusually severe weather marked by low temperatures, drought and then floods. The population, which for two centuries had been growing steadily, stagnated or went into decline. By the early seventeenth century the economy was being supported by a vast inflow of silver to pay for Chinese exports. However, a European trade depression in the 1620s, and the interruption of trade with the Philippines and Japan in the 1640s, reduced the inflow of silver, damaged the silk industry and drove up the price of grain.

The collapse of the dynasty was precipitated by peasant rebellions. James W. Tong has shown that the incidence of rebellions and banditry was far higher in the second half of the Ming dynastic period than in the first. These incidents were not a response to social change, because they were more common in the less commercialized parts of the country. Nor were they a response to the grosser examples of misgovernment, because the rise in incidents of violence was gradual and incremental. Tong concluded that the main reason for the increase was the decline of the coercive capacity of the state. This encouraged peasants, in times of hardship, to suppose that their best chance of survival was to become outlaws.[14]

Tong's conclusion was supported by the record of the rebellions, which began in 1628 in northern Shaanxi and eventually caused the downfall of the dynasty. Shaanxi was an impoverished area which had shared none of the prosperity enjoyed by the Yangzi provinces and which may have been more severely affected by the deteriorating climate than the south of the country. The security of the area, in so far as it depended on military garrisons, had broken down. The situation was exacerbated by administrative shortcomings: many official posts were vacant and the officials present failed to organize relief to combat a disastrous famine. The result was a rebellion that might have been defeated if the pacification programme which had been implemented had not been interrupted, in 1629, by the first major

Manchu raid into China. After the Manchu withdrawal government troops crushed the most obvious manifestations of rebellion, but the survivors became mobile raiders and the centre of
rebel activity moved south to the area between the Yellow and
Yangzi rivers.

In the late 1630s, when the rebellions again seemed on the
verge of extinction, further Manchu raids diverted attention to
the north. The leaders of the two main rebellions, Li Zicheng in
Henan and Zhang Xianzhong in Sichuan, began to display political ambitions. Li Zicheng, who was puritanical in his lifestyle,
managed to attract members of the gentry to his side, and after
he had captured Xiangyang in 1643 he established an
administrative structure and announced tax reductions. The following year he declared the foundation of a new dynasty and
marched on Beijing. Even at this point it should have been possible for the Ming to offer effective resistance, but it had lost control of large areas of the country, its military forces had collapsed, it was bankrupt and the will to resist had almost disappeared. On 24 April 1644 the rebels entered Beijing and that
same night the emperor hanged himself.

THE MANCHU INVASION

The Manchus were descendants of the Jurchen tribes who had
founded the Jin dynasty in 1122. By the sixteenth century the
Jianzhou Jurchen, who in 1635 were to adopt the name Manchu,
were living in the vicinity of the Changbai mountains in the east
of present-day Jilin. There they hunted, practised agriculture and
traded extensively with the Chinese. By the late Ming period the
area occupied by the Changbai Jurchen was designated a 'commandery', implying that it had been incorporated into the frontier defence system, although in truth Chinese control of the area
was superficial and depended largely on the exploitation of
vendettas between the Jurchen tribes.

The transformation of the Changbai Jurchen territory into the
Manchu state was largely the work of Nurhaci (1559–1626). He
unified the Jurchen tribes of his region through a mixture of
aggression and marriage alliances and then cultivated relations
with the Chinese. In 1589 he was granted a title by the Wanli

emperor and in the following year he headed a tribute mission to Beijing. Through the 1590s he traded profitably in ginseng and horses, and took advantage of the disruption caused by Hideyoshi's attempted invasion of China. In 1599 he began to organize the entire Jurchen population into banners. Groups of 300 households were designated a company and 50 companies formed a 'banner' – the name referring to the patterned flag borne by each group. Initially there were four banners, later the number was increased to eight Manchu banners and in addition there were eight Mongol and eight Chinese banners. In peacetime the banners served as administrative units and in times of war they formed the destructive cavalry forces of the Manchus.

By 1603 Nurhaci's rapid rise to power had alarmed the Chinese, and a boundary was defined between his lands and those of Chinese settlement. In the years that followed, Nurhaci, by employing Chinese officials and by adopting bureaucratic methods of government, transformed his confederation of Jurchen tribes into a Manchu state. At the same time he obtained the allegiance of the Jurchen tribes who had yet to place themselves under Chinese protection. In 1616 he announced the foundation of the Latter Jin dynasty and two years later, having justified his actions in a document entitled the 'Seven Great Vexations', he seized the important trading post and garrison town of Fushun, near present-day Shenyang. Nurhaci awarded the Chinese commander of the town a high military rank and married him to his granddaughter. A large Chinese force was dispatched to recover the town, but it was routed. By the end of 1621 Nurhaci had gained control of the whole of Liaodong and was appealing to Chinese officials and settlers to come over to his side.

The Manchu advance then stalled for eight years. After the occupation of Liaodong the Manchus were ruling perhaps one million Chinese. Some important Chinese families switched to the Manchu side, but many Chinese were treated as slaves or were forced to accept Manchu bannermen into their households. In 1623 a Chinese attempt to poison the Manchus' food and water supplies was punished harshly. Two years later the Chinese revolted and Nurhaci concluded that he could not rely on the Chinese population as a whole to support him. At about the same time the Ming strengthened their defences by deploying cannon supplied by the Portuguese to defend their garrisons beyond the Great Wall. As the Manchus did not yet possess firearms this presented a major obstacle to their advance. When Nurhaci died in 1626 the Chinese used the opportunity to negotiate peace terms.

The new ruler Abahai managed to placate the Liaodong Chinese, and the Manchu advance resumed. In 1629, in a spectacular raid, Abahai crossed the Great Wall, captured four Chinese cities and reached the walls of Beijing. It was this raid which disrupted the pacification campaign directed against the peasant rebellions in Shaanxi. In 1634–5 Abahai subdued the Chahar Mongols, which allowed him to claim the succession to Genghis Khan and the Yuan dynasty. In 1638 he personally led a force which defeated the Korean Yi dynasty and forced it to send tribute to the Manchus. However, Abahai realized that the Chinese could not be subjugated by military force alone, and from 1631 he began to adopt features of Chinese government, including the Six Boards and the Censorate, alongside Manchu institutions. He introduced an examination system and made increasing use of Chinese collaborators in government and Chinese troops, now organized into banners. From Chinese artillery experts he obtained the technology for casting cannon. That his ambitions exceeded those of his father was made clear in 1636 when he dropped the dynastic name of Jin in favour of Qing, signifying 'clear' or 'pure', a challenge to the Ming, or 'bright' dynasty. Abahai's adoption of Chinese practices led Franz Michael to declare, 'It was the Chinese system, Chinese officials and Chinese ideas that enabled the Manchus to conquer China.' However by the mid-1630s Abahai had become wary of excessive sinicization and had insisted on the maintenance of Manchu values and tribal virtues.

In 1643 Abahai died and, after a succession dispute, it was agreed that the throne should go to his five-year-old son, with the new emperor's uncles Dorgon and Jirgalang acting as regents. By now the Ming dynasty, faced with uncontrollable peasant rebellions, was on the verge of collapse. The two regents had to decide whether to continue Abahai's policy, which concurred with the aristocratic tribal traditions of the Manchus, of remaining in the Manchu homelands and raiding China when they pleased, or whether to abandon that stratagem and occupy China. Dorgon, ambitious to increase his power, favoured the latter course. It was at this point that the issue of Chinese collaboration became a crucial factor. The most powerful Chinese commander on the north-east frontier was Wu Sangui. When the rebel leader Li Zicheng captured Beijing he immediately attempted to persuade Wu Sangui to come over to his side. However, according to a popular story, Li Zicheng had already seized and violated Wu Sangui's concubine, the famous courtesan Yuanyuan, and for this reason Wu Sangui decided to reject Li's overtures and to negotiate with the Manchus. A less romantic explanation of Wu Sangui's decision is that his failure to respond promptly to Li Zicheng's invitation led Li to suspect that the general was not to be trusted. He therefore ordered the slaughter of all members of Wu Sangui's family to be found in Beijing, and it was for this reason that the general turned to the Manchus. Dorgon may have calculated that he could not defeat the combined forces of Wu Sangui and Li Zicheng, but with the former on his side he was able to inflict a crushing defeat on the rebel leader's forces.

In June 1644 Dorgon entered Beijing and issued an edict in which he reassured the population that the Manchus had avenged the overthrow of the Ming by those he described as 'roving bandits', and he added,

> In the counties, districts, and locales that we pass through, all those who are able to shave their heads and surrender, opening their gates to welcome us, will be given rank and reward, retaining their wealth and nobility for generations. But if there are those who resist us disobediently, then when our Grand Army arrives, the stones themselves will be set ablaze and everyone will be massacred.[15]

The Manchu forces quickly drove Li Zicheng's troops out of north China, and before the end of 1645 both rebellions had been defeated. The rump Ming court made Nanjing its capital and attempted to negotiate a settlement with the Manchus. The Manchu response was to launch an attack on the Yangzi provinces. This stage of the conquest witnessed the most spirited Chinese resistance and the fiercest Manchu reprisals. At Yangzhou, a city situated near the junction of the Grand Canal and the Yangzi river, opposition to the Manchu advance was headed by Shi Kefa. After their first attack had been repelled, the invaders used cannon to breach the city walls and then ordered the city to be sacked as a deterrent to further defiance. Modern nationalist writers have taken the ten-day massacre at Yangzhou as proof of Manchu ruthlessness and have regarded Shi Kefa as the epitome of patriotic Chinese resistance.

At Jiangyin, about 100 miles upriver from Shanghai, the initial reaction of the elite to the Manchu advance was to comply with the demand that the tax and population registers should be handed over. However, in June 1645 news reached the city that the Manchus were imposing the regulation which required men to wear their hair in the Manchu style, that is with the head shaved, apart from a patch at the back where the hair was allowed to grow and was braided into a queue. This gave rise to a resistance movement in which elite and popular elements came together in a brief alliance. The Manchu response was to stamp out opposition ruthlessly. At Jiangyin the elite was divided in its resistance and the slaughter was actually perpetrated by Chinese troops. Scenes such as these prompted Lynn A. Struve to challenge the view which she claimed was the standard in textbooks: that the Ming–Qing transition was relatively short and smooth, both institutionally and culturally.[16]

Nanjing fell to the Manchus in June 1645 and the Ming court fled south. The Manchus then paused to quell a rebellion among their supporters and to consolidate their position in the Yangzi valley. The invasion of the south began in 1649 and in the following year Guangzhou was captured and sacked by Shang Kexi, a Chinese bannerman who had switched to the Manchu side in 1634. Resistance in mainland China had now effectively ended. The last Ming emperor fled to Burma and was captured and executed in 1662.

In the meantime a challenge to the Manchus had come from Zheng Chenggong, known in the West as Koxinga, a man who was both pirate and patriot, who had established his base near Xiamen. Zheng Chenggong commanded a large naval force, which he used to dramatic effect in 1659 when he sailed up the Yangzi and besieged Nanjing. However, he had expended little effort on obtaining support from the Chinese population and a Manchu attack on his forces besieging the city forced him to withdraw. Despite this defeat Zheng Chenggong remained a serious threat. To deny him economic support the Manchus ordered the coastal population of the provinces of Guangdong, Fujian and Zhejiang to move several miles inland. Zheng Chenggong died on Taiwan in 1662, but resistance from his family and supporters continued for a further twenty years.

THE CONSOLIDATION OF MANCHU RULE

From the moment that Dorgon had committed the Manchus to the conquest of China the question of how the Manchus should behave as rulers had been raised. Dorgon had read the history of the Jin dynasty, and was well aware of the tension which could arise between a sinicized emperor supported by a Chinese bureaucracy, and a non-Chinese nobility accustomed to the use of military power. Moreover he knew that the Chinese bureaucracy itself was split between those who accepted the Manchu presence and those who did not.

Dorgon's response was to perform a balancing act directed at reassuring the Chinese while retaining the confidence of the Manchus. When he had entered Beijing he had ordered a mourning service and funeral for the last Ming emperor. The heavy taxes of the late Ming period were reduced and tax concessions were given to war-torn areas. He declared 'The empire is a single whole. There are no distinctions between Manchus and Hans', and he initiated a Manchu–Chinese diarchy by inviting all Ming metropolitan officials to remain in their posts and to perform their duties alongside Manchu appointees. An extensive programme of reforms proposed by Ming officials was adopted. The examination system was continued, in a form advantageous to northerners who had long suspected that the system favoured men from the south. On the other hand care was taken to assert Manchu dominance. The requirement that Chinese should adopt the queue as a symbol of subordination has already been mentioned. Although the Manchu–Chinese diarchy suggested parity, the top metropolitan posts were held by Manchus, and of the Chinese appointed many were bannnermen who had submitted to the Manchus before the conquest. Although some tax relief was offered to the Chinese population, this economic gain was outweighed by the need for land on which to settle banner troops.

Up to one million acres of land was confiscated from Chinese
farmers in Zhili, who were forced to move to other parts of
northern China. Ironically this measure did not benefit the
Manchu bannermen greatly, for they lacked knowledge of agricultural techniques and many soon became destitute.

Dorgon had been an ambitious and scheming ruler, and after
his death in 1650 the Manchu court was beset by a period of
intense factional rivalry. At first Jirgalang became influential but
from 1653 a dominant faction grouped itself around the Shunzhi
emperor, who by now was old enough to play a role in government. The young emperor was a vigorous if erratic ruler, who
encouraged a programme of reform for the most part initiated by
'twice-serving ministers', that is officials who had previously
served under the Ming. Shunzhi died in 1661, probably of smallpox, leaving a will which is now recognized as a partial forgery.
The self-deprecatory remarks inserted in the will show that
Shunzhi had aroused the opposition of the Manchu conquest
elite for activities which they regarded as too favourable to the
Chinese. He admitted to having reversed Dorgon's policy of
restricting the political influence of the eunuchs, by creating the
Thirteen Offices, a personal bureaucracy of eunuch advisers.
Shunzhi's purpose in this may have been to assert his authority
against his Manchu opponents. He confessed to having spent too
much time with Buddhist monks, to having allowed the German
Jesuit Adam Schall to exercise too much influence at court, to
having favoured Chinese officials and Ming institutions and to
having disregarded the Manchu advisers and bondservants who
had served his predecessors. Moreover he had culpably shown
greater devotion to his consort, posthumously known as the
Empress Xiaoxian, who to his grief had died in 1660, than to his
mother. The will named his seven-year-old son as his heir, who
was to reign as the Kangxi emperor, and prescribed that during
his minority power was to be exercised by a regency composed
of four Manchus from the imperial bodyguard.

The four regents, of whom the best known was Oboi, held
power until 1669. In that period they reversed some of the lega-
cies of Shunzhi's reign and attempted to reassert Manchu dominance. The Thirteen Offices were abolished, the late emperor's
Buddhist advisers were expelled and a persecution of Jesuit missionaries was commenced. In the metropolitan government,

Manchu institutions such as the Council of Deliberative Officials, the membership of which included the commanders of the Manchu and Mongol banners and the Manchu and Mongol presidents of the Six Boards, were given greater responsibility at the expense of Chinese institutions such as the Grand Secretariat.

In the provinces the task of enforcing Manchu dominance was more difficult to complete. Few Manchus were proficient enough in Chinese, let alone experienced enough in administration, to discharge the duties of a provincial appointment. As a consequence the regents continued Dorgon's policy of appointing many Chinese bannermen to senior provincial positions, although their first move was to replace many of those already in post. Later in the regency some Manchus were appointed as governors and governors-general, but as these appointments were of Oboi's close associates they were resented by other Manchus. Another problem concerned the relationship between the Manchu conquerors and the Chinese rural elite, particularly those who lived in the great commercial and cultural centres along the southern stretch of the Grand Canal. Their initial acquiescence to Manchu rule concealed a persistent Ming loyalism and a resentment over what they perceived to be unfair treatment on matters such as official appointments and taxation. In 1661 a protest outside the Confucian temple in Suzhou over the ruthless collection of tax resulted in the trial and execution of 18 members of the gentry on charges of treason and the subsequent deprivation of many gentry of their degrees. Two years later at Hangzhou all suspected of involvement in the production of a history of the Ming dynasty, which contained phrases which might be construed as critical of the Manchus, were the victims of a violent persecution.

The regency suffered from persistent factionalism, with Oboi eventually emerging as the winner, and he continued to dominate the government after 1667 when Kangxi reached his majority. However, two years later the emperor ordered the arrest of Oboi, and arraigned him and his supporters on charges of usurping his authority and many other faults. Oboi was imprisoned and died soon afterwards. Kangxi thereupon assumed full responsibility for government.

Shortly after Kangxi's accession the Qing dynasty faced the

most severe threat of the period of consolidation. The tension
between a metropolitan desire to centralize control and a provincial or regional desire for autonomy has been a recurrent theme
in Chinese history. At the end of the Han and the Tang dynasties,
and again after the fall of the Qing, China had fragmented into
independent states or warlord regimes. A similar fragmentation
threatened the Qing in the 1660s. The origin of the threat lay in
the reliance that the Manchus had placed on Chinese collaborators and turncoats at the time of the conquest. Four collaborators, all of whom came from Liaodong, were of particular note.
Three of them, Shang Kexi, Kong Youde and Geng Zhongming,
had crossed to the Manchu side in the 1630s. The fourth, Wu
Sangui, had famously changed his allegiance in 1644. For their
services they had been granted the title of prince and had then
been commissioned to pacify the south. Kong Youde had been
cut off by Ming forces at Guilin in 1652 and had committed suicide, but the others not only completed the pacification, but also
carved out for themselves semi-independent fiefdoms, Wu
Sangui in Yunnan and Guizhou, Shang Kexi in Guangdong, and
Geng Jingzhong, the grandson of Geng Zhongming, in Fujian.
Such was the power of these three 'feudatories', as they are
called, that Wu Sangui, for example, not only enjoyed virtual
suzerainty over the two provinces he controlled directly, but he
also had the right to make administrative appointments in neighbouring provinces and he could claim a subsidy of 10 million
taels a year for the upkeep of his army.

In 1673 Shang Kexi requested permission to retire and to pass
control of Guangdong to his son. The Council of Deliberative
Officials accepted his retirement, but refused to make the appointment, effectively abolishing the feudatory. This put pressure
on the other feudatories to resign. Both Geng Jingzhong and Wu
Sangui tendered their resignations, but it was the view of the
majority of the Council that Wu Sangui did not expect his resignation to be taken seriously and that it would therefore be prudent to refuse it. Instead the Kangxi emperor took what has been
described as the 'most courageous step' of his reign, by deciding
to accept the resignation and disband the three feudatories,
knowing full well that this was likely to precipitate a civil war.

In December 1673 Wu Sangui ordered the murder of the governor of Yunnan, decreed the revival of Ming customs and pro-

claimed the Zhou dynasty. He obtained the support of four provinces so quickly that the rumour went around Beijing that the Manchus were about to withdraw to the north-east. However, Kangxi was made of sterner stuff. He put down unrest in the capital and ordered the suicide of Wu Sangui's son, who had been kept in Beijing as a hostage. Nevertheless the rebellion continued to spread and by the end of 1674 virtually all the south and west of the country was in rebel hands, with only Shang Kexi in Guangdong remaining loyal. Kangxi personally directed the military campaign against the rebels, and increasingly relied on Chinese rather than Manchu commanders, who in many cases had proved incompetent. Through his efforts, and through adroit diplomacy, the rebellion was slowly confined and, after Wu Sangui's death in 1678, gradually extinguished. A factor in the defeat of the rebellion was the use of cannon cast under the supervision of the Jesuit missionary Ferdinand Verbiest. More important than any military consideration was the contest for Han Chinese support. Even Ming loyalists found it difficult to support Wu Sangui, who was regarded as a double traitor. The lower Yangzi area, the key economic area where previously resentment of the Manchu presence had been strongest, was won over through the remission of taxes and the restoration of gentry status to those who had lost it as a punishment for the 1661 protest.

After the defeat of the rebellion, one further task remained to be completed before the empire was secure. This was the subjugation of Taiwan, which until 1681 had been held by the son of Zheng Chenggong, who had joined the rebellion of the Three Feudatories and had for six years established an enclave on the mainland. In 1683 a large Manchu fleet, led by a former supporter of Zheng Chenggong, captured the Penghu (Pescadores) islands and then occupied Taiwan. In the following year Taiwan was incorporated into the empire as a prefecture of Fujian province and the policy of removing the coastal population was finally rescinded.

THE LATER YEARS OF KANGXI'S REIGN, 1684–1722

In the remaining years of Kangxi's long reign the Manchu rulers

became accepted as a legitimate Chinese dynasty and Manchu–
Chinese antagonism ceased to be an important factor in politics.
This was achieved by Kangxi committing himself whole-heart-
edly to the business of being a Chinese emperor. He was
extremely hard-working, reading and commenting on an average
of 50 memorials a day, as well as holding audiences and performing routine tasks such as reviewing death sentences. He also
travelled extensively and commented

> On tours I learned about the common people's grievances by
> talking with them, or by accepting their petitions. In northern
> China I asked peasants about their officials, looked at their
> houses, and discussed their crops. In the South I heard pleas
> from a woman whose husband had been wrongly enslaved,
> from a travelling trader complaining of high customs dues,
> from a monk whose temple was falling down, and from a man
> who was robbed on his way to town of 200 taels of someone
> else's money that he had promised to invest – a complex
> predicament, and I had him given 40 taels in partial compen-
> sation.[17]

Kangxi prided himself on his military knowledge gained
through his direction of the campaign against the rebellion of the
Three Feudatories. In the 1690s he took the field in two campaigns against the Dzungar. The background to this situation was
Russian expansion across Siberia, the establishment of a Russian
trading station at Nerchinsk, and, in 1656, the construction of a
fort at Albazin on the Amur river. At that time the Manchu position in China was too insecure to risk driving the Russians out,
but in 1685 Kangxi concluded that the moment had come, and he
ordered an attack on Albazin. However, he recognized the danger
of the Russians allying with the Dzungar, the western branch of
the Mongol tribes. As soon as Albazin had been captured he
sought a settlement with Russia. The negotiations between the
two states were handled by Jesuit missionaries and resulted in
the Treaty of Nerchinsk, 1689, the first treaty signed by China
which accepted the principle of diplomatic equality with another
state. The treaty demarcated the frontier between China and
Russia, keeping the Amur river in Chinese hands. This settlement left Kangxi free to attack the Dzungar, whose leader

Galdan was threatening to unite the Mongol tribes. The emperor led campaigns in 1696 and 1697 which resulted in the defeat of the Dzungar and the suicide of Galdan. The Dzungar remained a threat throughout Kangxi's reign, but in 1717 they rashly invaded Tibet and this gave Kangxi a pretext to intervene and establish a Chinese presence in Lhasa.

Kangxi's government for the most part continued the practices of the Ming, but there were three significant innovations. One of these was the development of the Imperial Household system. Before the conquest the Manchus had kept household or agricultural slaves, many of whom were ethnic Chinese, and their descendants became hereditary slaves or bondservants. From 1615 the bondservants of the emperor and of the Manchu princes were organized into banner companies. The Imperial Household was derived from the bondservant companies of the banners commanded directly by the emperor, with the supervising officials becoming his officials and the rank and file his personal servants. The development of the Imperial Household had been interrupted by Shunzhi's decision to revive the eunuch-controlled Thirteen Offices. In 1661 Kangxi formally established the Imperial Household Department to control the eunuchs and to manage the emperor's affairs. By the late eighteenth century the Imperial Household, which was situated in the Forbidden City, employed some 1600 officials and engaged in a wide variety of administrative and commercial activities on the emperor's behalf.

The Imperial Household belonged to what was known as the 'inner court', the realm of the emperor, as opposed to the 'outer court', the realm of the bureaucracy. The outer court operated in accordance with statutory provisions and administrative precedent, but the inner court operated according to the emperor's will. The outer court communicated with officials through open channels, whereas the inner court – and this was the second innovation in the Kangxi period – used the 'palace memorial' system, a means of communicating directly and secretly with correspondents in the provinces. Many of these correspondents were bondservants serving in the provinces, often in the south, who supplied the emperor with confidential information on provincial affairs and the conduct of officials.

The third significant innovation of Kangxi's reign was the

extensive employment of foreigners, in particular European Jesuits, at court. The Jesuit mission in Beijing had been established in the closing years of the Ming dynasty, and although the Jesuits had helped the Ming by supplying them with cannon, the missionaries' technical expertise enabled them to retain their position in China after the Manchu conquest. Shunzhi had been impressed by the German Jesuit Adam Schall, who was a noted astronomer. During the Oboi regency the Jesuits fell out of favour with the Manchu elite, because of their association with the Shunzhi emperor, and also with those Chinese who recognized the challenge they presented to Chinese culture. For a time during Kangxi's reign the Jesuits at court enjoyed a position of trust similar to that of Chinese bondservants. The vulnerability of their position was demonstrated in 1664 when Adam Schall, who had been given the responsibility of preparing the imperial calendar, was accused of inaccuracy amounting to treason and sentenced to death, the sentence later being rescinded. Schall died in 1666 and his position was taken by Ferdinand Verbiest who more than restored the Jesuits' position by defeating his Chinese opponent with a display of superior skill in a further dispute over the calendar. Kangxi employed other Jesuits as architects, mathematicians and artists, and as diplomats in the negotiation of the Treaty of Nerchinsk.

In 1692, after Jesuit missionaries had successfully treated the emperor for malaria by prescribing quinine, Kangxi issued an 'edict of toleration' permitting the teaching of Christianity and he commissioned Jesuits to make a cartographic survey of the empire. However, the Jesuits were already under attack from other Christian groups for their willingness to compromise with the Chinese practice of ancestor worship as required by Kangxi. The Pope sent Charles Maillard de Tournon as a special legate to the Qing court to resolve the issue. He was received in audience by Kangxi, but the emperor would not agree to allow a representative of the Pope to reside in Beijing, nor would Maillard de Tournon accept the Jesuit accommodation on the matter of rites. When the papal legate indicated that Jesuits who observed the compromise were liable to be excommunicated, the emperor ordered all missionaries either to accept the compromise and agree to remain in China for life or to leave the country. After Kangxi's death further negotiations took place, but no agreement could be reached and in 1742 the papal bull *Ex Quo Singulari* forbade Christians to perform the Chinese rites. Some European missionaries remained in Beijing, but the proselytization of Christianity was forbidden and its practice by Chinese converts was driven underground, although it continued to make progress in some provinces, for example in Sichuan.

One of the most memorable of Kangxi's decisions in the later years of his reign was his announcement in 1712 that the number of *ding*, or tax-collection units, should be frozen permanently and should not take account of the rise in the population. This decision was represented as an act of benevolence, as a peace dividend, and as fulfilment of the sentiment that 'the hallmark of good government is to keep the burden of taxation light'.[18] Although Kangxi may have been pleased to view his policy in that light, the reasons for his action were less estimable. Since the conquest the dynasty had been faced with mounting problems over the collection of tax. In the early years an attempt had been made to simplify and centralize the tax system, but it remained extremely complex and vulnerable to under-collection and corruption. Moreover, when young, Kangxi had been made aware of the political risks of enforcing tax payments and thereafter had found it expedient to act leniently on these matters. On several occasions he granted generous tax amnesties, he failed to deal harshly with cases of official corruption, and he took no steps to deal with the problem of 'hidden land', that is recently reclaimed land which did not appear on the tax registers.

Kangxi's later years were clouded by worries over the succession. In 1676 he had followed the Chinese imperial custom and had named the eighteen-month-old Yinreng, his second son and his only son born to an empress, as his heir apparent. At first the relationship between father and son was good, and in 1696, when Kangxi left Beijing to campaign against Galdan, he appointed Yinreng as regent. But soon after his return Kangxi began to hear reports that Yinreng was engaging in immoral behaviour and for the next 15 years, as these damning reports multiplied, the emperor vacillated between denouncing his son and reinstating him as his heir. Finally in 1712 Yinreng was declared insane and deposed. Until he lay on his deathbed Kangxi refused to name who should succeed him. Then, according to one version of events, he nominated his fourth son, who was to reign as the Yongzheng emperor. However, the new emperor was to stand accused of having usurped the throne, which should have gone to Kangxi's fourteenth son, and in addition, to having poisoned his father, accusations that may have had their origin in the factional in-fighting which marked court politics during the long succession crisis.

THE YONGZHENG EMPEROR, r. 1723–35

The relatively short reign of Yongzheng was notable for the emperor's energetic attempt to introduce reforms. The first of these was in response to the circumstances under which he had come to the throne. In September 1723 he introduced a new succession system which departed from both the Chinese tradition of appointing the eldest son born of an empress, and the Manchu custom of the heir being selected from the ruler's sons according to merit and with the approval of influential members of the imperial family. Now the emperor was to select his heir from any of his sons and put the candidate's name into a sealed box. His choice would not be revealed to anyone, including the candidate himself, until after the emperor's death. Another reform, also directed at curbing the power of the Manchu princes, was the bureaucratization of the banner system. The background to this measure was the sharp decline in the value of the banner forces as military units and the emergence of strong cliques within the Five Inferior Banners headed by the Manchu princes. Yongzheng deprived the princes of control of companies within the banners and placed the banners under uniform administrative rules. He established banner schools which aimed at preserving the distinctive elements of Manchu and Mongol culture, and took steps to improve the economic condition of the bannermen.

The emperor also reformed the dynastic governmental machinery. The palace memorial system, referred to above, undermined the censorial system by enabling the emperor to access confidential information directly. To complement this arrangement Yongzheng developed the 'court letter', a direct and confidential instruction to provincial officials. This change was part of a much more important reform, which had its origins under Kangxi, and which was to be developed further by Yongzheng. The reference is to the Grand Council, the inner-court council, comprising equal numbers of high-ranking Chinese and Manchu officials, which met daily in the presence of the emperor and which enabled him to deal efficiently with the greatly-increased volume of business requiring his attention. Although the Grand Council, as a permanent body vested with broad powers, did not appear until early in Qianlong's reign, in 1729 Yongzheng created a forerunner body to co-ordinate the campaign against the Dzungar, the most important war of his reign.

The Kangxi emperor had bequeathed to his successor a state treasury that was nearly empty. The reason for this was not Kangxi's extravagance, nor was it excessive military expenditure, but the large deficit between the amount of tax levied and the amount of tax received. This deficit had two main causes: loss at the point of collection, and the proportion retained at the provincial level of government. Whereas Kangxi had adopted a relaxed attitude on fiscal matters, Yongzheng immediately instituted a crusade against official corruption. More originally he initiated a reform connected with the 'meltage fee', a surcharge on the land tax which supposedly compensated for losses when silver collected as tax was melted down into standard ingots. The excessive imposition of this surcharge, which might add 40 per cent to the land tax, was both an abuse and an indication that officials were grossly underpaid. Oertai, a Manchu official noted for his frugality, contrasted his salary as a governor-general, which amounted to 180 taels per annum, with his expenses in office, which amounted to 6000 taels. Yongzheng acknowledged this problem and legalized the meltage fee to supplement official salaries and to provide public funds for projects such as replenishing community granaries. Yongzheng's reform, however, did not touch upon the fundamental weakness of the fiscal system, which was that it was not able to extract more than 5 per cent of the gross national product of a predominantly agrarian economy, a proportion inadequate to discharge the responsibilities of a modern government.

Yongzheng involved himself energetically in many other aspects of ruling. He was determined to enforce ideological conformity among the literati, and he followed his father in promoting Neo-Confucianism in the form of the School of Principle, which favoured moral imperatives such as the total subjection of women, the indisputable authority of fathers and the unquestioning loyalty of subjects to rulers. In 1670 Kangxi had circulated his *Sacred Edict*, which expounded these principles in the form of 16 maxims. In 1724 Yongzheng reissued the edict with his own amplified instructions. Examination candidates were required to memorize the maxims and scholars were required to expound them twice monthly at Confucian temples. Yongzheng used the case of Zeng Jing, a Hunan scholar who had described the Manchus as barbarians and Yongzheng as an usurper, as propaganda to support the claim that the mandate of heaven had been transferred to the Manchus because of the degeneracy of the Ming dynasty.

Another example of Yongzheng's vigorous approach to ruling concerned the ethnic minorities in the south. In the past imperial policy towards these groups had relied upon the *tusi* or tribal headman system, whereby minorities were ruled by their own tribal leaders, who were given official ranks, and the people themselves were left alone. In the eighteenth century, with the Han Chinese population increasing steadily, pressure on areas occupied by ethnic minorities increased and incidents multiplied. Yongzheng found the tribal headman system incompatible with the principle of universal and absolute rule, and he began the process of bringing the minority groups into the provincial administrative system. This involved the 'pacification' of minority groups such as the Miao and their subsequent sinicization.

Yongzheng's reputation as a ruler is mixed. He stands accused of having usurped the throne and of having disposed ruthlessly of his brothers who threatened to contest his claim. On the other hand he has been hailed as 'the greatest centralizer and stabilizer' of the Qing dynasty, who 'revitalized the state administration, and fostered a time of economic prosperity'.[19] He ruled as an autocrat, largely freeing himself from dependence on the bureaucracy and reliance on the Manchu princes. Yet his objective was not simply power, for he showed compassion for his subjects, notably in his efforts to emancipate the 'mean' people, occupational groups such as prostitutes and actors, and the Tanka or boat people of south China, who were excluded from public service and were not allowed to marry members of the 'good' population.

THE QIANLONG EMPEROR, r. 1736–95

The Yongzheng emperor was succeeded by his fourth son, to be known as the Qianlong emperor. Yongzheng had concealed the name of his heir, and the future emperor and his half-brother closest to him in age were given the same education and administrative experience to prepare them equally for the throne. Both attended the Palace School for princes and studied Manchu texts and Confucian classics and both learned painting, calligraphy and writing poetry, received instruction in archery and the use of firearms, and went hunting.

When he became emperor Qianlong continued the autocratic tendencies of his father's government. In the early years of his reign the Grand Council took its definitive shape. The imperial princes lost their seats on the council, their places being taken by Manchu and, for the first time, Chinese officials in the approximate ratio of two Manchu appointments to one Chinese. Ironically, in the course of the reign the Grand Council became so effective a decision-making body that the need for the emperor to direct its deliberations declined. A willingness to appoint Chinese officials, as opposed to Chinese bannermen, was also evident in provincial appointments. In most other respects the operation of the bureaucracy remained unchanged. The examination system continued in full force and appointments to the civil service were dominated by degree-holders. Competition for official appointments became severe and success in the examinations went increasingly to families which had previously placed a member in the bureaucracy, or which could afford to use the purchase system to gain an advantage. Notwithstanding the autocratic tendencies at the centre, the bureaucracy was now too large, and its procedures too complex, to be a simple instrument of the emperor's will, a situation which the Qianlong emperor apparently understood.

* * *

During the eighteenth century the Qing empire doubled its territorial size. Qianlong's contribution to this massive expansion came principally in Tibet and Xinjiang. A Chinese presence in Lhasa had been established during his grandfather's reign, but Chinese influence was undermined by Dzungar intrigues, which in 1750 led to a civil war. Qianlong's response was to instate the Dalai Lama as the temporal ruler of a state enjoying internal autonomy, while at the same time declaring a Chinese protectorate over the country. In 1793, in a further assertion of China's dominant role, Qianlong decreed that the future Dalai Lama should be chosen by lot, and sent a golden urn to Lhasa for that purpose. In Xinjiang the Dzungar continued to offer a challenge until between 1755 and 1757 Qing forces virtually wiped them out, forcing the survivors to accept the name of Eleuth. Zhaohui, the Manchu general who led these expeditions, later defeated a Muslim revolt and extended Chinese control to the Pamirs.

Although the early Manchu rulers had demonstrated a willingness to experiment in matters of foreign relations, Qianlong generally followed the practices of the tributary system. The most developed form of the system applied to relations with Korea which on average sent a tributary mission to China three times a year. The tributary relationship was regarded as providing benefits to both parties, with China granting commercial privileges in exchange for recognition of China's claim to be the Middle Kingdom. China also accepted some responsibility for the well-being of tributary states, for example in 1788 a Chinese force was dispatched to Annam to assist the king to put down a rebellion.

The Qing court valued foreign trade more than is commonly supposed, but it was also mindful of the potential dangers of foreign contacts in the south, a region of suspect loyalty. In 1684 restrictions on foreign trade were eased, but it remained under close regulation. A superintendent of maritime customs, known to Europeans as the Hoppo, was stationed at Guangzhou; only those Chinese merchants who belonged to the monopolistic group known as the Cohong were allowed to take a share of the trade, and they were required to guarantee the debts of the foreign traders. At first foreign trade was permitted at a number of southern ports, but this proved difficult to regulate and from 1760 maritime trade was confined to Guangzhou. By the eighteenth century, by far the most important participant in this trade was Great Britain. British trade was monopolized by the East India Company, which handled the tea trade, China's most substantial export.

In Qianlong's reign the economy appeared to be thriving. Its basis remained agriculture, with rice, wheat and millet the most important crops, although in some regions cotton, silk and tea were of major significance. Commerce was well-developed, with perhaps 20 to 30 per cent of agricultural production reaching the market. Exchange banks, sometimes known as 'Shanxi banks' because many were operated by merchant families from Shanxi, served to transfer government and private remittances from one part of the country to another. Some industries, in particular the iron, cotton and ceramic industries, were large and sophisticated. These industries had been well-established by the early seventeenth century, and it has been suggested that at that point China was on the verge of an industrial revolution, but that development was delayed by the Manchu invasion. Marxist historians have also descried the 'sprouts of capitalism' appearing in the eighteenth century and have claimed that an impending industrial revolution was then aborted by the impact of Western imperialism.

This view has been rejected by most Western historians. Albert Feuerwerker described the eighteenth-century industrial growth as 'a few possibly proven instances of fairly large-scale handicraft enterprises' and found no reason to suppose that these represented the first stage on the road to modern industrial production.[20] Mark Elvin referred to the state of the Chinese economy as 'quantitative growth, qualitative standstill'. He considered various explanations for China's failure to industrialize at this stage, including those of inadequate capital and political obstruction, but rejected them in favour of what he termed the 'high-level equilibrium trap'. He pointed out that the Chinese economy had achieved a high level of sophistication within the confines of traditional technology. However, in the eighteenth century the population had grown from an estimated 150 million persons to double that figure. Little new land was available for cultivation and yields per acre were nearly as high as could be achieved using the available technology. At some point between 1750 and 1775 the amount of food available per capita began to decline, which led to a reduction of demand per person for goods other than those needed for bare survival and a fall in the cost of labour. Under these circumstances there was no case for investing in technological improvements.[21]

These views continue to carry a good deal of weight, but two

recent studies suggest they may understate the Qing government's interest in the management of the economy. One refers to
the state granary system which the Qing dynasty, like its
predecessors, operated to store grain for distribution to peasants
in time of famine. Previously Qing famine-control measures had
been described as 'useful up to a certain point' but 'never free
from the effects of official ineptitude, indifference, and corruption'.[22] However, this new study has concluded that the granary
system demonstrated not only that the state wished to intervene
positively in people's lives, but also that it had the capacity to do
so.[23] Another study has analysed the debate conducted in the
eighteenth century on the issue of state intervention in the management of the economy as opposed to reliance on self-regulat-
ing market mechanisms. An example of this was Qianlong's
decision in 1737 to promulgate a ban on liquor preparation in
northern China, on the grounds that fermenting grain 'wasted' it
and aggravated the risk of famine. The ban proved difficult to
enforce and fell into disuse, but not before it had been criticized
on the grounds that for some poor peasants, converting part of
their grain to liquor was a vital source of cash income and intervention was not in their best interests. Later in Qianlong's reign,
government policy became more favourable to legitimate commercial operations and some officials began to express the idea
that economic liberalism benefited society as a whole.[24]

What has been said so far about Qianlong's reign has emphasized its stability and achievement, and indeed that is how it was
regarded at the time. However, it is often said that during Qianlong's reign the first signs of dynastic decline appeared, and that
some of the indicators of decline presaged not only the collapse
of a dynasty but also the beginning of the end of the imperial
system of government. To test these allegations three issues will
be explored: literary and intellectual life, popular religion and
the rise of rebellion, and bureaucratic corruption.

The Qianlong emperor posed as a patron of the arts. He wrote
poetry and commissioned scholarly enterprises, the most ambitious of which was the compilation of the *Complete Library of
the Four Branches of Literature*, a collection of the 3500 works
deemed to be the best in the Chinese literary tradition. The selection and editing of this collection provided employment for an
army of scholars. However, the enterprise had a darker side, for

it was also a literary inquisition aimed at identifying and destroying any literary works which contained disrespectful references to the Manchus. Because scholars were involved in collecting, rather than in original scholarship, and because they were forced to collude in a form of censorship, the whole project has been seen as repressive and stultifying. The project has been presented as typical of much eighteenth-century scholarly activity. The famous novel *The Scholars*, written by Wu Jingzi in the 1740s, contained an ironic description of misplaced intellectual activity, which involved an examination system that concentrated on literary skills and a system of appointment which promoted officials who were more concerned with pleasing their superiors than improving the lot of the common people. This accusation of intellectual sterility has been challenged by Benjamin A. Elman, who has argued that the main emphasis of scholarly activity, the careful textual studies of the Confucian classics, required the use of empirical methods and exact scholarship, the basic tools of research and scientific investigation.[25]

The dominance of Confucian ideology and of literati culture obscures the importance of popular religion and popular culture to the mass of the people. A vivid example of this was the 'sorcery scare' of 1768. A rumour swept the lower Yangzi region that sorcerers were stealing men's souls by clipping off their queues. The rumour grew so strong that the emperor, suspecting that queue-cutting masked sedition, ordered officials to arrest suspected sorcerers. Although the rumour had died down by the autumn, it had revealed incipient social strains which may have derived from a changing economy, population pressure, increased migration, and the growth of an underclass of displaced persons.

Among popular religions the most widespread was the White Lotus religion, whose adherents worshipped a supreme deity called the Eternal Mother. The religion suffered from periodic state persecution and as a consequence it had no central organization, being composed of small communities linked only by visits from peripatetic teachers. The White Lotus religion found many of its converts among recent migrants and other less settled groups in society and it had a particular appeal for women. For the most part the religion existed to satisfy the spiritual needs of the believers and to provide them with social support, but it did also contain a millenarian message which predicted a coming apocalypse marked by the arrival of the Maitreya Buddha, the emissary of the Eternal Mother. The White Lotus religion provided the inspiration for the uprising led by Wang Lun in Shandong in 1774. The rebels were soon defeated, but not before they had exposed the incapacity of the Chinese Army of Green Standard and the Manchu banner troops sent against them. Twenty years later the White Lotus religion provided the inspiration for the first major popular rebellion to threaten the dynasty. This arose in the mountainous region between the upper waters of the Yangzi and Yellow rivers, an area which had received many recent migrants. The rebellion was not suppressed until the government had permitted local gentry to raise militia forces and employ mercenaries, and had sanctioned the movement of the population into strategic hamlets, thereby denying the rebels food and fresh recruits.

The third issue, that of bureaucratic corruption, was commonly cited as a cause of dynastic decline. Yongzheng had attempted to treat what he regarded as the root cause of corruption, the inadequate salaries paid to officials, by providing extra stipends for 'cultivation of incorruptibility'. In Qianlong's reign these reforms were modified and, according to Madeleine Zelin, officials were even more handicapped than they had been 50 years previously, and 'corruption became a threat to the very survival of the unified Chinese state'.[26] The increase in corruption was illustrated by reference to a Manchu bannerman named Heshen, who was Qianlong's favourite throughout the last 25 years of his life. Heshen was to be accused of having built up an extraordinary network of patronage which corrupted a large part of the civil and military establishment and contributed to the growth of unrest and the rise of rebellion. It was claimed that during the White Lotus rebellion (1796–1804) Heshen had allowed the emperor to believe that the campaign was achieving success, while he embezzled large sums of money intended for military supplies. For this, Qianlong's successor, the Jiaqing emperor, had Heshen arrested and then allowed him to commit suicide. Heshen's career would seem to prove the seriousness of corruption, although it must be said that the White Lotus rebellion had other causes and that the difficulty in suppressing it was only partly Heshen's fault. However, it is not accepted unanimously that corruption was undermining the Qing government. Albert Feuerwerker has pointed out that corruption was probably no more prevalent under the Qing than under earlier dynasties, and has suggested that corruption might be described as the use of inducements to make a bureaucratic system of government work.[27]

5

China in the Late Qing

THE FIRST OPIUM WAR, 1839–42

In 1792 Great Britain, concerned about the security of its tea trade with China and keen to expand British commercial activity throughout Asia and into the Pacific, sent an embassy to China headed by Lord Macartney. Macartney had been instructed to negotiate a treaty of commerce and to obtain permission for Great Britain to accredit a resident minister at the Qianlong emperor's court. He was told to request the opening of ports additional to Guangzhou and the provision of a base for British merchants which was closer to the tea- and silk-producing areas than was Guangzhou. Macartney took with him as gifts samples of British manufactures, including a planetarium, chandeliers, two howitzers, three carriages and items of Wedgwood pottery, hoping thereby to secure new markets in China for British products.

Macartney was granted an audience with the emperor, but he refused to follow the protocol governing tribute missions and perform the kotow. In two edicts addressed to the king of England, Qianlong rejected all Macartney's requests. He was told that to allow a British national to reside in Beijing to take care of trade was 'contrary to all usage of my dynasty and cannot possibly be entertained'. The existing arrangements relating to trade were confirmed. The emperor supposed that Macartney had requested freedom to propagate Christianity – which he had not done – but such a concession was refused. Finally the emperor referred to the gifts which Macartney had brought. These he said would be accepted out of consideration for the spirit in which they had been sent, but he added,

> As your Ambassador can see for himself, we possess all things. I set no value on objects strange or ingenious, and have no use for your country's manufactures.[1]

Various explanations have been advanced for why the mission returned empty-handed. Macartney opined that the Chinese, having once been very civilized, were now when compared to Europeans a 'semi-barbarous people'. For J. K. Fairbank the reason why the Qing court clung so tenaciously to the performance of the kotow was because it functioned to legitimize its rule. Many writers have implied that the Qing court insisted on maintaining ceremonial supremacy because it could not adjust rationally to the demands of a new commercial age. James L. Hevia rejected that as an Eurocentric view and pointed out that in practice the Qing dynasty did not insist on a fixed ritual. Friction occurred on the occasion of the Macartney embassy because court officials failed to organize the ritual process properly. Only later was Macartney's embassy to be described as a failure and that conclusion used to justify Britain forcing China to accept foreign trade and foreign representation.[2] In a review of Hevia's interpretation, Joseph W. Esherick accepted that the kotow was not the issue, for it was probable that a modified form of the ceremony had been agreed. However, he reiterated that the embassy was a failure because it achieved none of its principal objectives, for the Qianlong emperor had refused all requests relating to trade and diplomatic representation.[3]

In the early eighteenth century British trade with China had been monopolized by the British East India Company and had comprised the exchange of Chinese tea for British woollen and metal goods. By the 1760s the value of tea exports greatly exceeded that of British imports and the balance had to be made up with silver. In 1784 the British government passed the Commutation Act which cut tea duties sharply. The demand for tea increased and tea duties continued to provide a large proportion of the British government's revenue. To offset the trading deficit raw cotton was exported from India to China on board 'country ships' owned by private British merchants. Alongside this legal commerce there was a small but lucrative trade in opium, which was grown on the Company's territory in Bengal and smuggled into China.

Although the Qing court had eventually allowed the resumption of maritime trade, it remained suspicious of foreign intercourse. It was for this reason that from 1760 foreign maritime trade was confined to Guangzhou, and Chinese participation in it was restricted to the group of merchants known to Westerners as the Cohong. As they were held responsible for the debts of foreign merchants, they protected themselves by setting aside a share of their profits in what was known as the Consoo fund. Foreign traders were subject to the Eight Regulations and were only allowed to remain in Guangzhou during the trading season. Relations between British and Chinese merchants were generally good, but in 1784 an unfortunate incident occurred which revealed only too clearly the disparities between Chinese and Western concepts of legal responsibility and of legal process. A British merchant ship, the *Lady Hughes*, fired a salute and accidentally killed two Chinese officials. Chinese law required that the person responsible should be surrendered to the authorities. The unlucky gunner was handed over reluctantly and immediately strangled. As time passed the confinement of trade to Guangzhou became increasingly irksome to the private traders, and it was they who promoted the idea of sending a mission to China, which resulted in the Macartney embassy.

After the Napoleonic Wars, which had confirmed Britain's position as the world's leading naval power, several events contributed to a rise in tension between Britain and China. In 1816 Lord Amherst headed a second embassy to the Manchu court, but his requests for improvements in the arrangements for trade were rejected abruptly. Opium smuggling began to escalate, one reason being a reduction in the price of Bengal opium. By the 1820s the value of the drug being imported was so large that the balance of trade shifted against China and the deficit had to be made up in silver, allegedly causing a silver drain and making it more difficult for peasants to pay land taxes, which had to be rendered in silver. Evidence of the growth of addiction prompted Ruan Yuan, the governor-general of Guangdong and

Guangxi, to take vigorous action. He drove the opium smugglers out of Aomen, but this only resulted in the trade extending along the coast eastwards and led to the greater involvement of secret societies in its operation.

In 1834 the East India Company's monopoly of the China trade, which had long been the subject of criticism by free traders, came to an end. The British government now assumed responsibility and Lord Palmerston, the British Foreign Secretary, appointed Lord Napier as superintendent of trade in China. Palmerston instructed Napier that on arrival in China he should open direct communication with the authorities in Guangzhou, with a view to discussing improvements in the arrangements for trade. Napier proceeded to Guangzhou without waiting to receive permission, as Chinese regulations required, and with only two frigates in support. There he was refused a meeting and only allowed to leave under humiliating circumstances. This débâcle strengthened the contention of those in favour of free trade – notably William Jardine, the most successful trader in opium, and the Manchester Chamber of Commerce – that China should be forced to open additional ports.

While this was happening, a debate was taking place between officials and degree-holders in Beijing on how to stop opium smuggling. One group argued that, as the smuggling could not be prevented, the only practical response was to legalize and tax the importation of opium and to allow the growth of the opium poppy in China. This proposal aroused the fury of a group of degree-holders known as the Spring Purification circle. This group, which had formed in the 1830s, modelled itself on the Donglin academy of the late Ming period and claimed that scholars had the right of *qingyi*, that is of moral censure. In 1836 the Spring Purification circle played a part in persuading the Daoguang emperor to reject the proposal to legalize the opium trade and to support a moral crusade against opium consumption. This crusade would involve the gentry of Guangdong and would threaten addicts with the death penalty if they did not agree to give up the habit.

In December 1838, Lin Zexu, the governor-general of Hubei and Hunan and a supporter of the Spring Purification group, was appointed imperial commissioner, with instructions to proceed to Guangzhou and carry out a comprehensive suppression of the

opium trade. When Lin reached Guangzhou he immediately
enlisted local gentry in a campaign against consumers and
ordered the arrest of 60 notorious opium dealers. He then turned
to deal with the foreign suppliers, first writing a letter to Queen
Victoria (which was never delivered) in which he pointed out
that as opium was prohibited in her country, she should use her
influence to prevent its production in territories under her control. On 18 March 1838 Lin ordered the Cohong merchants,
whom he regarded as no better than wealthy smugglers, to call
upon the foreign merchants to hand them their stocks of opium
within three days. They were also to require the foreigners to
sign a declaration stating that they would either cease trading in
opium or suffer death. In the meantime foreign trade was suspended and the foreign merchants were kept under house arrest
in the trading area outside Guangzhou known as the Thirteen
Factories. Lin also attempted to arrest Lancelot Dent, whose firm
Dent and Co. was heavily involved in opium smuggling. Charles
Elliot, the new superintendent of British trade in China, advised
the British merchants to surrender their opium and sign the declaration. He sent an urgent dispatch to Palmerston informing him
that the foreign community was being kept under duress, and
that he had guaranteed that the merchants would be compensated
for the loss of their opium stocks. After having been kept in
detention for seven weeks the foreign community was allowed to
go to Aomen. In July some drunken British sailors killed a
Chinese farmer. Elliot, recalling the *Lady Hughes* case, refused
to hand over the culprits. Lin Zexu responded by forcing the
Portuguese authorities in Aomen to request that the British
depart, whereupon they moved across the Pearl river estuary to
Xianggang.

Palmerston learned of the detention of British subjects and
Elliot's guarantee on 21 September 1839. Prompted by William
Jardine, on behalf of the opium interest, and by other British
merchants keen to sell textiles to China, he obtained agreement
for the dispatch of an expeditionary force to China with instructions to compel the Chinese to abolish the Cohong, to cede an
island base and to compensate British traders for the loss of
opium.

The war which ensued fell into two phases. In the first phase
the expeditionary force, headed by Charles Elliot and his cousin

Admiral George Elliot, blockaded Guangzhou, and then moved north, seizing the island of Zhoushan and threatening Tianjin and Beijing. At this point the emperor dismissed Lin Zexu and authorized Qishan, the Manchu governor-general of Zhili, to negotiate with Elliot. In January 1841, Elliot and Qishan agreed the Convention of Chuanbi, which accepted British demands, including the cession of the island of Xianggang. This agreement was rejected by both sides, as having conceded too little or too much. Qishan was disgraced and Elliot was replaced by Sir Henry Pottinger.

While a larger British expeditionary force was being assembled, an obscure but significant episode occurred near Guangzhou. After the agreement had collapsed, Elliot landed troops north of Guangzhou. As he knew that he had not got enough men to occupy a city of half a million people, he coerced the city authorities into promising the British a ransom of six million dollars for refraining from attack. In the meantime local gentry leaders had raised a militia and were harrying the British troops. On 29 May 1841, near the village of Sanyuanli, they ambushed a British patrol, killing one man and injuring several others. This skirmish came to represent the beginning of Chinese popular resistance to foreign invasion, and was later to be contrasted with the Manchu court's self-interested willingness to compromise with the imperial powers.

In the second phase of the war Pottinger moved up the coast and captured Xiamen, Zhoushan and Ningbo. In May 1842, having received reinforcements, he captured Zhapu, overcoming heroic resistance by Manchu soldiers whose families preferred death to capture. After Shanghai had been occupied and Pottinger had begun to move up the Yangzi, the emperor authorized the negotiations which resulted in the Treaty of Nanjing, which was signed on 29 August 1842. The treaty provided for the opening of five ports, Guangzhou, Xiamen, Fuzhou, Ningbo and Shanghai, to British trade and residence; the cession of Xianggang to Britain; the abolition of the Cohong; equality in official correspondence, and agreement on a fixed tariff. In addition China was to pay Britain $21,000,000 to cover the costs of the war and the value of the opium which had been confiscated. The treaty made no reference to the opium trade.

The Treaty of Nanjing was the first of the treaties between

China and the West which have been dubbed 'unequal treaties', because they conferred benefits on the Western powers without offering advantages to China in return. These treaties had four characteristic features: the opening of treaty ports; extraterritoriality, that is the removal of foreigners from the jurisdiction of Chinese courts; external tariffs fixed by treaty; and the 'most-favoured-nation' clause, which guaranteed that signatories of unequal treaties would share all benefits granted to other powers. The Nanjing settlement was supplemented by the Treaty of the Bogue, which provided for extraterritoriality and contained a most-favoured-nation clause. In this treaty, import tariffs were fixed at an average 5 per cent of the value of the goods. Similar treaties were negotiated by the United States and France. France also obtained an imperial edict which granted toleration to Roman Catholicism, a concession which was extended shortly afterwards to other Christian sects.

An extensive historiographical debate has arisen about the origins of the Opium War. Karl Marx, in articles for the *New York Daily Tribune* written in the 1850s, asserted the centrality of the opium trade to the origins of the war. However, modern Western historiography was long dominated by the view expressed by the Harvard historian John K. Fairbank, that opium was 'the occasion rather than the sole cause' of the war, which he argued arose essentially from a conflict between Eastern and Western cultures.[4] More recently the importance of the opium trade to Britain has been re-emphasized. According to D. K. Fieldhouse, 'it formed an integral part of the pattern of British economic activity in India and was in some ways fundamental to it.[5]

FROM THE FIRST OPIUM WAR TO THE *ARROW* WAR OF 1856–60

Both sides soon expressed their dissatisfaction with the Nanjing settlement. On the British side there had been high hopes that the opening of additional ports would lead to a large increase in trade, but after a short improvement the anticipated bonanza did not occur. Although a report made to the House of Commons in 1847 suggested that this was because of the lack of demand in the Chinese market, the suspicion remained that the real reasons were the obstructiveness of Chinese officials and the imposition of internal transit duties. Immediately after the conclusion of the Treaty of Nanjing, Pottinger and Qiying enjoyed a diplomatic honeymoon, but after 1844, when Pottinger was replaced by J. F. Davis, relations between Britain and China began to deteriorate. A particularly contentious issue was the 'Guangzhou city question', a dispute over whether the Treaty of Nanjing had given British subjects the right of trade and residence within the walls of Guangzhou, and if it had, when they would be allowed to exercise that right. In 1847 Davis lost patience and ordered the capture of the forts guarding the approaches to Guangzhou. Qiying was forced to promise entry into the city in two years' time.

On the Chinese side, the years immediately after the first treaty settlement were marked by the imperial court's willingness to be conciliatory in the management of 'barbarian affairs'. This policy was endorsed by Muchanga, the Daoguang emperor's chief minister. As Muchanga and Qiying were both Manchus, this willingness to appease the foreigners was later attributed to a desire to preserve the Manchu dynasty at the expense of the Chinese national interest. However, conciliation was a risky policy as it contrasted with the anti-foreignism of the majority of Chinese officials and of the local gentry around Guangzhou. In 1848 the emperor dismissed Qiying and appointed Xu Guangjin as governor-general of Guangdong and Guangxi and commissioner for foreign affairs. Xu, a Chinese, had already shown that he was responsive to local opinion. Ye Mingchen, who took over as governor of Guangdong, was also known for his xenophobia.

As April 1849, the agreed date for British entry into Guangzhou, approached, Xu Guangjin abandoned the conciliatory policy and allowed local gentry to raise militia to oppose the entry. He then took the even more desperate gamble of forging an imperial edict ordering him to respect the will of the people. Sir George Bonham, the new governor of Xianggang, accepted a further postponement, a concession which was greeted by the Chinese as a victory and commemorated by the granting of imperial honours to Xu Guangjin and Ye Mingchen, but which was deeply resented by the local British community. The anti-foreign direction of Chinese policy became even more marked after the Daoguang emperor's death in 1850, for his successor, the Xianfeng emperor, dismissed Muchanga and in 1852 promoted Ye Mingchen to the positions held by Xu Guangjin.

These incidents, and this hardening of attitudes, might have led to a second war in the early 1850s but other considerations prevailed. The rise of rebellion – the Taiping rebels captured Nanjing in 1853, and the Red Turbans rebels overran Guangdong in 1854 – forced the Chinese authorities to act circumspectly. British diplomats had assumed that the Treaty of Nanjing would be subject to revision after 12 years, that is in 1854, and it was only then that they realized that the Chinese had no intention of reopening questions which they regarded as settled. The outbreak of the Crimean War in March 1854 provided another reason for delaying what was now regarded as an overdue settlement of issues with China.

In October 1856 Chinese officials boarded the *Arrow*, a small ship claiming British registration, and seized the crew on suspicion of piracy. This incident was treated by Sir John Bowring, the Governor of Xianggang, as an insult to the British flag and he sanctioned a naval attack on Guangzhou. In response Ye Mingchen suspended foreign trade, the foreign factories were burned down and rewards were offered for the killing or capture of an Englishman. When news of these events reached London Lord Palmerston, now prime minister, was criticized for his handling of affairs in China and his government was defeated in a vote of censure. However, Palmerston won the ensuing election and obtained a mandate to send an expeditionary force to China. This force, headed by the Earl of Elgin, included a French contingent dispatched to obtain compensation for the judicial murder of a French missionary.

After a delay occasioned by the need to divert forces to help suppress the Indian Mutiny, Elgin captured Guangzhou, sent Ye Mingchen as a prisoner to India, and placed the city under an allied government headed by the thrusting British consul, Harry Parkes. The allied forces then moved north, seized the Dagu forts and reached Tianjin, at which point the emperor decided to negotiate. In the Treaty of Tianjin, concluded in June 1858, China agreed to open ten more treaty ports, to allow foreigners, including missionaries, to travel in the interior of China, to accept changes relating to external tariffs and new arrangements governing transit duties, to legalize the opium trade, and to accept a resident British minister in Beijing. The opening of the treaty ports on the Yangzi was to be deferred until the Taiping rebellion had been defeated.

Treaties containing similar terms were signed between China and France, the United States and Russia. American interest in the Pacific had been growing rapidly in the 1850s. It was an American expedition which in 1853 had forced Japan to end the policy of seclusion. Russia's involvement stemmed from the forward policy in Siberia, which it had pursued since the late eighteenth century. In 1849, N. N. Muraviev, the governor-general of eastern Siberia, dispatched an expedition to explore the Amur river valley. Finding it devoid of Chinese garrisons, he established a trading post, which he named Nikolaevsk after the tsar. During the Tianjin negotiations the Russian diplomat Count Putiatin pretended to act as a mediator between China and the Western powers. In the meantime Muraviev took advantage of China's weakness to obtain the Treaty of Aigun, which ceded to Russia all land north of the Amur river and provided for Sino-Russian administration of the territory between the Wusuli river and the sea.

In June 1859 the allied representatives returned to China to ratify the treaties. When they attempted to pass the Dagu forts they found the river blocked and in the action which followed the allies suffered heavy casualties. When news of this victory reached Beijing, hardliners at court advocated the abrogation of the treaties and the renewal of the war. However, in the following year the allies returned with a much larger force, outflanked the Dagu forts, and marched on Beijing. A group of British and French diplomats and soldiers, headed by Harry Parkes, was captured and maltreated. In revenge Elgin ordered the burning of the Summer Palace, the collection of buildings designed by Jesuits in the eighteenth century. Elgin then entered Beijing where he signed an additional convention which committed China to opening Tianjin as a treaty port, to ceding the Jiulong (Kowloon) peninsula opposite Xianggang to Britain, and to paying an additional indemnity. One month later, in November 1860, China was manoeuvred into ceding to Russia the vast expanse of territory east of the Wusuli river. This allowed Russia to establish a naval base at Vladivostok.

THE RISE OF REBELLION

Between 1850 and 1873 China experienced a sequence of rebellions and uprisings which came close to overthrowing the Qing dynasty. The greatest of these was the Taiping rebellion (1850–64), which for much of its course was centred on Nanjing, thereby splitting the country in two. The Nian rebellion (1853–68) had its base area in northern Anhui. In Yunnan (1855–73) and Gansu (1862–73), Muslim rebels threatened the secession of these provinces from China. In 1853 secret society members captured Shanghai and Xiamen and in the following year the Red Turbans nearly captured Guangzhou.

In Confucian historiography the rise of rebellion marked a stage in the dynastic cycle. When dynasties were founded they were headed by virtuous rulers who enjoyed the mandate of heaven. However, it inevitably happened that their successors and their officials could not maintain the standards which their predecessors had set and the quality of government declined. Rebellions arose which overthrew the dynasty and the dynastic cycle began again under a new leader. Some modern historians have adapted this concept, explaining the dynastic cycle in administrative rather than in moral terms. Dynasties were founded by active rulers supported by a modest court and an efficient bureaucracy. They exercised effective military authority and extended the frontiers of the empire. Later in the cycle the court became extravagant and the bureaucracy corrupt. The armed forces deteriorated and could no longer defend the over-extended frontiers. The burden of taxation increased and was heaped ever more oppressively on those least able to pay, thereby provoking the rebellion which was to overthrow the dynasty.

These rebellions are commonly described as 'peasant rebellions', a term which may imply that they arose from peasant immiseration, that the leaders were peasants, or that the great majority of the participants were peasants. However, the term has also acquired a political implication. Mao Zedong described the hundreds of uprisings which had punctuated Chinese history as 'peasant revolutionary wars'. They arose because of the ruthless economic exploitation of the peasantry by the landlord class and were therefore an expression of the class struggle. Moreover these wars 'alone formed the real motive force of China's historical evolution'.[6]

The mid-nineteenth-century rebellions may be located in the downward phase of the dynastic cycle. The White Lotus rebellion of the late eighteenth century became a major threat because of the ineffectuality of the armed forces and the misappropriation of funds by Heshen, the Qianlong emperor's favourite. This decline was not continuous, for Qianlong's successor, the Jiaqing emperor, attacked corruption and attempted to curb court extravagance. But the roots of corruption and inefficiency in state enterprises went deep, as the prolonged and unsuccessful attempt to revitalize the grain-tribute administration, the agency which transported the rice collected as tax from the provinces of the Yangzi delta to Beijing, had demonstrated.

However, the most important factor undermining the dynasty was a new phenomenon: the unprecedented growth of the population. In the eighteenth century the population of China had doubled, increasing from about 150 million to about 300 million people. This rise had occurred in a period of prolonged peace, at a time when there were no major outbreaks of epidemic disease. Until the end of the eighteenth century population growth had been matched by increases in the food supply, part of which came from the slow diffusion of new crops, notably maize, sweet potatoes and peanuts, which had been introduced into China from America in the late Ming period. Population increase encouraged extensive migration away from densely populated delta regions to less exploited hilly regions. A notable example of this movement occurred in the Yangzi highlands, where migrants known as 'shack people' cleared hillsides and planted the new crops, their activities causing serious erosion and flash floods. Migration weakened administrative control because migrant communities were unstable and unruly and could not readily be incorporated into the *baojia* framework. In some areas, for example in southern Guangxi, friction arose between the established Chinese population and recent arrivals, who were often Hakka or *kejia* ('guest people') Chinese, who spoke a different dialect. Population growth led to a rise in the number of candidates in the official examinations and heightened the already fierce competition for bureaucratic appointments. Administrative tasks became more complex and officials took on supernumerary personnel to enable them to fulfil their duties. They were paid by increasing the unofficial levies imposed on taxpayers.

A number of connections have been identified between the Opium War, Western imperialism, and the rise of rebellion. Karl Marx, writing in 1853, attributed the rise of the Taiping rebellion to the effects of defeat. 'Before the British arms,' he wrote, 'the authority of the Manchu dynasty fell to pieces.'[7] It has been suggested that the opium trade, and the consequent outflow of silver, altered the exchange rate between copper and silver, thereby increasing the land tax paid by poor farmers. It may also have exacerbated the contraction of the economy between 1825 and 1850, which led to a rise in unemployment. The opening of Shanghai as a treaty port put out of work many thousands of porters and boatmen who had been employed in transporting tea to Guangzhou. One of the tasks of the British navy, after the seizure of Xianggang, was to expel the pirate fleets from local waters. Some moved up the Xi (West) river, where they joined the rebels in the early stages of the Taiping rebellion.

In north China, rebellion was often associated with the White Lotus religion. In the south, the more common association was with the secret societies commonly known in the West as the Triad. These had originated on Taiwan in the seventeenth century and had as their claimed political objective the overthrow of the Qing and the restoration of the Ming. In times of peace they provided mutual support for their members who engaged in criminal activities such as piracy, smuggling and racketeering. When disturbances occurred the societies were quick to take advantage of the situation. In the eighteenth century the societies spread across southern China, gaining recruits among mobile groups, such as porters and boatmen, and among bandits, smugglers and pirates. From about 1840, when feuding between rival lineages became increasingly commonplace, the societies began to gain recruits from the settled peasantry of the Pearl river delta.

THE REBELLIONS

Hong Xiuquan (1814–64), the future leader of the Taiping rebellion, was a Hakka Chinese who came from the district of

Huaxian in Guangdong. In 1836, when in Guangzhou for the provincial examinations, he was handed a collection of Christian tracts entitled *Good Words to Admonish the Age*. The following year, having again failed the examinations, he fell ill, and had a series of dreams in which a venerable man presented him with a sword with which to exterminate demons, and a middle-aged man, whom he called elder brother, fought at his side against devils. In 1843 Hong failed the examinations for a fourth time and after returning home picked up the tracts he had been given seven years previously. They seemed to provide him with the key to his dreams: the venerable man was God the Father, the middle-aged man his son, Jesus Christ, and Hong himself was God's Chinese son, who had been entrusted with the task of restoring the true faith to China.[8]

Hong began by announcing his vision to his family and making his first converts, who included his cousin Hong Ren'gan and a fellow school-teacher, Feng Yunshan. They removed the Confucian tablets from the village school, and the hostility which this aroused may have prompted their decision to travel to Guangxi and make converts among the Hakka living there. In 1847 Hong returned to Guangzhou and for some months attended the church run by a fundamentalist Southern Baptist missionary, Issachar J. Roberts. When he returned to Guangxi he found that Feng Yunshan had assembled a congregation of some 2000 Hakka peasants and miners, known as the God Worshippers' Society, who were bound together not only by religion but also by the experience of the communal strife between the Hakka and the earlier Chinese settlers. After Feng Yunshan had been arrested on a charge of planning rebellion, two new leaders emerged, Yang Xiuqing, a charcoal burner later known as the Eastern king, and Xiao Chaogui, a poor hill farmer, who became the Western king. Both claimed spirit possession, Yang as the mouthpiece of God the Father, and Xiao as that of Jesus Christ. In the summer of 1850 the God Worshipper movement entered a millennial phase. In anticipation of an imminent second coming the adherents abandoned their houses and began to assemble near the village of Jintian. There they deposited their valuables in a sacred treasury and practised segregation of the sexes. In January 1851, after having been attacked by gentry-led militia and government troops, Hong Xiuquan declared the establishment of the *Taiping*

Tianguo, the Heavenly Kingdom of Great Peace and he himself assumed the title of the Heavenly king.

The rebellion which followed went through several phases. In September 1851 the Taipings captured the small walled city of Yongan and over the next few months they created a military organization, established a collective leadership and, using a captured printing press, published various documents including a new calendar. Yongan was besieged by government troops, but in April 1852 the Taipings broke out and began a spectacular northern advance, during which they collected a following estimated at over a million people. In March 1853 they captured Nanjing and committed what later proved to be the strategic error of making the city their capital. Later that year a northern expedition came close to capturing Beijing. Over the next seven years a stalemate ensued, with the rebels occupying the middle Yangzi and government troops and gentry-led militia being unable to dislodge them. In 1856 a power struggle within the collective leadership resulted in the death of the Eastern king and many of his followers. In 1859 Hong's cousin, Hong Ren'gan, re-joined the movement. Under his leadership, and that of Li Xiucheng, the Loyal king, the Taipings' most successful military commander, the rebellion revived and in 1862 the rebels nearly captured Shanghai. Then the tide turned, the rebels losing control of the Yangzi above Nanjing to forces raised by gentry leaders, and of the Yangzi delta region to similar forces supported by the British. In July 1864 Nanjing was recaptured and Hong Xiuquan committed suicide.

The Taiping rebellion had many aspects and has been the subject of numerous interpretations. Like nearly all great rebellions in Chinese history it had a religious inspiration. In the early years its followers were required to refrain from the use of tobacco, opium and alcohol, the practice of gambling, and engaging in sexual relations. The Christian elements in Taiping religion at first raised hopes among Protestant missionaries that the movement presaged the mass conversion of China. Later most Westerners found fault with Taiping religion, which they regarded as blasphemous, and they alleged that the rebel leaders were hypocrites and their followers did not observe the religious tenets. The rebellion has been hailed as an expression of a nationalist spirit, directed against Manchu oppression and committed to achieving 'a complete reform of China's social, economic, political, and military institutions', an allusion in particular to the ambitious programme of reform proposed by Hong Ren'gan but never implemented.[9]

The rebellion is often described as a revolution, a reference to the ambitious plans to remake society contained in a document entitled *The Land System of the Heavenly Dynasty*. This prescribed that land should be classified according to its fertility and then divided up among the population, with equal shares for men and women. Each family would be allowed to retain such proportion of the produce that it required for its own consumption, and the rest would be deposited in the public granary. The population was to be divided into groups of 25 families, each headed by a sergeant, who would be responsible for the religious education of the children. The same system provided the military organization of the Taiping state and defined the arrangements for the promotion and demotion of individuals.

This land system, which has been attributed to Yang Xiuqing, the Eastern king, displayed revolutionary intentions which accord with the interpretation of the rebellion as a class movement directed against landlords. However, there is not a great deal of evidence of its implementation. In areas under Taiping control some attempt was made to introduce the 25-family system, but no redistribution of land took place. In the later stages of the rebellion, when the Taipings occupied Jiangnan, they did not redistribute land, although they did attempt to improve the position of tenants by requiring them to pay the land taxes – which gave them a claim to the ownership of land in cases where the landlord had fled – and by enforcing a reduction in the amount of rent payable. This did not amount to a complete restructuring of property relations in the countryside, but it was a blow struck at the dominance of rural landlords.

The Nian rebellion (the word *nian* simply means group) arose in the harsh terrain north of the Huai river, an area which had been affected by the White Lotus rebellion half a century previously. Nian groups of bandits gained influence throughout the area by establishing mutually advantageous relationships with the leaders of local communities. In 1851 the Yellow river began to shift to its northern course and two years later the Taipings established themselves at Nanjing. The Nian chieftains profited from both developments to set up local defence organizations, which purported to be loyal, but which in reality were an extension of Nian influence. In 1856, perhaps in response to the example of the Taiping rebellion, the Nian chiefs chose Zhang Luoxing to be their leader and adopted elements of a political programme, claiming that they had risen up 'to rescue the impoverished, eliminate treachery, punish wrongdoing, and appease the public indignation'.[10] In 1857 they entered into an informal alliance with the Taiping rebels, with Zhang Luoxing being given the title of a Taiping king.

One reason for the Nian rebels' success was their use of cavalry, and it was to combat this strength that in 1860 the Mongol Prince Senggelinqin was given the task of defeating them. By spring 1863 he had captured and executed Zhang Luoxing and had driven the other Nian leaders out of their 'nest area' in northern Anhui. However, this provoked the Nian to adopt a new strategy of hit-and-run raids. In 1865, when in pursuit of the Nian rebels after such a raid, Senggelinqin was ambushed and killed.

In the meantime two major Muslim rebellions had arisen in south-west and in north-west China. In both cases the underlying cause was the discriminatory treatment of the large Muslim population and the failure of imperial officials to curb the excesses of the local Han Chinese settlers. In the south-west, in Yunnan, the precipitating factor was a dispute over the control of a silver mine. In 1856 the disorder turned into open rebellion with the Muslims headed by Du Wenxiu establishing an independent state with its capital at Dali. Du Wenxiu ruled with the assistance of a Chinese bureaucracy and entertained some hope of recognition by Britain and France. In the north-west, many Muslims had adopted the New Teaching, a mystic form of Islam, and this had brought them into conflict with other Muslims and with Han Chinese. Rebellion broke out in 1862 after a Taiping detachment had traversed the area, provoking both Muslims and Han Chinese to form armed corps. By 1864 Muslim rebels headed by Ma Hualong had occupied much of Gansu.

THE DEFEAT OF THE REBELLIONS

In 1860, when the Taipings were on the verge of capturing

Shanghai and the Western allies were marching on Beijing, the Qing dynasty appeared to be on the verge of collapse. Its recovery and survival for a further half-century was due to a variety of factors, including the limitations of the rebellions and the eventual marshalling of an effective opposition to them.

From its inception the Taiping rebellion had suffered from internal problems. The religious fanaticism of its leaders had denied it popular support and had brought about the internecine strife of 1856. Hong's religious vision caused him to adopt Nanjing as his capital when an all-out assault on Beijing might have succeeded. In 1861 the failure of Li Xiucheng, the Loyal king, and Hong Ren'gan, the Shield king, to co-ordinate their campaigns led to the loss of the key city of Anqing on the middle Yangzi and to the eventual military defeat of the Taiping movement. The other rebellions did not even claim the coherence or the dynastic pretensions of the Taiping Heavenly Kingdom, and apart from the brief liaison between the Taiping and the Nian, no effort was made to co-operate in the overthrow of the Qing.

Such an account of the shortcomings of the rebellions suggests that it was remarkable that they lasted so long. In many respects the rise and persistence of rebellion was an indicator of the limited capacity of the traditional forces of the Manchu dynasty. The main response was to mount an ineffective blockade of Nanjing, a tactic which left them vulnerable to the Taiping counter-attack of 1860, which virtually destroyed the imperial command. Nevertheless when Nanjing fell in 1864 the court was quick to claim credit for the defeat of the rebellion.

Western historians, writing in recent years, have ascribed the main role in the defeat of the rebellions to the new military formations known as the regional armies. When the Taipings swept across Hunan in 1852 the only resistance came from local defence organizations led by the gentry. It was obvious that better-trained and better-equipped forces were needed to oppose the rebels, and it was at this point that the famous Hunanese scholar-official Zeng Guofan (1811–72) began to play a key role. In 1852 he was permitted to return home to observe the customary mourning period for his mother and soon after was ordered by the emperor to recruit and drill militia. Zeng exceeded his instructions and began to recruit mercenaries and to organize an army based on the principles enunciated by Qi Jiguang, who in the sixteenth century had played a notable part in defeating the Japanese pirates. Zeng's army, to be known as the Hunan army, was organized like a Confucian family, with senior officers recruiting their followers on the basis of personal links and with moral exhortation taking the place of impersonal discipline. To pay for this force, at first Zeng obtained permission to sell ranks and titles. However, from 1853 he began to utilize the *lijin*, a new tax on goods in transit, to pay his troops at a rate higher than that paid to regular soldiers. The Hunan army played a crucial role in preventing the Taipings from occupying Hunan in 1854 and in recapturing Anqing in 1861.

In 1862 Li Hongzhang, a former assistant of Zeng Guofan, organized the Anhui or Huai army on the pattern of the Hunan army, although he paid more attention to the adoption of Western arms and military drill. This force assisted in the defence of Shanghai and subsequently achieved the defeat of the Nian rebellion. A reorganized branch of the Hunan army, under the command of Zuo Zongtang, was instrumental in the suppression of the north-west Muslim rebellion.

When the Taiping rebellion broke out, the British government adopted a policy of strict neutrality between the rebels and the insurgents. However, the 1858 Treaty of Tianjin opened the Yangzi as far as Hankou to foreign trade once the rebellion had been suppressed – a provision which made a Manchu victory advantageous to Britain. Active intervention only began in 1862, when British forces assisted in the defence of Shanghai and British ships transported Zeng Guofan's troops down the Yangzi. In Shanghai the foreign community raised a force to be known as the 'Ever-Victorious Army', at one time commanded by Captain Charles Gordon, which co-operated with Li Hongzhang's Huai army in recovering the cities of the Yangzi delta.

THE TONGZHI RESTORATION

The Xianfeng emperor died in 1861 and was succeeded by his infant son, who reigned as the Tongzhi emperor until his death in 1875. Shortly after the emperor's accession a coup at court ousted the officials held responsible for the recent disasters and replaced them with Prince Gong, the emperor's uncle, and

Wenxiang, a senior Manchu official. Also involved in the coup was the emperor's mother, a concubine named Yehonala. Now known as the Empress Dowager Cixi, she was to become the most powerful figure at court until her death in 1908.

During the Tongzhi emperor's reign a 'restoration', that is to say a temporary reversal of the dynasty's decline, was claimed to have taken place. The task of restoration encompassed the defeat of the rebellions, the recovery of dynastic authority, and the repair of the damage caused. The last of the rebellions, the north-west Muslim rebellion, was finally defeated in 1873. The recovery of territory was not yet complete, however, for in 1871 Russia had seized the opportunity presented by the rebellion to occupy the Ili valley in the area then known as Chinese Turkestan. Any loss of territory in Inner Asia implied a betrayal of the achievement of the earlier Manchu emperors. Whereas some senior officials, including Li Hongzhang, argued that priority should be given to coastal defence, the decision was taken to risk war with Russia rather than lose Ili. The crisis was settled in 1881 by the withdrawal of Russia under the terms of the Treaty of St Petersburg, and three years later the region became Xinjiang province.

The recovery of dynastic authority was a more difficult objective – and the extent to which it was achieved has become one of the main points of debate in late Qing history. In this debate two distinct but overlapping issues have emerged, namely the position of the gentry and the emergence of regional power centres.

In the early nineteenth century the gentry, by strict definition the holders of degrees and titles obtained by examination or purchase, numbered about 1.1 million. Only a small minority of them held office, but the remainder performed a vital role in ensuring local control, assisting officials in the performance of their duty and maintaining ideological conformity. In return for their services the gentry occupied a privileged position with regard to the payment of taxes and access to officials. The Qing dynasty recognized the importance of maintaining control of the gentry group. It did this by regulating the quota of candidates who would pass the examinations, by restricting the sale of titles and by requiring the gentry to pursue what has been called 'a life of examination'. It also excluded the gentry from certain key roles: the organization of the mutual security system known as the *baojia*, the collection of taxes, and engagement in military activity unless expressly required to do so.

The mid-nineteenth-century rebellions had a profound effect on the gentry's position. To raise funds the court relaxed restrictions on the sale of degrees and titles. It later rewarded provinces where gentry had contributed to the defeat of rebellion, by raising quotas. As a consequence the total number of gentry rose to about 1.45 million, the largest percentage increases being in those awarded higher degrees and those who obtained degrees by purchase. The gentry's exclusion from the collection of taxes was compromised by the introduction of the *lijin* tax. The prohibition on gentry involvement in military activities had been infringed, since endemic disorder and the effects of the Opium War had encouraged the development of *tuanlian*, gentry-led village defence organizations, an early stage in the increasing militarization of Chinese society. The *tuanlian* were supplemented by mercenary forces hired by gentry associations and eventually by the regional armies, which, although not the instrument of the gentry, owed much to gentry support. The consequent reduction in the dynasty's ability to control the gentry was reinforced by a gentry demand for 'local self-government'. Before the rebellions the view was being expressed that the local administration of the district magistrate had become corrupt and ineffective, and that its functions would be discharged more efficiently by the gentry. This case was taken up at the time of the restoration by the distinguished scholar Feng Guifen, who was an adviser to Li Hongzhang, the governor of Jiangsu. As a result of these changes, although no formal transfer of responsibilities took place from the traditional bureaucratic system to the gentry as a group, a shift in the balance of power at the local level became apparent.

The application of the term 'regionalism' to late Qing China implies that the rebellions brought about a transfer of power from the centre to the regions and into the hands of semi-independent regional leaders. Regionalism was a recurrent feature of periods of dynastic weakness. Symptomatic of its onset was the failure of the dynasty to enforce the rules devised to ensure its dominance, notably the rotation of officials, the 'law of avoidance', the freedom to make appointments, and most importantly the separation of civil and military offices. It has been argued that these rules were flouted by Zeng Guofan and Li Hongzhang, who combined the holding of official positions with the command of regional armies. Zeng Guofan held office in his home province of Hunan and allegedly secured the appointment of his protégé Li Hongzhang to the governorship of Jiangsu. Li Hongzhang was later appointed governor-general of the metropolitan province of Zhili, in which position he served for the unprecedentedly-long term of 25 years. Both Zeng and Li played a leading role in establishing military industries and Li Hongzhang went on to found a commercial empire. However, it is questionable whether their accumulation of influence amounted to regionalism. Both men remained ideologically committed to the support of the dynasty, and the breaches of the system of control were exceptions rather than the rule and may be interpreted as a response to the circumstances created by the rebellions and the challenge of the West.

The rebellions, and their suppression, had caused enormous loss of life and severe economic dislocation. Some areas, for example parts of southern Anhui, were almost completely depopulated. Several million lives were lost in Gansu as a result of the north-west Muslim rebellion. Westerners living in China at the time of the Taiping rebellion estimated that it had cost 20 to 30 million lives, a figure which Ho Ping-ti has since rejected as too low. The rebellions brought some relief from population pressure, particularly in the lower Yangzi region, and this effect was evident even a century later. But the population of China as a whole recovered quickly and probably surpassed its 1850 peak before the end of the century.[11]

After the defeat of the rebellions, the Qing government introduced various measures to relieve the needy and to rehabilitate the agricultural economy. Areas of abandoned land were repopulated by sponsored migration, settlers were supplied with tools and planting materials, and irrigation schemes were repaired. Gentry leaders were encouraged to open or reopen schools and to refurbish libraries. The examination system, which had been discontinued in areas affected by rebellion, was reinstated and it was estimated that after the restoration some two million candidates were presenting themselves annually for examinations at various levels. Education officials were given special instructions to ensure that the *Sacred Edict*, the series of maxims first produced by the Kangxi emperor, was expounded regularly. As it was believed that the burden of the land tax had played an important part in inciting the common people to support the rebellions, taxes were remitted or cancelled in areas which had suffered badly. In a widely publicized gesture the grain tribute paid by the Susongtai circuit in Jiangsu province, which was levied at an exorbitant rate, was slashed.

Such is the evidence to support the case that a genuine restoration did take place. Mary Wright, who wrote the classic study of the restoration, remarked,

> not only a dynasty but also a civilization which appeared to have collapsed was revived to last for another sixty years by the extraordinary efforts of extraordinary men in the 1860s.[12]

However, no effort could reverse the changes in the role of the gentry and even the achievements of the restoration were of doubtful validity. The economic measures taken showed that the restoration leaders had no concept of an economy which was other than agrarian and self-sufficient. The only political change introduced was the establishment, on a temporary basis, of the office known as the Zongli Yamen to deal with foreign affairs. Furthermore the much-vaunted reduction of the Susongtai grain tribute had more to do with achieving an advantageous accommodation between the local elite and the bureaucracy than with relieving the plight of poor peasants.

SELF-STRENGTHENING

Since the Opium War, concern had been expressed about the superiority of the West in terms of military technology. In 1842 Wei Yuan, a scholar and adviser to Lin Zexu, had outlined a plan for maritime defence. He referred to the traditional strategy of 'using barbarians to control barbarians', but he also recommended 'building ships, making weapons, and learning the superior techniques of the barbarians'.[13] In 1860 Feng Guifen, the essayist referred to above as an adviser to Li Hongzhang, called for the adoption of Western knowledge, the manufacture of Western weapons, and the establishment of translation offices and institutions where students would study Chinese classics and also Western languages and mathematics. This led him to enunciate a famous principle:

> If we let Chinese ethics and famous [Confucian] teachings serve as an original foundation, and let them be supplemented by the methods used by the various nations for the attainment of prosperity and strength, would it not be the best of all pro-cedures?[14]

Later in the century Zhang Zhidong encapsulated the same senti-ment in the phrase 'Chinese learning as the base, Western studies for use'. This became the slogan of *ziqiang* or 'self-strengthen-ing'.

In the 1860s the most prominent exponents of self-strengthen-ing were the three senior provincial officials, Zeng Guofan, Li Hongzhang and Zuo Zongtang, all of whom had played a leading role in the defeat of the rebellions. They received some support from Prince Gong and from the Zongli Yamen, the 'office for general management', which had been established in March 1861 to handle relations with the Western powers and *yangwu* or 'foreign matters'. Their activities did not amount to a national policy and *yangwu* remained peripheral to the mainstream of intellectual activity in China until the 1890s.

The first self-strengthening projects included the establish-ment of foreign-language schools in Beijing, Shanghai, Guangzhou and Fuzhou. The first principal of the Tongwenguan, the Beijing school, was W. A. P. Martin, an American missionary who later translated many important Western-language texts into Chinese. At about the same time a number of arsenals were set up which pioneered the introduction of Western technology. In 1862, having captured Anqing, Zeng Guofan set up an arsenal there to manufacture weapons to use against the rebels and he also made the first, albeit unsuccessful, attempt at building a steamship.

The manufacture of weapons and ships to standards compara-ble with those of the West was a tall order, and to accelerate the process attempts were made to buy in foreign technology. In 1863 Zeng Guofan sent Rong Hong (Yung Wing), the first Chinese to receive a degree from an American university, to the

United States to purchase 'machines to make machines'. Buying in foreign technology was not only expensive, but also entailed a risk of dependency. In 1861 Robert Hart, who later became inspector-general of the Imperial Maritime Customs, suggested to Prince Gong that China should buy a steam flotilla from Britain. It was only after the flotilla had reached China that it was disclosed that the ships would remain subject to British control, whereupon they were sent back to Britain.

In 1865 two more ambitious self-strengthening projects were commenced. The Jiangnan arsenal in Shanghai consolidated a number of smaller ventures initiated by Zeng Guofan and Li Hongzhang. The arsenal was equipped with machinery purchased in the United States and it employed Halliday Macartney, a British doctor, as a technical adviser, and a number of Western technicians. Its first task was to supply small arms and ammunition to Li Hongzhang's Huai army for its campaign against the Nian rebels. It later concentrated on launching steamships, which incorporated much Western technology, but which proved very costly to build. In the 1870s it also manufactured Remington rifles under licence, but these were both more expensive and less accurate than rifles produced in the West. The other venture was the establishment of a shipyard at Fuzhou by Zuo Zongtang. This combined a complete ship-building facility with a naval school. The project used French technicians and was funded from the revenues of the Fuzhou customs. By 1874 the shipyard had launched 15 ships, but these were costly to produce and technically obsolescent.

In 1872 Li Hongzhang sent a memorial to the court in which he argued that the self-strengthening programme should be widened to include industrial ventures and transport facilities to support them. This was the beginning of the *fuqiang*, or 'wealth and power' stage of self-strengthening, marked by the establishment of profit-oriented ventures. The first of these was the China Merchants' Steam Navigation Company, founded by Li Hongzhang to compete with foreign shipping, which was taking over China's coastal and riverine commerce. This venture was organized as a *guandu shangban*, that is an 'official-supervision merchant-management' enterprise, a form of organization to be adopted in other *fuqiang* ventures. In these enterprises officials were appointed to the management, but merchants supplied the capital and operated the company. Typically the enterprise was granted a monopoly to ensure its profitability. The China Merchants' Steam Navigation Company had a monopoly for the sea transport of tribute rice from the Yangzi delta to Tianjin. At first the company operated quite effectively under the management of Tang Tingshu, who was an official in that he had acquired a title by purchase and was an expectant sub-prefect. His real expertise derived from his having been a compradore, or Chinese agent, of Jardine, Matheson and Company in Shanghai and he had considerable experience of operating a joint-stock steamship enterprise. In 1876 the China Merchants' bought the merchant fleet of the American-owned Shanghai Steam Navigation Company. However, after the dismissal of Tang Tingshu, Sheng Xuanhuai was appointed director-general. Sheng, who came from a family of officials and who had come to prominence as Li Hongzhang's deputy in economic matters, considered his principal task to be the protection of his and the company's financial interests, and under his direction the opportunity to establish a genuine modern company was lost.

In 1872 Li Hongzhang had pointed out the importance of establishing heavy industry in China and six years later he followed this up by opening the Kaiping coal mines at Tangshan, 60 miles north-east of Tianjin. The project, which was managed by Tang Tingshu, employed British engineers and introduced the latest Western technology, including gas lighting. It began production in 1881 and its output soon began to offset the cost, in foreign exchange, of imported coal. However, from the outset the mine encountered difficulties. Mining was believed to harm the *fengshui*, the spirits of wind and water, and miners were regarded as a subversive group. The problem of transporting coal from the pithead to Tianjin had not been solved, because a request for permission to construct a railway had been withdrawn in anticipation of a refusal by the court. In the event, a tramway was constructed, and a locomotive christened the 'Rocket of China' was built surreptitiously. The project was given retrospective approval, and so became China's first permanent railway.

A number of other self-strengthening enterprises deserve a brief mention. In 1877 Zuo Zongtang established a woollen mill at Lanzhou in Gansu province which pioneered the application of steam power to industry in China. Sheng Xuanhuai was largely responsible for the establishment, in 1880, of the Imperial Telegraph Administration, which went on to create a national network of telegraph lines. The largest industrial enterprise, another venture initiated by Li Hongzhang, was the Shanghai Cotton Cloth Mill, which was given a ten-year monopoly of the use of foreign textile machinery. In 1892 it produced 4 million yards of cloth, but the following year the mill was destroyed by fire. The mill was not insured and the loss was very heavy. Nevertheless the enterprise had demonstrated that it was profitable to invest in modern machinery to produce textiles.

Most accounts of self-strengthening present it as an inadequate policy which initiated some rather unsuccessful ventures. A comparison is sometimes made with the Japanese government's role in pioneering successful enterprises. The government later sold these enterprises and they became the nucleus of the industrial empires of the *zaibatsu*. The evidence of China's failure is detected in the short term in the exposure of China's military weakness in the Sino-Japanese War of 1894–5, and in the long term in the delay before China eventually established a modern industrial base.

Having concluded that self-strengthening was a failure, many writers have then sought to explain why this occurred. Some cite cultural obstacles, referring to the strength of China's cultural tradition and to the incompatibility of Confucianism with the priorities of a modern state. Reference is made to the famous objection made in 1866 by Woren, a Mongol Grand Secretary, to the proposal that the Beijing language school should open a department of mathematics and astronomy and that students should be encouraged to study these subjects by offering them increased stipends and rapid promotion. Woren replied, 'Your slave has learned that the way to establish a nation is to lay emphasis on propriety and righteousness, not on power and plotting.'[15] Alternatively Chinese obscurantism is held responsible, the often-quoted example being the case of the short stretch of railway which was built to connect Shanghai and Wusong. This railway, which was constructed by a British consortium in 1876, was later bought by Chinese officials and destroyed. Their action was derided as irrational and superstitious, but it has been shown that they destroyed the railway because it had been built on

Chinese soil by Westerners who had not obtained permission, and because a fatality on the line had aroused local peasants and threatened disorder.

A second line of explanation concerns the role played by central government. The Qing court has been castigated as obstructive, and the Empress Dowager has been accused of being preoccupied with her own selfish interests. It has frequently been alleged that she misappropriated funds allocated for the purchase of naval ships and used them to refurbish the Summer Palace and to build the famous marble barge still to be seen there. However, most of the expenditure on the palace came after the disastrous naval defeat of 1894, and that débâcle was occasioned principally by the inadequate training of the sailors and the faulty tactics of the fleet. The argument that the Chinese government was indifferent towards, or even hostile to, industrial and commercial undertakings has also been challenged, and in recent years arguments have been put forward which suggest that government economic activity, though falling far short of management of the economy, was more constructive and more extensive than has hitherto been recognized.

Albert Feuerwerker suggested that the 'official-supervision merchant-management' system itself played a part in China's failure to transform the economy in the last four decades of the Qing dynasty. He argued that it encouraged regionalism; that it relied too heavily on raising capital from Chinese merchants in the treaty ports – merchants who looked for quick profits and whose capital was always inadequate; that it continued bureaucratic practices and failed to introduce modern management techniques; that it ensured that the enterprises were vulnerable to official exactions; and that it gave the enterprises an unfair advantage over private activity by the provision of monopoly privileges.[16]

A further line of explanation, one which will be dealt with more comprehensively in the next section, is that self-strengthening was inhibited by Western imperialism. The military threat from the West forced China to concentrate, in the first instance, on the establishment of modern military industries. Defeat in war weakened the authority of central government and burdened it with indemnities, so curtailing investment. However, the self-strengthening enterprises also benefited from the Western presence. A number of foreign experts were employed to establish shipyards and mines. The missionary John Fryer translated technical and scientific texts for the Jiangnan arsenal and edited the *Chinese Scientific Magazine*, which appeared between 1876 and 1892. Foreigners taught in the language schools and Chinese students were sent to America.

WESTERN IMPERIALISM IN THE LATE QING PERIOD

After the conclusion of the Treaty of Tianjin and the Convention of Beijing in 1858–60, the Western powers occupied a privileged position in China. Recognizing the impossibility of altering that situation in the short term, through the 1860s the Chinese government, as represented by the Zongli Yamen, the prototype foreign office, pursued a policy of co-operation. However, the increased Western presence in the country, particularly in the form of missionaries, was a constant cause of friction. In 1870 a massacre of French nuns at Tianjin was punished by the execution of officials held responsible and the imposition of an indemnity. In 1876 the murder near the Burmese frontier of Augustus Margary, a British official, was settled by the Zhefu Convention, which opened the upper Yangzi to foreign trade.

In the meantime the imperial powers were encroaching on China's periphery. The loss to Russia in 1858–60 of the territory north of the Amur and east of the Wusuli rivers has already been mentioned. In 1871 some 54 inhabitants of the Liuqiu islands who had been shipwrecked on the Taiwan coast were murdered by aborigines. Three years later Japan sent a punitive expedition to Taiwan to avenge the murders and then laid claim to the Liuqiu islands, which were incorporated into Japan.

In 1862 France forced the ruling Nguyen dynasty to cede to her the southern part of Vietnam, known as Cochin China. France then obtained the right to navigate the Red river in north Vietnam and in 1874 negotiated a treaty which described Vietnam as an independent state which was willing to accept French protection. In 1880, after Jules Ferry had become premier, France established fortresses on the Red river and took steps to bring the country under French control. China, in the person of Li Hongzhang, responded cautiously, merely encouraging the irregular force known as the Black Flags, composed in part of former Taiping rebels, to harass the French. But then in 1882 Henri Rivière, a French naval officer commanding a minute force, seized Hanoi and precipitated a direct confrontation.

Between 1883 and 1885 France and China fought a sporadic campaign for the control of north Vietnam. After a year of conflict Li Hongzhang and a French naval captain, F. E. Fournier, agreed that if China would withdraw from Vietnam and recognize French treaties with that country, France in return would not demand an indemnity, and would undertake not to invade China and not to make disparaging remarks about China in future treaties. Both countries immediately rejected the agreement. For France it implied that China would retain suzerainty over Vietnam. In China the settlement was denounced by a hardline pressure group known as the *qingliu*, or 'party of purists'. There followed a second phase of the conflict, which was notable for three incidents. The first was the heroic defence of the Chinese outpost at Bac Le, which convinced *qingliu* supporters that China had the capacity to repulse Western troops. However, the second incident, a French attack on the Fuzhou shipyard and the destruction of all but two ships of the Fujian fleet, revealed China's naval weakness only too clearly. Negotiations had resumed when a third incident, the recapture of Langson from the French, precipitated the fall of the French government and made it easier for Li Hongzhang to obtain a settlement. By the Treaty of Tianjin of 1885, China recognized the French protectorate over Vietnam and offered France economic opportunities in south-west China.

China's most important and most regular tributary relationship was with Korea. Korea, like Japan, had adopted a policy of international seclusion, but this policy came under threat after Japan had been 'opened' by the United States in 1853. From 1867 the Zongli Yamen began to suggest to the Korean court that resistance was not practical and that she would be advised to open her ports voluntarily. As a consequence, in 1876 Korea signed an unequal treaty with Japan. From 1879 Li Hongzhang took charge of Chinese relations with Korea, and it was with his encouragement that Korea signed a treaty with the United States, thus denying Japan exclusive access. He also secured a commercial treaty and dispatched a young soldier, Yuan Shikai, to create a modern

Korean army. In the meantime Japan had also become involved in Korean internal affairs, for the most part encouraging the modernizing faction at court, whereas Chinese support went to the more conservative members. In 1884, while China was involved in war with France, pro-Japanese Koreans headed by Kim Ok-kyun attempted a coup, which failed. This prompted China and Japan to conclude the Tianjin Convention, under which the two countries agreed to withdraw their troops from Korea, to cease training the Korean army and to forewarn the other party of any intention to send troops to Korea. In effect China surrendered her claim to exclusive suzerainty in Korea, which now had the status of a co-protectorate of the two countries.

This compromise survived until 1894, when two events occurred. In March Kim Ok-kyun, the leader of the pro-Japanese group, was murdered in Shanghai by the son of a victim of the 1884 coup. His body was returned to Korea in a Chinese warship, an arrangement which was found offensive by the increasingly vociferous proponents of expansionism in Japan. Meanwhile the threat of a popular movement, the Tonghak insurrection, led the Korean government to appeal to China for assistance. These events gave Japan a pretext for sending troops to Korea. Li Hongzhang attempted to negotiate a settlement, but when the Japanese navy sank the *Kowshing*, a Chinese troopship bringing reinforcements to Korea, war became inevitable.

Despite expectations of a Chinese victory, the contest was brief and one-sided. On land, units from Li Hongzhang's Huai army were defeated at Pyongyang. In September 1894, 12 ships from Li Hongzhang's Beiyang fleet engaged 12 Japanese warships off the mouth of the Yalu river. Four Chinese ships were incapacitated and the remainder took refuge at Weihaiwei, where they were later destroyed. These defeats ruthlessly exposed the limitations of military self-strengthening. China was forced to accept the humiliating terms of the Treaty of Shimonoseki, under which China recognized the independence of Korea and ceded Taiwan, the Penghu or Pescadores islands, and the Liaodong peninsula in southern Manchuria to Japan. Japan also acquired unequal treaty rights in China, and these were supplemented by the right to establish industry in the treaty ports, a right which, by the most-favoured nation principle, devolved to the other treaty powers.

China's defeat, and the terms of the Treaty of Shimonoseki, precipitated a scramble for China. In 1891 Russia had started to construct the Trans-Siberian railway to strengthen her position in East Asia. The cession of the Liaodong peninsula to Japan threatened these plans and provoked the Triple Intervention, whereby Russia, abetted by France and Germany, forced Japan to relinquish the peninsula in exchange for a larger indemnity, a humiliation which was to play a part in the coming of the Russo-Japanese War a decade later. In return for this support, in 1896 Li Hongzhang negotiated a secret alliance with Russia which permitted construction of a railway across Manchuria to Vladivostok. It also provided for mutual assistance in the event of a Japanese attack on China, Korea, or Russian possessions in East Asia.

Prussia had negotiated an unequal treaty with China in 1861 and after unification German economic interest in China had grown steadily, being surpassed only by that of Britain. In the 1890s Germany became committed to a drive to world power and in China this was translated into a desire to obtain a naval base and a sphere of influence. The murder in 1897 of two German Catholic missionaries provided justification for the seizure of Qingdao in Shandong province. China was forced to grant Germany a 99-year lease on Jiaozhou bay and concessions for the construction of railways and the extraction of coal. France, not to be outdone, obtained commercial concessions in south-west China and a lease on Guangzhouwan, on the mainland opposite Hainan island. Hitherto Britain, as the satisfied power, had opposed the division of China into spheres of influence. She now sought compensation in the form of a lease on Weihaiwei in Shandong, guarantees for her economic interests in the lower Yangzi, and a 99-year lease on what became known as the 'New Territories', on the mainland opposite Xianggang.

The scramble for concessions was accompanied by a rapid increase in foreign investment in China. For example, France took a large share in the Russo-Chinese Bank, which financed the Chinese Eastern Railway, the line constructed across Manchuria. Belgium played an important part in the financing and construction of the Beijing–Hankou railway, which was completed in 1905. After the Treaty of Shimonoseki had permitted the establishment of industries in the treaty ports, foreign investment in industry increased quickly. The treaty had imposed a large indemnity and for the first time China began to borrow heavily on the international money market.

One of the most extensive and acrimonious debates in modern Chinese history has concerned the economic effects of Western imperialism. According to Karl Marx, and to subsequent generations of Marxist writers, its effect was disastrous. Marx, writing in 1853, noted that the opium trade had caused a silver drain and that the importation of British cotton goods had disrupted the Chinese handicraft industry. The provision in the unequal treaties for foreign control of China's tariffs has been condemned as a device to prevent China imposing import duties to increase revenue and to protect new industries. In the treaty ports, Western commerce and industry enjoyed legal protection and other advantages, and was thus able to outstrip Chinese enterprises. Having defeated China in war, the imperial powers imposed indemnities which encumbered the Chinese government, and extorted concessions which gave them a stranglehold over much of China's heavy industry and communications.

In response to this indictment, some Western economic historians have argued that the evidence of exploitation is either misunderstood or grossly exaggerated. Referring to cotton textiles, Albert Feuerwerker remarked that foreign imports did not destroy the handicraft industry, which in the 1930s was still producing 61 per cent of the cotton cloth woven in China. Instead it forced it to evolve. He pointed out that much handicraft industry was the result of rural poverty, which obliged peasant families to use their surplus labour to supplement their incomes by any means possible. When the import of cotton yarn and cotton cloth began to increase significantly after the treaty settlement of 1858–60, it was machine-made yarn which was in greater demand, because it was both cheaper and stronger, and for this reason it displaced locally-produced yarn. Cloth woven with machine-made yarn, at first imported but later made in China, became widely accepted. The import of foreign-made cloth did increase, but at a lower rate and its principal market was in urban areas. At the same time the distribution of the cotton textile industry changed and more advanced machinery was introduced.[17]

A similarly complex interaction has been traced by Robert

Gardella with reference to the tea industry. In the eighteenth century tea had risen to be China's most important export and until the 1880s exports grew rapidly and prices rose. However by 1900 dominance of the black tea market in Britain and the British Empire had passed to India and Ceylon. In 1908 a provincial assemblyman from Fujian, a major tea-producing area, identified a number of reasons for this disastrous decline. He alleged that Westerners applied the principles of nationalism to the tea industry. Not only did they employ mechanization to greater effect and use better planting methods, but their newspapers also slandered the Chinese tea industry as unsanitary. In China, however, commercial knowledge was not well disseminated, the commercial spirit was dissipated and the Chinese were unable to organize and deal with foreign obstacles. In the twentieth century, attempts were made to revive the tea trade by reducing taxation, by making greater use of machinery in planting and processing, by organizational innovation and by improving quality control, but the lost markets were never recovered. From this, Robert Gardella concluded that although the opening of China to world trade initially had a beneficial effect on tea production, the pre-modern state of the Chinese economy prevented the transformation of the tea industry. On the other hand the production and marketing revolution initiated by the corporate plantations of India and Ceylon responded effectively to rising world demand and brought China's tea boom to an end.[18]

CHRISTIAN MISSIONARIES IN CHINA

Christian missionaries have been described as the cultural arm of Western imperialism and have been accused of having denationalized many Chinese converts and having disintegrated both the body and the spirit of the nation.[19] This sweeping indictment by a Nationalist writer is testimony to the bitterness which Christian mission activity in China has aroused.

Up to the early nineteenth century, Christianity had made little progress in China. The Catholic mission to China, which the Jesuits had initiated in the sixteenth century, had by the eighteenth century become subjected to restriction and persecution, although in some provinces, for example Sichuan, Christian communities had survived and expanded. Robert Morrison of the London Missionary Society, the first Protestant missionary sent to China, reached Guangzhou in 1807, but only made his first convert seven years later. In the 1830s a few missionaries were sent to China by several European Protestant mission societies and others came from the United States, a notable early arrival being Dr Peter Parker, the first medical missionary to China, who established a hospital in Guangzhou.

The position of Christian missionaries in China was transformed by the provisions of unequal treaties and associated agreements. In 1844 and 1846 France obtained edicts which removed many of the restrictions on Christian activity. In the settlement of 1858–60 the French treaties contained clauses which allowed missionaries to move freely about the country and to purchase or rent sites for missions in the interior. By virtue of the most-favoured-nation clause these rights devolved to the other treaty powers, and the extraterritorial agreements protected not only Western missionaries, but also mission property and mission converts. Under these conditions mission activity increased rapidly. In 1844 Roman Catholic missions claimed to have only 240,000 converts, by 1901 this figure had risen to over 720,000, and it had doubled again by 1912. Protestant missionaries always asserted that their criteria for conversions were more stringent than those of the Catholics. In 1853 there were only 350 Protestant communicants, by 1889 the figure had risen to over 37,000, and by 1914 to over a quarter of a million. By that time over 5000 foreign missionaries were working in China, missions had been established in all of China's 18 provinces, at least 250 medical missions and hospitals were operating, and over 2000 mission schools, some of which educated girls, had been opened. Missionaries had also started secondary schools and had founded universities which offered a Western curriculum.

Despite the sincere endeavour of many missionaries, the Chinese response to their religious message and social activities was at best disappointing and at worst violently hostile. The bitterest opposition came from the gentry, who reacted against what they saw as a threat to their position in rural society. Christianity had long been rejected by Confucian scholars as intellectually spurious. Zeng Guofan attacked the Taiping rebels for having plagiarized a foreign religion and for having precipitated an unprecedented crisis in the history of traditional Confucian moral principles. In 1861 a pamphlet entitled *A Record of Facts to Ward Off Heterodoxy* began to circulate, which set out to arouse hostility to Christianity by alleging, for example, that Christian missionaries habitually sexually abused children placed in orphanages.

From the 1860s anti-missionary incidents became commonplace. In 1862, an attempt to re-establish the French Lazarist mission at Nanchang resulted in a riot incited by members of the local gentry. In 1868, the Protestant China Inland Mission, whose leader Hudson Taylor was appalled by the thought that a million Chinese were dying every month without God, opened a station at Yangzhou. The building was soon attacked by a mob and Taylor called for assistance. Four British gunboats were sent to Nanjing, and Zeng Guofan, the governor-general, was forced to dismiss the officials held responsible for the disorder. In 1870, the Catholic orphanage in Tianjin was attacked by a crowd which believed that the orphans were being abused. Some 19 foreigners were killed and the incident nearly provoked a war between France and China. After incidents such as these the Chinese government had to agree to humiliating terms of settlement. After the Tianjin massacre the senior Chinese officials involved were sentenced to life-long exile, 18 Chinese were executed and a fine of 280,000 taels was levied.

NATIONALISM AND REFORM

The later Manchu rulers had copied the model of a Confucian emperor so closely that by the beginning of the nineteenth century, although anti-Manchu feeling had not entirely disappeared, it had ceased to be a political issue. However, the Opium War aroused xenophobia and defeat raised questions about the extent of the Manchu commitment to the national interest.

The development of nationalist sentiment can be traced by referring to various incidents. The skirmish at Sanyuanli in 1841 had briefly encouraged the notion that the Chinese people, led by the gentry, could resist the foreigner. This event has been taken as an example of proto-nationalism. In 1859, the defiance at the Dagu forts showed that foreign naval strength could also be challenged, even though that might lead to further humiliation. However, after 1860 the court followed a co-operative policy with the Western powers and the leaders of the self-strengthening movement adopted a pragmatic attitude towards borrowing from the West. This aroused the anger of scholars and officials such as Woren, who rejected any compromise with the West. In 1875 they made their presence felt when they protested against the dispatch of Guo Songtao to London to apologize for the murder of Augustus Margary. The first settlement of the Ili crisis in 1879 was opposed by Zhang Zhidong, a leading member of the *qingliu* or 'party of the purists'. During the Sino-French War, Zhang Zhidong, now governor-general of Guangdong and Guangxi, inveighed constantly against Li Hongzhang, accusing him of being willing to betray China's national interests. The disastrous defeat in the Sino-Japanese War destroyed the credit of the self-strengtheners and raised acute fears for the nation's survival. In its aftermath, in response to the scramble for China, a determination to embrace all practical means to preserve China may be observed, for example in the rights recovery movement, which brought together officials, gentry and merchants in endeavours to recover concessions granted to the foreign powers. From these incidents and from the social changes which occurred in the late nineteenth century, there developed the sentiment which may properly be called Chinese nationalism.

THE 100 DAYS' REFORMS, 1898

Defeat in the Sino-Japanese War and the subsequent scramble for China had a momentous effect on Chinese intellectuals, who responded violently to what they perceived as the threat of national extinction. A few – the most notable example being Sun Zhongshan – abandoned not only the Manchu dynasty, but also the system of imperial government, and began to plot a revolution. Others were so shocked that they proposed radical reforms to the system. Among them was Kang Youwei, a scholar from Guangdong, who had already achieved notoriety for his reinterpretation of the classical texts. When the terms of the Treaty of Shimonoseki became known, Kang Youwei circulated a petition which called for the rejection of the treaty and the introduction of a wide range of reforms. At the same time some senior provincial officials, for example Zhang Zhidong, the governor-general of Hunan and Hubei, pressed ahead with a range of practical reforms, such as the introduction of electric lighting to Changsha and the inclusion of Western subjects in the syllabus of the *shengyuan* degree.

Kang Youwei's chance came two years later. By this time he had published another disquisition on the classical texts, in which he had argued that Confucius, although claiming to revive the past, had in fact been a reformer. Kang's reputation as a radical thinker gained him an audience with the young Guangxu emperor, who since 1889 had exercised nominal authority, the Empress Dowager having officially retired. At that meeting Kang Youwei suggested to the emperor that he might bring about a 'revolution from above' similar to that achieved by the Meiji government in Japan 30 years previously. His suggestion was received and for a 100 days, starting from 11 June 1898, the emperor with the assistance of Kang Youwei and two other reformers, Liang Qichao and Tan Sitong, promulgated 40 edicts proposing wide-ranging reforms. They included the abolition of the formal examination composition, the 'eight-legged essay'; the creation of a ministry of agriculture; the phasing out of the Army of the Green Standard and the raising of a national conscript army. The only political reform proposed was to extend the right to send memorials to the emperor, a right hitherto granted only to senior officials, to all subjects.

On 21 September the Empress Dowager brought the reform programme to an abrupt halt. With the backing of Yuan Shikai, who after his service in Korea had organized the Beiyang Army in Zhili, she ordered the arrest and execution of the leading reformers on the grounds that they had been plotting a coup. Kang Youwei and Liang Qichao escaped, but Tan Sitong was among those executed.

The obvious reason for the failure of the reform programme was the opposition of the Empress Dowager who has been portrayed as an implacable opponent of reform. However, her long-term support of Li Hongzhang suggests that she did not object to reform if it did not threaten her position. Many writers have accepted the view put forward by H. B. Morse, that the emperor and Kang Youwei were impractical reformers, whose over-ambitious reform programme threatened a wide variety of vested interests, including the gentry who were uneasy about the change in the examinations, senior officials who were dismayed by the loss of their privileges, and Manchus who resented the loss of their sinecures.[20] Undoubtedly the reforms were handled in a politically inept manner, but it should be remembered that Zhang Zhidong had introduced a similarly wide range of reforms in Hunan and that opposition there only arose when radical reformers proposed unacceptable measures such as promoting intermarriage with the white race. Jack Gray has suggested recently that the Empress Dowager intervened because the reforms threatened to remove her power of patronage and because the changes in the rules relating to communications raised the spectre of 'people's rights'.[21]

THE BOXER UPRISING

Scarcely had the repercussions of the Hundred Days' reforms died down before the Qing court was faced with a very different sort of crisis, a major peasant uprising in north China.

The origins and objectives of the Boxer Uprising have been subject to a variety of interpretations. The event has often been referred to as a rebellion, implying that the Boxers were antidynastic. In fact the Boxers never rebelled against the Qing, and in 1900, when threatened with a foreign attack on the capital, the court declared its support for the Boxers. The Boxers have been described as descended from the White Lotus rebels of the early nineteenth century, but it has been pointed out that in their day the Boxers were regarded as a new phenomenon and that they did not share the White Lotus belief in the Eternal Venerable Mother or the coming of the Maitreya Buddha. Nor is there a clear connection between the Boxers and the martial arts associations which were common in Shandong where the uprising had its origins.

The Boxer movement arose in Zhili and Shandong, an area of high population density which in 1876 had experienced a severe famine. In 1898 the Yellow river burst its banks and caused extensive flooding. Two years later a prolonged drought inflicted further loss of life. The region had also suffered from Western economic imperialism, for example the importation of machine-spun yarn had affected the cotton-growing areas in the west. Several missionary societies were active in the area, the most aggressive being the German Steyl Society. The murder of two missionaries from this society had served as the pretext for the German seizure of Jiaozhou bay in 1897. Banditry was an endemic problem and to combat it the governor of the province had permitted the formation of militia forces. This provided a cover for the emergence, in the south of the province, of the Big Sword Society, a martial arts society which became prominent in the conflict between Christian congregations and the rest of the population.

The movement to be known as the Boxers derived from a group calling itself Spirit Boxers, which appeared in north-west Shandong in 1896. The group, which professed the simplest ethical principles – 'respect your parents, live in harmony with your neighbours' – engaged in ritual boxing, which was not a martial art but an activity originally associated with healing, and later developed as an invulnerability ritual which provided protection against the power of the Christians. They also practised spirit possession, believing that any adherent who was pure in heart could become possessed of a particular spirit. From about 1898 the Spirit Boxer movement began to grow and to threaten Christian converts. The following year the name of the movement was changed to 'Boxers United in Righteousness' and clashes between the group and Christians became increasingly common and violent.

At first, provincial officials attempted to maintain an even-handed policy towards the Christians and the Boxers. However as the situation deteriorated some officials, including Yu Xian the governor of Shandong, were accused by foreigners of complicity with the Boxers. Late in 1899 Yu Xian was dismissed and replaced by Yuan Shikai, but by this time the court's policy was beginning to change. In January 1900 the Empress Dowager, who was alert to the danger of seeming to be hostile to a popular movement, issued an edict which urged officials to distinguish between outlaws and those law-abiding citizens who practised ritual arts to protect themselves.

By May 1900, groups of Boxers were appearing on the streets

of Beijing and Tianjin. Most were young men, but a group known as the Red Lantern Society comprised young women, who it was said could ride on clouds and kindle fire to burn the warships of the Westerners. By June the threat to foreigners was so serious that Britain sent a force of 2000 men under Admiral Seymour to protect the legations in Beijing. The Boxers cut the Tianjin–Beijing railway line and forced Seymour to withdraw. In retaliation the Western powers seized the Dagu forts.

On 21 June, the Empress Dowager threw in her lot with the Boxers and issued a 'declaration of war', which laid the blame for the disorder on foreign aggression. In some parts of north China officials came out on the Boxers' side, the most notorious example being that of Yu Xian, now governor of Shanxi, who rounded up and executed 44 men, women and children from missionary families. However, in Shandong Yuan Shikai suppressed the Boxers and in other parts of China senior officials distanced themselves from what was happening in the north.

In Beijing the foreign population was besieged in the legations for 55 days. The siege was raised on 14 August when a relief expedition reached Beijing. There followed an orgy of looting. The allies sent out punitive expeditions under the German Field Marshal von Waldersee, which inflicted heavy punishment on towns which had been the scene of Boxer activity. The Boxer Protocol, setting out the terms acceptable to the allies before they would withdraw, provided that ten officials including Yu Xian should be executed and that others should be required to commit suicide or to suffer banishment. It also stipulated the dispatch of apology missions to Germany and Japan, the destruction of the Dagu forts, and the suspension of the examinations for five years in cities where the Boxers had been active. Finally an indemnity of 450 million taels was levied, payable in instalments over 39 years. To facilitate payment the tariff on external trade was raised.

The Boxer Uprising had several important consequences. The indemnity imposed a heavy and long-lasting financial burden, although the United States took the lead in waiving payment and using part of the proceeds to establish Qinghua University in Beijing. While the allied powers were marching to the relief of the Beijing legations, Russian troops had occupied Manchuria. After the settlement Russia failed to withdraw as promised and this aroused Chinese nationalist feeling and contributed to the rise of tension between Japan and Russia. The uprising left a contradictory legacy: foreigners in the 1920s used the spectre of Boxerism to delegitimize Chinese nationalism, but writers sympathetic to that cause invoked the Boxers as 'a dramatic example of ordinary Chinese peasants rising up to rid China of the hated foreign presence'.[22]

THE LATE QING REFORMS

When the allied forces entered Beijing, the Empress Dowager and the court fled ignominiously to Xi'an. In January 1901, after having reflected on the gravity of the situation, Cixi issued a decree calling upon senior officials to submit proposals for reform. The most important submission came from Zhang Zhidong and Liu Kunyi, two of the most senior provincial officials. They suggested a programme of reforms relating to education, the military, the economy and the operation of government. This was adopted as a basis for action and a start was made even before the Empress Dowager returned to the capital in January 1902.

Educational reform began in 1901 with the abolition of the 'eight-legged essay'. An edict required all prefectures to establish middle schools and all districts to establish primary schools. In these schools, Western subjects would be taught alongside the traditional syllabus. Another edict approved the sending of students to study abroad and provided that on their return they would be eligible for the award of degrees. In September 1905, after the defeat of Russia in the Russo-Japanese War, the empress dowager took the momentous step of announcing the immediate ending of the imperial examinations.

The need for military reform had been made abundantly clear by the defeats of the Sino-Japanese War, and in the years after that disaster new armies had been raised, notably by Yuan Shikai whose Beiyang Army, based at Xiaozhan near Tianjin, was China's best-trained and best-equipped force. In 1901 the traditional military examinations were abolished and the first steps were taken to disband the Army of the Green Standard and to replace it with a new national army. In 1906 an army ministry was created, as part of a process intended to impose central control over all the armed forces in the empire. After the death of the Empress Dowager and of the Guangxu emperor in 1908, Prince Chun, the new emperor's father, made a determined effort to place Manchus in leading positions in the army and navy.

Several reforms with economic implications were introduced although nothing like a programme for economic development was attempted. A change of attitude towards merchants was evident in the promulgation of a commercial code and the establishment of a ministry of commerce. This new ministry was responsible for railway construction, which hitherto had been the field of action of provincial merchant and gentry groups that had recovered rights alienated to foreign interests. In 1911 the government negotiated a loan from a consortium of British, French, German and American banking interests, to be used to develop Manchuria, to reform the currency, and to buy out the provincial railway companies, and in particular the company which held the right to build the Guangzhou–Hankou railway. This issue was to be one of the precipitating factors of the 1911 revolution.

The case for a constitutional monarchy had been argued persuasively by the reformer and writer Liang Qichao, who, after the failure of the Hundred Days' reforms, had fled to Japan. In 1905, after the Japanese victory over Russia had seemed to betoken the victory of constitutionalism over autocracy, the Empress Dowager had announced her conversion to constitutionalism and sent missions abroad to study constitutional systems. In 1908 a programme was announced which provided for the promulgation of a constitution in 1916 and for the convening of a parliament in the following year. In the meantime, provincial assemblies were to be elected by an electorate composed of men over the age of 25 who either had an educational qualification or owned property. The provincial assemblies were only allowed to discuss a limited range of topics and to make recommendations to the provincial authorities. These assemblies began to meet in 1909 and soon became a forum for critical comments on the policies of central government. Pressure on government to accelerate the reforms led in 1910 to a decision to promulgate the constitution in 1912 and to convene the parliament in the following year.

The late Qing reforms were once dismissed as a futile attempt by a dynasty to defer its inevitable fall. More recently several writers have argued that the reforms contributed to that débâcle. Frederic Wakeman noted how the reforms accelerated the formation of new elites who were to play a large role in the fall of the dynasty.[23] He was referring to the educational reforms which destroyed the basis of the dynasty's control over the gentry and created a new category of educated youth, and to the military reforms, which led to the recruitment of soldiers inspired by nationalism and apprehensive of Manchu dominance. Other writers have emphasized the negative impact of the reforms, which were expensive, often ineffective and fell far short of the hopes of those who had looked forward to the establishment of a genuine constitutional monarchy.

6

. . . .

Republican China, 1911−49

On 10 October 1911, a date thereafter known as the 'Double Tenth', a mutiny headed by New Army officers broke out at Wuchang. They seized the city and obtained the support of the Hubei provincial assembly, which declared the province independent from the empire. By December all the provinces of central and southern China had followed suit. A republic was declared and Sun Zhongshan (Sun Yatsen) was invited to become provisional president. The Qing court appealed to Yuan Shikai, the most influential military commander in the north, to come to its support, but instead he decided to support the republic and to force the emperor to abdicate.

Between 1912 and 1916 Yuan Shikai ruled, first as president and then as emperor. His death in 1916 left a political vacuum and until 1928 the government in Beijing exercised only symbolic authority over the country, real power resting in the hands of warlords. During these years several important events took place: the May Fourth Movement, the name given to the political and cultural movement which climaxed in 1919; the founding of the Chinese Communist Party (CCP) in 1921; the reorganization of the Guomindang, or Nationalist Party; and the Northern Expedition of 1926–8 which led to the nominal reunification of the country.

Between 1928 and 1937 the Guomindang attempted to transform China into a modern state, while at the same time harassing the CCP, with which it had split in 1927. In 1931 Japan seized

Manchuria but Jiang Jieshi, now leading the Guomindang, refused to respond. He preferred to pursue the Communists, who set out on the Long March in 1934. By 1936 Japanese encroachment on north China forced Jiang Jieshi to agree an united front with the Communists, and in the following year the Sino-Japanese War broke out. After an initial period of heroic resistance, the Guomindang retreated to Chongqing while the Communists fought on from their base at Yan'an. After the defeat of Japan in 1945, the Guomindang and CCP fought a civil war which resulted in the Communist victory of 1949.

THE SOCIAL BACKGROUND TO THE REVOLUTION

By the beginning of the twentieth century major changes were taking place in Chinese society, particularly in the treaty ports where Western influence was most apparent. The traditional elite, the gentry, no longer relied on the examination system to justify its position. Wealthy gentry families moved into the cities and employed members of the lower gentry to manage their rural estates. Although the gentry affected to despise commerce, many engaged in commercial activities and on occasion joined with merchants, forming what has been described as a 'merchant-gentry alliance'.

The opening of China to world trade and the emigration of many thousands of Chinese to the Americas and South-east Asia had led to the emergence of a new merchant class. This included compradores, a Portuguese term first used to describe the agents of Western firms who handled the Chinese side of the business, but later applied to those who engaged in foreign trade or utilized their familiarity with Western business methods. It also included wealthy Overseas Chinese who invested part of their fortunes in China. The great majority of the new merchant class were owners of small enterprises which were affected by the changing economic environment. To protect their interests they formed chambers of commerce, which in 1904 were given official recognition.

The late Qing educational and military reforms had also contributed to the process of social change. The number of modern schools rose from 35,787 with an enrolment of 1,006,743 pupils in 1907, to 87,272 schools with an enrolment of 2,933,387 pupils in 1912. It has been said of these schools, where ill-prepared teachers taught a syllabus which was divorced from Chinese reality, that they 'did more to encourage protest and demands than to consolidate the imperial monarchy'.[1] A small but influential group of students went overseas. Many of them went to Japan where they studied a variety of subjects, but the main lesson they learned was the importance of nationalism, for they received constant reminders of the strength of Japan and the weakness of their own country.

Since the formation of the regional armies, the status of the military, which by tradition was very low, had begun to rise. After the abolition of the traditional military examinations and the creation of the new armies, a new class of professional soldiers began to appear. Young men from good families were sent abroad to study, usually to Japan, where they encountered the idea that the army might take the lead in defending and regenerating the nation. When they returned to China they became officers in the New Army units, of which the most prominent were the Beiyang Army formed by Yuan Shikai in the north and the Self-Strengthening Army raised by Zhang Zhidong at Nanjing.

In the years before the 1911 revolution other groups in Chinese society began to play a political role, albeit a minor one. The Treaty of Shimonoseki had permitted the establishment of foreign-owned industry in the treaty ports. In Shanghai and a few other cities an industrial proletariat had begun to form, numbering about 661,000 by 1912. Workers, many of whom were women, were often recruited as contract labour, which left them entirely dependent on the contractor to negotiate their conditions of work, which were usually very poor. Under these circumstances the first industrial strikes took place and a labour movement began to form.

The cities also became the forum for mass political protests. In 1905 a boycott was organized in Shanghai and several other cities to protest against the restriction of Chinese immigration into the United States. In 1908, after the Chinese government had been forced to apologize abjectly over an incident concerning a Japanese ship, the *Tatsu Maru*, street demonstrations took place in Guangzhou, and Japanese goods were burned. Among the demonstrators were many women who urged their supporters to wear rings engraved with the words 'National Humiliation'.

These signs of change were referred to as 'Young China'. Young China was, of course, an urban phenomenon; rural China remained, if not unchanging, at most only remotely affected.

THE REVOLUTIONARY MOVEMENT

In the Guomindang version of the history of the 1911 revolution the revolutionary movement, headed by Sun Zhongshan, played a key role in the overthrow of the Manchus. Modern historians have been less convinced of the centrality of the revolutionaries in the events that led to the fall of the Qing dynasty and the collapse of the imperial system. Mary Wright suggested that at most the revolutionary movement created a revolutionary tradition. In 1911 it was too frail an instrument to be able to bring about a revolution on its own.[2]

Despite this disclaimer, the record of the early revolutionaries and their organizations is of interest. Sun Zhongshan (1866–1925), the founder of the first revolutionary group, was born near Guangzhou and studied in Xianggang where he was baptized a Christian. He lived for a time with his brother in Hawaii before returning to Xianggang to study medicine. Having become interested in politics, in 1894 he offered his services to Li Hongzhang, but his offer was ignored and thereafter he abandoned thoughts of reform and turned to revolution. He formed a revolutionary organization in Honolulu and in the following year he was involved in an abortive attempt to capture Guangzhou. In 1896 he was kidnapped by the Chinese authorities on the streets of London and would have been smuggled back to China for trial and execution had he not contacted friends, who publicized his plight in the *Globe* and secured his release. Sun came into contact with Kang Youwei and Liang Qichao, the leading Chinese nationalists in exile in Japan, but he did not accept their plans for a constitutional monarchy or their links with the gentry reform movement. Instead he preferred to seek funds from Overseas Chinese and to attempt uprisings with the help of secret society members.

Nationalist accounts of the revolution have emphasized the

contribution of Sun Zhongshan at the expense of that of other revolutionary figures. Zou Rong (1885–1905), like many other Chinese students living in Japan, became a revolutionary when Russia failed to withdraw troops from Manchuria after the Boxer Uprising. His manifesto, *The Revolutionary Army*, published in the comparative safety of the International Settlement of Shanghai, contained a violent attack on the Manchus. He was imprisoned for issuing inflammatory writings and died in gaol at the age of 19. Qiu Jin (1875–1907) was also a student in Japan, where she took up the cause of women's liberation. This she believed would only be achieved in conjunction with China's political liberation. On her return to China she joined the Zhejiang Restoration Society, became involved in an attempted revolutionary coup and was executed. Huang Xing (1874–1916), a more conventional revolutionary, came from Hunan. After studying in Japan he returned to his home province where he established the Society for China's Revival. A feature of this society was its early recognition of the importance of infiltrating the armed forces.

In 1905 Sun Zhongshan, with the support of Huang Xing, formed the Tongmenghui, or Revolutionary Alliance, in Tokyo. The alliance, which brought together a number of revolutionary organizations, adopted a manifesto written by Sun which contained a four-point programme: drive out the Manchus, restore China, establish a republic, and equalize land-ownership. The first revolutionary stage would be a military dictatorship, which would be followed by a period of one-party government or 'political tutelage' and eventually by the introduction of democracy.

Over the next few years several abortive revolutionary incidents occurred. In 1906, at Pingliuli in eastern Hunan, the Gelaohui or Elder Brother Society, in conjunction with dissident miners and soldiers, attempted an uprising. Some students from the Revolutionary Alliance took part and the rebels variously called for the establishment of a republic or the restoration of a Chinese Empire. However, the rebels were no match for well-armed government soldiers. In 1910, Huang Xing and other revolutionaries organized a mutiny in the ranks of the Guangzhou New Army, but the mutiny broke out prematurely and was easily suppressed. Nine months later the Alliance was involved in the

Guangzhou revolt, which turned into a devastating defeat for the Guangdong revolutionaries.

THE 1911 REVOLUTION

Although the revolutionary attempts had dramatized the challenge to Manchu rule, at the beginning of 1911 there was no expectation that China was on the verge of a revolution. However, two incidents were to precipitate a crisis and expose the weakness of the Manchu dynasty and the frailty of the imperial system.

The first incident derived from the issue of railway construction. In 1908 Zhang Zhidong had begun to negotiate an international loan, part of which was to be used to finance the construction of a national railway network, a plan which threatened the interests of the consortia formed by merchants and gentry to build provincial railway lines. Zhang Zhidong died in 1909 and his place was taken by Sheng Xuan-huai, a bureaucratic capitalist who had previously run the Hanyeping Coal and Iron Company at Hanyang. Sheng was a leading exponent of railway nationalization and he already stood accused of selling out China's rights by borrowing from foreigners. In May 1911 Sheng proposed the nationalization of all the noncompleted railways for which provincial gentry-merchant capital had been raised. When investors learned that they would only recover part of their investment, loud protests were expressed, particularly in Sichuan. The Sichuan Railway Protection League, a body with strong links with the provincial assembly, was established, mass meetings were held and a campaign of civil disobedience began. The governor-general of the province arrested the League's leaders, broke up demonstrations and called for military reinforcements. Nevertheless, by September local militia and secret societies, led in some cases by members of the Revolutionary Alliance, virtually controlled the province.

The second incident had its origins in the military modernization which began after the Sino-Japanese War and continued with the late Qing reforms. The new armies recruited better-educated soldiers, many of whom were susceptible to nationalist propaganda. After revolutionary attempts like the Pingliuli uprising had demonstrated that it was futile to oppose the new armies, revolutionaries had tried to infiltrate them. This was done most successfully in Hubei, where the New Army units were stationed at Wuhan, the triple city on the Yangzi, which included Hankou with its important foreign concession. In 1908 a group calling itself the Political Study Society, which had links with the local treaty-port press, was formed among soldiers of the 41st Regiment of the Hubei Army. The society was broken up but the revolutionaries regrouped in early 1911 to form the Literature Society.

In 1911 other events contributed to the development of a revolutionary atmosphere. Central China, and Hankou in particular, had suffered from an economic depression. Severe flooding of the Yangzi and Han rivers had cost an estimated 2,500,000 lives. In April one of the much-vaunted constitutional reforms at last came into effect: the appointment of a responsible cabinet. However, it was composed of eight Manchus, one Mongol and only four Chinese. Then came the controversy over the nationalization of the railways, which resulted in some units of the Hubei Army being sent to Sichuan to suppress a movement for which many soldiers felt some sympathy.

By October, it has been said, 'Central China lacked only the spark that would light the prairie fire.'[3] The Literature Society, together with other revolutionary organizations in Hubei and Hunan, had planned an insurrection for the middle of the month. The plot was discovered and this forced the revolutionaries to advance the date to 10 October. With surprising ease the revolutionaries seized Wuchang, on the opposite bank of the Yangzi from Hankou. They set up a military government, which was supported by the Hubei provincial assembly. Having declared independence from the empire and the establishment of a republic, they sent messages to other provincial assemblies and New Army units inviting them to follow suit. By early December 1911 all the provinces of south and central China had seceded from the empire.

The fate of the Qing dynasty, however, remained undecided. The most important of the new armies, the Beiyang Army, which was stationed in the north, was less responsive to revolutionary propaganda and did not react immediately to events in central China. Yuan Shikai, the army's creator, had been dismissed in

January 1909. In November 1911 the Manchus invited him back to serve as prime minister. Yuan, who had also been approached by the revolutionaries, accepted the offer from the court. Imperial forces recaptured Hankou but were repulsed at Nanjing, and this reverse may have convinced Yuan that the future lay with the revolution. He encouraged the Qing dynasty to abdicate with the promise of a generous settlement, and in March 1912 he succeeded Sun Zhongshan as president of the new republic.

Many issues relating to the 1911 revolution have been the subject of debate, not least whether the event – which was followed soon after by the decline of the republic into warlordism – should be counted as a genuine revolution. Two issues are of particular interest: the motivation of the gentry, and the part played by the revolutionaries. In the past the gentry group had transferred its allegiance to a new dynasty when it felt that the old dynasty could no longer secure its interests. It has been suggested that in 1911 some gentry leaders, particularly those who had played a prominent role in the provincial assemblies, were motivated by constitutionalism, that is to say their main aim was constitutional reform and the establishment of a parliament. They abandoned the dynasty because they lost faith in the Qing commitment to political reform. However, for many other members of the gentry dynastic decline, the rise of violence, the activities of the secret societies, all spelled out danger. They sided with the revolution because they believed the New Army units could best preserve order, and because they saw in the situation the opportunity to enhance their own power at local and provincial level.

The role of the revolutionaries was ambiguous. The Revolutionary Alliance did not contribute directly to the Wuchang coup. Sun Zhongshan himself was in the United States and read of the event in a newspaper. The Wuchang rebels persuaded Li Yuanhong, a New Army brigade commander who was not a revolutionary, to head the government. By November almost all the revolutionary leaders had concluded that Yuan Shikai held the key to the success of the revolution. When Sun Zhongshan returned to China in December he was apprehensive that more fighting might lead to foreign intervention and he too, albeit reluctantly, turned to Yuan and resigned the presidency to him. From this sequence of events one might deduce that although the revolutionaries and Sun Zhongshan had helped create the political atmosphere in which the 1911 revolution took place, they had little control over the events which ensued.

THE PRESIDENCY OF YUAN SHIKAI

The critics of Yuan Shikai have accused him of betraying the 1898 reformers, of deserting the Qing dynasty and of abandoning the republic to make himself emperor, at all times acting on selfish motives. His biographer E. P. Young, while admitting that Yuan had faults, has suggested that throughout his presidency he pursued policies which he believed to be in the best interests of his country. Apprehensive of foreign pressure on China's sovereignty, he set out to centralize the administration through reforms, which were introduced in stages to reduce the risk of disorder.[4]

According to the constitution of the new republic, the president exercised considerable power, but was required to share that power with the prime minister and the provisional parliament. Tang Shaoyi, the first prime minister, and four other cabinet ministers were members of the Revolutionary Alliance, which also held about one-third of the seats in the provisional parliament. This arrangement soon proved unmanageable. In June, Tang and the other Alliance members of the cabinet resigned after a row over a foreign loan. In August, Yuan Shikai announced that the first parliamentary elections would take place at the end of the year. In preparation the Alliance amalgamated with four minor parties and renamed itself the Guomindang, or Nationalist Party. In the elections the Guomindang, headed by Song Jiaoren, who had drafted the constitution, won a majority in both houses of parliament. The new party immediately began to criticize some of the actions of Yuan's government, particularly its willingness to take foreign loans, and began to demand that the power of parliament should be increased. Yuan Shikai's response was to have Song Jiaoren assassinated.

There followed the event known as the Second Revolution. In April 1913 Yuan Shikai, without the prior consent of parliament, contracted a 'Reorganization Loan' of $25,000,000 from a British, French, German, Russian and Japanese consortium. The loan, which was secured on the revenue of the salt monopoly, was ostensibly intended to re-finance China's existing debts and to pay for a reform of the administration. However, Yuan's opponents were sure that he intended to use it to bankroll a campaign of suppression against his political opponents. This suspicion was confirmed in June when Yuan dismissed three military governors, including Li Liejun, the governor of Jiangxi, with whom he had already clashed. Li Liejun thereupon declared his province independent and tried to rally military support. But Yuan had anticipated the danger and although his opponents captured Nanjing and threatened Shanghai, by September the attempted revolution had been crushed.

After the Second Revolution Yuan established himself as a dictator. Martial law was declared, newspapers were closed down, opposition members of parliament were arrested and many thousands of people were killed. The Guomindang members of parliament were expelled and the party itself proscribed. Yuan then dissolved the provincial assemblies, thereby tampering with the interests of the gentry. At the same time, Yuan introduced several measures some of which, for example his attempt to revise the fiscal relationship between the province and central government, continued his policy of centralization. Other reforms, for example one which aimed to provide education for all Chinese boys, and another which sought to raise standards of agriculture, hinted at a wider agenda of social improvement.

At the time of the Second Revolution, Yuan had justified his actions on the grounds of national unity. In 1915 his commitment to that cause was tested severely by the presentation by Japan of the notorious document known as the 'Twenty-one Demands'. When the First World War broke out, Japan opportunistically declared war on Germany and seized the German base at Qingdao in Shandong. In January 1915 the Japanese government presented to Yuan Shikai 21 demands divided into five groups, which included the transfer to Japan of all German interests in Shandong, the extension of Japan's lease on the Liaodong peninsula, the grant of further commercial rights in Manchuria, and joint Sino-Japanese control of the Hanyeping industrial complex. The fifth group required the Chinese government to use Japanese advisers in its military, police and financial administrations, thereby turning China into a 'second Korea'. The doc-

ument was leaked to the Chinese press and an outburst of patriotic protests followed. Britain and the United States expressed
concern but advised that China would have to accept the ultima-
tum. On 7 May 1915, Yuan acceded to the first four groups of
demands but deferred agreement on the fifth group. That day
was to be commemorated as the day of national humiliation and
Yuan's prestige was never to recover from his compromise on
the issue.

Yuan's willingness to compromise has been attributed to his
desire to become emperor. His opponents had long suspected
him of cherishing that ambition, but he only became committed
to it in 1915 after the presentation of the Twenty-one Demands.
He believed that a restoration was the preference of the mass of
the population, which had never accepted the republic. He was
encouraged in this view by Dr F. J. Goodnow, his American
political adviser, who argued that China's history and traditions
made her more suited to a monarchy than to a republic. Despite
evidence of opposition to his plans, in December Yuan accepted
an invitation from his supporters to become emperor and on 1
January 1916 his reign began.

The monarchical venture was not a success. Intellectual criticism was led by Liang Qichao, who in the past had been an
advocate of a constitutional monarchy, but who now believed
that the mystique of the monarchy had been destroyed irrevoca-
bly. Japan and the Western imperial powers expressed doubts
about the wisdom of the move and Japan began to supply funds
to Yuan's political opponents. The most serious opposition came
from a group of military men headed by Cai E, the military governor of Yunnan. Having protested in vain against Yuan's monarchical plans, in December 1915 Cai E declared Yunnan independent, and in the following month he led his troops into Sichuan.
Yuan dispatched units of the Beiyang Army, which should have
been able to defeat Cai E easily, but a combination of Cai E's
enterprising military tactics and the defection of Yuan's supporters led to the loss of Sichuan. By now support for Yuan Shikai
was crumbling rapidly and in March he abandoned his claim to
the monarchy. Three months later he died.

THE WARLORD ERA, 1916–28

Yuan Shikai's death left a political vacuum which in the short term proved impossible to fill. His rejection of the republic had discredited parliamentary democracy, but his ventures into dictatorship, and his restoration of the monarchy, had shown that neither alternative had enough support. In the ensuing period the central government ceased to exert national authority, and effective power fell into the hands of military governors or warlords.

The origins of warlordism has been the subject of a lively debate. Franz Michael argued that Chinese history showed a pattern of recurrent decline in the authority of the central government and the development of regionalist power centres; that the nineteenth-century rebellions had left a legacy of regionalism, and the collapse of the empire completed the disintegration and ushered in the era of warlordism.[5] Other writers, for example Jerome Ch'en, have suggested that warlordism in China was a modern phenomenon which could be traced to the effects of military modernization. According to Ch'en, Yuan was the founder of the Chinese modern army and his legacy to the republic was a large number of warlords. When he was alive, they supported him; when he was dead, they fought amongst themselves.[6] Recently Edward A. McCord has pointed out that warlords emerged during the continuing crisis of political authority that followed the fall of the imperial system, a crisis which revolved around issues such as the relative powers of president and parliament and the relationship between the civil and military power.[7]

Yuan Shikai was succeeded as president by Li Yuanhong, the 1912 constitution was revived and there was a brief period of national unity. This was destroyed by disputes between Li and Duan Qirui, a general in the Beiyang Army, in the first instance over the validity of the 1912 constitution, which in some eyes had been superseded by the constitution introduced by Yuan Shikai in 1914, and secondly over whether China should enter the war against Germany. In July 1917 the vacillations of the Beijing government encouraged Zhang Xun, known as the 'pig-tailed general' because his troops had retained their queues, to march into Beijing and briefly to restore the last Manchu emperor. He was quickly expelled and Duan Qirui regained control. However, Li Yuanhong was forced to resign the presidency, his

place being taken by Feng Guozhang, another former commander under Yuan Shikai. In 1918 Duan Qirui outraged nationalist
opinion by accepting the 'Nishihara loans' provided by Japanese
interests to advance their claims in Manchuria.

From this point onwards the Beijing government, although it
continued to receive the recognition of the foreign powers,
ceased to exercise effective authority over the nation. Over the
next decade, the distribution of power was fluid, but it may be
indicated in broad outline by saying that initially north and central China was divided between the supporters of Duan Qirui,
who formed the Anhui or Anfu clique, and the supporters of
Feng Guozhang, who formed the Zhili clique. In 1920 the Zhili
clique, with the support of the Fengtian or south Manchurian
clique headed by Zhang Zuolin, otherwise known as the Old
Marshal, defeated the Anfu clique. The Zhili and Fengtian
cliques then fought two wars; the second, in 1924, was a major
conflict which resulted in the break-up of the Zhili clique. From
1924 a somewhat more stable situation emerged, the principal
warlord regimes being those of the Old Marshal in Manchuria;
that of Feng Yuxiang, the 'Christian General', in the north-west;
Yan Xishan, known as the Model Governor, in Shanxi; Sun
Chuanfang, a former member of the Zhili clique, in the lower
Yangzi provinces; Wu Peifu, the 'Philosopher Marshal', in the
middle Yangzi; and in the south-west the Guangxi clique.
Around Guangzhou, Sun Zhongshan, with the consent of the
local warlord Chen Jiongming, maintained a precarious existence.

Although warlord regimes were extremely diverse, they did
have some common features. Most warlords had a military background and many had previously been military governors of
provinces. They all maintained armies which were personally
loyal to them, and all – with the exception of Feng Yuxiang who
has been described as a 'mobile warlord' – commanded a territorial base. Armies had to be paid and warlords used a variety of
levies to supply their financial needs. Part of their revenue came
from taxes, for example the land tax, which were normally
payable to the government. Another part of their revenue derived
from monopolies on consumer goods, the sale of opium, charges
on businesses and railway companies. Warlords were frequently
short of funds and they then used unorthodox methods, for

example printing their own currency, to supplement their income.

Warlords did differ in terms of the ideologies they projected. James Sheridan identified three main categories: conservative warlords, for example Wu Peifu, who was a committed Confucianist; reactionary warlords, for example Zhang Xun, who attempted to restore the Qing; and reformist warlords, who included Feng Yuxiang and Yan Xishan. The former, who had become a Christian in 1914, insisted that his troops should not drink, gamble, use opium or visit prostitutes. He selected recruits on the basis of physical fitness and expected his men to train vigorously. The latter, who controlled the poor province of Shanxi, promoted primary education and literacy, and initiated campaigns against foot-binding and prostitution.[8]

The warlord period has usually been regarded as a disastrous episode in China's history. Central government had collapsed, Outer Mongolia and Tibet had become semi-independent, intellectuals had withdrawn from public service, warfare was endemic, the economy was neglected and Western imperialism continued to make inroads. Wen Yiduo, one of China's best-known modern poets, wrote bleakly in the late 1920s:

This is a ditch of hopelessly dead water.
No clear breeze can raise half a ripple on it.
Why not throw in some rusty metal scraps,
Or even some of your leftover food and soup?[9]

Nevertheless the warlord period had some positive aspects. Despite their self-seeking tendencies, most warlords subscribed to the cause of Chinese nationalism. During the First World War, largely because of the preoccupation of the European powers with the conflict in Europe, China's exports had boomed and modern industries had expanded sharply. This trend continued after the war, with the index of industrial production rising by 300 per cent in 1916–28. The traditional emphasis on ideological conformity was replaced by intellectual freedom, which enabled the cultural change known as the May Fourth Movement to take place. The political disintegration left the way open for the emergence of new political parties and it is in these years that the Chinese Communist Party (CCP) was founded and the

Guomindang was reorganized and began its bid to reunify China.

On 4 May 1919 the news reached Beijing that the Paris Peace Conference had decided that the former German interests in Shandong, which had been seized by Japan during the war, should not be returned to China but retained by Japan. A crowd of 3000 students assembled at the Tiananmen and marched on the foreign legations. The march was blocked by the police, so the students diverted to the house of Cao Rulin, the minister of communications who had negotiated the Twenty-one Demands and who had arranged the Nishihara loans, and burned his house down. The police then intervened and arrested 31 students, one of whom later died of his injuries. The incident rapidly turned into a national protest, with demonstrations occurring in many other cities and a boycott of Japanese goods being declared. The government responded indecisively, at first arresting more students and then capitulating to their demands. Cao Julin resigned from the government and the government itself fell shortly afterwards. The Chinese delegation at Versailles refused to sign the concluding agreement.

This incident was the central event in the intellectual or cultural movement which is known as the May Fourth Movement. Its main themes were an attack on Confucianism, an enthusiasm for new ideas, and a literary revolution. The movement emerged at a time of rapid social change, marked by the growth of the coastal cities and the rapid increase in the number of students at universities and colleges – by 1919 about 4,500,000 students had received an education which included some Western-style studies. The most prestigious institution was Beijing National University, which had been founded in 1898 as a training centre for officials, but which was transformed into the leading academic institution committed to the promotion of liberal ideas, by its chancellor Cai Yuanpei (1868–1940). He brought to the university a number of leading academics, including Hu Shi (1891–1962), who had studied with the philosopher John Dewey at Columbia University, and Chen Duxiu (1879–1942), who had founded the journal *New Youth* in Shanghai in 1915. Its first editorial had called upon the youth of China to cast off the conventions of the past and to embrace the individualism and utilitarianism of the West. Chen Duxiu and Li Dazhao (1888–

1927), the university's librarian, were to be the joint founders of the CCP.

The 1911 revolution had dismantled the political framework of the Confucian state, but the Confucian tradition remained dominant in the family, particularly in the wealthy extended families from which many of the first generation of Westernized intellectuals came. This tradition was now attacked fiercely in the pages of *New Youth*. In December 1916, Chen Duxiu, who himself came from a wealthy Anhui family and who had taken, but failed, the provincial examinations, published an article entitled 'The Way of Confucius and Modern Life'. In it he criticized Confucian teaching on filial piety and on the subservience of women, noting in particular the prejudice against the remarriage of widows. Confucius, he remarked, lived in a feudal age and the ethics, social mores and political institutions he advocated belonged to a feudal age.

Classical Chinese literature was written in a condensed and allusive form which made it accessible only to those with a classical education. By the end of the nineteenth century the demand for newspapers, popular fiction and translations of Western works had resulted in the production of a large amount of writing in the vernacular, but the classical form continued to be used for all serious literature. In 1917 Hu Shi published an article in *New Youth* in which he called for a 'literary revolution', which would supplant the classical style with the vernacular for all forms of literary expression. The following month Chen Duxiu demanded,

> Destroy the aristocratic literature which is nothing but literary chiselling and flattery, and construct a simple, expressive literature of the people.[10]

The consequence was the emergence of a true vernacular literature. One of the first and greatest exponents of this was Lu Xun (1881–1936), whose short story 'A Madman's Diary' appeared in *New Youth* in April 1918. In 1921 the ministry of education decreed that the vernacular should be used in all primary school texts.

The third strand in the intellectual ferment of the May Fourth Movement was the diffusion of a wide range of ideas from the

West. By the late nineteenth century many of the key concepts of Western thought, including Social Darwinism and socialist and anarchist ideas, had been translated into Chinese. In November 1918, in an article in *New Youth* entitled 'The Victory of Bolshevism', Li Dazhao attempted to explain the tenets of Bolshevism, and in the following year he used an entire issue of the magazine to discuss Marxism. In January 1919 Chen Duxiu was still arguing that only science and democracy could 'cure the dark maladies in Chinese politics, morality, learning and thought',[11] but he, like many others, lost faith in Western democracy after the betrayal of China at Versailles. Hu Shi adopted the pragmatic philosophy of John Dewey, who was lecturing in China between 1919 and 1921. This made him doubt that ready-made ideologies, such as anarchism or Marxism, which he called 'isms', could provide the solution to China's problems. He asked rhetorically what was the sole aim of this new thought. His answer was: to re-create civilization, but civilization was not created *in toto*, but by 'inches and drops'.[12] His leaning to gradualism contrasted with the revolutionary preferences of Li Dazhao and Chen Duxiu, an indication that the intellectual unanimity of the May Fourth period, brought about largely by the nationalistic fervour of the times, would not last.

THE FOUNDING OF THE CHINESE COMMUNIST PARTY AND THE REORGANIZATION OF THE GUOMINDANG

Many Chinese were to be proud of having belonged to the May Fourth generation, for they regarded those years as the starting point of modern Chinese history. Among them was Mao Zedong (1893–1976), who came from Hunan where his father had begun life as a poor peasant. Mao was a student at the time of the 1911 revolution and a political activist when the May Fourth Incident occurred. By 1920, Chen Duxiu and Li Dazhao had started a Marxist study group at Beijing University and Mao Zedong had started his own group in Changsha, the provincial capital of Hunan. In April of that year Grigori Voitinsky, representing the Third Communist International, visited China to assist in the formation of a Communist party. First a Socialist Youth League was organized and contact was made with the group of students from

Hunan and Sichuan – among them Deng Xiaoping – who were being sent to France on a part-study–part-work scheme. In July 1921, at a girls' school in the French Concession in Shanghai, the First Congress of the CCP was held. Neither Chen Duxiu nor Li Dazhao was present on that occasion, though Chen Duxiu was chosen as secretary-general of the Party in absentia. There is some uncertainty about the decisions taken at that meeting, but probably it was agreed that the Party should concentrate on promoting the labour movement.

Between 1921 and 1923, China experienced what has been described as 'the first big wave of labour struggles'.[13] Communist historiography has claimed that the CCP played the major role in directing the struggle, but Guomindang activists also played their part and the rise of unrest was apparent before the CCP had been formed. The most successful industrial action was the Xianggang seamen's strike, which began in January 1922 and which had as its central issue the discrepancy between the wages of white and Chinese seamen. The strike spread to Guangzhou and Shanghai, eventually involved 120,000 workers, and resulted in the Xianggang seamen receiving a wage rise of 15 to 30 per cent. Later that year the Communist-supported Labour Secretariat organized a congress in Guangzhou which was attended by delegates who claimed to represent 300,000 workers. But then, when the labour movement seemed about to take off, a strike of railway workers on the Beijing–Hankou line led to disaster. The local warlord, Wu Peifu, perhaps with the encouragement of the Western powers, broke up the strike, killing 35 of the strikers, including the branch secretary of the union of the Jiangnan depot in Hankou, who was beheaded on his own station platform.

After the Guomindang had been expelled from the Beijing parliament in 1913 it moved to Guangzhou, where it maintained a shadowy existence with the unreliable support of Chen Jiongming, the local warlord. It was these circumstances which made Sun Zhongshan receptive to the overtures of Maring, the Comintern agent whom he met in 1921. In the previous year, Lenin had persuaded the Comintern that in colonial countries, a term which included China, Communists should collaborate with bourgeois-democratic movements. Maring concluded that the Guomindang should be regarded as such a movement, and he obtained Sun Zhongshan's agreement that members of the newly-formed CCP should be allowed to join the Guomindang as individuals and that an united front should be formed by the two parties.

Sun Zhongshan had already begun a reorganization of the Guomindang. A new constitution had been adopted which refined the manifesto commitment of the Revolutionary Alliance to three principles: nationalism, democracy, and the people's livelihood. Now the Comintern, in the person of Mikhail Borodin who had arrived in Guangzhou in October 1923, assisted in making further changes. The party was reorganized on Bolshevik lines, although Sun Zhongshan retained personal leadership, a diversion from the Leninist model. Through the efforts of Sun Fo, Sun Zhongshan's son, who was mayor of Guangzhou, a significant improvement was made to the party's finances. Most importantly, in May 1924 a military academy was opened at Huangpu (Whampoa), south of Guangzhou. The academy, headed by Jiang Jieshi (Chiang Kaishek) (1887–1975), who had recently returned from Moscow, was to train a National Revolutionary Army, which would be used to reunify China.

In the meantime the Guomindang, with Communist support, was attempting to organize mass movements. Liao Zhongkai, leader of the left wing of the Guomindang, promoted a revival of the Guangzhou labour movement, which led to a series of strikes and a strengthening of union discipline. One notable protest, the Shamian affair of July 1924, was directed against Western imperialism and the unequal treaties. Contact was made with the peasants, now recognized as an important component in the revolutionary struggle. In 1922 Peng Pai, the son of a landlord, who had joined the Socialist Youth League, had begun to work among the peasants of his home district in eastern Guangdong. Two years later the Guomindang established a Farmers' Bureau, headed by Peng Pai, which organized peasant associations and supported peasants in disputes with landlords.

However, the more successful the Guomindang was in creating a mass following, the more it alienated the merchants and landlords who provided its principal support. This situation was illustrated dramatically in the autumn of 1924, when a group of Guangzhou merchants, infuriated by the heavy taxes imposed by the Guomindang and its encouragement of the labour movement, raised a militia and smuggled arms into the city. Ironically this militia was defeated by soldiers from the Huangpu military academy, although their commander Jiang Jieshi had already voiced his suspicion of the infiltration tactics of the CCP.

In March 1925, Sun Zhongshan, who had long been a sick man, died of cancer. His death was commemorated in services nationally, but his memory might then have faded if an incident had not inflamed nationalist sentiments in China to a degree that outstripped the response to 4 May 1919. On 30 May 1925, police commanded by a British officer fired on Chinese demonstrating in the Nanjing Road in Shanghai, killing 12 people. Protests followed in cities throughout China. In Guangzhou, on 23 June, British troops fired on a rally and killed 52 demonstrators. This precipitated the Guangzhou–Xianggang strike, which lasted 16 months and seriously disrupted the trade and services of Xianggang.

Since 1924, discussions had been taking place in Guomindang and CCP circles of a northern expedition to reunify China. In the autumn of that year the defeat of Wu Peifu, the dominant figure in central China, by the combined forces of Feng Yuxiang, the Christian General, and Zhang Zuolin, the warlord of Manchuria, encouraged Sun Zhongshan as he had made an agreement to share power with the latter. However, Borodin advised that the military strength of the northern warlords was still too great, and the expedition was postponed.

The Northern Expedition was eventually launched in July 1926. By then the National Revolutionary Army and its allies had some 150,000 men and was assisted by Russian military advisers. Against it were arrayed the large but inferior forces of Wu Peifu in central China, Sun Chuanfang in the east and Zhang Zuolin in the north. The Nationalist forces advanced rapidly through Hunan, and only encountered stiff resistance from Wu Peifu's army as they approached Nanchang, the provincial capital of Jiangxi. According to Harold Isaacs, a left-wing American journalist, this rapid progress was due to the help given to the Guomindang forces by the mass movements. Other writers have been more sceptical, arguing that it was only after the revolutionary armies had arrived that the mass movements, which had been kept in check by the warlords, began to play an important role.[14]

Whether the response came before or after the arrival of the Nationalists, there is no doubt that the Northern Expedition did set off a wave of popular movements. In the Hunan countryside the number of peasants belonging to peasant associations rose dramatically. This prompted Mao Zedong, who had been head of the Guomindang Peasant Movement Training Institute in Guangzhou, to return to Hunan in December 1926 and make his celebrated investigation into the peasant movement. In his report he predicted that 'in a very short time, several hundred million peasants . . . will rise like a tornado or a tempest'.[15] The arrival of the Nationalist armies in the Yangzi cities also brought about a surge of revolutionary spirit in the cities, made manifest in a wave of industrial strikes and heightened student activism.

The relationship between the Guomindang and the CCP was already under severe strain. In March 1926, Jiang Jieshi, suspecting that the crew of a gunboat named the *Zhongshan* was about to kidnap him, seized the boat and then carried out a purge of Communist supporters in Guangzhou. Borodin calmed things down and persuaded the CCP to continue the united front with the Guomindang. The Northern Expedition exposed the different agendas of the two parties, and the likelihood of an open disagreement increased as Jiang Jieshi and the eastern wing of the National Revolutionary Army approached Nanjing and Shanghai. On 24 March the expeditionary force entered Nanjing and some of its troops looted the foreign consulates and killed several foreigners. In response, British ships laid down a protective barrage which killed a number of Chinese. Jiang Jieshi, determined not to antagonize the Western powers, blamed the Communists for the attack and executed some of the soldiers held responsible for looting. In Shanghai, Communist leaders, including Zhou Enlai, future prime minister of the People's Republic, had mobilized city workers, in particular those of the Commercial Press and the Shanghai Post Office, against the warlord Sun Chuanfang. In March 1927 they seized control of the city. Jiang Jieshi then entered Shanghai and immediately began to use his contacts with the Western powers, with wealthy bankers and industrialists, and with underworld figures such as 'Smallpox Jinrong', leader of the Green Gang, to raise a force of mobsters to strike at the labour unions. On 12 April they attacked, killed several hundred union members and handed the city over to Jiang Jieshi.

Notwithstanding the events in Shanghai, in Wuhan the united front between Guomindang and Communists survived. One reason for this was that Stalin, currently engaged in his power struggle with Leon Trotsky, had staked his ideological reputation on continuing the alliance with the 'bourgeois-democratic' Guomindang, and as a consequence Borodin and the Comintern had to support that policy. Another reason was that the leader of the Guomindang government in Wuhan was Wang Jingwei, regarded by many as Sun Zhongshan's heir, who was on the left wing of the party. The key political issue was whether the two parties should carry through an agrarian revolution, and if so, from whom should land be confiscated and to whom should it be distributed. Confused and ill-informed instructions from Moscow threw the CCP into disarray. The threat of a rural revolution lost the Guomindang support and at the same time the deteriorating military situation forced Wang Jingwei to act. In July Communists were expelled from the Guomindang, Wuhan was placed under martial law and a repression of the CCP began.

The CCP, with Comintern encouragement, now turned to armed revolt. On 1 August, National Revolutionary Army units sympathetic to the Communist cause seized and briefly held Nanchang. They then marched south, apparently hoping to find support in eastern Guangdong where Peng Pai had achieved success with the peasant associations. In the meantime Mao Zedong had been instructed to organize a peasant insurrection in Hunan. The event, known as the Autumn Harvest uprising and celebrated as evidence of Mao's inspired recognition of the role that poor peasants were going to play in the revolution, turned into a disaster. The peasant forces were easily defeated and Mao and the few survivors were forced to flee into the mountains. Despite these reverses, in December the CCP Politburo, with encouragement from the Comintern, promoted an insurrection in Guangzhou which has become known as the Guangzhou Commune. The uprising was ill-prepared, there was little popular support, and Zhang Fakui, commander of the Nationalist forces acted promptly and put down the revolt with great severity. This incident, it has been claimed, 'turned Chinese public opinion against the Communist Party and Soviet Russia'.[16]

The events of 1927 discredited Wang Jingwei and the left wing of the Guomindang, and enabled Jiang Jieshi to consolidate his position. In April 1928, having secured the co-operation of two important warlords, Feng Yuxiang and Yan Xishan, he recommenced the Northern Expedition against the remaining warlord armies headed by Zhang Zuolin, the warlord of Manchuria. The second half of the expedition, now simply a military campaign, was marked by two important incidents. In late April the Nationalist forces captured Jinan, the provincial capital of Shandong, which had a substantial number of Japanese residents. The Japanese government had already voiced its concern that the Northern Expedition might endanger Japanese interests in China. The arrival of the Nationalist forces at Jinan prompted the dispatch of two Japanese divisions to protect Japanese nationals. A clash between Nationalist and Japanese troops followed but Jiang Jieshi, ignoring Chinese protests against this infringement of China's sovereignty, patched up the incident and the National Revolutionary Army continued its advance upon Beijing. Then the Guandong Army, the force safeguarding Japanese interests in Manchuria, attempted to influence events. Suspecting that the warlord Zhang Zuolin would oppose any extension of Japanese influence in Manchuria, on 4 June Kwantung Army officers assassinated him by blowing up his train. However, his son Zhang Xueliang took his place and gave his support to the Nationalists. Before the end of June, Nationalist forces entered Beijing, so completing the Northern Expedition.

THE NANJING DECADE, 1928–37

The Guomindang made Nanjing its capital because the southern capital was closer to its main power centre on the lower Yangzi. Beijing was now renamed Beiping, that is 'Northern Peace'. The ten-year period between 1928 and the Japanese invasion in 1937 is known as the Nanjing decade. The record of the Guomindang in these years provides the evidence on which to judge the success of its attempt to create a modern nation-state.

China in the Nanjing decade was a country of startling contrasts. In the coastal cities the indications of modernization and Westernization were widespread if superficial. In Shanghai in 1929 there were 2326 factories employing nearly 300,000 workers, 70 per cent of whom were women or children. In 1933 more than 80 per cent of Chinese-owned industry was located in the eastern and southern coastal provinces and in Manchuria.

In contrast, the pattern of rural life appeared to be unchanging, although allegations were being made that China was facing an agrarian crisis. The evidence for this is contradictory. According to Albert Feuerwerker, until 1937 the total output of agriculture probably kept pace with the growth of population, which he considered a creditable performance in view of the lack of significant technological improvements.[17] However, Chen Han-seng, who observed conditions in Guangdong in the early 1930s, recorded that some peasants were reduced to such abject poverty that they sold their daughters, or joined those who had migrated to work in the European colonies of South-east Asia. Chen's study suggested that the main causes of peasant immiseration were the exploitation of landlords and the effects of Western imperialism. A modern study of the peasant economy of Hebei and Shandong in the same period concluded that peasants' living standards were rising and that the main obstacle to their increased prosperity was not landlord exploitation but the absence of any coherent programme for improving agricultural technology.[18]

The Guomindang, following Sun Zhongshan's political programme, which had assumed that China was not yet ready for democracy, established a one-party dictatorship. In 1931 it issued a provisional constitution which created a five-branch system of government, comprising the executive, legislative, judicial, examination and control bureaux. This structure was a curious mixture of traditional and modern features. The examination bureau, which supervised entry to the civil service, and the control bureau, which supposedly stamped out corruption, were reminiscent of the imperial system, whereas other aspects of the government displayed Western influence. The Guomindang's Central Political Council nominally exercised executive control, but after 1930 Jiang Jieshi obtained such dominance that both the Guomindang and the government lost effective authority. Jiang's dominance was achieved by manipulating factions within the army, the party and the government. In the army his support came from former cadets at the Huangpu Military Academy where he had been commandant. Within the party

Jiang Jieshi was aided by the 'CC clique' led by his close friends the Chen brothers, whose influence derived in part from their involvement with the secret police. A less formal grouping, known as the Political Study clique, provided Jiang with support from professional organizations. Jiang also benefited from other personal connections. In 1927 he had married Song Meiling, the sister of Sun Zhongshan's widow. Song Meiling's other sister was married to Kong Xiangxi (H. H. Kung), a leading banker, and her brother Song Ziwen (T. V. Soong) was a Harvard graduate and a noted financial expert. Because of these nepotic connections, the Communists described the Nanjing government as the rule of the 'Four Big Families'.

The ideological stance of the Nanjing government was also ambiguous. Although many of its supporters were of the May Fourth generation and had participated in the attack on Confucianism, Jiang Jieshi was a follower of Zhu Xi, the twelfth-century Neo-Confucianist. Whereas Sun Zhongshan had admired Hong Xiuquan, the Taiping leader, Jiang Jieshi extolled the achievements of Zeng Guofan, who had led the opposition to the rebellion. During the Nanjing decade Confucianism was reinstated and Confucius's birthday was made a public holiday. Confucianism was also an important element in the New Life Movement which Jiang Jieshi launched in 1934. This aimed to encourage the practice of the four Confucian virtues of propriety, justice, honesty and self-respect while at the same time it disseminated Western ideas on hygiene. The New Life Movement also had a Christian content, with Jesus being held up as a model to emulate, and members of the Young Men's Christian Association (YMCA), which was very active in social work in Chinese cities, being asked to give it support.

In 1931 a group of Huangpu officers formed an elitist organization later known as Blue Shirts, because they wore Chinese-made cotton cloth as a demonstration of their commitment to China's national interest. They aimed to revive the Guomindang and make Jiang Jieshi a dictator. They also played a leading role in the New Life Movement. The Blue Shirts' open admiration of Mussolini, their strident anti-Communism and their use of violence, has led to them being described as a fascist organization and to Jiang Jieshi being accused of harbouring fascist sympathies.

The economic record of the Nanjing government has been the subject of conflicting assessments. In 1957 Douglas S. Paauw argued that the government had neither developed the agricultural sector, nor had it encouraged saving and investment in the modern industrial sector, and as a consequence the overall picture was one of economic stagnation.[19] On the other hand, Thomas G. Rawski calculated that China's annual rate of per capita output growth exceeded 1 per cent during the interwar years, a rate comparable with that achieved by Japan between 1897 and 1931.[20]

The most impressive aspects of the economic record concerned financial institutions, communications, and the growth of the modern industrial sector. In the 1920s China still lacked a unified currency, and foreign exchange and banking facilities were largely in the hands of foreigners. In 1927 Jiang Jieshi had asked his brother-in-law Song Ziwen to develop a financial strategy for the government. Among Song's achievements were the rescheduling of China's foreign debts, the introduction of a Chinese silver dollar, and the abolition of the the *lijin*, the tax on internal trade. He also established a central bank and specialized banks to deal in foreign exchange, to provide credits for peasants, and to finance the development of transportation.

His reforms were not entirely successful. Throughout the Nanjing decade, because of heavy military spending, government revenue covered only about 80 per cent of its expenditure. The financially sound way to increase government revenue was to tax the agricultural sector efficiently, but the Guomindang lacked the authority and the trained personnel to achieve this. To cover the deficit the banks sold large quantities of heavily-discounted government bonds, very often to officials, thereby increasing government liabilities and diverting private investment into speculation. Bureaucratic capitalism became even more marked after Song Ziwen was replaced in 1933 by Kong Xiangxi. Faced with the crisis caused by the United States' silver-buying programme, the Bank of China was forced to issue new shares and to exchange these for government bonds. As a consequence the government holding of bank assets rose from 20 per cent to over 70 per cent.

At the beginning of the Nanjing decade China had about 8000 miles of railway track and about 18,000 miles of motorable road.

Ten years later a further 5000 miles of railway had been built, the length of motorable roads had increased to 69,000 miles and a further 10,000 miles of road were under construction. In addition a national air line had been established which operated scheduled services and carried air mail. This expansion of modern communications created work and investment, helped to integrate economic regions and strengthened the sense of national identity. In other respects the achievement was less creditable. Much of the labour used was conscripted and peasants were often not permitted to use the new roads because they had been built for military purposes. Over half the new railway mileage had been built in Manchuria, which from 1931 was under Japanese control.

During this period the modern industrial sector grew rapidly from a small base. Impressive advances were achieved both in new industries, for example electricity generation, and in older industries such as coal, where output grew at 7 per cent per annum. However, this growth was heavily concentrated in the treaty ports and in Manchuria, a high proportion of the larger enterprises were foreign owned and much of the Chinese share of modern industry was in consumer goods, with perhaps three-quarters of the output by value being in textiles and foodstuffs.

Of fundamental importance to China's economic regeneration was the raising of output and the improvement of productivity in the agricultural sector. Reference has already been made to the issue of an agrarian crisis during the interwar years. To add to their difficulties, between 1931 and 1935 farmers suffered a sharp fall in income occasioned by the world depression and the outflow of silver. The Guomindang was aware of the problem of peasant immiseration and it took some steps to relieve it. In 1930 it passed a land law which restricted rent to three-eighths of the main crop, but this was never enforced. A National Agricultural Research Bureau was set up in 1932 and measures were introduced to extend credit to farmers through the agricultural co-operative movement. However, most of the loans went to landlords and little of what they borrowed was invested in the land. In retrospect these measures appear woefully inadequate and the commitment of the Guomindang to a transformation of the countryside is suspect.

The Guomindang had signalled its intention to develop education as a means of creating a modern nation-state. When it came to power it passed detailed laws covering all forms of schooling and in 1930 Jiang Jieshi himself became minister of education. Advice was received from the League of Nations on a national plan of educational reform and 1940 was chosen as the date for the introduction of compulsory education. The educational record during the Nanjing decade was very uneven. The proportion of children attending primary and secondary schools increased, but the provision was much better in the cities than in the countryside. In 1932 only 15 per cent of the children enrolled in primary schools were girls. Many private schools continued to operate and missionary societies ran over 3000 primary schools. The most ambitious attempt to extend educational opportunities was made by the National Association for the Promotion of Mass Education, led by Dr James Yen, an American-educated Christian. The literacy campaign it promoted was part of a broader rural reconstruction movement pioneered at Yen's centre at Ding Xian in Hebei.

Colleges and universities were concentrated in the coastal cities. Universities made heavy use of staff who had trained abroad and who based their teaching on foreign texts and examples. Many universities were underfunded and their students suffered economic hardship. The Guomindang tried to clamp down on political activity in universities, but students were frequently involved in protests, notably in 1935 and 1936 when a wave of nationalism swept the campuses. Nevertheless, a scholarly community grew up, which engaged in research and publication. A notable achievement was the founding in 1928 of the Academia Sinica, a national research institute.

The Guomindang had come to power on a wave of nationalist sentiment and it had declared that it intended to get rid of the unequal treaties. However in 1927, in Hankou, in Nanjing and yet again in Shanghai, it strove to avoid antagonizing the Western powers, and after it came to power it used diplomatic measures rather than threats of violence to achieve its aims. In 1928 the United States took the lead in returning tariff autonomy and between 1929 and 1931 Britain voluntarily surrendered concessions in Hankou, Jiujiang, Zhenjiang and Xiamen, and the leased territory of Weihaiwei. Other concessions remained in foreign hands and negotiations to end extraterritoriality had made little progress before the outbreak of war with Japan changed the priorities of China's foreign relations.

The record of the Guomindang government in the Nanjing decade has been variously assessed. For Robert E. Bedeski its major achievement was the establishment of a new and sovereign Chinese state system, which implied the expansion of state sovereignty, the creation of national institutions and the improvement in China's international stature.[21]

Other writers have been less convinced about the party's commitment to the national interest, arguing that the basis of its support was a coalition between rural landlords and Shanghai capitalists. Its character demanded that it should compromise with the warlords, avoid confrontation with vested interests in the countryside and treat Western imperialism with the utmost caution.

THE CHINESE COMMUNIST PARTY, 1928–35

The series of disasters which had overwhelmed the CCP in 1927 forced a re-evaluation of the Party's strategy. At the Sixth Party Congress, held in Moscow in June 1928, Li Lisan took over as secretary-general from Qu Qiubai, who was condemned for his 'leftist opportunist deviation'. A surprisingly optimistic view was taken of the situation in China, but for the time being it was agreed to concentrate the Party's efforts on the countryside. When Li Lisan returned to China he acknowledged the importance of the rural bases which Mao Zedong and others had established, but his commitment remained to the cities and to the industrial proletariat. His authority was weakened by the presence of the 'Twenty-eight Bolsheviks', a group of Moscow-trained Chinese Communists who considered it their task to rebuild and redirect the Party.

Perhaps because of the weakness of his position, perhaps because he genuinely believed that the world depression and the Guomindang's involvement in a war with the warlords Feng Yuxiang and Yan Xishan meant that the time was ripe, in 1930 Li Lisan embarked on another attempt at an armed uprising. The plan was to foment strikes and demonstrations in Changsha, Wuhan and Nanchang, and then for the newly formed Red Army to capture those three cities. The coup was launched in the summer of 1930, and the greatest success was achieved at Changsha, which was held for ten days. However the Red Army was inadequate for the task, the popular response was half-hearted and the support of some rural-base leaders, notably of Mao Zedong, was withheld, and the result was a disaster. In the following year Pavel Mif, the new Comintern representative, arrived in China. Under his direction Li Lisan was condemned for blind opportunism and the Twenty-eight Bolsheviks took over leadership of the Party.

After the failure of the Autumn Harvest uprising Mao Zedong had retreated to the mountain range on the borders of Hunan and Jiangxi known as the Jinggangshan, where he joined up with two bandit chiefs. In April 1928 Zhu De brought in the survivors from the attack on Nanchang. Later Peng Dehuai, a future minister of defence, arrived with a group from Hunan. These forces, the nucleus of the Red Army, were soon called into action to repel Guomindang attacks. Before the end of the year Mao had concluded that the Jinggangshan area was too small and too rugged to be a suitable base area, and in January 1929 he moved east to Ruijin in southern Jiangxi.

The Ruijin area became the most important of several Communist rural bases. For Mao Zedong, possession of a rural base was an essential part of his revolutionary strategy. He likened a base to a person's buttocks – without buttocks one would be unable to sit down and regain one's strength. At the Ruijin base he began to put into practice three key policies, the first of which was to make the Red Army a disciplined and politicized force. Already at Jinggangshan Mao had enunciated the basic principles of guerrilla warfare: 'The enemy advances, we retreat; The enemy camps, we harass; The enemy tires, we attack; The enemy retreats, we pursue', and had required every soldier to know the Three Rules: to obey orders, to take nothing from the peasants, and to pool all captured goods. However, it was evident from remarks made by Mao at the Gutian conference held in December 1929 that many Red Army soldiers still lacked discipline and did not understand the aims of the revolution or the role that the army was expected to play. In future, political officers were appointed to help the army mobilize the masses and set up new regimes. At least one in three soldiers had to be a Party member. The army was intended to be democratic, the soldiers wore no badges of rank, all received the same pay and all shared in the discussion of any proposed action.

The second policy concerned revolutionary land reform, that is the confiscation of land from landlords and its redistribution to poor peasants. This policy had only been adopted by the CCP at its Fifth Congress in April 1927, on the eve of its split with the Guomindang, and there was no agreed line on whether land should also be confiscated from rich peasants, that is peasants who owned more land than they could farm with their own labour. At the Ruijin base Mao Zedong introduced a moderate policy which allowed rich peasants to retain their land. Villages were encouraged to form revolutionary committees, which first classified the inhabitants of the village as landlord, rich peasant, middle peasant and poor peasant and then applied the agreed redistribution of land.

The third policy concerned social reform and in particular the position of women in Chinese society. At the time of the May Fourth Movement Mao Zedong had criticized arranged marriages and during his investigation of the peasant movement in Hunan he had written approvingly of the formation of women's associations which challenged the authority of husbands. In 1930 he carried out a study of Xunwu in south-east Jiangxi to provide himself with recent and detailed information on a rural community. Among the matters he studied was the effect of permitting freedom of marriage and divorce. In his report he argued that male peasants opposed the emancipation of women only because they were uncertain of the outcome of land reform.

Mao's position in the Jiangxi soviet was unchallenged until 1931, when members of the Central Committee abandoned their undercover existence in Shanghai and moved to Ruijin. Later that year the Chinese Soviet Republic was established at Ruijin, with Mao Zedong its first president, although his authority and policies were now being challenged by the Twenty-eight Bolsheviks. The Soviet Republic immediately passed a radical land law which provided for the confiscation not only of landlords' land but also the land of rich peasants. It also approved a marriage law which defined marriage as 'a free institution between a man and a woman'. Both men and women could apply for a divorce and divorced women were given some economic protection. There immediately followed a spate of divorce petitions.

The survival of the rural soviets was threatened by developments from both within and without. In December 1930 the Nationalist Army made its first determined attack on the Communist bases in southern Jiangxi, but was forced to withdraw. The attack coincided with the Futian Incident, which involved the alleged infiltration of the Jiangxi action committee by the pro-Guomindang Anti-Bolshevist League. There followed a mutiny in a Red Army unit and a purge by Mao Zedong of his suspected opponents. In July 1931 Jiang Jieshi took personal command of the Nationalist forces investing the Communist bases, which now numbered 300,000 men, and he was making good progress when the campaign was called off because of the Japanese occupation of Manchuria. This respite, and a Comintern declaration that the world depression would lead to a world revolutionary upsurge, encouraged the Twenty-eight Bolsheviks to denounce Mao Zedong's tactics of mobile guerrilla warfare as over-cautious. Mao lost his place on the Party's Military Council and the strategy promoted by Zhou Enlai of positional warfare and capturing cities was adopted.

In the Jiangxi central base the CCP had begun to apply its revolutionary land policy. Many landlords were dispossessed and others were killed, but it soon became apparent that some landlords and rich peasants were concealing the extent of their landholdings. In June 1933 a Land Investigation movement was launched, originally with Mao Zedong's support, to identify cases of evasion. Later Zhang Wentian, one of the Twenty-eight Bolsheviks, took charge and the investigation became increasingly oppressive. In November 1933 the Guomindang Nineteenth Route Army, stationed in Fujian province, mutinied in protest against Jiang Jieshi's failure to oppose Japanese encroachment on China. Whereas Zhou Enlai was in favour of assisting the rebels, Mao Zedong counselled caution. While the Communist leadership was arguing, Jiang Jieshi stepped in and crushed the mutiny and a great opportunity for the Communists was lost.

In October 1933 Jiang Jieshi commenced his fifth encirclement campaign. This comprised both a major military offensive and a comprehensive political campaign. The Nationalist Army, which now numbered over 750,000 men in the field, was supported by German advisers and equipped with heavy guns and aeroplanes. To counter the Communist tactic of mobile warfare it had ringed the Jiangxi central base with 15,000 blockhouses. On the political front the Guomindang attempted to match CCP propaganda by requiring the officers in its armies to wear the same uniform and eat the same food as their men. The population of the areas around the Communist bases was required to support a blockade of all essential supplies. It was at Nanchang in 1934, while he was planning the fifth extermination campaign, that Jiang Jieshi launched the New Life Movement, which was in part a response to the threat of Communism.

The CCP's decision to abandon the Jiangxi base and set out on the Long March was probably taken in May 1934, although the departure was delayed until October. The main reason for going was the deteriorating military situation, although it has been suggested that the over-zealous application of the Land Investigation movement had lost the Party much popular support. Approximately 86,000 people set out from the Jiangxi base while some 20,000 sick and injured and a force of 30,000 soldiers remained behind. After breaking through the Guomindang blockade with surprising ease, the Red Army marched due west and crossed into Hunan and then Guangxi. The first major engagement was the crossing of the Xiang river north-east of Guilin, where the Red Army lost about half its strength. In January 1935 the Communists captured Zunyi in northern Guizhou and there an important conference took place. The main issue was the military failure which had resulted in the abandonment of the Jiangxi base. The policies pursued by the Politburo and by the military leadership, which included Otto Braun, the Comintern military adviser, were criticized and by implication those advocated by Mao Zedong were endorsed. Although Mao did not become Party leader at this point, his rise to power had begun.

The marchers left Zunyi with the intention of joining up with Zhang Guotao's Fourth Front Army, which had moved from its original base in Anhui to Sichuan. Various final destinations were under discussion, with Mao Zedong proposing moving north to oppose the Japanese. First the upper waters of the Yangzi river had to be traversed, which meant marching far to the west to shake off the Nationalists, and finally crossing the

Jinsha or Golden Sands river. The marchers then turned north, through areas inhabited by sometimes hostile minority groups. Then came the most celebrated incident of the march, the crossing of the Dadu river by the Luding Bridge, an ancient chain suspension bridge guarded by a Guomindang machine-gun post. The next obstacle was the Great Snowy Mountain, where hundreds of men died from exposure. In June the two main branches of the Red Army met at Mao'ergai in north Sichuan. On the surface the reunion between Mao Zedong and Zhang Guotao was cordial, but past differences and political rivalries soon appeared and whereas Zhang Guotao chose to move west to Xizang, Mao Zedong continued northwards through Gansu, where he encountered one final physical challenge, the vast swamp of the Great Grasslands.

In October 1935 Mao Zedong and the First Front Army reached the north Shaanxi rural base. The Long March had extended over 5000 miles and less than 20,000 of those who had set out arrived at its final destination. Many years later Mao Zedong was to speak sadly of the thousands who died, and the obligation felt by the survivors that their sacrifice should not have been in vain. As a result of the march the main theatre of Communist operations was transferred from the south to the north.

THE SINO-JAPANESE WAR, 1937–45

After having occupied Manchuria in 1931, Japan continued to encroach on north China. In the following year China and Japan fought an undeclared war in Shanghai, and the Chinese Soviet Republic in Jiangxi declared war on Japan. However, Jiang Jieshi, recognizing the weakness of his position, refused to allow China to be drawn into hostilities, declaring that the Japanese were a disease of the skin, but the Communists were a disease of the heart. By 1936 Hebei and Inner Mongolia had established autonomous governments under Japanese protection.

Protests against Jiang Jieshi's policy came from various quarters and were particularly vociferous on university campuses. The Guomindang treated student political movements with suspicion, on the grounds that as the nationalist revolution had been completed student agitation must be fomented by the Communists. The student movement of 9 December 1935 challenged this view. It began when Beiping police attempted to suppress a student protest against Japanese plans to turn areas of north China into autonomous regions, and it then spread to many other cities. Pressure on Jiang Jieshi to change his mind also came from the National Salvation Association, founded by the journalist Zou Taofen. Among the supporters of the association was Zhang Xueliang, the 'Young Marshal' of Manchuria, whose father had been killed by the Guandong Army in 1928. Zhang had moved his forces into north China and had reluctantly taken on the task of suppressing the Communists in Shaanxi. In December 1936, Jiang Jieshi flew to Xi'an to encourage Zhang to campaign more vigorously. However, the Young Marshal took him prisoner and detained him until Jiang Jieshi had agreed to end the civil war and lead the resistance to Japan.

Early in 1937 the Guomindang and the CCP negotiated a second united front. The Communists agreed to abandon armed insurrection and cease confiscating landlords' land. In return the Guomindang undertook to end the attacks on Communist bases, release political prisoners and prepare to resist Japan. On 7 July 1937, an incident at Lugouqiao (Marco Polo Bridge) near Beiping led to full-scale war between China and Japan.

The first phase of the war, which lasted until October 1938, was marked by a rapid Japanese invasion and some heroic Chinese opposition. In north China, Japanese troops advanced along the main railway lines and Chinese forces fell back in disorder. However, in Shanghai, Chinese resistance was better organized and more determined. Chinese ground forces surrounded the Japanese settlement and in a tragic error Chinese aeroplanes bombed the International Settlement. The battle for Shanghai continued for three months, until Japanese troops landed on the coast to the south of the city and forced the Chinese forces to fall back on Nanjing. Jiang Jieshi had ordered that the capital should be defended to the last man, but his orders were ignored and on 12 December Japanese troops entered the city and perpetrated the atrocities known as the 'rape of Nanjing'. The Nationalist government transferred the capital to Chongqing, a thousand miles up the Yangzi river. Chinese troops continued to fight and in April 1938 obtained a significant victory, when forces under

Li Zongren defeated a large Japanese force at Tai'erzhuang, near Xuzhou. In June, in an attempt to delay the Japanese advance on Wuhan, Jiang Jieshi ordered the Yellow river defences near Kaifeng to be breached. In October, however, Wuhan fell and in the same month Guangzhou was occupied.

In December 1937 Japan offered Jiang Jieshi peace terms, but he refused them because they required recognition of Manzhouguo, the puppet regime which had been established in Manchuria under the last Chinese emperor. As Japan could not force Jiang to surrender, the alternative solution was to establish puppet regimes in the parts of China now under Japanese control. In December 1938, Wang Jingwei, leader of the left wing of the Guomindang, defected from the Nationalist side and offered himself as leader of a collaborationist regime with its capital at Nanjing. This regime was to last throughout the war, although Wang himself died in 1944. It claimed to be an independent government exercising authority over much of central and south-east China. It maintained diplomatic relations with Japan and Germany and had its own armed forces and the trappings of a government, though its dependence on Japan was never in doubt.

The Nationalist government claimed to govern an area containing nearly half the population of China, although in truth its political authority was weak. It had lost control over the lower Yangzi provinces, its main political base, and now it had to rely on local power-holders, for example Long Yun in Yunnan. This weakness was not immediately apparent, for at the beginning of the war the Guomindang and Jiang Jieshi enjoyed a wave of national and international support. Before the move to Chongqing, Jiang Jieshi had been given the title of director-general of the Guomindang and he was also chairman of the Military Affairs Commission. In a gesture towards broadening the basis of the Guomindang's support, a People's Political Council was formed which contained representatives of minor parties and even Communists. In addition the Three People's Principles Youth Corps was created to mobilize the nation's youth and revitalize the Guomindang. However, Jiang Jieshi 'did not understand this form of modern pluralistic politics'.[22] In 1942, after independent members of the People's Political Council had criticized the government, the Guomindang was given the majority of the seats on the council, which thereafter was of little importance.

Relations with intellectuals and students also soured. When Japan invaded China, universities migrated to areas outside Japanese control. Staff and students from Beijing National University, Qinghua, and Nankai University, Tianjin, made their way to Kunming in Yunnan where they formed the National South-West Associated University. But the university's liberal values were not acceptable to the increasingly autocratic rule of the Guomindang, and the Three People's Principles Youth Corps had cells on the campus and spied on the staff and students. Before the end of the war the political strains within the Guomindang were evident. At the Guomindang's Sixth Party Congress, the government was described as corrupt and inefficient and Jiang Jieshi was accused of having become increasingly dictatorial.

To conduct a war of resistance, the Nationalist government had to establish a war economy within the Free Zone, as the area under its control was called. This was a demanding task, as much of the region was economically backward. Nevertheless, at the beginning of the war an heroic attempt was made to shift industrial plant and skilled workers from areas threatened by the Japanese invasion to the Free Zone. The government established a National Resources Commission which took control of heavy and technical industry. Between 1939 and 1943, industrial output grew rapidly, coal output doubled, over a 1000 miles of rail track were built, electricity production increased seven-fold, and after the closing of the Burma Road in 1942 had cut petroleum supplies to the amount which could be brought in by air, ingenious attempts were made to produce liquid fuels from alternative sources. However, the industrial growth began from a very small base, industrial output was insufficient to satisfy demand and the rate of growth declined sharply after 1943, when the Free Zone began to experience an industrial crisis.

The industrial crisis was a symptom of a deeper economic malaise which manifested itself in inflation. During the Nanjing decade the government had been unable to balance its budget and had borrowed heavily. With the move to Chongqing it had lost its main sources of revenue, in particular customs duties, and it now incurred heavy wartime expenditure. It tried to recover control of the land tax from the provincial authorities, and in order to secure food supplies for its troops, it began to collect taxes in grain, but these measures did not solve the problem of inadequate revenue. Between 1942 and 1945 inflation rose at over 230 per cent annually. Official salaries declined sharply and this encouraged corruption. Because of the shortage of commodities, in particular petrol, a flourishing black market grew up.

The vast majority of the population of the Free Zone were peasants. To fight a war of resistance effectively their co-operation was essential, as the Communists were to show. However, the evidence suggests that the policies which the Guomindang pursued alienated peasant support. Although inflation generally benefits primary producers, because government regulations required grain to be sold at fixed prices and transported to collecting stations, poor peasants incurred costs which more than doubled their tax burden. As the gap in incomes between rich and poor in the countryside widened, landlord–tenant conflicts reached epidemic proportions. The consequences of the government imposing heavy exactions to feed its troops were revealed in the Henan famine of 1942–3, which left five million people starving, many to death. Peasants also bore the main burden of conscription, which nominally applied to all males between the ages of 18 and 45, but which inevitably fell most heavily on poor families.

After the heroic resistance of the first year of the war, the main Nationalist forces were withdrawn to the Free Zone to regroup and retrain. Thereafter the Nationalist armies remained largely on the defensive, although the casualty record shows that the fighting between Nationalists and Japanese never stopped. Between 1939 and 1941, Chongqing and other cities held by the Nationalists were bombed incessantly. The only land link with the outside world available to the Nationalists was the Burma Road, which had been built at immense human cost in 1938 and was to close in 1942 after the Japanese invasion of Burma.

At the beginning of the war the Nationalists and Communists had reached agreement about the zones in which the Red Army was to be allowed to operate. In addition to its forces in the north, now renamed the Eighth Route Army, the CCP raised the New Fourth Army in Jiangxi. In October 1940 Nationalist commanders, who regarded the Communist operations south of the Yangzi as an infringement of the agreement on zones, ordered the New Fourth Army to move north. Its failure to comply fully led to fighting between Nationalist and Communist forces which effectively ended the united front.

The Japanese invasion of China was condemned by the United States, and from December 1938 American aid began to reach the Nationalist side. After the Japanese attack on Pearl Harbor in December 1941 the two countries became allies. General Joseph W. Stilwell ('Vinegar Joe'), a former military attaché to China, was sent to Chongqing with the task of encouraging Jiang Jieshi to go on the offensive against Japan. However, to Stilwell's annoyance, Jiang Jieshi refused to commit his troops to support the British in Burma and keep the Burma Road open. Nor would he agree to Stilwell's suggestions on how the Nationalist army, which numbered about 3,800,000 men, might be made more effective. In April 1944, when it seemed that the war in China had stalemated, Japan launched Operation Ichigo. The short-term objective was to disable the best National armies and to deny the United States the use of Chinese airfields. The longer-term strategy was to establish a land supply route across China to Hanoi, which would ensure that although Japan might lose the war with the United States, she could not be evicted from China. The operation resulted in a major Japanese victory, which exposed the corruption and inefficiency of the Nationalist government and left the Nationalist forces weaker than at any other time during the war.

THE CCP DURING THE SINO-JAPANESE WAR

At the end of the Long March Mao Zedong had established his headquarters at Yan'an, a city in north Shaanxi. There, under his leadership, the CCP was to develop political, social and economic policies which were to transform the Party and gain it mass support.

At Yan'an, Mao Zedong consolidated his position as Party leader. His two main rivals were Zhang Guotao, the veteran Party leader whose disagreement with Mao on the Long March has already been noted, and Wang Ming, the most influential of the Twenty-eight Bolsheviks. Zhang Guotao, having lost much of the New Fourth Army, finally reached Shaanxi in late 1936.

Although his disagreements with Mao were patched up, his defection to the Nationalists in April 1938 was no great surprise. Wang Ming's position rested on the support he received from the Comintern, and at first his political influence outweighed that of Mao Zedong. However, he held no military command and he had no experience of conducting a rural revolution, and after the outbreak of war he lost influence.

Mao Zedong also strengthened his position by laying claim to the ideological leadership of the Party. In 1938–40 he wrote three key works: 'On the New Stage', 'The Chinese Revolution and the Chinese Communist Party' and 'On New Democracy'. In the first he called for the 'sinification of Marxism', arguing that if Marxism was to mean anything to China it had to be imbued with Chinese peculiarities, 'We must put an end to writing eight-legged essays on foreign models.' In the second he reviewed Chinese history, emphasizing the key role of peasant revolts, and pointing out that earlier peasant revolts had failed because they had not been led by the proletariat and the Communist Party. In 'On New Democracy' he repeated Lenin's argument that in colonial societies revolution would be accomplished in two stages, the first of which would be bourgeois-democratic and the second socialist. 'New democracy' was the term used by Mao Zedong to denote the point – which he identified with the May Fourth Movement – when the revolution began to be led, not by the bourgeoisie alone, but by a 'joint revolutionary–democratic dictatorship of several revolutionary classes'. After the Communist victory, which he now began to anticipate, there would be a place for the bourgeoisie, or at least that part of it which had not allied with feudalism or imperialism, in the new state.

During the Sino-Japanese war the CCP underwent a drastic reorganization. At the beginning of the war, as refugees flocked to Yan'an, the membership of the Party had soared to 800,000. Many of the new members knew little of Marxism and did not accept Party discipline. In February 1942, after a series of military setbacks and political disagreements, Mao Zedong launched a rectification campaign. Cadres (trained leaders) were required to attend a Party school, at which Mao gave lectures in which he identified the main errors threatening the Party, including 'subjectivism', by which he meant the claim to superiority of cadres who had theoretical knowledge but no down-to-earth experience. In another lecture he argued that art and literature must serve the masses. The rectification campaign did not amount to a purge, but a number of intellectuals were forced to make a self-criticism and all cadres were expected to study Mao's writings and to strive to improve the quality of their work.

*   *   *

Yan'an was the capital of the Shaanxi–Gansu–Ningxia (Shaan–Gan–Ning) Border Region. By 1944 the Communists claimed to control four 'border regions', which stretched across much of China north of the Yellow river. There were also about a dozen other 'liberated areas', most of which were in central China. In the border regions representative governments were established. All men and women over the age of 16 could vote and the 'three-thirds' system was adopted, which meant that the Communists restricted themselves to one-third of all elected positions, the rest being shared between 'progressive' (petty bourgeois) and middle-of-the-road (middle bourgeois or enlightened gentry) candidates.

Like the Guomindang, the CCP had to develop a self-sufficient war-time economy. Shaanxi was a very poor area which had suffered badly in the 1928–33 famine, when many peasants had been forced to sell their land. Before the Long Marchers had arrived the local soviet had already begun to confiscate and redistribute landlords' land. Under the united front agreement the CCP had agreed to stop confiscations, and throughout the war it adhered to that policy except in the case of landlords who collaborated with the Japanese. Instead, from 1942 it promoted a Rent and Interest Reduction campaign. A rent ceiling of 37.5 per cent of the crop – the figure endorsed but never applied by the Guomindang – was enforced strictly. A programme of land registration was introduced and security of tenure was improved, measures which threatened the privileged position of landlords and rich peasants. The border region government was desperate for tax revenue and by 1941 the tax burden was heavy, although it had eased by 1943. In that year a campaign was launched to develop a more productive economy organized on co-operative principles. At the same time attempts were made to increase industrial production using primitive technology and surplus labour.

At Yan'an, important experiments were made in the delivery of mass education. Many primary schools were *minban* schools, that is schools paid for and run by the people, who hired the teacher and suggested the curriculum. Their priority was for the pupils to become literate, but literacy was closely connected with the needs of the world of work, and schools closed at harvest time. In secondary schools, courses were reduced from six to three years, the curriculum was simplified and all students did at least 20 days of productive labour a year. In 1941 Yan'an University was founded, and here too study was combined with productive labour and emphasis was placed on political study.

While these policies were being pursued the Communists were also fighting a war. In 1937 the Eighth Route and New Fourth armies had 92,000 men. Although these troops did engage the Japanese forces at the time of the invasion, for the next two years they restricted themselves to guerrilla tactics, leaving the Nationalist armies to take the brunt of the Japanese attack. Faced with an elusive enemy the Japanese commander General Tada instituted a 'cage policy', sealing off the Communist areas within a cage of blockhouses and trenches. In 1940 the Communist forces, now numbering 500,000 men, launched the Hundred Regiments' campaign, which broke out of the cage and inflicted heavy losses on the Japanese. Their response was to counterattack and to carry out ruthless reprisals against civilians suspected of harbouring the Communists. As a consequence the population of the areas under Communist control fell sharply and the strength of the Eighth Route Army declined from 400,000 to 300,000 men.

The reason for the Communist change of tactics which turned into a disaster is disputed. The campaign may have been launched because the Nationalists were believed to be about to negotiate a settlement with Japan. An attack would expose the contrast between Communist patriotism and Nationalist defeatism. During the Cultural Revolution Peng Dehuai, who had led the attack, was held responsible and accused of megalomania. Whatever the reason for the change of tactics, thereafter the Communist forces reverted to guerrilla activity and small-scale attacks, frequently on the forces of the puppet regimes rather than on the Japanese army.

There is no doubt that the balance of power between Nationalists and Communists shifted during the Sino-Japanese War. One reason for this was that the Japanese invasion and Operation Ichigo gravely damaged the Nationalists' military capacity. Another was that Jiang Jieshi's government earned a reputation for being undemocratic, corrupt and inefficient, whereas the Communists at Yan'an took pains to project a contrasting image. In 1944 John S. Service, a member of an United States observer group, travelled from Chongqing to Yan'an. He was so struck by the apparent contrast between the two regimes that when he reached Yan'an he wrote 'we have come into a different country and are meeting a different people'.[23] This image was manipulated and the Communists were no democrats. In the 1942 rectification movement the target of the Yan'an forum on literature and art was intellectual freedom. One of the victims of the rectification movement was Ding Ling, China's foremost woman writer, who in a story entitled 'When I was in Xia Village' had criticized male Communist cadres for having double standards on sexual morality. For this she lost her post of literary editor of the Yan'an newspaper *Liberation Daily* and was sent to work in the countryside for two years. Perhaps the most important consequence of this contrast of images was the increased scepticism of the United States towards Jiang Jieshi as a reliable ally.

The Communist success in the war years has been explained in a number of ways. In 1962 Chalmers Johnson observed that whereas before the war the Communists had made little progress in mobilizing the peasants on their side, during the war they obtained a mass following in the countryside. The alliance between the Eighth Route Army and the peasantry was born in the aftermath of the Hundred Regiments' campaign, when the Japanese adopted the 'three-all' – 'kill all, burn all, destroy all' policy. The alliance, according to Johnson, 'derived partly from nationalism (hatred of the invader), but to a large extent it was purely a matter of survival'.[24] Johnson's view was challenged by Donald G. Gillin, who argued that when the Red Army entered Shaanxi at the end of the Long March it received popular support because it advocated revolutionary land reform. After the Japanese invasion, the elite responded to the appeal of nationalism, but peasants were happy to work for the Japanese, who paid good wages. Only when the Eighth Route Army resumed its attack on landlords, did it recover popular support. His argument was developed by Mark Selden, who discussed the significance of the 'Yan'an Way', the range of reforms which the Communists introduced at Yan'an after 1942, which he described as a bold and effective response to the war-aggravated problems of rural society.[25]

It may be that it was a combination of factors which gave the Communists their success. The war saved them from extinction at the hands of the Nationalists. At Yan'an the Communist leaders astutely emphasized the Party's role in leading resistance to Japan. The 'Yan'an Way' policies were not new, for they had been pioneered in the Jiangxi period. The Communists had learned from their mistakes and in the border regions they had the security and the time to implement a modified version of those policies consistently.

CIVIL WAR AND COMMUNIST VICTORY

The bombing of Hiroshima and Nagasaki by the United States in August 1945 brought the Sino-Japanese War to an abrupt end and left the Nationalists and Communists jostling for advantages. Although, under the Yalta agreement of February 1945, the Japanese forces were to surrender only to the Nationalists, the Communists also occupied territory held by the Japanese and seized Japanese weapons. Immediately after the bombing of Hiroshima the Soviet Union finally declared war on Japan and proceeded to occupy Manchuria. In response, the United States assisted the Nationalist forces to return to north-east China and to Manchuria, but by the time they had arrived the Chinese Communists had already entrenched themselves in the countryside.

In December 1945 General George C. Marshall took up his post as ambassador to China and in January 1946 he persuaded the Nationalists and Communists to agree to a ceasefire. A Political Consultative Conference was convened, a range of political and military issues were decided, and Jiang Jieshi announced that one-quarter of the Nationalist army would be demobilized. However, neither Nationalists nor Communists were sincere in their search for a peaceful settlement and there was no superior power to enforce the agreements they had made.

The Soviet forces began to withdraw from Manchuria in March 1946, taking with them industrial machinery in lieu of war reparations. Chinese Communist troops took their place and by May the ceasefire had ended in Manchuria. General Marshall continued his peace mission until the end of the year, although well before then it was clear that both sides were using the pretence of negotiations as a cover for their preparations for war.

At the start of the conflict it appeared that the Nationalists held a clear advantage. They controlled China's major cities and the country's industrial base. Their armies numbered more than twice as many men as the Communists' and they were supported by an air force and a small navy. Although the United States placed an embargo on the shipment of arms to China in July 1946, this was rescinded within less than a year and the Nationalists were not short of weapons. Nevertheless within three years they were driven from the mainland.

The civil war may be divided into three stages. The first stage, which lasted from July 1946 to June 1947, began with the Nationalists occupying the main cities of Manchuria as far north as Changchun and recovering large areas of north China, including Yan'an, which was captured in March 1947. The People's Liberation Army, as the Communist forces were now named, adopted new tactics, surrendering territory but harassing and destroying the Nationalist forces. Lin Biao, the commander of the Communist forces in Manchuria, carried out lightning attacks which halted and then reversed the Nationalist advance.

In the second stage of the civil war, which began in June 1947, the People's Liberation Army overran much of Manchuria and north China apart from the key cities and main lines of communication. In June, Communist forces crossed the Yellow river and cut off Xi'an, and then began to isolate concentrations of Nationalist forces. By March 1948 the Nationalists' hold on Manchuria was reduced to three cities. From the middle of the year the power balance had begun to shift in the Communists' favour – by now the People's Liberation Army had over 1,500,000 troops and had seized large quantities of weapons and equipment.

The final stage began in the autumn of 1948. By November Lin Biao had captured Shenyang, and Manchuria had fallen to the Communists. He then moved into north China and in January

1949 he took Tianjin. Each of these victories was accompanied by the surrender of thousands of Nationalist troops and the seizure of vast quantities of materiel. Between November 1948 and January 1949, in the area between the Huai river and the Longhai railway, the decisive battle of Huai-Hai was fought. Communist forces methodically cut off and then forced to surrender a Nationalist force of 300,000 men. After this battle Nationalist resistance north of the Yangzi came to an end. In April 1949 Communist forces captured Nanjing and in the following month Shanghai fell. In December Jiang Jieshi and two million of his supporters, taking with them China's foreign reserves and art treasures, fled to Taiwan.

A wide variety of explanations have been given for the Communist victory. At the time, accusations were levelled against the United States for having failed to support the Nationalists adequately with military and economic aid. Even if that accusation were true it is difficult to prove that it had a decisive influence on the outcome of the civil war. A more convincing argument is that the Nationalist defeat was a military disaster which can be explained in military terms. Major-General David Barr, writing in early 1949, gave his appreciation of why the Nationalists were losing on the battlefield. They had made a major strategic error in trying to recover Manchuria. The leadership of the Nationalist army was very poor and contrasted sharply with the brilliance of some of the Communist military leaders. The Nationalists had resorted to a defensive strategy which allowed them to be surrounded and forced to surrender. Finally the morale of the Nationalist troops, who were poorly paid and badly treated, was very low and they frequently deserted.

Clausewitz famously said that 'war is nothing more than the continuation of politics by other means'. The civil war had its origin in a political struggle and it was success in that struggle which was to determine the outcome of the war. On the one hand the Nationalists, through errors and omissions, lost the political struggle, on the other hand the Communists profited from the Nationalists' mistakes and presented themselves as a moderate, efficient and patriotic alternative to Nationalist rule.

It may be argued that the Guomindang had begun to lose the political struggle during the Nanjing era, when it had failed to live up to the expectations of a modernizing government. Alternatively it may be suggested that the Nationalists forfeited support during the Sino-Japanese war by ceasing to fight the enemy and by ignoring urgent political, social and economic issues.

After 1945 the Guomindang government made further mistakes which eventually destroyed its basis of support. The mistakes began as soon as the Guomindang government returned to Nanjing. Many expected that those who had collaborated with the Japanese would be punished, but only a few notorious collaborators were executed and others were allowed to retain their jobs. Guomindang officials were accused of commandeering Japanese property, whereas industrialists and merchants whose property had been seized by the Japanese received no compensation. When the Nationalists reoccupied Manchuria, such was their suspicion of the local leadership that they appointed outsiders to administrative posts and thereby presented the Communists with a grievance to exploit. When the Nationalists returned to Taiwan, which had been a Japanese colony for 50 years, they treated the native Taiwanese more harshly than the Japanese had done, and provoked a serious uprising.

Much of the blame for the outbreak of the civil war had fallen on the Guomindang. The most coherent criticism came from radical students who believed that the Guomindang should have persisted in forming a coalition government with the Communists. They regarded the close links between the Nationalists and the United States with suspicion and particularly resented the continued presence of American troops on Chinese soil. In December 1946, two United States marines were accused of raping a student at Beiping University. This provoked a series of demonstrations on campuses throughout the country at which anti-American and anti-government sentiments were expressed. Student agitation continued throughout the civil war and other issues, for example the economic hardships of students and intellectuals, helped to turn university communities against the government. The Guomindang insisted that this hostility was fomented by Communists and there probably was an underground Communist organization supporting the protests. However, the agitation could be explained readily by reference to government incompetence and the brutal suppression of student demonstrations.

Two other issues served to alienate the Guomindang's basis of support: the lack of political progress, and economic mismanagement. Sun Zhongshan had prescribed that after a period of political tutelage by the Guomindang a constitutional form of government would be introduced. A constitution had been drafted in 1936 and the Political Consultative Conference held in January 1946 had agreed to introduce it forthwith. However, the Guomindang commitment to constitutionalism was undermined by the Renovationist faction, which would not accept that the Guomindang should give up its monopoly of power. The constitution was promulgated on 1 January 1947, and elections for a National Assembly were held later in the year, but the elections were condemned as a farce and the sessions of the National Assembly ended in uproar. By now the Guomindang was regarded as too corrupt, too intolerant of minority parties, and too indifferent to the issue of civil liberties, to be able to introduce a constitutional form of government.

Monetary inflation had already set in during the war. It started to accelerate in 1946 and by mid-1948 the Shanghai wholesale price index (September 1945 = 100) had risen to 1,368,049 and the economy was on the verge of collapse. In August the government replaced the worthless *fabi* with the gold *yuan* note, without previously having attempted to balance the budget or to back the new currency with reserves. Hopes of a currency stabilization loan from the United States were dashed. When the new currency was issued the rich were urged to turn over their gold and foreign currency holdings to the government in exchange for certificates. In October the government, in an attempt to reduce the budgetary deficit, raised taxes on consumer goods. This prompted a rush to stockpile goods, disastrous shortages and within three months the collapse of the currency reform. So disastrous was the gold *yuan* experiment that some observers at the time regarded it as the main cause of the government's fall.

*   *   *

The shortcomings of the Guomindang only supply half the explanation for the shift in the political balance. The other half lies in the CCP's success in winning the battle for hearts and minds, particularly in the countryside. Revolutionary land reform has been seen as the key factor in this success. The CCP had renounced land reform as part of the second united front agreement. However, on 4 May 1946 a directive was issued which authorized the seizure of land from collaborators, and the Outline Agrarian Law, published on 10 October 1947, provided for the confiscation of all land belonging to landlords and for its division among the total population. These measures sanctioned the violence against landlords already occurring in many villages in north China, which amounted to a rural revolution.

A programme of revolutionary land reform only attracted peasant support under certain conditions. When CCP cadres returned to Manchuria in 1945 they found that the simple promise of land was not enough to bring the peasants over to their side. What was needed was an 'equation of revolutionary transformation', which meant convincing poor peasants that those who supported the Communists in the civil war, by supplying them with taxation, military and labour service and food, would receive a share of the landlords' land and would participate in new decision-making bodies after the revolution. This promise was only credible if the peasants were confident that the revolution would not be reversed. In many parts of north China it was not landlordism which afflicted poor peasants, but low wages, high taxes and the arbitrary exercise of power by the local elite. To obtain their support CCP cadres had to awaken peasants to their condition of exploitation and give them the confidence to act against it. To do this they organized 'struggle meetings' at which the poorest of peasants were encouraged to voice their grievances. Cadres would then encourage, but not lead, a movement to seize the goods of members of the exploiting class and to wreak vengeance on them.

The CCP also encouraged the formation of women's associations and implied that the revolution would lead to their emancipation. Both the new marriage law, which gave women rights relating to divorce and custody of children, and revolutionary land reform, which gave women a share of the redistributed land, provided reasons why rural women should support the revolution.

It is not easy to determine the relative importance of the armed struggle and the mass campaigns in the CCP's victory in the countryside. No mass campaign could succeed if there was a risk of the Guomindang forces returning and the local elite recovering power, for if this occurred terrible reprisals would take place.

In one Henan village a returning landlord shot or buried alive a member of every family which had supported the Communists. Land reform, and more generally the overthrow of the system of exploitation, provided the motivation for peasants to join the revolution, but their participation depended on the Communists being able to convince them that their oppressors would not return.

The final act of the civil war was played out in the cities. Here student unrest, the alienation of the intellectuals, corrupt and undemocratic government and chaotic economic conditions had undermined the position of the Guomindang. However, the Communists had lost touch with the industrial proletariat and had little experience of dealing with urban populations. In August 1945 the Communists captured Zhangjiakou (Kalgan), 200 miles north-west of Beijing. Here they engaged in an urban experiment to demonstrate that they could administer a city more effectively than the Nationalists. Collaborators were arrested, streets were cleaned and beggars and prostitutes were found alternative employment. The workers were unionized and wages were raised, but private businesses were left untouched. A reputation as honest and effective administrators served the Communists in good stead when the cities of north China fell into their hands in 1949. Beiping was occupied in January 1949 without a shot being fired. The People's Liberation Army enforced strict discipline and no looting took place. Workers and students co-operated in restoring production and maintaining essential services. The gold *yuan* notes were replaced with 'people's notes', or *renminbi*, and an attempt was made to curb inflation. Political groups opposed to the Guomindang were invited to participate in a coalition government. As the Nationalists fell back in disorder, the disciplined Communist approach allayed panic and ensured that the final stage of the civil war was concluded swiftly.

7

China since the 1949
Revolution

The half-century since the Communists took power in China may be divided into two main phases: a revolutionary phase, which lasted until the death of Mao Zedong in 1976, and a pragmatic phase, which extended to the death of Deng Xiaoping in 1997 and which still continues.

In the first phase Mao Zedong attempted to translate the revolutionary commitment of the CCP into practice. This led to a sequence of policies referred to as the Soviet period, 1952–8, the Great Leap Forward and its aftermath, 1958–65, and the Cultural Revolution, from 1966 to Mao Zedong's death a decade later. Although these divisions obscure major continuities throughout the period and beyond, they do provide a convenient framework within which to examine developments.

THE PERIOD OF CONSOLIDATION, 1949–52

Until 1952 the main effort of the new government was expended on consolidating its control. No organized resistance remained in China Proper after the Guomindang's precipitate departure from the mainland. Nevertheless there was a real danger of subversion and to guard against this, in September 1949 the country was divided into six military regions and joint military and administrative commissions began to exercise power. The CCP referred to the border regions as the 'old liberated areas' and the rest of

China as 'new liberated areas'. In the old liberated areas the Communist leadership was already established, but in the new areas much remained to be done. Guangzhou, for example, was not occupied until two weeks after the establishment of the People's Republic of China. In the new liberated areas most senior Guomindang officials had fled and the first task was to find people with the skill and political reliability to take over their posts and to keep essential services functioning. In this the student body played an important part.

Four tasks needed to be addressed immediately. The first was to define the political characteristics of the new state. In September 1949 a People's Political Consultative Conference was convened and an Organic Law and a Common Programme were adopted. The former established a 'democratic dictatorship' led by the CCP; the latter guaranteed basic human rights and promised equality for women, the continuation of revolutionary land reform, the development of heavy industry, and safeguards of the rights of minority peoples. The second task was to gain control of the economy, which meant curbing inflation. This was achieved by increasing government revenue by creating a unified fiscal system (for the first time since 1928 land taxes accrued to central rather than to provincial government) and by selling bonds. At the same time various strategies were employed to keep government expenditure under control, for example requiring the army to be partly self-sufficient.

The new government was intent on asserting control over all territory deemed to be part of China. The three provinces of Manchuria were now fully integrated into China. Tibet, which had been autonomous since 1913, was 'liberated' by the People's Liberation Army in 1950 and later became the Xizang Autonomous Region. However, Outer Mongolia, which had become the Mongolian People's Republic in 1924, remained independent. As for Taiwan, in October 1949 a Communist force tried but failed to seize the island of Jinmen (Quemoy). The rebuff showed that an invasion of Taiwan would be a major operation, and the matter was postponed.

The fourth priority task concerned foreign relations. During the Second World War China had been treated flatteringly by the United States as a great power, but in the post-war period and the civil war China's international status had declined to that of a client state. The CCP aspired to present China as an independent and unaligned power, but in 1949, in the atmosphere of the Cold War, it seemed that China must 'lean to one side', which meant seeking an alliance with the Soviet Union. In December 1949 Mao Zedong left China for the first time in his life to go to Moscow and negotiate with Stalin. Although there was a show of cordiality between the two, neither man fully trusted the other and the negotiations were prolonged and difficult. The outcome was the Sino-Soviet Treaty of Alliance and Mutual Assistance. Its most important provisions were a promise of mutual support in the event of an attack by Japan, and a Soviet advance of $300 million in credits to China.

The implications of the alliance with the Soviet Union soon became apparent. In June 1950 civil war broke out between North and South Korea. After North Korean troops had virtually overrun the south, the United Nations sent forces to assist South Korea. At the same time the United States interposed its Seventh Fleet in the Taiwan Straits to prevent China using the opportunity to invade the island. By November 1950 the United Nations' forces had not only invaded North Korea, but were within 50 miles of the Yalu river, the frontier with China. At that point China intervened on a massive scale and drove the United Nations' forces back to the 38th parallel, the boundary between North and South Korea. The war then stalemated and a truce was signed in June 1953.

China's decision to intervene in the war was most probably occasioned by the collapse of the North Korean army and the threat of a United Nations' force, in effect an United States' force, becoming poised on its north-east frontier. Chinese participation in the war was significant in a variety of ways. Although the Chinese forces, led by Peng Dehuai, achieved remarkable success, the war exposed serious military weaknesses and a decision was taken to modernize the People's Liberation Army and to develop the air force. The war cost over 700,000 Chinese casualties, among them Mao Zedong's son, and China incurred very heavy debts to the Soviet Union for the purchase of arms. China's involvement also deepened the rift with the United States, which now became committed to the support of the Nationalists on Taiwan. In China the threat of war was used to whip up support for the regime, for example through the Resist America, Aid Korea campaign. It was also invoked to justify a harsher line against all persons suspected of not giving the regime their full support.

During these years the programme of revolutionary land reform was completed. The Agrarian Reform Law of 1950 extended land reform to the new liberated areas. Its purpose was explained by Liu Shaoqi, who was second to Mao Zedong in the Party hierarchy: it was not only to end the feudal exploitation of the landlord class, it was also to preserve a rich peasant economy to enable the revival of agricultural production. Land reform had been completed by 1952 except in areas occupied by national minorities, which were exempted. By then about 43 per cent of China's cultivated land had been confiscated and redistributed, with about 60 per cent of the rural population benefiting. Many poor peasants, who by definition owned little or no land and survived by selling their labour, now became middle peasants. The importance of this measure in terms of consolidating peasant support behind the regime cannot be underestimated. However, the reform was achieved at a high cost. Estimates of the number of landlords and rural power-holders who died range from 200,000 to two million. The redistribution on average gave a poor peasant just over a quarter of an acre of land, which did little to solve the problem of land shortage. Official estimates of grain production indicate that between 1949 and 1952 output rose by 12.6 per cent. The increase may reflect the post-war recovery and perhaps a greater effort from peasants who did not have to surrender much of their crop to landlords. Without fresh inputs, however, this rise in output could not be sustained.

During these years several other measures helped to consolidate the CCP's position. In 1950 a Marriage Law was introduced which replaced the 'feudal' marriage system with the 'New Democratic' marriage system. Women were allowed to choose their partner freely and given equal rights relating to divorce, custody of children, and property. After the law had been promulgated, women's associations led a mass campaign to publicize the changes and a sharp rise in the number of divorces followed. Nevertheless, in rural areas many features of the traditional marriage system survived.

Steps were taken immediately to increase educational opportunities for the masses. Those whose schooling had been interrupted by war were offered accelerated programmes of study and many millions of adults attended winter study classes and spare-time schools. Teachers were re-educated, school texts were revised and political study classes were held. Most Western missionary educators left the country and their schools and universities were nationalized. By 1952 about 60 per cent of children eligible for primary education were in school, and impressive increases had been recorded in the numbers attending secondary schools and colleges.

It was essential that the new government should gain the confidence of the industrial and business communities. At the time of the Communist victory economic activity in the cities was virtually at a standstill and public utilities were out of commission. Once order had been restored it was made clear that for the time being the more traditional sector of the economy would not be reformed. At the same time the government took steps to discourage strikes and to negotiate moderate wage claims. However, the modern economic sector was immediately affected by the departure of most foreigners and those Chinese industrialists who had close links with the Guomindang. Their enterprises were immediately taken under state control. In April 1951, systematic confiscation of foreign assets began with the nationalization of the property of Shell Oil.

By early 1951 it had become apparent that the period of reconstruction and moderation was coming to a close. The apprehension aroused by the Korean War was utilized by the CCP to justify the launching of mass campaigns which were to have a profound impact on Chinese society. Three major campaigns were initiated: against suspected counter-revolutionaries, against corrupt cadres, and, in the 'Five Antis' campaign, against capitalists. The campaign against counter-revolutionaries began with mass rallies and denunciations and was followed by arrests and executions. In the Guangzhou region alone over 28,000 people were executed and in the country as a whole as many as 500,000 to 800,000 people may have been killed. The campaign against corrupt cadres had its origin in the shortage of trained cadres when the CCP came to power. This had led to the recruitment of cadres whose class origin or personal commitment were unsatisfactory. Perhaps 10 per cent of Party cadres were now weeded out. The Five Antis campaign was an attack on wealthy capitalists, who, it was claimed, were defrauding the public through a variety of economic crimes. Capitalists who were found guilty were forced to pay heavy fines and to accept state control of their enterprises. These mass campaigns mobilized the population and attacked the web of personal friendships and obligations which typified relationships within the business community.

Another indicator that fresh initiatives were imminent was the establishment in 1952 of the State Statistical Bureau and the announcement that a census would be held on 30 June 1953. The declared result was that the People's Republic of China, excluding Taiwan and the Overseas Chinese, had a population of 582,603,417. From figures collected later it has been calculated that at the time of the census the Chinese population was growing at about 2 per cent per annum. The census has been described as no more than an enumeration of the population and the results have been disputed, but as there is no good reason why the results should have been falsified they represent the best available evidence of the magnitude of China's population at that time.

THE SOVIET PERIOD, 1953-8

In 1953 the Communist leadership began to implement its policy of socialist transformation and economic development, that is to say the transfer of ownership from private to public hands and the introduction of centralized economic planning. In September the First Five-Year Plan was introduced and the collectivization of agriculture began.

The influence of Soviet Russia on China was already apparent in a variety of forms, but now with the adoption of state planning the Chinese debt to Soviet Russia was even more noticeable. When selecting a development model which gave priority to heavy industry, which involved the construction of large-scale, capital intensive and technologically-advanced plants, and which assumed the institutional transformation of the agricultural sector, which was to supply much of the capital required, China was following the path recommended by Lenin and implemented by Stalin. That China should be willing to become so dependent on a foreign power was surprising, but only the Soviet Union was willing to contribute to the heavy investment which the Chinese leadership believed was an essential element in the country's transition to socialism.

China now received Soviet assistance in the form of expert advice, extensive economic aid and the introduction of Soviet methods, for example in industrial management. Initially 156 major industrial enterprises, including 7 iron and steel plants, 24 power stations and 63 machinery plants were supplied, many of them in kit form for assembly in China. Later another 125 projects were approved. Some 11,000 Soviet specialists were sent to China to supervise the installation and the operation of plants and to provide technical assistance and 28,000 Chinese students were sent to Russia to study.

The period of the First Five-Year Plan saw a number of other important initiatives. Hitherto most of China's modern industry was concentrated in the coastal cities and the north-east. Now, as a matter of policy, industrial complexes were sited in the interior. Major steel complexes were constructed at Wuhan and in Inner Mongolia, and an oil refinery was built at Lanzhou in Gansu province. To service these plants a large investment was made in new railways, including the construction of a line from Xi'an to the Xinjiang oil-fields. In these new industrial complexes the Soviet model of 'one-man management' was introduced. This system, which was associated with centralized planning and the setting of production targets, replaced management committees and worker representation with an authoritarian system. Workers who in the Yan'an period had responded to ideological incentives, now did piecework, or were placed on steeply-graded salary scales.

Soviet influence was also apparent in education, particularly in universities and colleges, which were reorganized on Soviet lines. Russian academic advisers assisted in the planning of courses and Russian textbooks were used widely. Expenditure on higher education tripled between 1952 and 1957 and the number of students, one-third of whom studied engineering, rose sharply. Students from poor families received free tuition and maintenance grants. In return many pledged themselves to the '8:1:50' schedule: eight hours of sleep and one hour of exercise a day and 50 hours of work a week.

*   *   *

The socialist transformation of society also implied the collectivization of agriculture. The arguments in favour of this step were both economic and political. One consequence of revolutionary land reform had been even greater fragmentation of agricultural holdings. Peasants farming small, scattered holdings could not accumulate capital for investment and could not maintain the sustained rise in output and productivity needed to feed the growing population and to release surplus labour for industry. The Soviet Union had collectivized agriculture in the 1930s and it was capital derived from the agriculture sector which had provided investment in industry. It was also apparent that, since land reform, many poor peasants had sold the land they had been given. In 1955 Mao Zedong complained that there had been a spontaneous growth of capitalist elements in the countryside.

In the Yan'an period co-operative farming had been encouraged in the form of mutual aid teams, which pooled their resources in terms of labour and draught animals. After a period of experimentation, from 1954 mutual aid teams were encouraged to amalgamate to form agricultural producers' co-operatives. In these, families retained their titles to their plots, but their land was farmed co-operatively, and crops were divided according to the amount of land and labour supplied by each family. On 31 July 1955, while this change was still under way, Mao Zedong called for a sharp increase in the rate of collectivization. In the winter of 1955–6 co-operatives began to be merged into Advanced Producers' Co-operatives. These were collective farms in which private land-ownership was abolished and members were remunerated on the basis of their labour alone. By the end of 1956 the socialist transformation of agriculture was virtually complete.

China's experience of collectivizing agriculture has often been compared favourably with that of the Soviet Union. There, collectivization was opposed by the rich peasants, or kulaks, and several million of them lost their lives. Various explanations for China's more favourable record have been proposed, for example that China's rich peasants were neither as numerous nor as established a feature of rural society as were the kulaks. Another suggestion is that collectivization in China was better timed, in that only a short period had elapsed since land reform, and the capitalist tendencies in the countryside, against which Mao Zedong had warned, had not become firmly established. Collectivization, it has been claimed, appealed to the rational self-interest of peasants and was carried through by local cadres who had a clear grasp of the situation. Mao Zedong's call for accelerating the programme was not as headstrong as has been suggested. It was based on a well-informed appreciation of the situation and was occasioned mainly by political considerations. Such explanations assume that in China collectivization was unopposed, and it is true that at the time there was little sign of disagreement with the policy. Since decollectivization some dissenting voices have been heard. In 1984 a Shandong farmer recalled:

> When we had advanced co-ops I was the head of one. Quite the little activist I was in those days. When the call went out to form co-ops I put everything my parents had bought – the land, the ox, the donkey and all – into the co-op. At night I was grieving over losing them, but during the day I was taking the lead, trying to talk other people into joining – and trying to talk myself into it too.[1]

Undoubtedly the achievements of these years of socialist transformation were impressive. During the First Five-Year Plan period China's industrial output doubled, the most spectacular increases being recorded in the output of steel, oil and chemicals. These rates of growth probably exceeded those of the Soviet Union at the time of its First Five-Year Plan, but it should be remembered that China owed the Soviet Union a share of the credit, as about 50 per cent of the industrial investment made during the First Five-Year Plan derived directly or indirectly from the Soviet Union. The debt did not only cover investment, for the Soviet provision of plant, blueprints and technicians has been described as 'one of the largest transfers of technology in world history'.[2] During the same period China collectivized agriculture and carried through an extensive programme of social reforms, notably in education. Between 1949 and 1956 primary school enrolment rose from 24.3 million to 64.2 million, middle school enrolment from 1 million to 6.2 million and in higher education the number of students quadrupled to 441,000.

THE GREAT LEAP FORWARD AND THE SINO-SOVIET SPLIT

In 1958 China embarked on a radical, even utopian programme to 'complete the building of socialism ahead of time, and carry out the gradual transition to communism'.[3] Behind this rapid change of pace, if not direction, lay a complex set of interactions within the Party, the economy, industrial management, educational strategy and international relations.

One indication of the strain imposed by revolutionary change was the disillusionment of the intellectuals, that is to say the educated elite, most of whom had welcomed the Communist victory in 1949. At first the CCP had tolerated what was seen as the intellectuals' bourgeois individualism, but in 1955 a harder line was adopted. A mass campaign was launched against the poet Hu Feng who had criticized the Party's insistence that culture should be proletarian. The campaign was used to warn intellectuals not to oppose the First Five-Year Plan or the collectivization of agriculture.

In 1956 Premier Zhou Enlai commented that to promote the economy and to reform the bureaucracy the Party needed the support of intellectuals. In May, Mao Zedong, who was engaged in a Party debate over the pace of co-operativization, endorsed the changed line by announcing 'Let a hundred flowers bloom, a hundred schools of thought contend.' After some hesitation intellectuals began to criticize the competence of cadres, for example for interfering in scientific research. When Mao heard of the Hungarian uprising of November 1956, he attributed it to the isolation of the Hungarian Communist Party from the masses and the intellectuals. In February 1957, in a speech entitled 'On the Correct Handling of Contradictions Among the People', he argued that 'non-antagonistic contradictions' could exist in a communist society and that their resolution by discussion would speed up progress to socialism. His ideas encouraged intellectuals to believe that the open expression of their opinions would be welcomed and many articles critical of the Party, of educational policies and even of Mao Zedong himself were published. Students from Beijing University began to put up posters criticizing officials on 'democracy wall', a stretch of wall near the Forbidden City. However, in June the CCP counter-attacked with an Anti-Rightist campaign. The most outspoken critics of the Hundred Flowers movement were singled out for punishment and other intellectuals were forced to participate in their denunciation. One of the most famous victims was the writer Ding Ling, who was accused of having opposed the Party leadership in literary work. She refused to admit her faults and was sent to redeem herself through labour on a farm near the Soviet border.

Some writers have accused Mao Zedong of treacherously encouraging intellectuals to criticize the Party and then siding with the Party in persecuting them. Merle Goldman has suggested that the Hundred Flowers movement developed a momentum of its own which went beyond the Party's intention and this dismayed Mao. Thereafter he rejected the intellectuals as the key to economic development and instead he became concerned with what he saw as insufficient revolutionary consciousness among educated young people.[4]

Notwithstanding the economic achievements of the First Five-Year Plan, as an economic strategy it had serious shortcomings. Investment had been concentrated on heavy industry, which had grown at a rate five times faster than that of agriculture. The increase in agricultural output had done little more than feed the growing population. Although the industrial sector had grown, it had not created the large numbers of jobs needed to reduce unemployment in the cities. More jobs would be created if the consumer industries were expanded but these were restricted by shortages of raw materials. In a speech entitled 'On the Ten Great Relationships', given in 1956, Mao Zedong had expounded a theory of relationships, or as he defined it 'contradictions' in economic development. The first contradiction was between industry and agriculture and between heavy industry and light industry. His conclusion was that although heavy industry must continue to be given priority, agriculture and light industry must also be developed, a strategy which came to be called 'walking on two legs'.

Other dissatisfactions included a reaction against the 'one-man management' system. This system had been associated with Gao

Gang, the chairman of the State Planning Commission, who in 1954 had been accused of plotting against Liu Shaoqi and had committed suicide. At the Eighth Party Congress, which began in September 1956, the 'one-man management' system was criticized and replaced by a system of collective leadership with the Party in command. The extensive Russian influence on education was also challenged and from 1956 attempts were made to speed up the expansion of education, particularly at junior middle school level.

Relations with the Soviet Union had improved after Stalin's death in 1953, and when Khrushchev and Bulganin visited China in 1954 it seemed that the two countries had achieved a relationship of equality and mutual respect. However, in February 1956 Khrushchev delivered his secret speech denouncing Stalin. Mao Zedong resented Khrushchev's failure to give him warning of the speech, which Mao believed was liable to cause dissension in the Communist world at a time when unity was essential. Disagreement on the issue exposed ideological differences, for example over the inevitability of war with the capitalist powers, which Khrushchev now denied. The attack on Stalin's personality cult may also have caused Mao Zedong to be concerned about his own posthumous reputation. Despite these differences Mao Zedong visited Moscow for the second time in November 1957, soon after the Soviet Union had launched Sputnik, an achievement which led Mao to praise the achievements of the Soviet Union and to declare that 'The East Wind is prevailing over the West Wind.'

*   *   *

In late 1957, while a Second Five-Year Plan was being considered, indications began to multiply that the conservative economic strategy was about to be replaced by a radical programme. In the countryside a massive programme of irrigation using the labour of 100 million peasants was rushed through. In November the *People's Daily* gave prominence to the slogan 'More, better, faster, cheaper'. At a speech given at the Supreme State Conference on 28 January 1958, Mao Zedong declared that 'It is possible to catch up with Britain in 15 years,' and shortly afterwards production targets for both agriculture and industry were raised dramatically. In that same speech Mao had declared

'In making revolution one must strike while the iron is hot – one revolution must follow another, the revolution must continually advance.' This was his theory of 'permanent revolution', a process which embraced both the economic substructure and the social superstructure of society. The Great Leap Forward which was soon to follow, which has been described as 'more the product of a social vision than an economic plan', may be connected with Mao's concept of revolutionary change.[5]

In April 1958, 27 Advanced Producers' Co-operatives in Henan decided to amalgamate and form a commune. They did so without formal direction from the centre, although the encouragement given to the large irrigation schemes of the previous winter had implied tacit approval for the creation of larger units. Other co-operatives followed suit and in August communes received official approval. Before the end of the year the 700,000 Agricultural Producers' Co-operatives had been reorganized into 24,000 People's Communes, each with an average of 5,000 families. In the autumn, communes were also organized in urban areas. The model for these was the Zhengzhou Spinning and Weaving Machine Plant commune in Henan, which was centred on the factory but which also farmed some land.

The main economic benefit of communes was the mobilization of labour for large-scale labour-intensive projects. To maximize the release of labour, the private plots which peasants had been allowed to keep in the Agricultural Producers' Co-operatives were abolished and rural markets ceased to function. To enable women to participate in productive labour, crèches and nurseries were introduced, collective kitchens were organized and a free food system was introduced. The labour thus made available was employed on major construction projects, such as the Ming Tombs Dam near Beijing, and also used to develop rural industry. Following reports of an abundant harvest, communes were encouraged to prospect for local sources of iron ore and to construct their own 'backyard steel furnaces'.

During the Great Leap Forward, vastly-increased targets were set for industrial production. The target for steel output, fixed in February 1958 at 6.2 million metric tons, was already a 19 per cent increase on the previous year's production. In August, Mao endorsed raising it to 10.7 million tons and a few weeks later he even suggested the figure of 12 million tons. To achieve such targets over a range of industries, hundreds of new state projects were started. Between 1957 and 1960 the number of people employed in state industries doubled to over 50 million, which placed an immense strain on the system of food procurement from the countryside. This vast workforce was encouraged by ideological exhortation to work excessively long hours on plant which was over-used and under-maintained.

That the Great Leap Forward was more than a leap for economic growth was demonstrated by other aspects of the movement. In September 1958 a 'great leap' in education was announced. In part this was a matter of rapidly expanding educational opportunity, particularly in the countryside. Primary school enrolment rose by 20 million and there were large increases in the number of students at secondary and tertiary level. Some 30,000 agricultural middle schools and about 400 'red and expert' universities were opened. At the same time important changes took place in the operation of the educational system. The new schools were run on the *minban*, or 'run-by-the-people' principle, productive labour was introduced into the curriculum in all schools and at all levels, and students were encouraged to voice their criticisms of teachers. Another feature of the communes was the revival of the people's militia and the arming of the peasantry. The need for military preparedness was justified by the crisis of August 1958 caused by the declaration that China intended to 'liberate' Taiwan. It was also a challenge to the professional leadership of the People's Liberation Army, and a reminder of the 'people's war' fought in Yan'an days. The communes also briefly offered women an escape from the double burden of domesticity and work. This was most warmly embraced in the urban communes where women, who in the past had been restricted to the home, took a leading role in organizing child-minding arrangements and other features of the commune which were a break from the traditional family structure.

The euphoria of the Great Leap in 1958 was to be followed by disillusionment and dissension in the following year. By then it had become apparent that reports of a bumper harvest had been exaggerated and that the industrial targets which had been set were unrealistic. An early response to this realization was to reorganize the communes, making the production brigade, in effect the former Advanced Producers' Co-operative, the level at which ownership and decision-making was fixed. Communal eating was ended and steps were taken to restore private plots and to reopen rural markets.

As the retreat from the Great Leap Forward began, the political conflict which had simmered under the surface at least since 1956 came out into the open. At the Party's Central Committee meeting held in Wuhan in December 1958, Mao had agreed to step down as Chairman of the People's Republic, and in April 1959 that position was taken by Liu Shaoqi. Although Mao retained the chairmanship of the Party, he later claimed that after the Wuhan meeting he was treated like a 'dead ancestor'. In July, at a conference held at Lushan, Mao Zedong received a letter from Peng Dehuai, a veteran of the Long March who was now Minister of Defence, warning him that the achievements of the Great Leap Forward were being exaggerated. Mao chose to publish the letter and to attack Peng Dehuai openly at the conference. As Peng had recently returned from Moscow, Mao accused him of having conspired with Khrushchev to criticize the communes and also to cancel the offer of nuclear aid for China. Subsequently Peng Dehuai was replaced at the ministry of defence by Lin Biao, a close supporter of Mao. Critics of the Great Leap Forward were intimidated and a second Great Leap began in 1960. A feature of the second Great Leap was the extensive introduction of urban communes, in an attempt to make urban areas more self-sufficient. Mistaken agricultural policies, bad weather and the withdrawal of the Soviet technicians in July had by mid-1961 forced the abandonment of the second Great Leap.

The Great Leap Forward has excited controversy as an economic strategy and its failure has been seen as having momentous consequences for China. Before the full extent of the disaster precipitated by the Great Leap Forward was known, some Western economists, for example Alexander Eckstein, contended that the strategy of using China's underemployed labour to invest in agriculture, for example by large-scale irrigation projects, was appropriate for a densely-populated underdeveloped country. The reason for failure was not faulty strategy but hasty and ill-planned implementation and the adverse circumstances which have already been mentioned.[6] Nicholas Lardy was much more critical of the strategy, which was based on what he regarded as a misunderstanding of the constraints facing Chinese agriculture, a reference to Mao's belief that larger agricultural units would capture significant economies of scale. The projects undertaken by mobilized labour, most particularly the irrigation projects, were poorly designed, and reduced rather than raised yields. In addition the massive growth in the industrial workforce drove grain procurement in 1959 up to nearly 40 per cent of the harvest.[7]

The release of demographic data in the 1980s revealed that the Great Leap Forward had a disastrous effect on China's population. The decline in food production and the breakdown in the system of distribution had set off a famine unprecedented in the twentieth century. The cumulative increase in mortality has been estimated as somewhere between 16 and 27 million deaths. The famine, which was at its height in 1960, was felt most severely in rural areas and in certain provinces, with Anhui alone suffering about 2 million deaths. These figures may be compared with the loss of life in the Soviet Union at the time of the collectivization of agriculture, which has been estimated at 5 million deaths. The Party's response to this tragedy was wholly inadequate. In part this was because of lack of accurate information: the system of gathering statistics had collapsed and had been replaced by grossly exaggerated claims of increases in output. In part it was because after the Lushan conference many Party leaders, including Chen Yun, the Party's most senior economist, remained silent.

The Great Leap Forward and its consequences played a significant role in deepening the Sino-Soviet dispute. The origins of the dispute may be traced back to incidents in the history of the rise of the CCP, to the negotiation of the Treaty of Alliance and Mutual Assistance in 1950, to Sino-Soviet relations during the Korean War, to Khrushchev's secret speech denouncing Stalin in 1956, and to the tensions which had emerged at the time of Mao's visit to the Soviet Union in November 1957. However, it was the Great Leap Forward which brought these tensions out into the open. The rejection of Soviet economic methods, the trumpeting of the initial achievements of the Great Leap Forward, and the hailing of the communes as a short cut to communism, all threatened to deprive the Soviet Union of its claim to be the 'ideological and economic leader of the socialist camp'.[8] The tensions were heightened in 1958 and 1959 by various international crises, beginning with the United States' landings in Lebanon. On the day that Khrushchev arrived in Beijing his cautious response to this crisis was criticized in *Red Flag*, the Party's journal. Soon after, the Chinese threat to 'liberate' Taiwan was treated coolly by the Soviet Union. The Tibetan revolt in spring 1959, and the flight of the Dalai Lama to India, posed a threat to China, but again the Soviet Union did not offer firm support.

The rupture followed shortly after. In June 1959 the Soviet Union rescinded the offer of nuclear assistance it had made two years previously. At the same time, reports of critical remarks made by Khrushchev about the communes reached Mao's ears. In April 1960 *Red Flag* openly criticized the Soviet Union's policy of peaceful co-existence. This, and its rejection of China's economic policies, led the Soviet Union to announce in July that its technicians would be withdrawn in two months. Thus began a diplomatic estrangement which was to last until 1985.

PRELUDE TO THE CULTURAL REVOLUTION

The years following the disaster of the Great Leap Forward were dominated by economic reconstruction and educational and political adjustment. Steps were taken to restore the agrarian economy. In 1959 the brigade had replaced the commune as the unit of accounting and private plots had been restored. Up to 30 million people were relocated from the cities to the countryside, so allowing a large reduction in cereal procurements. Under Chen Yun's direction an 'agriculture first' economic strategy was developed. Believing that the mobilization of labour alone could not solve China's agricultural problems, Chen increased state investment in agriculture, expanded the production of agricultural machinery and chemical fertilizers and developed a 'high and stable yield' area policy, which encouraged regions which already produced large quantities of grain to concentrate on expanding cereal production. In the industrial sector many state enterprises were closed down and a partial return was made to the one-man management practices of the First Five-Year Plan. As a result of these policies, by 1965 agricultural output had returned to the level achieved in 1957, although in the meantime the population had risen by 80 million. Industrial output recovered even more quickly and by 1963 a period of sustained growth had begun, aided by the development of new industries, most notably the petrochemical industry. This recovery was remarkable for two reasons: it was achieved at a time when China was technologically isolated, and when the development of nuclear weapons – China's first nuclear test took place in October 1964 – was absorbing high technology sources.

In education the principle of 'walking on two legs' – which in this context meant the provision of regular, quality schools and mass-based work-study alternatives and the combination of study and productive work – was not abandoned, but it was modified extensively. The number of pupils in elementary schools fell from 93 million in 1960 to 69 million in 1962. Most of the agricultural middle schools, where students had studied the Chinese language and practical subjects in the morning and had worked in the fields in the afternoon, were closed. Likewise few of the 'red and expert' universities survived, one exception being the Jiangxi Communist Labour University, which continued to serve as a model for work-study and agricultural education. Central authority over education was reasserted and the amount of productive work required of staff and students was limited. Significantly 'keypoint schools', which had been introduced at the time of the Great Leap Forward, were retained. In them talented children were taught by selected teachers in a well-equipped environment.

*   *   *

In the post-Great Leap Forward period political leadership was provided by Liu Shaoqi, supported by Deng Xiaoping, (the general secretary of the CCP), the economist Chen Yun; and Peng Zhen, the 'mayor' of Beijing. Mao Zedong had largely withdrawn from the day-to-day management of affairs, but his views were represented by his wife Jiang Qing, who was active in the field of cultural affairs, and by Lin Biao, the minister of defence. Zhou Enlai, the premier, remained uncommitted to either side.

The nature of the contest between these two groupings has been interpreted in a variety of ways. One way is to regard it as a power struggle between Mao Zedong and his critics. Although differences between Mao and other Party leaders can be traced back many years, it was only after the disaster of the Great Leap Forward that Mao Zedong found himself excluded from political power. Subsequent events: the Socialist Education movement, the promotion of Mao's personality cult, Lin Biao's reforms of the People's Liberation Army, and the Cultural Revolution, may all be taken as an assault on Mao's political rivals, Liu Shaoqi and Deng Xiaoping.

Mao Zedong's relationship with the CCP had altered drastically since 1949. At that time, when the Party was transforming itself into the government of China, Mao's authority and ideological leadership had been unchallenged. In 1956, at the Eighth Party Congress, the Party constitution was revised by deleting reference to Mao Zedong's thought as part of the CCP's guiding ideology and by making it easier for white-collar workers to become members of the Party. The Politburo was enlarged and important positions were filled by technocrats. At the same time it was recognized that the government was becoming more bureaucratic and increasingly divorced from the masses and a campaign for Party rectification was launched. The changes effected did not satisfy Mao and his hostility towards the Party was apparent in his speech 'On the Correct Handling of Contradictions Among the People', which he gave in February 1957. Among the contradictions he identified was one between the leadership and the masses, which at the time he described as a non-antagonistic contradiction. His hostility increased markedly during the period of recovery after the Great Leap Forward. At the 7000 cadres' conference held in 1962 he made an outspoken attack on Party bureaucrats, who he accused of being arrogant. By now he had concluded that the relationship between the Party, which for him represented privileged power-holders, and the masses was an antagonistic contradiction. As such a contradiction could not be resolved by rectification, the Party would have to be smashed.

Other interpretations of the origins of the Cultural Revolution emphasize differences in the revolutionary objectives of the two sides. Mao had managed to persuade many, though not all, Party leaders to support the launching of the Great Leap Forward. In 1962, when the true extent of the disaster became apparent, Deng Xiaoping openly criticized the communes and socialist relations of production and hinted at the abandonment of collectivized farming. Speaking at a Communist Youth League conference he said that he favoured any form of production which would rapidly restore and increase agricultural output. Famously he quoted a Sichuan proverb 'Yellow or white, a cat that catches mice is a good cat.'[9] This issue, and other causes of dispute earned Deng Xiaoping and Liu Shaoqi condemnation as 'capitalist-roaders', and led to their being accused of following the revisionist course set by Khrushchev in the Soviet Union. Mao Zedong's loss of confidence in the Party and its leaders led him to look to the next generation in his search for revolutionary successors.

The first rounds of the struggle were fought in the context of the Socialist Education movement, which was launched in 1963. Mao shared common ground with other Party leaders in believing that apathy and corruption among Party cadres in the countryside was widespread. In a document later known as the 'Former Ten Points', which Mao himself had drafted, poor and lower-middle peasant associations were given the task of investigating cadre corruption and restoring the collective principle in farming. In September Deng Xiaoping issued a document known as the 'Later Ten Points', which supported many of the anxieties voiced in the previous document, but which called for the formation of urban-based work teams to carry out the rectification. In the winter of 1963–4 Wang Guangmei, Liu Shaoqi's wife, spent six months incognito investigating examples of cadre abuse. In September of the following year Liu Shaoqi, using information gathered by his wife, produced a third document, the 'Revised Later Ten Points', which painted a gloomy picture of the situation and proposed that large work teams should visit selected communes, investigate them thoroughly and deal severely with cases of cadre corruption. The dispute separating Mao and Liu Shaoqi was now becoming clear: whereas Liu regarded the central issue to be cadre corruption and the appropriate action to be the reimposition of Party authority, for Mao the issue was the revisionism which had appeared at all levels in the Party. In January 1965, Mao convened a conference and issued yet another document, the 'Twenty-three Articles' which made it clear that the target of the campaign was not the corruption of local cadres, but the actions of those people holding positions of authority in the Party who were taking the capitalist road.

In the meantime other controversies had arisen which widened the gap between Mao and his critics. Mao had long favoured the use of revolutionary models and in 1964 he promoted Dazhai Brigade in Shanxi as a model because its peasants, through their self-reliance and commitment to collective farming, had transformed the barren land they farmed and had raised its yields five-fold. The slogan coined was 'In agriculture learn from Dazhai'. Other brigades were called upon to emulate the selfless commitment of the people of Dazhai and to adopt their workpoint system, which rewarded political awareness as well as physical effort. However, later that year a work team investigating Dazhai concluded that the production figures had been grossly exaggerated. Nevertheless, Mao's influence protected the reputation of the brigade, which continued to serve as a model until Mao's death.

Mao had greater success in mobilizing support in the People's Liberation Army. Peng Dehuai, who had been appointed Minister of Defence after the Korean War, had introduced a series of reforms intended to turn the army into a professional force. When he was replaced by Lin Biao in 1959, the latter had continued the modernization programme and in October 1962, when the border dispute between India and China turned into a war, the People's Liberation Army achieved a rapid and overwhelming victory. Lin Biao also supported the nuclear programme which resulted in China detonating an atomic device in October 1964. However, Lin was also politically ambitious and he determined to make the armed forces an example of revolutionary zeal. He promoted the case of the model soldier Lei Feng who had died in 1962 at the age of 20 when trying to help a comrade. In 1964 the army's political department produced an early version of the compilation which was to become the *Quotations from Chairman Mao Zedong*. In return for his support Mao endorsed a campaign based on the slogan 'Learn from the People's Liberation Army'. In 1965 Lin, in an article entitled 'Long live the Victory of the People's War!', anticipated a confrontation between the United States and national liberation movements. In the article, he praised Mao Zedong extravagantly for his leadership in the war of resistance against Japan, which he described as a genuine 'people's war', in which the Party had relied on the masses, not on machines.

Two other issues were important in the years preceding the launching of the Great Proletarian Cultural Revolution, and were to be central to that event. The first was education, with particular reference to access and opportunity. In the aftermath of the Great Leap Forward fresh emphasis had been placed on educational standards and the use of examinations. By the early 1960s the educational system was 'probably more elitist than it had been a decade earlier'.[10] In a speech given at the Tenth Plenum of the Eighth Central Committee in September 1962, Mao Zedong had warned 'never forget the class struggle'. However, it appeared that the experiments in mass education which had appeared at the time of the Great Leap Forward had been forgotten and that a 'two-track' educational system had been established, which worked to the advantage of urban children, in particular the children of Party cadres. Mao criticized these developments at the Spring Festival Forum of 1964. He argued that the current period of schooling was too long, that too much reliance was placed on examinations, that too much deference was paid to teachers and that a stronger link should be established between education and production.

The other issue was culture. In 1942, in his 'Talks at the Yan'an Forum on Literature and Art', Mao had argued that the arts should serve the revolution and should do so by endorsing proletarian values. In the early 1960s, however, a number of novels and plays had appeared which contained implicit comments on political issues. The most notorious example was an opera written by the historian Wu Han entitled *Hai Rui Dismissed from Office*. Hai Rui, an upright sixteenth-century Ming official, had been dismissed by the emperor because he had protested against the confiscation of land from peasants. The opera was widely recognized as a criticism of Mao's actions at the time of the Great Leap Forward. In response Mao called upon his wife Jiang Qing, herself an erstwhile film star, to formulate a policy statement on culture. She teamed up with Kang Sheng, a former member of the Politburo who had specialized in issues relating to revisionism and counter-revolution. She also found allies in the Shanghai Party chief, Zhang Chunqiao, and the literary critic Yao Wenyuan, who were later to achieve notoriety as members of the 'Gang of Four'. In 1964 her efforts seemed to have born fruit when a 'Group of Five', headed by Peng Zhen and including Kang Sheng, was formed to carry out a cultural rectification. However, it soon became apparent that the efforts of the Group of Five did not satisfy the radicals, as Jiang Qing and her supporters may be called. In November 1965 Yao Wenyuan published a critical review of *Hai Rui dismissed from Office* in *Liberation Army Daily*, the organ of the People's Liberation Army. Wu Han, who as deputy mayor of Beijing happened to be Peng Zhen's immediate subordinate, was forced to make a self-criticism. This political infighting set the stage for the Cultural Revolution.

THE GREAT PROLETARIAN CULTURAL REVOLUTION

The Great Proletarian Cultural Revolution, to give it its full title, began in May 1966 and lasted in its active phase until April 1969. Its reverberations continued until Mao Zedong's death in September 1976 and the arrest of the Gang of Four in the following month.

The official launch of the Cultural Revolution was preceded by a period of manoeuvring. In the People's Liberation Army, Lin Biao was engaged in a struggle with Luo Ruiqing, his Chief-of-Staff. When the United States had started to bomb North Vietnam in February 1965, Luo Ruiqing had advocated a policy of improving relations with the Soviet Union and making preparations to give material support to North Vietnam. Lin Biao, on the other hand, argued that the Vietnamese should fight a 'people's war' and that China should only offer moral support. The difference of opinion between the two men resulted in Luo Ruiqing being forced to make a self-criticism, and to his dismissal. At the same time cultural issues were becoming increasingly divisive. The Group of Five issued a document known as the 'February Outline', which tried to limit consideration of the bourgeois tendencies in *Hai Rui Dismissed from Office* to an academic discussion. However, Mao Zedong complained that the Group had obscured class lines and had encouraged rightist sentiment. He described Wu Han as an 'academic warlord' and Peng Zhen, the leader of the Group, as a 'Party warlord'.[11] This manoeuvring phase ended with the Politburo meeting which began on 4 May. Lin Biao used the occasion to accuse Luo

Ruiqing and Peng Zhen of having plotted a coup against him and other radicals. At the end of the meeting the Politburo issued the 'May 16 Circular', which alleged that the Party had been infiltrated by bourgeois revisionists. It also announced the dissolution of the Group of Five and the appointment of a Cultural Revolution Group to be led by Chen Boda, the editor of *Red Flag*, and including Jiang Qing and Kang Sheng.

In the 'Fifty Days' between 16 May and 5 August two conflicting tendencies were apparent. Liu Shaoqi, who may have already been regarded by Mao Zedong as a revisionist, was placed in charge of implementing the Cultural Revolution. At the same time covert encouragement was being given to radicals in the universities to challenge Party leaders. On 25 May, Nie Yuanzi, a philosophy teacher at Beijing University, put a big-character poster on the canteen wall which attacked the university president for having supported the February Outline. The university authorities responded by trying to suppress the radical movement, but on 1 June Mao Zedong authorized the broadcasting of the contents of the poster. This resulted in a rash of big-character posters critical of educational policies and educational leaders appearing in schools and colleges throughout the country. Liu Shaoqi dispatched over 400 workteams to schools, universities and various government agencies to carry out a rectification campaign, and at the same time attempted to assert Party authority over the radical student movement. At Qinghua University in Beijing the conflict between Party leaders and radicals was personalized. Wang Guangmei, Liu Shaoqi's wife, was a member of the workteam, whereas Jiang Qing lent her support to the radicals.

Up to this point Mao Zedong had remained in Hangzhou, distancing himself from the struggle. On 16 July he made his famous swim in the Yangzi river, covering nine miles downstream in 65 minutes. Two days later he returned to Beijing and on 1 August he indicated his support for the use of the term 'Red Guard', which had been coined in May by student radicals at Qinghua University Middle School. On 5 August he published his own big-character poster entitled 'Bombard the Headquarters', which accused the workteams of 'adopting the reactionary stand of the bourgeoisie'. On 8 August, at a meeting of the Eleventh Plenum of the Central Committee of the CCP (from which some of Mao's opponents were excluded), a document known as the 'Sixteen Points' was adopted, which set out the purpose of the Cultural Revolution:

> to struggle against and overthrow those persons in authority who are taking the capitalist road, to criticize and repudiate the reactionary bourgeois academic 'authorities' and the ideology of the bourgeoisie . . . and to transform education, literature and art and all other parts of the superstructure not in correspondence with the socialist economic base. . . .[12]

By now numerous Red Guard organizations had appeared in schools and colleges, and on 18 August Mao Zedong reviewed the first of many Red Guard rallies in Tiananmen Square. The impression given was that this was a movement united in its revolutionary purpose and adulation of Mao Zedong. In fact from an early stage the Red Guard movement was split by factionalism, which derived from the educational policies that had been adopted after the Great Leap Forward. The main division lay between those students who came from the 'five kinds of red' family background – that is to say who were the children of workers, peasants, soldiers, cadres or revolutionary martyrs, – and those who came from 'bourgeois' backgrounds. The former, who had enjoyed preferential educational treatment in the 1960s, supported the workteams which Liu Shaoqi had sent into schools, and by extension they supported the Party. The latter, who felt that they had been overlooked academically, began to form their own rebel organizations and to challenge the workteams.

At the end of the Eleventh Plenum Mao Zedong had addressed a rally of Red Guards and had encouraged them to make revolution throughout the country. In schools and colleges, administrators and teachers were subjected to criticism and often publicly humiliated, and the same treatment was meted out to some Party officials. Lin Biao had called for the destruction of the 'four olds': old ideas, old culture, old customs and old habits. Red Guard groups took this as an invitation to destroy anything which might be described as representing bourgeois culture, whether it be works of art, foreign clothing, hairstyles, or even street names which made reference to the past. Red Guards also took advantage of free rail travel to visit Beijing and other parts of the country to attend rallies and to enjoy the experience of 'revolutionary tourism'.

By October it was apparent that the Cultural Revolution Group intended to challenge the Party establishment and that a fierce power struggle lay ahead. The Group accused 'persons in authority' of having taken the capitalist road, and Liu Shaoqi and Deng Xiaoping were forced to make self-criticisms. Red Guard groups in the provinces, often incited to action by delegates from Beijing Red Guard organizations, attacked local Party officials. After the 'five red' qualification for Red Guard membership had been relaxed, Red Guard organizations became more daring. In November they were permitted to enter factories and communes and to challenge the Party monopoly of relations with peasants' and workers' organizations.

In January 1967 an incident known as the 'Shanghai storm' epitomized the collapse of Party provincial authority. The Shanghai workforce included many thousands of casual labourers and contract workers who enjoyed none of the benefits enjoyed by employees in the state sector. The tensions deriving from their economic situation were exploited by Shanghai radicals with the encouragement of the Cultural Revolution Group. On 6 January the mayor and other municipal officials were forced to resign, and rebel organizations, with the support of the People's Liberation Army, seized control of factories and offices. A new city government was formed, supposedly modelled on the Paris Commune of 1871. Its representatives were elected in a secret ballot by members of factory organizations. The Party authorities were entirely swept aside. By the end of January similar 'seizures of power' had occurred in cities throughout the country, although in some cases these had been stage-managed by Party officials.

The resultant confusion led Mao and the Cultural Revolution Group to reject the Paris Commune model and to endorse the creation of a new power structure, the revolutionary committee, which comprised representatives of the mass organizations, Party cadres and the People's Liberation Army. Each of these groups contained radical and conservative elements and in the first half of 1967 there was incessant infighting. Party cadres fought to protect themselves from criticism, the mass organizations struggled amongst themselves, and even in the armed forces radical and conservative elements were in competition. At the same time the Red Guard press openly criticized Liu Shaoqi and Deng Xiaoping.

The danger of the situation was made manifest by an incident which occurred in Wuhan in July. The commander of the Wuhan Military Region, who had supported an organization of conservative workers known as the 'Million Heroes', was accused of repressing the radical mass organizations. A delegation from the Cultural Revolution Group, accompanied by Zhou Enlai, went to Wuhan and found in favour of the radicals, whereupon the Million Heroes attacked the delegation. To resolve the dispute Zhou Enlai was forced to bring in outside military forces and to dismiss the Wuhan military commander. By the end of August China was on the verge of civil war. Red Guard and other mass organizations were obtaining arms and fighting pitched battles in the streets. Jiang Qing was voicing criticism of leaders of the People's Liberation Army, thereby threatening to undermine the army's shaky authority. The foreign ministry, which was headed by Marshal Chen Yi, an ally of Zhou Enlai, was seized by the radicals, and the British legation in Beijing was burned down.

The crisis forced Mao Zedong, supported by Zhou Enlai and Lin Biao, to adopt measures to restore stability. Some of the radicals were purged from the Cultural Revolution Group, and the People's Liberation Army was empowered to suppress disorder. The army encouraged the study of the 'little red book', the *Quotations from Chairman Mao Zedong*, to provide a basis for a revolutionary consensus. In September the first steps were taken towards the reconstitution of the Party. After a further upsurge of campus violence in spring 1968, Red Guard organizations were disbanded. The process of forming revolutionary committees was accelerated and finally completed in September 1968. In the following month, at the Twelfth Plenum of the Central Committee, Liu Shaoqi was officially expelled from the Party. Finally, at the Ninth Party Congress, held in April 1969, a new Party leadership, with Lin Biao identified as Mao's successor, was agreed. A report from Lin Biao to the Congress marked the conclusion of the first stage of the Cultural Revolution.

Mao Zedong is reputed to have said that the Cultural

Revolution consisted of 70 per cent achievements and 30 per cent mistakes. This estimate was based on the alleged aims of the event: reversing the trend towards revisionism, getting rid of bourgeois influences and placing 'politics in command'. Since Mao Zedong's death, however, few have regarded it so favourably. An account of the revolution published in Xianggang in 1986 concluded,

> For China the Cultural Revolution remains a colossal catastrophe in which human rights, democracy, the rule of law, and civilization were unprecedentedly trampled. Not only was the president [Liu Shaoqi] persecuted to death, tens of millions of innocent people were also attacked and maltreated.[13]

The direct impact of the Cultural Revolution on the economy was limited. Although political disruption was extensive, industrial and agricultural output only declined temporarily and by 1970 output was already surpassing previous peak levels. The indirect impact was more serious, for it left China's planners 'severely constrained by fears of political reprisals'.[14] It also had a lasting influence on industrial management. During the 'Shanghai storm' the conservative labour unions had been accused of trying to bribe the workers with the promise of higher wages. The radicals had countered this by introducing ideological incentives and by appealing to the *Quotations from Chairman Mao Zedong* for guidance. Other changes gave workers a share in management and required cadres to participate in labour. Soon after the Cultural Revolution, material rewards were reintroduced, but the influence of the revolution could still be detected in a management style which sought to compromise between 'one-man management' and worker participation in management, which resulted in management by revolutionary committee.

The Cultural Revolution left its most enduring imprint on education. Between 1968 and his death in 1976 Mao Zedong 'presided over the most radical set of reforms to be imposed upon China's modern school system' this century. The aim of these reforms was to reduce the 'three great distinctions', between town and country, industry and agriculture, and mental and manual labour.[15] To achieve this the school curriculum was shortened, more time was spent on political education and all pupils and students were required to participate in manual labour. In the countryside, middle schools were run by communes and primary schools by production brigades. Primary school teachers were paid in work points based on the collective's annual income. National college examinations were abolished and colleges selected students from those recommended by their work units. A typical innovation of the time was the 'July 21 Workers' University', exemplified by the institute attached to the Shanghai Machine Tools Plant. There workers and peasants with good political credentials and extensive practical experience followed a shortened course which combined technology, political thought and manual labour. After graduation they returned to their original place of work.

After Mao Zedong's death the official line was that 'not one good thing' could be said of these years of educational reform. Suzanne Pepper, however, has suggested that, like the French Revolution for Charles Dickens, they were both the best of times and the worst of times. On the positive side the most important achievement was the expansion of educational opportunity. Between 1969 and 1977 primary school enrolment rose from 100 million to 146 million pupils and ordinary secondary school enrolment from 20 million to 67 million pupils. The disadvantages experienced by children who lived in rural areas were somewhat reduced by a redistribution of resources. The main negative criticism of the reform programme was that it lowered educational standards, the most severe impact being on tertiary education. Most universities and colleges did not resume regular intakes until the early 1970s. Some four million secondary students, who formed the 'Red Guard generation', were 'rusticated', that is sent to the countryside on rural assignments, where they remained for up to ten years. When tertiary education was resumed, the challenge to academic education continued. A notable protest was made in 1973 by a student named Zhang Tiesheng who, when taking the cultural test for entry to a provincial college, handed in a blank examination paper. His explanation was that he, unlike other entrants, had been unable to study because he had been working. His action was cited as a praiseworthy example of 'going against the tide' which was restoring academic standards.

FROM THE CULTURAL REVOLUTION TO THE DEATH OF MAO ZEDONG

During the Cultural Revolution the People's Liberation Army had been called upon to restore order and later to form a part of revolutionary committees. In 1967, People's Liberation Army officers headed 21 of the 27 provincial revolutionary committees. Two years later, at the Ninth Party Congress, Lin Biao, the minister of defence, was named as Mao's successor. A new Politburo was chosen, 55 per cent of the membership of which came from the military. Some Western observers suggested that in China, as in some other Third World countries, the army was in the process of displacing the Party.

Over the next two years Mao Zedong, motivated either by his belief that 'the Party should command the gun', or by his growing suspicion of Lin Biao, took steps to restore the authority of the Party and to undermine Lin Biao's standing. While the army continued to perform its political role, a start was made to reconstituting the Party and revising the state structure. In late 1969 the army was told that it should pay greater attention to military training, an indication that it would soon be relieved of its political responsibilities. In the meantime, differences had emerged between Lin and Mao on the issue of the future direction of China's foreign policy. Whereas Lin believed that in international relations China should ally with oppressed and revolutionary peoples, Mao now endorsed cautious moves towards a rapprochement with the United States. Finally, at the Second Plenum of the Ninth Congress, held at Lushan in September 1970, events occurred which may have convinced Mao that Lin was not a suitable successor. Some months previously Lin had proposed that Mao should become head of state. This position, which after 1959 had been held by Liu Shaoqi, was due to be abolished in the new state structure. Mao rejected the offer, but Lin raised the matter again at the Second Plenum, perhaps expecting that Mao would refuse once more and that the position would then be awarded to him to signify publicly that he was Mao's heir. The persistence of Lin Biao and his supporters, who included Chen Boda, a former member of the Cultural Revolution Group, earned a rebuke from Mao Zedong.

After the Plenum a campaign was mounted to discredit Chen

Boda and in August 1971 Mao visited regional military commanders in central and south China to assure himself of their loyalty. According to allegations made later, Lin Biao realized that his time was up, so he authorized his son to devise the '571 plot', which involved killing Mao Zedong when he was aboard his special train. When the plot failed the conspirators attempted to set up a rival regime in Guangzhou. That plan also having collapsed, on 13 September Lin Biao, his wife and his son fled the country. They were killed when their plane crashed in Mongolia.

While these dramatic events were occurring, a major realignment had been taking place in China's foreign relations. At the time of the Cultural Revolution China had become diplomatically isolated. In March 1969 a dispute arose with the Soviet Union over the ownership of Zhenbao (Danansky) island on the Wusuli river. The incident, which may have been engineered by Lin Biao for his own ends, brought home to China the danger of the Russian nuclear threat and the concentration of Soviet forces on her frontier. From 1969 the possibility of improving relations with the United States was under discussion. In July 1971 Henry Kissinger, the United States' Secretary of State, made a secret trip to China to prepare the way for a visit by President Nixon in the following year. From the Chinese point of view Nixon's visit was a great success, as it resulted in an agreement on peaceful co-existence between the two countries without China having to make any concessions about the 'one China' policy and the claim to Taiwan.

After Lin's death the main domestic political issue was the succession to Mao. The struggle lay between the more pragmatic senior Party members, who included Zhou Enlai and Chen Yi, the former foreign minister, and the radicals, who included Mao's wife Jiang Qing, and Zhang Chunqiao and Yao Wenyuan, both from Shanghai. As Mao regarded none of them as potential successors, he first promoted an outsider, Wang Hongwen, a former worker in a Shanghai cotton mill, to the number three position in the Party hierarchy. Wang found that Zhou Enlai held all the key posts and this encouraged him to join Jiang Qing in the 'Criticize Lin Biao, criticize Confucius campaign', the real targets of which were Zhou Enlai and the former victims of the Cultural Revolution, who were now being rehabilitated. However, Zhou had recently been diagnosed as having cancer and the campaign misfired. Thereupon Mao Zedong decided to turn to Deng Xiaoping – the man who in 1967 had been described as the 'number two person in authority taking the capitalist road' – because his high reputation with the military and his political skills were much needed qualities.

Deng Xiaoping was rehabilitated in May 1973 and over the next year he initiated a number of overdue reforms. These included reducing the size of the People's Liberation Army and defining a long-term economic policy, described by Zhou Enlai as the 'Four Modernizations', which referred to agriculture, industry, defence, and science and technology. These reforms left him open to criticism from the radicals. When Zhou Enlai died in January 1976, Mao decided against appointing Deng as premier and chose instead Hua Guofeng, the former First Secretary of the Party in Hunan, who he believed was committed to the policies of the Cultural Revolution.

Jiang Qing, Zhang Chunqiao, Yao Wenyuan and Wang Hongwen, described by Mao as 'the Gang of Four', were infuriated by Hua Guofeng's elevation, and Jiang Qing criticized him openly. However, a demonstration in Tiananmen Square in March 1976 in memory of Zhou Enlai showed how unpopular the radicals were. Suspecting that the demonstration was connected with Deng Xiaoping, the Gang had it broken up ruthlessly, and Deng himself, on Mao's instruction, was removed from all his offices. In July an earthquake hit Tangshan, 160 miles south-east of Beijing, killing nearly a quarter of a million people. The Gang misread the situation, which was one of extreme apprehension, and issued an official message to survivors that they should 'deepen and broaden' the criticism of Deng Xiaoping's revolutionary line.

Mao Zedong died on 9 September 1976. The editorial of the *People's Daily* of 18 September claimed that 'Chairman Mao Will Live Forever in Our Hearts', but this uncritical assessment was not to survive for long. In June 1981 the Party accepted a wordy 'Resolution on Certain Questions in the History of Our Party'. Mao Zedong Thought, now described as the collective wisdom of the Party, was to remain 'a guide to action for a long time to come', but Mao himself was said to have made 'gross mistakes' at the time of the Cultural Revolution, although his contribution to the Party's success prior to then far outweighed those errors.

The Gang of Four assumed that the succession to Mao would fall to them, and at the memorial service held in Tiananmen Square on 18 September Jiang Qing stood beside Hua Guofeng when he read the eulogy. But on 6 October Hua Guofeng had the Gang arrested on the charge of plotting to usurp power. Four years late the Gang, and five military commanders who were accused of complicity in Lin Biao's attempted coup, were put on trial. Jiang Qing spoke in her own defence, arguing that she was merely 'Chairman Mao's dog'. She was given a suspended death sentence, later commuted to life imprisonment. She committed suicide in 1991.

THE ERA OF DENG XIAOPING

After Mao Zedong's death and the fall of the Gang of Four, Deng Xiaoping was restored to the offices he had held before the Tiananmen incident, but Hua Guofeng, who had previously been his subordinate, remained premier. Over the next four years Deng Xiaoping campaigned to secure the rehabilitation of the victims of the Cultural Revolution, and by implication the rejection of Mao Zedong's legacy, of which Hua Guofeng claimed to be the guardian. By 1980 he had isolated Hua who was then forced to resign as premier. In the early 1980s Deng delegated routine administration to two men from a younger generation, Hu Yaobang, who became Party secretary, and Zhao Ziyang, who succeeded Hua Guofeng as premier. Deng remained in effective control until 1987, when he resigned from the Central Committee, although he retained the chair of the Military Affairs Commission. He continued to dominate the political scene until his retirement from all official positions in 1990, and his influence was apparent until shortly before his death in February 1997.

Deng Xiaoping's political style was highly personalized and he was prepared to go to great lengths to settle private animosities. For example, he used his authority to secure a ten-year prison sentence for Nie Yuanzi, the philosophy teacher at Beijing University whose big-character poster had launched the Cultural Revolution. In Deng's opinion she was also responsible for the persecution by Red Guards of his son Deng Pufang, which led to him falling from a roof at the university in 1968 and becoming paralysed from the waist downwards.

Deng was no advocate of democracy but he accepted the case for some modest political changes. In 1980 the system of congressional elections, which had not operated since the Cultural Revolution, was revived and direct elections were held for some 2000 county-level congresses. Members of the National People's Congress, an indirectly-elected body which hitherto had met sporadically to rubber-stamp Party decisions, were now allowed to cross-examine ministers on their work and to table suggestions for government action. The 1982 constitution provided for the Congress to establish standing committees to deal with foreign, economic, and minority-nationalities' affairs. In September 1985 a special Party conference was convened to force the retirement from the Politburo of some of its most aged members. An attempt to reduce the gerontocratic character of government was certainly desirable, but Deng's motives may have been largely the settling of old scores.

These moves were subordinate to Deng's primary objective, which was to bring about a major shift in economic policy. In agriculture this implied the abandonment of collectivization and the adoption of a market economy. After the Great Leap Forward, modifications had been introduced to the communes, but the principles of public ownership of land, reliance on human labour as the main resource, and restrictions on private enterprise, had been retained. In the years from 1966 to 1978 the gross value of agricultural output had grown at 3.1 per cent per annum, sufficient to sustain the growing population but quite inadequate to raise living standards to a significant degree.

In 1979 two reforms were instituted which were to transform the agricultural sector. The first was to encourage peasants to maximize the use of their private plots and to sell their produce on the open market. By 1982 the private income of peasant families may have amounted to 38 per cent of family income. The second was the 'productive responsibility system', which was introduced in 1981. Although the collective ownership of land was retained, individual families could now take out contracts to cultivate plots of land with specified crops and could retain or sell any surplus produced in excess of their contract. These measures injected an entrepreneurial spirit into farming. The slogan

'To get rich is glorious' was coined and the 'ten thousand yuan' household appeared. In the years immediately after the introduction of these reforms the growth rate of grain output rose from 3.5 to 5 per cent per annum. In 1984 China's grain output topped 400 million tonnes for the first time. However, the improvement in rates of growth could not be maintained without new inputs, which meant the increased use of agricultural machinery, chemical fertilizer and electric power. Increase in rural incomes might still be achieved by diversifying production and by the encouragement of rural industry, but the fundamental problem of agriculture remained the shortage of arable land, which in 1987 amounted to only 0.1 hectare per capita.

In the ten-year period after 1979, China's gross national product grew at 9.2 per cent per annum. Part of this growth, as has been indicated, was achieved in the agricultural sector and more came in the hitherto much underdeveloped service sector. The key area of growth, however, was industry. In the 1970s China's industry still retained many of the characteristics of the Soviet period. The Ten-Year Plan launched in 1976 had concentrated investment on large-scale heavy-industrial projects which were set unrealistically-high production targets. By the 1980s the need to improve incentives for workers was apparent and this forced a switch to the production of consumer goods, which in turn encouraged the importation of foreign technology and the growth of foreign trade. After a period of adjustment, China experienced an economic boom which between 1981 and 1986 nearly doubled China's industrial output.

Although it had achieved an impressive rate of growth, China's industrial sector was still controlled by a centralized planning system which determined what an enterprise should produce, where it should obtain its raw materials and where and at what price it should sell its products. In the 1980s, with China suffering the consequences of an energy crisis, the need for change was apparent. In 1984 economic policy began to shift away from reliance on centralized planning towards the greater use of market forces. Two years later, state price control was replaced with a dual-price system, with state-set prices being used to subsidize favoured firms, but market-set prices controlling demand for materials in short supply. Although these reforms freed up the market, they also accelerated inflation and encouraged corrupt practices in the allocation of goods at state-set prices.

In December 1978 the policy of national economic self-sufficiency was abandoned. China began to accept loans and foreign investments and joined the International Monetary Fund and the World Bank. In 1979 four 'Special Economic Zones' were created at Zhuhai, north of Aomen (Macao), Shenzhen near Xianggang, Shantou, and Xiamen. The purpose of establishing these zones was to attract foreign capital to China. Foreign firms were offered advantageous terms for investment, suitable sites and a supply of cheap labour. Foreign direct investment quickly became substantial, most of it coming from Xianggang firms seeking cheap labour. It brought with it not only foreign exchange, but also new technology and management practices.

A number of social issues became topical in the 1980s, the most notorious being the 'one-child family' policy which was introduced in 1979. In 1953 the census had shown how rapidly China's population was growing and a birth control campaign was introduced, although this was abandoned during the Great Leap Forward. It was later revived, but during the Cultural Revolution birth control was denounced as an anti-Marxist heresy. In the 1970s, partly in response to a government campaign which imposed economic sanctions on families with more than three children, the fertility rate began to fall rapidly. Nevertheless the population continued to increase and this led the government in 1979 to adopt the draconian 'one-child family' policy. Couples who accepted a one-child family certificate received a generous package of benefits, whereas a couple who persisted in having a second child were liable to lose a percentage of their income and forfeit their private plot or responsibility plot. Some exceptions were made in the case of children born with congenital defects, and the policy generally did not apply to minority groups.

Many questions have arisen about the advisability of this policy. The need for drastic action was supported by the evidence of the 1982 census, which showed that China's population exceeded one billion. Nevertheless the policy flew in the face of the deeply-held belief that a family needed a son to preserve the ancestral line and to provide economic support. The enforcement of the policy involved the widespread use of abortion and sterilization and encouraged female infanticide. In 1984 it was recognized that the campaign was too coercive, and a wider range of exemptions was allowed. Since then the policy has been generally accepted and enforced in urban areas, but has been less successful in rural areas.

The introduction of the one-child family policy revived the debate about the status of women in modern Chinese society. The 1950 Marriage Law had appeared to confirm the Communists' promise that under the new regime women would occupy a position of economic and legal equality with men. Rural China remained a patriarchal society however, and although educational opportunities for girls and employment opportunities for women improved, women still laboured under the double burden of child-bearing and work. During the Great Leap Forward the provision of communal kitchens and nurseries offered women a brief glimpse of a less trammelled existence, but during the Cultural Revolution the class struggle was emphasized and feminist issues were dismissed as bourgeois preoccupations. In 1980 a new Marriage Law was passed, which confirmed the legal rights of women and raised the minimum age of marriage for men from 20 to 22 and for women from 18 to 20. If the position of women in Chinese society today is compared with that which they occupied before 1949, the argument that they have been liberated would seem incontrovertible. Yet few women achieve senior positions in employment or occupy important political roles, and the one-child family policy has proved a sharp reminder of the misogynism which still persists in Chinese society.

In the new constitution promulgated in 1982 it was reaffirmed that the People's Republic was a multinational state. This was in recognition of the fact that 8 per cent of China's population belong to one of the 55 national minorities. The largest single group, the Zhuang, who live in the south-west, number over 15 million. Other sizeable groups include the Hui, Chinese-speaking Muslims, and the Uighur, to be found in the north-west, and the Miao and the Tibetans in the south and west.

For the most part, China's minority nationalities occupy China's strategically-important border regions. The territories in which they predominate have been granted autonomous-region status, which affords them some economic and political freedom but does not give them the option of secession. Although the minority nationalities are encouraged to preserve features of their culture, the persistent migration of Han Chinese into the autonomous regions forces ethnic groups to adapt to the dominant Han Chinese presence. It is clear that the process of absorption, typical of the historic relationship between Chinese and neighbouring peoples, is continuing. In recent years Uighur nationalists have made some violent protests against the erosion of their independence, but the most notable opposition, which has received a good deal of sympathy in the West, has come from Tibet.

Tibet fell under Chinese political control in the eighteenth century and from time to time thereafter international agreements, for example the Anglo-Chinese agreement of 1906, acknowledged the region to be Chinese territory. In 1911 Outer Mongolia and Tibet seized the opportunity to break away from China. Two years later the Dalai Lama declared Tibet to be an independent state and this was recognized by Great Britain but never accepted by China. In 1950 Tibet was 'liberated' by the People's Liberation Army commanded by Deng Xiaoping, and was designated the Xizang Autonomous Region. Assurances were given that the region would continue to administer its internal affairs and that its social system would be left intact. However, the Chinese presence in Tibet, and in particular the challenge this posed to Tibetan Buddhism, led to rising tension. The Tibetan revolt of 1959 resulted in Chinese military intervention and the flight of the Dalai Lama to India. During the Cultural Revolution, many Buddhist monasteries were destroyed, in some cases by Tibetan Red Guards. After the Cultural Revolution reassurances were offered about Tibet's economic and cultural autonomy. Nevertheless, Tibetan opposition to the Chinese presence continued and in 1989 demonstrations in favour of Tibetan independence were crushed brutally.

During Deng Xiaoping's time as leader the relationship between the People's Republic of China and the Republic of China on Taiwan changed from one of military and political confrontation to one of economic co-operation. After the Guomindang defeat on the mainland, Taiwan, under President Jiang Jieshi, became a bastion of Nationalist resistance and an important part of the United States' strategy for the containment of Communism. This arrangement collapsed in 1971 when President Nixon visited Beijing and the People's Republic took the seat held by Taiwan at the United Nations. Nevertheless Jiang Jieshi persevered with the policy of confrontation with the mainland until his death in April 1975. He was succeeded as president by his son Jiang Jingguo, who initiated a policy of cautious political liberalization. He remained deeply suspicious of the People's Republic and his doubts about China's intentions increased in 1979 when relations between the United States and China were normalized. In 1981 Deng Xiaoping assured the people of Taiwan that China no longer planned to recover the island by force and that if it were reunited peacefully with the mainland its people would be allowed to retain a high degree of autonomy. Although no negotiations on reunification took place, trade between Taiwan and China began to increase rapidly and in 1987 Taiwan relaxed its foreign-exchange controls and removed its ban on travel to the mainland.

Deng Xiaoping also played a leading role in determining the future of Xianggang. The island itself had been ceded to Great Britain in perpetuity in 1842 but the New Territories, which were essential for Xianggang's survival as a viable unit, had only been leased to Great Britain on a 99-year term from 1898. After 1949 there was an expectation that the People's Republic would demand the immediate return of Xianggang, but Mao Zedong gave the matter a low priority. Twice over the next 20 years the security of Xianggang as a British colony appeared under threat. After the Great Leap Forward, Xianggang's resources were strained to the limit by an influx of thousands of refugees. In 1967, during the Cultural Revolution, Red Guards fomented the most serious disorder the colony had ever known. Notwithstanding these threats, the issue of Xianggang's future remained undecided.

When the colony's economy began to expand rapidly in the 1970s, this was so much to China's advantage that it seemed possible that the return of the territory to China would be postponed indefinitely. However, Deng Xiaoping had strong views on national unification and he suggested that Xianggang should receive an offer similar to that which had been made to Taiwan in 1981. After reintegration the territory would be allowed to retain a high degree of autonomy, a concept which was later described as 'one country, two systems'. In 1982 Margaret Thatcher, the British Prime Minister, visited Beijing and began the negotiations which resulted in the Anglo-Chinese agreement of 1984. Under this, Xianggang would revert to China in 1997 and become a Special Administrative Region. Its people would be allowed to retain their own social and economic systems for 50 years after that date.

*   *   *

Deng Xiaoping's record as paramount leader was to be tarnished by his handling of the democracy movement and by his role in the massacre which took place in the vicinity of Tiananmen Square on the night of 3–4 June 1989.

Since its founding, the CCP's attitude towards democratic freedoms has been very mixed. In 1919, Chen Duxiu declared that only the two gentlemen 'Mr Science and Mr Democracy' could 'cure the dark maladies in Chinese politics, morality, learning and thought'. However, Comintern influence on the Party led to Chen being expelled and to members being subjected to Party discipline. At Yan'an some intellectuals who had joined the Party ventured to criticize the lack of democratic rights. Mao Zedong responded in his 'Talk at the Yan'an Forum on Literature and Art'. Art, he said, must serve the masses, not the subjective interests of the artist. In protest against this denial of freedom Wang Shiwei, a young Communist activist, wrote an essay entitled 'Wild Lily'. For his temerity Wang was put on trial and later executed. The term 'wild lily' came to denote democratic dissent, and Wang Shiwei was later described as the CCP's first dissident.

In 1957, when Mao Zedong launched the Hundred Flowers campaign, intellectuals were given a brief opportunity to express their opinions. On Beijing University campus a 'democracy wall' was started, with one student calling for true socialism with democracy. When the strength of dissenting views became apparent, Mao abandoned the intellectuals and called upon Deng Xiaoping to lead an anti-rightist movement. During the Cultural Revolution, when Mao himself had declared that 'to rebel is justified', some Red Guards had published critiques of aspects of the Party in the Red Guard press. After the Cultural Revolution millions of Red Guards were sent down to the country. Many of them felt betrayed, either because they had been deprived of their educational opportunities, or because the cause to which they had been committed was rejected after Mao Zedong's death.

This was the background of the new democracy movement which appeared in 1978. At first this was not primarily a movement of intellectuals, its main participants being state-employed manual workers and technicians, who were later joined by former Red Guards who had drifted back to the cities. The first manifestation of the movement was the appearance of posters on a wall along Chang'an Avenue in Beijing. Among the contributions was a poster headed 'Democracy, the Fifth Modernization' by Wei Jingsheng, a man in his forties who worked as an electrician at Beijing Zoo while at the same time studying at Beijing University. Wei Jingsheng argued that free enterprise was the only economic system compatible with democracy. Other contributors to the democracy movement remained committed to socialism and argued that China's problems stemmed from the shortcomings of its bureaucracy.

The democracy movement began soon after Deng Xiaoping had been reinstated. His first response was to regard the activists as useful allies against the surviving Maoists and to give the movement his guarded support. However, his priority was economic modernization and in February 1979 he defined his political stance in 'four cardinal principles': that China should keep to the socialist road and that it should uphold the dictatorship of the proletariat, the leadership of the CCP, and the authority of Marxism–Leninism and Mao Zedong Thought. At the same time the 'four great freedoms': to speak out freely, to air views fully, to hold great debates and to write wall posters, – freedoms which had been formulated by Mao Zedong – were removed from the 1978 constitution. When Wei Jingsheng and others protested they were arrested and Wei was given a 15-year gaol sentence.

In the early 1980s the effects of China's increasing contact with the outside world alarmed some of the more conservative Party leaders. In 1983 a campaign was started against 'spiritual pollution', a reference to Western hairstyles, Beethoven's music, and other examples of capitalist decadence. The leadership was not united in this condemnation, and Hu Yaobang, who became general secretary of the Party in 1982, became known for making incautious remarks which were sometimes critical of

Marxism or positive about aspects of the West. Some intellectuals, the most famous of whom was the astrophysicist Fang Lizhi,
who had been a victim at the time of the Hundred Flowers and
who was now vice president of the University of Science and
Technology at Hefei, were also bold enough to question the
record of the CCP.

In December 1986 a student movement began at Hefei in
protest against the alleged rigging of elections to the people's
congresses. Whereas student movements had played a key role in
national history in 1919 and again in 1935, this was 'the first
sustained series of student demonstrations in the People's
Republic not directly sponsored or explicitly encouraged by top
party officials'.[16] The movement spread rapidly to Shanghai and
Beijing, the students were joined by other social groups and banners were displayed calling for democracy. As the movement
gained momentum Party leaders became increasingly concerned.
In January 1987 Fang Lizhi was dismissed and it was later
revealed that in the same month Hu Yaobang had been forced to
make a self-criticism and then made to resign for having allowed
the demonstrations to get out of hand. Zhao Ziyang took over as
Party secretary and in November 1987 Li Peng became acting
premier. Under this new leadership further efforts were made to
implement the Four Modernizations, but political reform
remained excluded from the agenda.

In April 1989 Hu Yaobang, who was popularly supposed to
have been a supporter of democracy, died of a heart attack.
Beijing students held demonstrations in his memory and at the
same time protested about corruption and nepotism in government and the introduction of new restrictions on students' choice
of employment after graduation. The seventieth anniversary of 4
May 1919, a date forever associated with democratic freedoms,
was marked by massive unofficial parades in Beijing and in
other cities. The Chinese leadership was surprised by the scale
of these demonstrations, and Zhao Ziyang and Li Peng disagreed
on how best to proceed. Tension began to rise when some of the
student demonstrators camping on Tiananmen Square began a
hunger strike to force the government to make political concessions. The situation was complicated by the arrival of the Soviet
leader, Mikhail Gorbachev, on 15 May for a state visit. On 19
May Zhao Ziyang visited some of the hunger strikers and gave

the impression that he was sympathetic to their demands. Li Peng took a harsher line and on the following day he issued emergency orders banning demonstrations and empowering the People's Liberation Army to take appropriate action. On the night of 22 May, and again two days later, Deng Xiaoping called together the Party elders to discuss the crisis. The leading advocate of decisive action was President Yang Shangkun, who argued that if the Party gave way it would fall from power and capitalism would be restored.[17] The student protesters remained resolute and on 29 May erected a statue of the Goddess of Democracy on Tiananmen Square. The first army units to arrive in Beijing appeared unwilling to use force against the demonstrators, but on the night of 3–4 June troops broke into the square and opened fire. It was later estimated that between 400 and 800 people had been killed, most of whom were not students and many of whom did not die in the square but in the surrounding streets.

Various reasons have been advanced to explain why the massacre occurred. The official Chinese version was that it was the suppression of an attempted coup by counter-revolutionaries who had foreign backing. The Party leadership was blamed and Zhao Ziyang was dismissed for having failed to take a firm line with the students. Deng Xiaoping concluded that Li Peng was also at fault, for he had bungled the containment of the movement and then had to order its suppression in a blaze of international publicity. To distance himself from those implicated, Deng arranged that Jiang Zemin, the mayor of Shanghai, should be promoted above Li Peng as secretary-general of the Party. In broader terms the tragic events of 3–4 June 1989 have been explained as a failure of China's political system. The economic reforms which began in 1978 might have eased tensions within the leadership and might have been accompanied by the development of institutions which would have promoted long-term political stability. Instead the reforms provided further grounds for dispute between reformers and conservatives. Because of this rift there was no agreement within the leadership on how to deal with the democracy movement, and policy see-sawed between concession and violent suppression.

After the Tiananmen Square massacre, those political activists who had not fled abroad were rounded up and imprisoned. For a time international outrage in the West was so great that it seemed possible that the Chinese leadership might find it necessary to make some political concessions. However, at the 1992 Party Congress Deng's 'four cardinal principles' were reaffirmed and the need to suppress political 'turmoil', a reference to the 1989 demonstrations, was reiterated. Nevertheless, economic reforms, which to hardline members of the leadership were the cause of political discontent, had by now become irreversible. Between 1989 and 1991 an attempt was made to restore centralized control of the economy, but in 1992 Deng Xiaoping, while making a tour of south China which included a visit to Shenzhen, proclaimed that China would adopt a 'socialist market economy', and this meant the end of price controls, a massive shakeout of workers in state enterprises, and the encouragement of private enterprise.

Epilogue

Deng Xiaoping's death on 19 February 1997 marked the end of an era, for he was nearly the last link with the early years of the CCP, but otherwise it brought little immediate change. Deng's wish to live to see the return of Xianggang to China was not granted, but that event took place as planned on 30 June 1997. The political leadership headed by President Jiang Zemin, which he had approved, remained in place. The economic modernization, which was his enduring legacy, forged ahead. Two of the most pressing economic tasks, the radical overhaul of state enterprises and the drastic reduction of the vast workforce relying on the 'iron rice bowl', or state employment, continued apace. The Three Gorges Dam project, the extraordinarily ambitious programme promoted by Li Peng to control the Yangzi river, remained on schedule despite the devastating floods of August 1998. In that same month the Chinese economy was not only strong enough to withstand the effects of the Asian crisis, but was even able to offer financial support to Russia. At the time of writing, it seems likely that Deng's legacy will remain intact into the twenty-first century.

Notes

The abbreviation *CHC* refers to *The Cambridge History of China*, ed. Denis Twitchett and John K. Fairbank. For full details, see 'Further Reading', pp. 309–10.

Notes to the Introduction
1. John W. Dardess, *A Ming Society: T'ai-ho County, Kiangsi, Fourteenth to Seventeenth Centuries* (Berkeley, CA: University of California Press, 1996).
2. Li Jun, *Chinese Civilization in the Making, 1766–221 BC* (London: Macmillan, 1996).
3. Paul A. Cohen, *Discovering History in China: American Historical Writing on the Recent Chinese Past* (New York: Columbia University Press, 1984) pp. 9–55.

Notes to Chapter 1 The Prehistory and Early History of China
1. D.C. Lau (trans. and ed.), *Mencius* (Harmondsworth: Penguin Books, 1970) p. 128.
2. Quoted in Derk Bodde, 'Feudalism in China', in Rushton Coulborn (ed.), *Feudalism in History* (Hamden, CT: Archon Books, 1965) p. 58.
3. Herrlee G. Creel, *The Origins of Statecraft in China: The Western Chou Empire* (Chicago: University of Chicago Press, 1970) p. 320.
4. Xueqin Li, *Eastern Zhou and Qin Civilizations* (New Haven: Yale University Press, 1985) p. 477.
5. Raymond Dawson, *Confucius* (Oxford: Oxford University Press, 1981) p. 76.
6. D. C. Lau (trans. and ed.), *Confucius: The Analects* (Harmondsworth: Penguin Books, 1979) pp. 74, 131.
7. W. T. de Bary et al. (eds), *Sources of Chinese Tradition*, 2 vols (New York: Columbia University Press, 1960) vol. I, p. 40.
8. D. C. Lau (trans. and ed.), *Lao Tzu: Tao Te Ching* (Harmondsworth: Penguin Books, 1975) p. 57.
9. Ibid., p. 59.
10. De Bary et al. (eds), *Sources of Chinese Tradition*, vol. I, p. 73.
11. Lau (trans. and ed.), *Confucius*, p. 143.
12. Lau (trans. and ed.), *Mencius*, p. 160.
13. De Bary et al. (eds), *Sources of Chinese Tradition*, vol. I, p. 104.
14. Hans Bielenstein, 'The institutions of Later Han', *CHC*, 1, pp. 491–519.

Notes to Chapter 2 From the Period of Division to the Tang
1. Patricia Buckley Ebrey, *The Aristocratic Families of Early Imperial*

China: A Case Study of the Po-ling Ts'ui Family (Cambridge: Cambridge University Press, 1978) p. 18.

2. W. J. F. Jenner, *Memories of Loyang: Yang Hsüan-chih and the Lost Capital (493–534)* (Oxford: Clarendon Press, 1981) p. 28.

3. Mark Elvin, *The Pattern of the Chinese Past* (London: Eyre Methuen, 1973) p. 55.

4. W. E. Soothill, *A History of China*, rev. edn (London: Ernest Benn, 1950) p. 40.

5. Arthur F. Wright, 'T'ang T'ai-tsung and Buddhism', in Arthur F. Wright and Denis Twitchett (eds), *Perspectives on the T'ang* (New Haven, CT: Yale University Press, 1973) pp. 239–63.

6. G. W. Robinson (trans. and ed.), *Poems of Wang Wei* (Harmondsworth: Penguin Books, 1973) p. 30.

7. Elling O. Eide, 'On Li Po', in Arthur F. Wright and Denis Twitchett (eds), *Perspectives on the T'ang* (New Haven, CT: Yale University Press, 1973) pp. 367–403.

8. Arthur Cooper (trans. and ed.), *Li Po and Tu Fu* (Harmondsworth: Penguin Books, 1973) p. 184.

9. Michael Sullivan, 'The heritage of Chinese art', in Raymond Dawson (ed.), *The Legacy of China* (Oxford: Oxford University Press, 1964) pp. 165–233.

10. Denis Twitchett, 'Introduction', *CHC*, 3, pp. 37–8.

11. Sechin Jagchid and Van Jay Symons, *Peace, War, and Trade along the Great Wall: Nomadic–Chinese Interaction through Two Millennia* (Bloomington: Indiana University Press, 1989) pp. 1–23.

12. Arthur F. Wright, *Buddhism in Chinese History* (Stanford: Stanford University Press, 1959) pp. 82–3.

13. E. Zürcher, 'Perspectives in the study of Chinese Buddhism', *Journal of the Royal Asiatic Society* (1982) part 2, pp. 161–76.

14. W. T. de Bary et al. (eds), *Sources of Chinese Tradition*, 2 vols (New York: Columbia University Press, 1960) vol. I, pp. 372–4.

15. Reigned 846–59, to be distinguished from his famous predecessor who reigned 712–56.

Notes to Chapter 3   The Song and Yuan Dynasties

1. Denis Twitchett and Klaus-Peter Tietze, 'The Liao', *CHC*, 6, p. 110.

2. Gungwu Wang, 'The rhetoric of a lesser empire: Early Sung relations with its neighbors', in Morris Rossabi (ed.), *China among Equals: The Middle Kingdom and Its Neighbors, 10th–14th Centuries* (Berkeley, CA: University of California Press, 1983) pp. 47–65.

3. E. A. Kracke, *Civil Service in Early Sung China, 960–1067* (Cambridge, MA: Harvard University Press, 1953, 1968) pp. 68–70.

4. John W. Chaffee, *The Thorny Gates of Learning in Sung China: A Social History of Examinations* (Cambridge: Cambridge University Press, 1985) pp. 182–3.

5. Winston W. Lo, *An Introduction to the Civil Service of Sung China: With an Emphasis on Its Personnel Administration* (Honolulu: University of Hawaii Press, 1987) pp. 92–3.

6. Mark Elvin, *The Pattern of the Chinese Past* (London: Eyre Methuen, 1973) pp. 113–99.

7. Charles O. Hucker, *China's Imperial Past: An Introduction to Chinese History and Culture* (London: Duckworth, 1975) p. 342.

8. Etienne Balazs, 'The birth of capitalism in China', in Etienne Balazs (ed. A. F. Wright), *Chinese Civilization and Bureaucracy* (New Haven, CT: Yale University Press, 1964) pp. 34–54.

9. Albert Feuerwerker, 'Chinese economic history in comparative perspective', in Paul S. Ropp (ed.), *Heritage of China: Contemporary Perspectives on Chinese Civilization* (Berkeley, CA: University of California Press, 1990) pp. 224–41.

10. John Meskill (ed.), *Wang An-shih: Practical Reformer?* (Boston: D. C. Heath, 1963).

11. James T. C. Liu, *China Turning Inward: Intellectual-Political Changes in the Early Twelfth Century* (Cambridge, MA: Harvard University Press, 1988) pp. 81–104.

12. Richard L. Davis, *Court and Family in Sung China, 960–1279: Bureaucratic Success and Kinship Fortunes for the Shih of Ming-chou* (Durham, NC: Duke University Press, 1986).

13. Peter J. Golas, 'Rural China in the Song', *Journal of Asian Studies*, 39.2 (1980) pp. 291–325.

14. Robert P. Hymes, *Statesmen and Gentlemen: The Elite of Fu-chou, Chiang-si, in Northern and Southern Sung* (Cambridge: Cambridge University Press, 1986) pp. 210–18.

15. Patricia Buckley Ebrey, *The Inner Quarters: Marriage and the Lives of Chinese Women in the Sung Period* (Berkeley, CA: University of California Press, 1993) pp. 4–6, 37–43, 199.

16. Frances Wood, *Did Marco Polo Go to China?* (London: Secker & Warburg, 1995); and Morris Rossabi, 'The reign of Khubilai khan', *CHC*, 6, pp. 414–89, at p. 463 n. 83.

17. Frederick W. Mote, 'Chinese society under Mongol rule, 1215–1368', *CHC*, 6, pp. 616–64, at p. 620.

18. Rossabi, 'The reign of Khubilai khan', p. 489.

19. Bayan of the Merkid, to be distinguished from Bayan of the Barin, the general who conquered the south.

20. Quoted in Hucker, *China's Imperial Past*, p. 400.

21. Ch'i-ch'ing Hsiao, 'Mid-Yüan politics', *CHC*, 6, pp. 490–560.

Notes to Chapter 4   The Early Modern Period: The Ming and the Early Qing

1. Frederick W. Mote, 'The rise of the Ming dynasty, 1330–1367', *CHC*, 7, pp. 11–57, at p. 48.

2. Edward L. Dreyer, *Early Ming China: A Political History 1355–1435* (Stanford, CA: Stanford University Press, 1982) p. 87.

3. F. W. Mote, 'The growth of Chinese despotism: A critique of Wittfogel's theory of Oriental Despotism as applied to China', *Oriens Extremus*, 8 (1961) pp. 1–41.

4. Dreyer, *Early Ming China*, p. 182.

5. The official salary of a county magistrate was about 5.2 taels per month.

6. Ray Huang, *Taxation and Governmental Finance in Sixteenth-Century Ming China* (Cambridge: Cambridge University Press, 1974) p. 60. A standard *mou* was approximately 6000 square feet, or one-seventh of an acre.

7. John W. Dardess, *A Ming Society: T'ai-ho County, Kiangsi, Fourteenth to Seventeenth Centuries* (Berkeley, CA: University of California Press, 1996) p. 82.

8. Huang, *Taxation and Governmental Finance*, p. 82.

9. Fang-chung Liang, *The Single-Whip Method of Taxation in China* (Cambridge, MA: Harvard University Press, 1970) p. 1.

10. Dardess, *A Ming Society*, p. 48.

11. Hilary J. Beattie, *Land and Lineage in China: A Study of T'ung-ch'eng County, Anhwei, in the Ming and Ch'ing Dynasties* (Cambridge: Cambridge University Press, 1979).

12. Ping-ti Ho, *The Ladder of Success in Imperial China: Aspects of Social Mobility, 1368–1911* (New York: Columbia University Press, 1967) pp. 92–105.

13. Timothy Brook, *Praying for Power: Buddhism and the Formation of Gentry Society in Late-Ming China* (Cambridge, MA: Harvard University Press, 1993) pp. 311–21.

14. James W. Tong, *Disorder under Heaven: Collective Violence in the Ming Dynasty* (Stanford, CA: Stanford University Press, 1991) pp. 192–203.

15. Quoted in Frederic Wakeman, Jr, *The Great Enterprise: The Manchu Reconstruction of Imperial Order in Seventeenth-Century China*, 2 vols (Berkeley, CA: University of California Press, 1985), vol. I, p. 317.

16. Lynn A. Struve (trans. and ed.), *Voices from the Ming-Qing Cataclysm: China in Tigers' Jaws* (New Haven, CT: Yale University Press, 1993) p. 2.

17. Jonathan D. Spence, *Emperor of China: Self-portrait of K'ang-hsi* (Harmondsworth: Penguin Books, 1977) p. 43.

18. A late seventeenth-century writer quoted in Helen Dunstan, *Conflicting Counsels to Confuse the Age: A Documentary Study of Political Economy in Qing China, 1644–1840* (Ann Arbor: University of Michigan, Center for Chinese Studies, 1996) pp. 151–2.

19. Pei Huang, *Autocracy at Work: A Study of the Yung-cheng Period, 1723–1735* (Bloomington: Indiana University Press, 1974) p. 21.

20. Albert Feuerwerker, *State and Society in Eighteenth-Century China: The Ch'ing Empire in its Glory* (Ann Arbor: University of Michigan Center for Chinese Studies, 1976) p. 84.

21. Mark Elvin, *The Pattern of the Chinese Past* (London: Eyre Methuen, 1973) pp. 285–315.

22. Kung-chuan Hsiao, *Rural China: Imperial Control in the Nineteenth Century* (Seattle: University of Washington Press, 1967) p. 144.

23. Pierre-Étienne Will and R. Bin Wong, *Nourish the People: The State*

Civilian Granary System in China, 1650–1850 (Ann Arbor: University of Michigan, Center for Chinese Studies, 1991).

24. Dunstan, *Conflicting Counsels*, pp. 203–45, 293.

25. Benjamin A. Elman, *From Philosophy to Philology: Intellectual and Social Aspects of Change in Late Imperial China* (Cambridge, MA: Harvard University Press, 1984).

26. Madeleine Zelin, *The Magistrate's Tael: Rationalizing Fiscal Reform in Eighteenth-Century Ch'ing China* (Berkeley, CA: University of California Press, 1984) pp. 265–6.

27. Feuerwerker, *State and Society*, pp. 74–5.

Notes to Chapter 5   China in the Late Qing

1. J. Mason Gentzler (ed.), *Changing China: Readings in the History of China from the Opium War to the Present* (New York: Praeger, 1977) pp. 23–8.

2. James L. Hevia, 'The Macartney embassy in the history of Sino-Western relations', in Robert A. Bickers (ed.), *Ritual and Diplomacy: The Macartney Mission to China, 1792–1794* (London: British Association for Chinese Studies, and the Wellsweep Press, 1993) pp. 57–79.

3. Joseph W. Esherick, 'Cherishing sources from afar', *Modern China*, 24.2 (April 1998) pp. 135–61.

4. John King Fairbank, *Trade and Diplomacy on the China Coast: The Opening of the Treaty Ports, 1842–1854*, rev. edn (Stanford, CA: Stanford University Press, 1969) p. 74.

5. D. K. Fieldhouse, *Economics and Empire 1830–1914* (London: Weidenfeld and Nicolson, 1973) p. 212.

6. Mao Zedong, 'The Chinese revolution and the Communist Party' (1940), quoted in Stuart Schram, *The Political Thought of Mao Tse-tung*, revised and enlarged edn (London: Frederick A. Praeger, 1969) p. 262.

7. Karl Marx, *New York Daily Tribune*, 14 June 1853, reprinted in Dona Torr (ed.), *Marx on China, 1853–1860: Articles from the New York Daily Tribune* (London: Lawrence & Wishart, 1968) pp. 1–2.

8. Jonathan Spence, *God's Chinese Son: The Taiping Heavenly Kingdom of Hong Xiuquan* (London: Harper Collins, 1996) p. 65.

9. Yu-wen Jen, *The Taiping Revolutionary Movement* (New Haven, CT: Yale University Press, 1973) p. 6.

10. Elizabeth J. Perry, *Rebels and Revolutionaries in North China, 1845–1945* (Stanford, CA: Stanford University Press, 1980) p. 130.

11. Ping-ti Ho, *Studies on the Population of China, 1368–1953* (Cambridge, MA: Harvard University Press, 1959) pp. 236–48, 275–8.

12. Mary Clabaugh Wright, *The Last Stand of Chinese Conservatism: The T'ung-chih Restoration, 1862–1874*, 2nd edn (Stanford, CA: Stanford University Press, 1962) p. ix.

13. Ssu-yu Teng and John K. Fairbank, *China's Response to the West: A Documentary Survey, 1839–1923* (New York: Atheneum, 1963) pp. 30–5.

14. Ibid., pp. 50–4.
15. Ibid., p. 76. It was customary for a Mongol to refer to himself as a slave when addressing the emperor.
16. Albert Feuerwerker, *China's Early Industrialization: Sheng Hsüan-huai (1844–1916) and Mandarin Enterprise* (New York: Atheneum, 1970) p. 30.
17. Albert Feuerwerker, 'Economic trends in the late Ch'ing empire, 1870–1911', *CHC*, 11, pp. 1–69.
18. Robert Gardella, *Harvesting Mountains: Fujian and the China Tea Trade, 1757–1937* (Berkeley, CA: University of California Press, 1994) pp. 81–3, 110–11, 170–4.
19. Leang-li T'ang, *China in Revolt: How a Civilization Became a Nation* (London: Noel Douglas, 1927), reprinted in Jessie G. Lutz (ed.), *Christian Missions in China: Evangelists of What?* (Boston: D. C. Heath, 1965) pp. 51–9.
20. Hosea Ballou Morse, *International Relations of the Chinese Empire*, 3 vols (New York: Longmans, Green, 1910–18), vol. III, pp. 158–9.
21. Jack Gray, *Rebellions and Revolutions: China from the 1800s to the 1980s* (Oxford: Oxford University Press, 1990) pp. 132–5.
22. Paul A. Cohen, *History in Three Keys: The Boxers as Event, Experience, and Myth* (New York: Columbia University Press, 1997) pp. 251–60.
23. Frederic Wakeman, Jr, *The Fall of Imperial China* (London: Collier Macmillan, 1977) p. 228.

Notes to Chapter 6   Republican China, 1911–49

1. Marianne Bastid-Bruguière, 'Currents of social change', *CHC*, 11, pp. 535–602 at p. 561.
2. Mary Clabaugh Wright, 'Introduction: The rising tide of change', in Mary Clabaugh Wright (ed.), *China in Revolution: The First Phase, 1900–1913* (New Haven, CT: Yale University Press, 1973) pp. 1–63.
3. Joseph W. Esherick, *Reform and Revolution in China: The 1911 Revolution in Hunan and Hubei* (Berkeley, CA: University of California Press, 1976) p. 175.
4. Ernest P. Young, *The Presidency of Yuan Shih-k'ai: Liberalism and Dictatorship in Early Republican China* (Ann Arbor: University of Michigan Press, 1977) p. 243.
5. Franz Michael, 'Introduction', in Stanley Spector, *Li Hung-chang and the Huai Army: A Study in Nineteenth-Century Chinese Regionalism* (Seattle: University of Washington Press, 1964) pp. xxi–xliii.
6. Jerome Ch'en, *Yuan Shih-k'ai, 1859–1916: Brutus Assumes the Purple*, 2nd edn (London: George Allen & Unwin, 1972) p. 214.
7. Edward A. McCord, *The Power of the Gun: The Emergence of Modern Chinese Warlordism* (Berkeley, CA: University of California Press, 1993) pp. 309–15.
8. James E. Sheridan, *China in Disintegration: The Republican Era in Chinese History, 1912–1949* (New York: The Free Press, 1975) pp. 183–206.

9. Julia C. Lin, *Modern Chinese Poetry: An Introduction* (London: George Allen & Unwin, 1972) p. 85.

10. W. T. de Bary et al. (eds), *Sources of Chinese Tradition*, 2 vols (New York: Columbia University Press, 1964), vol. II, pp. 156–67.

11. S. Y. Teng and J. K. Fairbank (eds), *China's Response to the West: A Documentary Survey, 1839–1923* (New York: Atheneum, 1963) p. 239.

12. Ibid., pp. 252–5.

13. Jean Chesneaux, *The Chinese Labor Movement, 1919–1927* (Stanford, CA: Stanford University Press, 1968) pp. 177–210.

14. Harold R. Isaacs, *The Tragedy of the Chinese Revolution* (London: Secker & Warburg, 1938) p. 126.

15. Stuart R. Schram, *The Political Thought of Mao Tse-tung*, revised and enlarged edn (New York: Frederick A. Praeger, 1969) pp. 250–9.

16. C. Martin Wilbur, 'The Nationalist Revolution: From Canton to Nanking, 1923–28', *CHC*, 12, pp. 527–720 at p. 690.

17. Albert Feuerwerker, 'Economic trends, 1912–1949', *CHC*, 12, pp. 28–127.

18. Han-seng Chen, *Landlord and Peasant in China: A Study of the Agrarian Crisis in South China* (New York: International Publishers, 1973); Ramon H. Myers, *The Chinese Peasant Economy: Agricultural Development in Hopei and Shantung, 1890–1949* (Cambridge, MA: Harvard University Press, 1970).

19. Douglas S. Paauw, 'The Kuomintang and economic stagnation 1928–1937', in Albert Feuerwerker (ed.), *Modern China* (Englewood Cliffs: Prentice-Hall, 1964) pp. 126–35.

20. Thomas G. Rawski, *Economic Growth in Prewar China* (Berkeley, CA: University of California Press, 1989) pp. xxi–xxi, 332, 344.

21. Robert E. Bedeski, 'China's wartime state', in James C. Hsiung and Steven I. Levine (eds), *China's Bitter Victory: The War with Japan 1937–1945* (New York: M. E. Sharpe, 1992) pp. 33–49.

22. Lloyd E. Eastman, *Seeds of Destruction: Nationalist China in War and Revolution, 1937–1949* (Stanford, CA: Stanford University Press, 1984) p. 43.

23. John S. Service, *Lost Chance in China: The World War II Despatches of John S. Service* (New York: Random House, 1974) pp. 178–81.

24. Chalmers A. Johnson, *Peasant Nationalism and Communist Power: The Emergence of Revolutionary China, 1937–1945* (Stanford, CA: Stanford University Press, 1962) p. 59.

25. Donald G. Gillin, '"Peasant nationalism" in the history of Chinese Communism', *Journal of Asian Studies*, 23.2 (February 1964) pp. 269–89; Mark Selden, *The Yenan Way in Revolutionary China* (Cambridge, MA: Harvard University Press, 1974).

Notes to Chapter 7   China since the 1949 Revolution

1. Xinxin Zhang and Ye Sang, *Chinese Lives: An Oral History of Contemporary China* (London: Penguin Books, 1989) p. 119.

2. Barry Naughton, 'The pattern and legacy of economic growth in the

Mao era', in Kenneth Lieberthal, Joyce Kallgren, Roderick MacFarquhar and Frederic Wakeman, Jr (eds), *Perspectives on Modern China: Four Anniversaries* (New York: M. E. Sharpe, 1991) pp. 226–54.

3. Mark Selden, *The People's Republic of China: A Documentary History of Revolutionary Change* (New York: Monthly Review Press, 1979) p. 402.

4. Merle Goldman, 'The Party and the intellectuals', *CHC*, 14, pp. 218-58.

5. Maurice Meisner, *Mao's China: A History of the People's Republic* (New York: The Free Press, 1977) p. 205.

6. Alexander Eckstein, *China's Economic Revolution* (Cambridge: Cambridge University Press, 1977) pp. 58–9.

7. Nicholas R. Lardy, 'The Chinese economy under stress, 1958–1965', *CHC*, 14, pp. 360–97.

8. Alan S. Whiting, 'The Sino-Soviet split', *CHC*, 14, pp. 478–538.

9. Benjamin Yang, *Deng: A Political Biography* (New York: M. E. Sharpe, 1998), p. 151. The quotation is usually rendered as 'Black cat or white cat. . . '.

10. Meisner, *Mao's China*, p. 285.

11. Jiaqi Yan and Gao Gao, *Turbulent Decade: A History of the Cultural Revolution* (Honolulu: University of Hawaii Press, 1996) p. 32.

12. David Milton, Nancy Milton and Franz Schurmann (eds), *People's China: Social Experimentation, Politics, Entry onto the World Scene, 1966–72* (Harmondsworth: Penguin Books, 1977) pp. 269–81.

13. Yan and Gao, *Turbulent Decade*, p. 529.

14. Dwight H. Perkins, 'China's economic policy and performance', *CHC*, 15, pp. 475–539 at pp. 482–3.

15. Suzanne Pepper, *Radicalism and Education Reform in 20th-Century China: The Search for an Ideal Development Model* (Cambridge: Cambridge University Press, 1996) pp. 381, 385.

16. Jeffrey N. Wasserstrom, *Student Protests in Twentieth-Century China: The View from Shanghai* (Stanford, CA: Stanford University Press, 1991) p. 304.

17. John Gittings, obituary of Yang Shangkun, *Guardian*, 15 September 1998.

Further Reading

The number of books on Chinese history available in English is already vast and is increasing rapidly. The following suggestions for further reading highlight a number of classic works and a selection from recent literature.

GENERAL THEMES

Recent general histories of China include: John K. Fairbank, *China: A New History* (Cambridge, MA: Harvard University Press, 1994); Ray Huang, *China: A Macro History* (New York, M. E. Sharpe, 1989); and Franz Michael, *China Through the Ages: History of a Civilization* (Boulder, CO: Westview, 1986).

Recent histories of modern China include: Rafe de Crespigny, *China this Century* (Hong Kong: Oxford University Press, 1992); John K. Fairbank, *The Great Chinese Revolution, 1800–1985* (New York: Harper and Row, 1986); Immanuel C.-Y. Hsü, *The Rise of Modern China*, 5th edn (Oxford: Oxford University Press, 1995); Richard T. Phillips, *China since 1911* (London: Macmillan, 1996); J. A. G. Roberts, *Modern China: An Illustrated History* (Stroud: Sutton Publishing, 1998); and Jonathan D. Spence, *The Search for Modern China* (London: Hutchinson, 1990).

The following works introduce key themes in Chinese history: S. A. M. Adshead, *China in World History* (London: Macmillan, 1988); Thomas J. Barfield, *The Perilous Frontier: Nomadic Empires and China* (Oxford: Basil Blackwell, 1979); W. T. de Bary, Wing-tsit Chan and Burton Watson (eds), *Sources of Chinese Tradition*, 2 vols (New York: Columbia University Press, 1960); Lloyd E. Eastman, *Family, Fields and Ancestors* (Oxford: Oxford University Press, 1988); Mark Elvin, *The Pattern of the Chinese Past* (London: Eyre, Methuen, 1973); J. K. Fairbank, *The Chinese World Order* (Cambridge, MA: Harvard University Press, 1968); Ping-ti Ho, *Studies on the Population of China, 1368–1953* (Cambridge, MA: Harvard University Press, 1959); Ramon H. Myers, *The Chinese Economy: Past and Present* (Belmont, CA: Wadsworth, 1980); Dwight H. Perkins, *Agricultural Development in China, 1368–1968* (Chicago: Aldine, 1969); Paul S. Ropp (ed.), *Heritage of China: Contemporary Perspectives on Chinese Civilization* (Berkeley: University of California Press, 1990); John E. Wills, Jr, *Mountain of Fame: Portraits in Chinese History* (Princeton, NJ: Princeton University Press, 1994).

The Cambridge History of China, General Editors Denis Twitchett and John K. Fairbank (Cambridge: Cambridge University Press, 1978–) is not a continuous history of China but a collection of essays on periods of Chinese history. The following volumes have appeared to date:

1 *The Ch'in and Han Empires, 221 BC–AD 220* (1987)
3 *Sui and T'ang China, 589–906, Part 1* (1979)
6 *Alien Regimes and Border States, 710–1368* (1994)
7 *The Ming Dynasty, 1368–1644, Part 1* (1988)
10 *Late Ch'ing, 1800–1911, Part 1* (1978)
11 *Late Ch'ing, 1800–1911, Part 2* (1980)
12 *Republican China, 1912–1949, Part 1* (1983)
13 *Republican China, 1912–1949, Part 2* (1986)
14 *The People's Republic, Part 1: The Emergence of Revolutionary China, 1949–1965* (1987)
15 *The People's Republic, Part 2: Revolutions within the Chinese Revolution, 1966-1982* (1991)

These volumes are referred to as *CHC*, 1, etc.

PREHISTORY AND EARLY HISTORY

The best introduction to themes in China's prehistory is still David N. Keightley (ed.), *The Origins of Chinese Civilization* (Berkeley: University of California Press, 1983). A new field of China's prehistory is introduced in Steven F. Sage, *Ancient Sichuan and the Unification of China* (New York: State University of New York Press, 1992). For an interpretation of China's formative period, see Li Jun, *Chinese Civilization in the Making, 1766–221 BC* (Cambridge: Cambridge University Press, 1996).

On the archaeology and history of the Zhou period, see Cho-yun Hsü and Katheryn M. Linduff, *Western Chou Civilization* (New Haven: Yale University Press, 1988); and Mark Edward Lewis, *Sanctioned Violence in Early China* (New York: State University of New York Press, 1990). On the literature of the period, see D. C. Lau (trans. and ed.), *Mencius* (Harmondsworth: Penguin, 1970), *Lao Tzu: Tao Te Ching* (Harmondsworth: Penguin, 1975), and *Confucius: The Analects* (Harmondsworth: Penguin, 1985). The best biography of Confucius is Raymond Dawson, *Confucius* (Oxford: Oxford University Press, 1981). On the Qin empire, see Derk Bodde, 'The state and empire of Ch'in', *CHC*, 1, pp. 20–102.

On the Han period, see several books by Michael Loewe, including *Everyday Life in Early Imperial China during the Han Period, 202 BC–AD 220* (London: Carousel, 1973), and *Crisis and Conflict in Han China, 104 BC–AD 9* (London: George Allen and Unwin, 1974); and Cho-yun Hsü, *Han Agriculture: The Formation of Early Chinese Agrarian Economy (206 BC–AD 220)* (Seattle: University of Washington Press, 1980).

THE PERIOD OF DIVISION AND THE SUI AND TANG DYNASTIES

On the Period of Division and the Sui dynasty, see Patricia Buckley Ebrey, *The Aristocratic Families of Early Imperial China: A Case Study of the Po-ling Ts'ui Family* (Cambridge: Cambridge University Press, 1978), W. J. F. Jenner, *Memories of Loyang: Yang Hsüan-chih and the Lost Capital (493–534)* (Oxford: Clarendon Press, 1981); and Arthur F. Wright, 'The Sui dynasty (581–617)', *CHC*, 3, pp. 48–149.

On the history and culture of the Tang period, see John C. Perry and Bardwell L. Smith (eds), *Essays on T'ang Society: The Interplay of Social, Political and Economic Forces* (Leiden: E. J. Brill, 1976); Edwin G. Pulleyblank, *The Background of the Rebellion of An Lu-shan* (London: Oxford University Press, 1955); Denis C. Twitchett, *Financial Administration under the T'ang Dynasty*, 2nd edn (Cambridge: Cambridge University Press, 1970); and Arthur F. Wright and Denis Twitchett (eds), *Perspectives on the T'ang* (New Haven: Yale University Press, 1973).

For an introduction to Tang poetry, see Arthur Cooper (trans. and ed.), *Li Po and Tu Fu* (Harmondsworth: Penguin, 1973). Aspects of Tang religion are dealt with in Stanley Weinstein, *Buddhism under the T'ang* (Cambridge: Cambridge University Press, 1987). Tang expansion southwards is treated imaginatively in Edward H. Schafer, *The Vermilion Bird: T'ang Images of the South* (Berkeley: University of California Press, 1967), and in socio-economic terms in Hugh R. Clark, *Community, Trade, and Networks: Southern Fujian Province from the Third to the Thirteenth Century* (Cambridge: Cambridge University Press, 1991).

THE SONG AND YUAN DYNASTIES

James T. C. Liu has written a number of important studies on Song China. They include *Reform in Sung China, Wang An-shih, 1021–1086 and his New Policies* (Cambridge, MA: Harvard University Press, 1959), and *China Turning Inward: Intellectual-Political Changes in the Early Twelfth Century* (Cambridge, MA: Harvard University Press, 1988). A number of books have been written about the Song bureaucracy and examination system. They include John C. Chaffee, *The Thorny Gates of Learning in Sung China* (Cambridge: Cambridge University Press, 1985); Richard L. Davis, *Court and Family in Sung China, 960–1279: Bureaucratic Success and Kinship Fortunes for the Shih of Ming-chou* (Durham: Duke University Press, 1986); and Winston W. Lo, *An Introduction to the Civil Service of Sung China, with Emphasis on Its Personnel Administration* (Honolulu: University of Hawaii Press, 1987). The emergence of the gentry is discussed in Brian E. McKnight, *Village and Bureaucracy in Southern Sung China* (Chicago: University of Chicago Press, 1971); and Robert P. Hymes, *Statesmen and Gentlemen: The Elite of Fu-chou,*

Chiang-si, in Northern and Southern Sung (Cambridge: Cambridge University Press, 1986).

For an influential discussion of economic developments under the Song, see Yoshinobu Shiba, *Commerce and Society in Sung China* (Ann Arbor: University of Michigan Press, 1970). Song foreign relations are dealt with in Morris Rossabi, *China Among Equals: The Middle Kingdom and Its Neighbors* (Berkeley: University of California Press, 1983).

On the Mongol conquest and Yuan China, see John D. Langlois, Jr (ed.), *China under Mongol Rule* (Princeton: Princeton University Press, 1981); Frederick W. Mote, 'Chinese society under Mongol rule, 1215–1368', *CHC*, 6, pp. 616-64; and Morris Rossabi, *Khubilai Khan: His Life and Times* (Berkeley: University of California Press, 1988).

THE MING AND EARLY QING PERIODS

On the founding of the Ming dynasty and its early history see Edward Dreyer, *Early Ming China: A Political History, 1355–1435* (Stanford: Stanford University Press, 1982); and Charles O. Hucker, *The Ming Dynasty: Its Origins and Evolving Institutions* (Ann Arbor: University of Michigan Press, 1978). On the Ming voyages, see J. V. G. Mills (trans. and ed.), *Ma Huan, Ying-yai sheng-lan: 'The Overall Survey of the Ocean's Shores' [1433]* (Cambridge: Cambridge University Press, 1970). Financial issues are dealt with in Ray Huang, *Taxation and Governmental Finance in Sixteenth-Century Ming China* (Cambridge: Cambridge University Press, 1974), and matters relating to gentry society are considered in Hilary J. Beattie, *Land and Lineage in China: A Study of T'ung-ch'eng County, Anhwei, in the Ming and Ch'ing Dynasties* (Cambridge: Cambridge University Press, 1979); Timothy Brook, *Praying for Power: Buddhism and the Formation of Gentry Society in Late-Ming China* (Cambridge, MA: Harvard University Press, 1993); and John W. Dardess, *A Ming Society: T'ai-ho County, Kiangsi, Fourteenth to Seventeenth Centuries* (Berkeley, University of California Press, 1996).

On the decline and fall of the Ming, see Ray Huang, *1587: A Year of No Significance – The Ming Dynasty in Decline* (New Haven: Yale University Press, 1981); James W. Tong, *Disorder under Heaven: Collective Violence in the Ming Dynasty* (Stanford: Stanford University Press, 1991); and James Bunyan Parsons, *The Peasant Rebellions of the Late Ming Dynasty* (Tucson: University of Arizona Press, 1970).

The rise of the Manchus and their conquest of China is dealt with at length in Frederic Wakeman, Jr, *The Great Enterprise: The Manchu Reconstruction of the Imperial Order in Seventeenth-Century China*, 2 vols (Berkeley: University of California Press, 1985). Vivid insights into that event are contained in Lynn A. Struve (trans. and ed.), *Voices from the Ming-Qing Cataclysm: China in Tigers' Jaws* (New Haven: Yale University Press, 1993).

On the early years of Manchu rule, see Robert B. Oxnam, *Ruling from*

Horseback: Manchu Politics in the Oboi Regency 1661–1669 (Chicago: University of Chicago Press, 1975); Lawrence D. Kessler, *K'ang-hsi and the Consolidation of Ch'ing Rule, 1661–1684* (Chicago: University of Chicago Press, 1978); and Jonathan D. Spence, *Emperor of China: Self-Portrait of K'ang-hsi* (Harmondsworth: Penguin Books, 1973).

On the middle years of the Qing dynasty, see Beatrice S. Bartlett, *Monarchs and Ministers: The Grand Council in Mid-Ch'ing China (1723–1820)* (Berkeley: University of California Press, 1991); Pei Huang, *Autocracy at Work: A Study of the Yung-cheng Period, 1723–35* (Bloomington: Indiana University Press, 1974); Harold L. Kahn, *Monarchy in the Emperor's Eyes: Image and Reality in the Ch'ien-lung Reign* (Cambridge, MA: Harvard University Press, 1971); Susan Naquin and E. S. Rawski, *Chinese Society in the Eighteenth Century* (New Haven: Yale University Press, 1987); and Madeleine Zelin, *The Magistrate's Tael: Rationalizing Fiscal Reform in Eighteenth-Century Ch'ing China* (Berkeley: University of California Press, 1984).

Two books pick out signs of tension in the late eighteenth century: P. A. Kuhn, *Soulstealers: The Chinese Sorcery Scare of 1768* (Cambridge: Cambridge University Press, 1990), and Susan Naquin, *Shantung Rebellion: The Wang Lun Uprising of 1774* (New Haven: Yale University Press, 1981).

CHINA IN THE LATE QING PERIOD

Of the extensive literature on the Opium wars, John King Fairbank, *Trade and Diplomacy on the China Coast: The Opening of the Treaty Ports, 1842–1854*, revised edn (Stanford: Stanford University Press, 1969), has become a classic. The Chinese perception of these events is presented in Frederic Wakeman, Jr, *Strangers at the Gate: Social Disorder in South China, 1839–1861* (Berkeley: University of California Press, 1966); and James M. Polachek, *The Inner Opium War* (Cambridge, MA: Harvard University Press, 1992).

The mid-nineteenth-century rebellions are dealt with in Philip A. Kuhn, *Rebellion and Its Enemies in Late Imperial China: Militarization and Social Structure, 1794–1864* (Cambridge, MA: Harvard University Press, 1970); Franz Michael and Chung-li Chang, *The Taiping Rebellion: History and Documents*, 3 vols (Seattle: University of Washington Press, 1966–71); Elizabeth J. Perry, *Rebels and Revolutionaries in North China, 1845–1945* (Stanford: Stanford University Press, 1980); Stanley Spector, *Li Hung-chang and the Huai Army: A Study in Nineteenth-Century Chinese Regionalism* (Seattle: University of Washington Press, 1964); and Jonathan Spence, *God's Chinese Son: The Taiping Heavenly Kingdom of Hong Xiuquan* (London: HarperCollins, 1996).

On late Qing themes, see Mary Clabaugh Wright, *The Last Stand of Chinese Conservatism: The T'ung-chih Restoration, 1862–1874*, 2nd edn (Stanford: Stanford University Press, 1962); Jonathan Ocko, *Bureaucratic*

Reform in Provincial China: Ting Jih-ch'ang in Restoration Kiangsu, 1867–1870 (Cambridge, MA: Harvard University Press, 1983). Economic history is dealt with in Albert Feuerwerker, *China's Early Industrialization: Sheng Hsuan-huai (1844–1916) and Mandarin Enterprise* (Cambridge, MA: Harvard University Press, 1958); Robert Y. Eng, *Economic Imperialism in China: Silk Production and Exports, 1861–1932* (Berkeley: University of California Press, 1986); Robert Gardella, *Harvesting Mountains: Fujian and the China Tea Trade, 1757–1937* (Berkeley: University of California Press, 1994) and Robert Lee, *France and the Exploitation of China, 1885–1901* (Hong Kong: Oxford University Press, 1989). On missionaries, see Paul A. Cohen, *China and Christianity: The Missionary Movement and the Growth of Chinese Antiforeignism, 1860–1870* (Cambridge, MA: Harvard University Press, 1963). On the emergence of nationalism, see John E. Schrecker, *Imperialism and Chinese Nationalism: Germany in Shantung* (Cambridge, MA: Harvard University Press, 1971).

On the 100 Days' reforms, the Boxer uprising and the late Qing reforms, see Luke S. K. Kwong, *A Mosaic of the Hundred Days: Personalities, Politics, and Ideas of 1898* (Cambridge, MA: Harvard University Press, 1984); Joseph W. Esherick, *The Origins of the Boxer Uprising* (Berkeley: University of California Press, 1987); Paul A. Cohen, *History in Three Keys: The Boxers as Event, Experience, and Myth* (New York: Columbia University Press, 1997); Marianne Bastid, *Educational Reform in Early Twentieth-Century China* (Ann Arbor: University of Michigan Press, 1988); Charlton M. Lewis, *Prologue to the Chinese Revolution: The Transformation of Ideas and Institutions in Hunan Province, 1891–1907* (Cambridge, MA: Harvard University Press, 1976).

REPUBLICAN CHINA

On the 1911 revolution, see Joseph W. Esherick, *Reform and Revolution in China: The 1911 Revolution in Hunan and Hubei* (Berkeley: University of California Press, 1976); Edward J. M. Rhoads, *China's Republican Revolution: The Case of Kwangtung, 1895–1913* (Cambridge, MA: Harvard University Press, 1975), and Mary Clabaugh Wright (ed.), *China in Revolution: The First Phase, 1900–1913* (New Haven: Yale University Press, 1973).

On Yuan Shikai, the May Fourth period and the warlord era, see Ernest P. Young, *The Presidency of Yuan Shih-k'ai: Liberalism and Dictatorship in Early Republican China* (Ann Arbor: University of Michigan Press, 1977); Tse-tsung Chow, *The May Fourth Movement: Intellectual Revolution in Modern China* (Cambridge, MA: Harvard University Press, 1960); Edward A. McCord, *The Power of the Gun: The Emergence of Modern Chinese Warlordism* (Berkeley: University of California Press, 1993); Arthur Waldron, *From War to Nationalism: China's Turning Point, 1924–1925* (Cambridge: Cambridge University Press, 1995).

The rise of the Nationalist Party and the record of the Nanking decade are discussed in Donald A. Jordan, *The Northern Expedition: China's National Revolution of 1926–1928* (Honolulu: University of Hawaii Press, 1976); Elizabeth J. Perry, *Shanghai on Strike: The Politics of Chinese Labor* (Cambridge: Cambridge University Press, 1995); Lloyd E. Eastman, *The Abortive Revolution: China under Nationalist Rule, 1927–1937* (Cambridge, MA: Harvard University Press, 1974) and Parks M. Coble, *The Shanghai Capitalists and the Nationalist Government, 1927–1937* (Cambridge, MA: Harvard University Press, 1986).

On the early history of the Chinese Communist Party, see Arif Dirlik, *The Origins of Chinese Communism* (Oxford: Oxford University Press, 1989); Fernando Galbiati, *P'eng P'ai and the Hai-lu-feng Soviet* (Stanford: Stanford University Press, 1985); Roy Hofheinz, Jr, *The Broken Wave: The Chinese Communist Peasant Movement, 1922–1928* (Cambridge, MA: Harvard University Press, 1977); Zedong Mao, *Report from Xunwu* (Stanford: Stanford University Press, 1990); and Benjamin Yang, *From Revolution to Politics: Chinese Communists on the Long March* (Boulder, CO: Westview Press, 1990).

For the Sino-Japanese War and the Civil War, see Lloyd E. Eastman, *Seeds of Destruction: Nationalist China in War and Revolution, 1937–1949* (Stanford: Stanford University Press, 1984); Chalmers A. Johnson, *Peasant Nationalism and Communist Power: The Emergence of Revolutionary China, 1937–1945* (Stanford: Stanford University Press, 1962); Mark Selden, *The Yenan Way in Revolutionary China* (Cambridge, MA: Harvard University Press, 1971); Steven I. Levine, *Anvil of Victory: The Communist Revolution in Manchuria, 1945–1948* (New York: Columbia University Press, 1987); and Suzanne Pepper, *Civil War in China: The Political Struggle, 1945–1949* (Berkeley: University of California Press, 1978).

CHINA SINCE THE 1949 REVOLUTION

On the period of consolidation, the First Five-Year Plan and the Great Leap Forward, see Lowell Dittmer, *China's Continuous Revolution: The Post-Liberation Epoch, 1949–1981* (Berkeley: University of California Press, 1987); Kenneth G. Lieberthal, *Revolution and Tradition in Tientsin, 1949–1952* (Stanford: Stanford University Press, 1980); Vivienne Shue, *Peasant China in Transition: The Dynamics of Development toward Socialism, 1949–1956* (Berkeley: University of California Press, 1980); Ezra F. Vogel, *Canton under Communism: Programs and Politics in a Provincial Capital, 1949–1968* (Cambridge, MA: Harvard University Press, 1969); Jasper Becker, *Hungry Ghosts: China's Secret Famine* (London: John Murray, 1996).

For the Cultural Revolution, see David Milton et al. (eds), *People's China: Social Experimentation, Politics, Entry on to the World Scene, 1966–72* (Harmondsworth: Penguin Books, 1977); and Jiaqi Yan and Gao

Gao, *Turbulent Decade: A History of the Cultural Revolution* (Honolulu: University of Hawaii Press, 1996).

On China in the 1980s and 1990s, see Barry Naughton, *Growing out of the Plan: Chinese Economic Reform, 1978–1993* (Cambridge: Cambridge University Press, 1995); Gregor Benton and Alan Hunter (eds), *Wild Lily, Prairie Fire: China's Road to Democracy, Yan'an to Tian'anmen, 1942–1989* (Princeton: Princeton University Press, 1995).

Biographies of Deng Xiaoping include Richard Evans, *Deng Xiaoping and the Making of Modern China*, revised edn (London: Penguin Books, 1997); and Benjamin Yang, *Deng: A Political Biography* (New York: M. E. Sharpe, 1998).

On social themes during the period, see Suzanne Pepper, *Radicalism and Education Reform in 20th-Century China: The Search for an Ideal Development Model* (Cambridge: Cambridge University Press, 1996); Judith Banister, *China's Changing Population* (Stanford: Stanford University Press, 1987); Colin Mackerras, *China's Minority Cultures: Identities and Integration since 1912* (New York: Longman, 1995); Margery Wolf, *Revolution Postponed: Women in Contemporary China* (Stanford: Stanford University Press, 1985).

Index